AAI - 4637

22.95
65J

# The
# Interactional
# View

BOOKS OF RELATED INTEREST

*Pragmatics of Human Communication*
by Paul Watzlawick, Janet H. Beavin, and Don D. Jackson

*Change: Principles of Problem Formation and Problem Resolution*
by Paul Watzlawick, John H. Weakland, and Richard Fisch

*Mirages of Marriage*
by William J. Lederer and Don D. Jackson

*Communication*
by Jurgen Ruesch and Gregory Bateson

*Uncommon Therapy*
*The Psychiatric Techniques of Milton H. Erickson, M.D.*
by Jay Haley

FORTHCOMING

*The Teaching Tales of Milton H. Erickson*
by Milton H. Erickson, M.D. and Sidney Rosen, M.D.

# THE
# INTERACTIONAL
# VIEW

Studies at the Mental Research Institute
Palo Alto, 1965–1974

*Edited and with a commentary by*

PAUL WATZLAWICK and JOHN H. WEAKLAND

W · W · NORTON & COMPANY

*New York · London*

W. W. Norton & Company, Inc., 500 Fifth Avenue, New York, N.Y. 10110
W. W. Norton & Company Ltd., 37 Great Russell Street, London WC1B 3NU

Published simultaneously in Canada by
Penguin Books Canada Ltd,
2801 John Street, Markham, Ontario L3R 1B4.

Library of Congress Cataloging in Publication Data
Main entry under title:
The Interactional view.
    Includes bibliographies and index.
    1. Family. 2. Family psychotherapy. I. Watzlawick, Paul. II. Weakland,
John H. III. Mental Research Institute. [DNLM: 1. Family therapy.
WM430 I622]
RC455.4.F3I57        616.8'915        76–44220

ISBN 0-393-01131-3

3 4 5 6 7 8 9 0

# Acknowledgments

On behalf of the Mental Research Institute and as the editors of this volume we want to express our gratitude to the authors and publishers of the papers for their permission to reprint them. Dr. Jackson's articles are reprinted here by special permission of his widow, Mrs. Angela Jackson. Specific acknowledgments and information about the original source can be found at the beginning of each contribution. The affiliations of the authors are mentioned in the List of Contributors.

Our thanks go to Mrs. Claire Bloom for her untiring help in preparing the manuscript.

P.W.
J.H.W.

# Contents

# List of Contributors

Janet Beavin Bavelas, Ph.D. Assistant Professor, Department of Psychology, University of Victoria, B.C. Former Research Associate, MRI.

Arthur M. Bodin, Ph.D. Research Associate, MRI. Co-Director, Emergency Treatment Center.

Norma H. Davies, Ph.D. Research Associate, MRI. Consulting Psychologist, Family Focus, Division of Physical Therapy, Stanford University School of Medicine.

Elaine E. Faunce, B.A. Technical Associate, University of Rochester Medical School, Rochester, New York. Former Research Associate, MRI.

Antonio J. Ferreira, M.D. Research Associate, MRI. Psychiatrist in private practice.

Richard Fisch, M.D. Research Associate, MRI. Director, Brief Therapy Center, MRI.

Jay Haley, M.A. Director, Family Therapy Institute, Washington, D.C. Former Research Associate, MRI.

Elaine Hansen, R.P.T. Clinical Instructor, Family Focus, Division of Physical Therapy, Stanford University School of Medicine.

Fred C. Hoebel, Ph.D. Research Associate, MRI. Director, Family Heart Project, MRI.

Don D. Jackson, M.D. Founder and First Director of MRI.

Alma Z. Menn, A.C.S.W. Research Associate, MRI. Principal Investigator and Project Director, Soteria Project, MRI.

Loren R. Mosher, M.D. Collaborator, Soteria Project, MRI. Chief, Center for Studies of Schizophrenia, National Institute of Mental Health.

Ann Reifman, B.A. Research Assistant, Center for Studies of Schizophrenia, National Institute of Mental Health.

Jules Riskin, M.D. Director, MRI. Clinical Associate Professor, Department of Psychiatry and Behavioral Sciences, Stanford University School of Medicine.

Carlos E. Sluzki, M.D. Research Associate, MRI. Adjunct Associate Professor of Psychiatry and Lecturer in Ambulatory and Community Medicine, University of California, San Francisco. Former Director, Center for Research in Psychiatry, Lanús Hospital, Lanús, Buenos Aires.

Elaine M. Sorensen, D.N.S. Research Associate, MRI. Project Director, Family Interaction Center, MRI.

Eliseo Verón, Ph.D. Director of Studies, École des Hautes Études en Sciences Sociales, Paris. Former Research Associate, Centro de Investigaciones Sociales, Instituto Torcuato Di Tella, Buenos Aires.

Paul Watzlawick, Ph.D. Research Associate, MRI. Clinical Associate Professor, Department of Psychiatry and Behavioral Sciences, Stanford University School of Medicine.

John H. Weakland, Ch.E. Research Associate, MRI. Associate Director, Brief Therapy Center, MRI.

Irvin D. Yalom, M.D. Professor of Psychiatry, Department of Psychiatry and Behavioral Sciences, Stanford University School of Medicine.

# Introduction

*Paul Watzlawick*

In his preface to volumes I and II of the papers written by members of the Mental Research Institute,[1] the founder and first director of our institute, Dr. Don D. Jackson, stated: "The papers included in these volumes cover a considerable span of time, substantive focus, and levels of generality, yet there is a unity in their manifest diversity."

This statement holds equally for the present volume, a representative sample of the nine books (and their fourteen foreign editions) and over 130 articles published by members and associates of MRI during the period 1965 to 1974. At first glance they seem to lack thematic cohesion. Yet while no common denominator is immediately apparent, there is a common basis of a more general and profound sort, one which concerns the essence rather than the details of our institute's interest. To clarify this, especially for the reader unacquainted with the work of MRI, some introductory remarks are in order:

MRI was founded in November 1958, at a time when family therapy was still in its infancy. Our institute was one of the few places where this new form of treatment, referred to as conjoint family psychotherapy, was explored, taught, and practiced. As the term implies, this method involves meeting with the members of a family at the same time and place rather than, for instance, treating family members individually and in separate sessions either by the same therapist or even by different therapists who may or may not communicate among themselves about their individual efforts.

It is not difficult to see that this approach to human problems entailed a significant departure from the monadic, intrapsychic treatment methods

[1] Don D. Jackson, ed., *Communication, Family and Marriage* (volume I) and *Therapy, Communication and Change* (volume II) (Palo Alto: Science and Behavior Books, 1968).

widely practiced at that time. Without going into unnecessary detail, it can be said that family therapy, as it has evolved during the last twenty years, is in our opinion not simply a new, additional treatment *method,* but first of all *a new way of conceptualizing human problems.* To emphasize this dual nature (conceptual framework *and* practical method) is neither novel nor trivial. It is not novel, because as early as 1922 Freud[2] already postulated the same distinction for psychoanalysis (in fact, he defined three aspects: a theory, a method of psychological investigation, and a therapeutic technique). Its nontriviality requires explanation:

Like other scientific conceptualizations, psychiatric theories are embedded in the *Zeitgeist* or the epistemology of their era. Seen in this perspective, psychoanalysis has all the unmistakable characteristics of a theory based on the first law of thermodynamics, with its almost exclusive emphasis on the phenomena of conservation and transformation of *energy.* In fact, it has variously been proposed that psychodynamics is based on the essentially hydraulic model of a fluid that has a somewhat viscous quality (the libido). The concept of causality underlying this model is of necessity a linear, unidirectional one, whereby event A effects (determines) event B whose occurrence in turn is the cause of event C, and so on from the past through the present and into the future. Within this framework all exploration and explanation is necessarily past-oriented, since in it the past is the cause of the present, and the understanding of the past therefore the precondition for change in the present.

Since approximately the end of World War II, however, a very different epistemology has gained increasing acceptance. Rather than basing itself on the concept of energy and its unidirectional causality, it is founded on the concept of *information,* that is, of order, pattern, negentropy, and in this sense on the second law of thermodynamics. Its principles are cybernetic, its causality is of a circular, feedback nature, and, with information being its core element, it is concerned with the processes of communication within systems in the widest sense—and therefore also with human systems, e.g. families, large organizations and even international relations.

This way of conceptualizing events is essentially new. "The truths of cybernetics are not conditional on their being derived from some other branch of science. Cybernetics has its own foundations." states Ashby.[3]

---

[2] Sigmund Freud, Two Encyclopedia Articles, (A) Psycho-Analysis, in *The Standard Edition of the Complete Psychological Works of Sigmund Freud* (London: New York: W. W. Norton, 1976), vol. XVIII, p. 235.

[3] W. Ross Ashby, *An Introduction to Cybernetics* (New York: John Wiley and Sons, 1963), p. 1.

It should be immediately clear that the conclusions that can be drawn from these foundations will not only differ from those derived from other, more orthodox theories, but are very likely to be wholly incompatible with them. This becomes most obvious in connection with change, the central concern of psychotherapy. Different as the classical theories of psychotherapy may be, their foundations in the first law of thermodynamics do provide a common denominator, and for all of them change is contingent on a sufficiently deep exploration and understanding of the causes in the past. In the cybernetic framework, on the other hand, a "transformation is defined, not by any reference to what 'really' is, nor by reference to any physical cause of the change [ . . . ]. The transformation is concerned with *what* happens, not *why* it happens," to quote Ashby (op. cit., p. 11) again.

For our readers who may be more interested in practical rather than epistemological considerations, this crucial difference can perhaps be illustrated by the following example:

For a relationship to be viable, there has to be a minimum of that kind of mutual understanding which is colloquially referred to as "knowing where one stands with the partner." What constitutes that minimum may vary greatly from one individual to another; for whatever reasons in their individual past some people get along with very little of it, while others need a lot. Assuming now that a husband belongs to the former class of people and his wife to the latter, a typical conflict will very probably arise in their marriage. Since the wife does not get enough information from her husband to know "where she stands" with him, what he thinks and feels about her and their shared life, etc., she is likely to try to get this information by asking him pertinent questions, watching his behavior, searching for further clues, and the like. In all probability he will find these behaviors excessively curious and intrusive. Notice that up to this point there is nothing even remotely "pathological" about their relationship. They simply operate with two different ideas about what their degree of understanding and closeness should be, and neither of these ideas is wrong *per se*—they are simply different. But the situation is unstable and unless they manage to decrease the discrepancy of their views, their interaction is bound to escalate. The more she seeks the missing information, the less likely he is to give it, and the more he withdraws and keeps her at a distance, the harder she will try to establish closeness. Both are thus caught in a "more-of-the-same" interaction[4] in which, typically, a solution is sought through increased effort of a certain kind while

[4] See note 2 on page 249.

in actual fact it is precisely this effort that precludes the solution. The rest of this fictitious, yet everyday story is easy to imagine. By the time professional help becomes necessary, her behavior satisfies the established clinical criteria of pathological jealousy.

Depending on his epistemological orientation, a psychotherapist confronted with this case will take one of two very different approaches. If he holds the view that emotional problems—and therefore this woman's pathological behavior—are determined by causes in the individual's past, he will quite logically attempt to uncover these past causes (the *why*), lead his patient to insight into them, and he will refrain from exerting any influence in the here and now before her underlying problem (of which her behavior is only the surface manifestation) has been analyzed and thus resolved. He may or may not interview the husband, but if he does, the information supplied by the latter will be considered to have only very limited importance, except for the fact that it will confirm and reinforce the clinician's impression that he is dealing with a deep-seated psychotic process. In accordance with *this* theory of the nature of psychiatric disorders he will, quite correctly and consistently, treat the woman's case in monadic, intrapsychic isolation and on the basis of the above-mentioned epistemology of a linear, unidirectional causality.

If, on the other hand, he takes into account the marital interaction as described in the foregoing, he will attempt to discover *what* is going on here and now and not *why* the spouses' respective attitudes evolved in their individual pasts. He will identify their pattern of interaction as well as their attempted solutions (the more-of-the-same quality of their escalating behaviors) and he will then design the most appropriate and effective therapeutic intervention into the present functioning of this human system.

It is not too difficult to see that these two procedures will differ to the point of incompatibility and what may be the most appropriate and correct course of action for the one may be tabooed for the other. What is not equally apparent is that these incompatibilities are the direct result of the discordant and discontinuous nature of the two *epistemologies* underlying the two procedures and not—as is often and naïvely assumed—of a more or a less correct view of the nature of the human *mind*. Or, to borrow Einstein's famous remark: It is the theory that determines what we can observe.

We are now in a position to return to the starting point, namely the claim that family therapy is first of all a new way of conceptualizing human problems, and only secondly a different therapeutic approach based on this conceptualization. This being so, the frequently asked question whether in a given case individual or family therapy is more indicated is moot.

This, then, is the common denominator of the otherwise apparently heterogeneous papers brought together in this volume, since it is this *perspective* and resulting *procedure* that constitutes the basis of most of the work performed at MRI. But it is not to be construed as a general theory of family therapy, because even within this burgeoning field there are many different schools of thought and of treatment methods. For instance, great efforts are being made by some family therapists to reconcile and combine the two epistemologies mentioned above (which in our opinion are discontinuous), to cast an amalgam of the intrapsychic and the interpersonal and to try to utilize the best of two worlds. In the same vein, other workers are trying to find a bridge over which individual treatment methods can be taken into the treatment of systemic pathologies.

# The
# Interactional
# View

# CHAPTER 1

# Theory

*This first chapter contains papers dealing with questions of family theory, the dynamics of interaction and human communication in general. Their common denominator is the perspective outlined in the Introduction, namely the study of human systems rather than of individuals in artificial isolation. In one way or another, they all emphasize the fact which philosophers of science have referred to as the incommensurabilitity of scientific evolution. To paraphrase Kuhn,[1] one of their main exponents, a new scientific paradigm is not simply the negation of a preceding one, nor its amplification in which the latter then continues to exist as a "special case," but there is a logical incompatibility between the two.*

*It would be preposterous to claim that from the outset our work was oriented along such advanced epistemological principles. Rather, what led us in this direction, for which we may invoke epistemological justification* a posteriori, *were eminently practical, mostly clinical considerations which we were able to conceptualize only after Gregory Bateson and his original research team at the Veterans Administration Hospital in Menlo Park had begun to apply anthropological and cybernetic rather than psychiatric principles to the study of families with an emotionally disturbed member.*

*The papers contained in this chapter were chosen to highlight important steps along this path leading from first formulations of a very pragmatic nature to later attempts at scientific presentations of a more formal (and therefore more widely applicable) quality.*

*"The Study of the Family," by Don D. Jackson, is the first fairly comprehensive presentation of the principles of family theory and therapy developed at MRI under his leadership. It deals briefly with the difference between the individual and the interactional viewpoints, the different con-*

[1] Thomas S. Kuhn, *The Structure of Scientific Revolutions*, 2nd ed., enlarged, in *Foundations of the Unity of Science*, ed. Otto Neurath, Rudolf Carnap, and Charles Morris (Chicago: University of Chicago Press, 1970).

*ceptualizations of causality underlying the two, and then introduces the
concept of family rules. In retrospect—ten years later—it is already difficult to appreciate how novel an idea this concept of rules as determinants
of behavior (rather than needs, drives, personality traits, etc.) was at the
time.*

# THE STUDY OF THE FAMILY

### Don D. Jackson, M.D.

For the past six years, we at the Mental Research Institute in Palo Alto
have been studying family interaction to see whether and how such interaction relates to psychopathology or deviant behavior in one or more
family members. The "normal" as well as the "disturbed" family is studied
in order to infer conditions conducive to mental health. Our approach
has been interaction-oriented because we believe that individual personality, character and deviance are shaped by the individual's relations with
his fellows. As the sociologist Shibutani has stated:

Many of the things men do take a certain form not so much from instincts as
from necessity of adjusting to their fellows. . . . What characterizes the interactionist approach is the contention that human nature and the social order
are products of communication. . . . The direction taken by a person's conduct is seen as something that is constructed in the reciprocal give and take
of interdependent men who are adjusting to one another. Further, a man's
personality—those distinctive behavioral patterns that characterize a given individual—is regarded as developing and being reaffirmed from day to day in
his interaction with his associates (14).

Thus, symptoms, defenses, character structure and personality can be
seen as terms describing the individual's *typical interactions which occur
in response to a particular interpersonal context.* Since the family is the
most influential learning context, surely a more detailed study of family
process would yield valuable clues to the etiology of such typical modes
of interaction.

This work has been supported by National Institute of Mental Health Grant
MH-04916, by the Robert Wheeler Foundation, and the Ampex Foundation.
    This paper was written with the assistance of Janet Beavin.
    Originally published in *Family Process* 4:1–20, 1965; reprinted with per-
mission.

## Problems of Family Study

Operating from this interactionist view, we began (as did many other family study centers) by studying families which had a schizophrenic member, to see whether or not these families had processes in common.[1] Various projects have since gone on to study families with delinquent, neurotic, or psychosomatically ill members.

Although our original approach—assessment of the family's influence on the individual patient—yielded many useful concepts, hunches, and observations, it also had inherent difficulties and potential fallacies. To study family process *per se* is difficult enough; to try to uncover the origins of pathology inevitably becomes part science and part crystal ball.

### *Problems of Theory*

When searching for one-to-one relationships between an identifiable family process and a characteristic individual response, it must be kept in mind that:

I. The same behavior in two people can spring from quite different interactional causes. Thus, according to the principle of equifinality, different causes may produce similar results; e.g., two different sets of family reactions may each produce a child who steals.

II. Behavior is multi-determined. A child is exposed to a vast number of learning contexts, all of which help to mold behavior.

III. Stress resulting from outside pressures on the family can exacerbate family processes destructive to a child's development. As a matter of fact, stress may so alter family processes that even after the circumstances producing it have ceased, there may be a "snowball" effect.

IV. Certain variables might be present which help to soften the effect of a destructive family process. A child might, by happy circumstance, escape the family often enough to form a protective relationship with a school teacher, for example. Another child might not come upon such an opportunity.

V. There is a possible importance of so-called constitutional factors, even though such factors are not independently assessable by present methods except in cases of severe mental deficiency.

[1] Before the formation of the Mental Research Institute in March 1959 I had worked five years with Gregory Bateson on his "Communication in Schizophrenia" project. Jack and Jeanne Bloch, Virginia Patterson and I studied the families of neurotic and autistic children at the Langley Porter Neuropsychiatric Institute from 1953 to 1956.

Most important of all, however, is to remain alert to the fundamental precariousness of using the symptom as a starting point from which to investigate family interaction. Families of schizophrenics, delinquents, and neurotics may be more alike than different, both in their formal structure and in their response to society's discovery that they contain a deviant member. (The Bateson group, when first studying families of schizophrenics, recognized all these problems. We labeled each index case *schizophrenia p* in order to signify: "This is a way of describing the *people* we are observing, and not of describing all schizophrenics.")

When the symptom is used as the starting point, the problem is further compounded by the fact that the psychiatric nosology, or system, for labeling deviance is not only individual-oriented but often idiosyncratic and not clearly related to observed behavior. Psychiatrists are often more interested in pinning the patient with a label than in studying how he got into the spot of being pinned. Psychiatric terms frequently include labels for different kinds of individual behavior, in widely varying interpersonal contexts; for example, the word "delinquent" covers children who steal, rape, beat up others, truant, etc. When labels that are used for individuals are extended to describe a *dyad,* they are unhelpful because they are undifferentiating. For example, the label "sadomasochistic," when applied to a couple, describes little; from our observations, almost all troubled marital pairs can be described this way.

All these impediments to family theory and research can be seen to be variations of two related conceptual issues:[2] individual versus interactional process, and linear versus circular causality. From our resolution of these issues will emerge general criteria of family theory by which the rest of this presentation will be guided.

*Individual versus Interactional Process*

We have just noted that to focus on a family because of the psychiatric symptom[3] of a family member introduces an inappropriate individual bias,

---

[2] To the proponents of a new theory falls the sometimes pedantic and arid, but more often illuminating, task of boring down to basic premises, to conceptual models and metatheoretical considerations, which those who have a broad framework of agreement, theoretically, need not constantly remind each other of. When alternative premises, methodologies, and data are proposed, the old and the new must be laid out side by side for comparison, and the newcomer has the duty to state with maximum possible clarity just what he does and does not assume.

[3] Or absence thereof, which amounts to the same thing.

making the analysis of interactional processes more difficult. But even if the object of study is ostensibly the family unit, any examination of the characteristics of the various individual family members remains in the domain of individual theory. When we say that the patient is disturbed but one or both of his parents cause this, or that various family members manifest perceptual, emotional, or cognitive disturbances, or that a family member other than the identified patient is "really" sick—in all these ways we may quantitatively increase the number of individuals under study, but the theory remains individual in orientation. It is only when we attend to *transactions between* individuals as primary data that a qualitative shift in conceptual framework can be achieved. Yet our grasp of such data seems ephemeral: despite our best intentions, clear observations of interactional process fade into the old, individual vocabulary, there to be lost, indistinguishable and heuristically useless. To put the problem another way, we need measures which do not simply sum up individuals into a family unit; we need to measure the characteristics of the supra-individual family unit, characteristics for which we presently have almost no terminology. We can only use this rule of thumb: the whole is more than the sum of its parts, and it is that whole in which we are interested.

## Linear versus Circular Causality

Much of the work done in the behavioral (and many other) sciences can be said, essentially, to be devoted to finding *causes* for given observed effects. These causes are supposed to be lineally related to their effects, i.e., event B happens (or happened) because event A is happening (or previously happened). Since longitudinal studies are, unfortunately, the exception, and cross-sectional or time-sample studies predominate our researches, this assumption has never been adequately tested. Still, despite an embarrassing simultaneity of observation, the "cause" and "effect" are treated as if they occurred in linear series and in the appropriate order. One important concept ignored by this theory is that of *feedback,* which proposes that information about event B impinges on event A, which then affects B, etc., in a circle of events which modify each other. Since psychological "events" seldom occur only once, but rather persist and overlap with maddening complexity, this circular model is often more appropriate than one which artificially abstracts such events from the intricate time sequence in which they occur.

When applied to the family, the notion of linear causality is particularly inappropriate and leads directly to several of the problems outlined earlier (especially equifinality, multi-determination of behavior and even the process whereby the patient is labeled). Faced with the undeniable fact that family members act constantly on each other, modifying each other's behavior in the most complex ways, a conceptual model which would have us delineate event A from event B, much less put them in causal order, is of little help. Furthermore, such goals are sterile because they must ultimately lead to unanswerable questions such as whether the parents of the schizophrenic are the way they are because they have an organically ill child, or the patient is schizophrenic because of his parents' behavior. The study of *present process* in the family, then, seems both more accurate and more fruitful.

(The "double-bind" theory (3) has been subject to considerable mis-understanding on this issue and provides us with a good example. It was not immediately clear in the original paper that there was no "binder" and no "victim" in the relationship described as a double bind, but rather two binder-victims. This is obvious when one realizes that there is no possible response to a double bind *except* an equally or more paradoxical message, so if neither can escape the relationship, it can be expected to go on and on until it matters little how it all got started. Thus, both for theory and for therapy, we do much better to study the present operation of this pathological interaction than to seek the ultimate villain.)

It follows that the first step must be to study family interaction *per se;* to study interaction patterns in families of *all* kinds, whether or not the family has a labeled symptom-bearer. The goal is to classify families in terms of how they characteristically interact, in other words, to try to build a typology of families. While this is being done it might also be possible to note any one-to-one relationships between certain kinds of family interaction and certain types of individual behavior. Such a task is, of course, Herculean, since one can look at family interaction in a variety of ways and draw from many different theoretical formulations. Our approach has been exploratory and crude. But while polyadic systems are unquestionably more complex than our present research strategies can assess, there is the curious fact that attention to such systems—because of their lawfulness—*simplifies* the observation of human behavior.

## Family Rules

Briefly stated, the major assertion of the theory to be outlined here is that *the family is a rule-governed system:* that its members behave among themselves in an organized, repetitive manner and that this patterning of behaviors can be abstracted as a governing principle of family life.

*Theoretical Background*

Both common sense and clinical observations argue for the organized nature of family interaction. If there were not some circumscription of the infinity of possible behaviors in which its members might conceivably engage, not only the daily chores but the very survival of the family unit would be in question. And, indeed, we can observe more or less strict divisions of labor and of power which comprise the cultural and the idiosyncratic "styles" of family life. (The latter may, for instance, bewilder the small child when he begins visiting friends' families and discovers they have a way of doing things which is alien to his privately held definition of family operations.)

We need not rely only on the practical argument that family life *must be* organized (and therefore, have "rules" of organization), nor on the commonly shared observation that family behavior *is* organized (and that we can and do infer the "rules" governing this organization). The theory of communication and interpersonal relations, even in its present infancy, permits logical deduction of the hypothesis of family rules. To accomplish this derivation, it is necessary to review a few pertinent aspects of communications theory.

In 1951, Bateson (1, see also 10) noted that communications[4] can be said to have two distinct aspects or functions, *report* and *command*. Most obviously, every communication bit conveys information of a factual nature which, presumably, can be evaluated in terms of truth and falsity, and can be dealt with logically as the "object" of communication; this is the communication *report;* e.g., "the streets are icy," "Darwinian evolution does not necessarily invalidate the concept of a Supreme Being," or a shake of the head.

But, in addition to this report, and of immeasurably more interest to our theory of interpersonal relations, the same communication bit also conveys a *command* which indicates *how this information is to be taken.* Although this theory holds for a wider variety of communicational phenomena, we will limit ourselves to human communication, where we will see that the command aspect can be paraphrased "this is how I define the relationship in which this report takes place, i.e., this is how *you* are to see *me* in relation to you." None of the examples above was in the im-

---

[4] By communication is meant *behavior* in the widest sense: words and their non-verbal accompaniments, posture, facial expressions, even silence. All convey messages to another person, and all are subsumed in our term "communication."

perative mood grammatically, yet each effectively defines the nature of the relationship in which it occurs. Even the (superficially) impersonal statement about Darwinian evolution is not the sort of opinion one renders to the barber or even to one's wife without defining the relationship in a highly specific manner.[5]

This definition may not be accepted; it may be rejected, countered, modified, or ignored. It may also be redundant—confirming a long-standing or stereotyped relationship agreement such as teacher-student. But the offering of a "command" and the response by the other are distinguishable issues. Their interaction will be taken up shortly. Here, we can summarize the general report-command theory of communication into terms suitable for the specific aspects of human communication: *Every message (communication bit) has both a content (report) and a relationship (command) aspect; the former conveys information about facts, opinions, feelings, experiences, etc., and the latter defines the nature of the relationship between the communicants.* It is the relationship level of communication which will be our primary focus in this paper.

In every communication, then, the participants offer to each other definitions of their relationship, or, more forcefully stated, each seeks to determine the nature of the relationship. Each, in turn, responds with his definition of the relationship—which may affirm, deny, or modify that of the *vis-à-vis*. This process, at the relationship level of interaction (communication), warrants close attention.[6]

One of the simplest examples is the behavior of strangers in public places (in an airplane, in a bar, waiting in line). They may exchange trivial comments which lead to, say, a "small talk" relationship being agreed upon; or one may seek such a relationship and the other may quell it; or they may mutually define theirs as a "stranger" relationship—a special relationship with its unique rules, rights, and expectations. Note especially that the *context* exchange in these circumstances (offering a cigarette, comments about the weather, chuckling "to oneself") is of little consequence; it may be false or virtually non-existent (feigned deafness, pretended concentration, simple ignoring). But the *relationship* struggle and

---

[5] The relationship of the report to the command aspect of communication can be seen to be one of logical levels. One classifies the other, but is also classified by the other. For the sake of exposition, we will leave this reciprocity implicit and speak of command as a "higher" level than report.

[6] In our view, the definition of the self, the relationship, and the other are an indivisible whole. We especially do not isolate or abstract the individual from the individual-in-this-relationship-with-this-other. This bias is implicit throughout the present work, and any tendency to read otherwise in the following will only lead to confusion.

resolution are definitive even in the unlikely case where they simultaneously decide to ignore each other.

If we now narrow our focus even more, from human communication in general to ongoing (perdurable) relationships only, we see that what is relatively simple and unimportant between strangers is both vital and complex in an ongoing relationship. An *ongoing relationship* may be said to exist when, for some reason, the relationship is (a) "important" to both parties and (b) assumed to be of long term duration, as is true of some business relationships, between friends and lovers, and especially in marital and familial relationships. When these conditions impinge on a relationship, the determination of the nature of that relationship cannot *not* be accomplished, nor can it be a haphazard process. The give and take of relationship definitions must stabilize or lead to a so-called runaway which would endanger the maintenance of this ongoing relationship, i.e. divorce, desertion, or disaster would ensue, and there would be no relationship to study.[7]

Thus, the population of families which is ours to study—those which remain family units—have stabilized the process of determining the nature of their relationship, "agreeing" on a mutually acceptable definition or at least on the limits for dispute. These relationship agreements, which are here called *rules*, prescribe and limit the individuals' behaviors over a wide variety of *content* areas, organizing their interaction into a reasonably stable system.

By way of illustration, we might speculate how rules must develop and operate in a new relationship: Boy meets girl on their first date. Take any aspect of the many behaviors involved; say, he arrives a little late. Suppose further that she delays her entrance (consciously or not) by exactly the amount of time he kept her waiting. He gets the message that she will not tolerate his keeping her waiting. At the same time, though, he cannot be sure whether this is just her mood tonight, or coincidence, or characteristic of her. If they are exceptional persons, they might discuss this "interchange," which would be a step toward resolution or change. But, whether they verbalize it or not, real change would require several repetitions of the corrected behavior. That is, if he were really unavoidably detained the first time, he would have to be on time the next several times to "prove" this. So suppose they still have this question, undiscussed, and unresolved. In the course of the evening, he decides they should go to a movie, and while she agrees, she picks the movie. He could decide he must treat her

---

[7] However, relationships do not necessarily terminate in actuality when they terminate in legality. Many divorced persons, for instance, remain intensely involved with each other and have even been known to participate in "marital" therapy.

as an equal and start practicing equality; she responds by treating him equally, that is, she does not overdo it and push him around. Within a few dates, they would have something which could last a lifetime—although of course we cannot prove this. Mate selection must be in large part the matching of certain expected behaviors (and self-definitions) in certain crucial areas.

At this point we must, proleptically, digress to lay to rest questions of "consciousness," "intention," "purposefulness," or any of a variety of other terms implying that extremely troublesome issue: Is the behavior motivated or not? (And if so, how?) To propose that every individual moves to determine the nature of his relationship with another would seem to imply a theory of the individual which is based upon an Adlerian motivation to power. This is emphatically not so. *No* theoretical assumptions about the individual have been or need be invoked, only assumptions on the nature of communication *qua* communication. Only the premise of a report-command duality of communication is necessary to our theoretical model. Similarly, although we find it convenient to say family members "agree" on relationship rules, we do not intend or need to assume that this is a conscious process. Most relationship rules are probably out of our awareness, but the issue is moot and irrelevant in this context.

### The Rule as Redundancy in Relationships

If a man from Mars were to hover outside some living room window any given night, he might discover four people sitting around a small table, passing pasteboard rectangles to one another and muttering such phrases as "one no-trump." After watching for awhile and noting redundancies in the players' behavior, our intelligent Martian could discern that what these people were doing was highly rule-governed. He might discover, for example, that spades are higher than clubs, that play goes from left to right, etc. He might or might not immediately discover certain other rules of bridge, depending on whether special circumstances arose while he happened to be watching. For instance, it is assumed that no one will cheat. If one partner gives the other a significant glance, his opponents scowl angrily as a warning that this behavior is on the road to out-and-out cheating. Or, a really clever extraterrestrial observer might realize that the players *could* gain advantage by cheating, and that since they consistently refrained from this behavior, it must be against the rules. However, groups who have played together for some time will follow rules that are not overtly evident and which could only be inferred by an outsider after long, patient observation and recording of redundancies. Even if he spoke English and queried the players, it might not occur to them to mention certain rules that they abide by but are not consciously aware of observing. For example, A may "know" that when B says "one no-trump," he usually has minimal points and therefore A needs a strong hand to raise B.

When the game is family relationships, behavioral scientists are alien observers. The rules of play are not known completely even to the participants. What confronts the observer is a plethora of behaviors (communications) from which rules can be inferred which "explain" the patterning of the behavior. Just as a relatively few rules permit games as complex as chess or bridge, so a few family rules can cover the major aspects of ongoing interpersonal relationships. (The comparative difficulties of deducing many possible behaviors from a few given rules and of inducing the rules from a wide variety of behaviors should, however, be obvious.)

In other words, a redundancy principle operates in family life. The family will interact in repetitious sequences in all areas of its life, though some areas may highlight these repetitions (or patterns) more quickly and systematically than do other areas.

The rule approach to the study of family interaction is similar to that of the biologist studying genes and to Bateson's approach to the study of the learning process. As Maruyama (13) describes the former, biologists were long puzzled by the fact that the amount of information stored in genes is much smaller than the amount of information needed to account for the structure of the adult individual. However, this puzzle is solved if one assumes that the genes carry a set of *rules* to generate information for the whole system. Similarly, Bateson (2) described "deutero-learning" or "learning to learn," which concisely governs the wider range of *what* is learned. Although the family-as-a-unit indulges in uncountable numbers of different specific behaviors, the whole system can be run by a relatively small set of rules governing relationships. If one can reliably infer the general rules from which a family operates, then all its complex behavior may turn out to be not only patterned but also understandable—and, as a result, perhaps predictable.

Again, we must emphasize the rule is an inference, an abstraction—more precisely, a *metaphor* coined by the observer to cover the redundancy he observes. We say a rule is a "format of regularity imposed upon a complicated process by the investigator," (8) thereby preserving the distinction between theoretical term and object of Nature which is also maintained by many of our more sophisticated colleagues in the natural sciences. A rule is, but for our paucity of expression, a formula for a relationship—No one shall control anyone else, Father shall overtly run the show but Mother's covert authority shall be respected, Husband shall be the wooer and Wife the helpless female. Such formulations are inferences, just as is the concept of gravity; they explain the data in the sense that they incorporate the relevant visible evidence *and* relate it to a larger heuristic framework.

### A Lexicon of Rules

I have come to refer to family relationship rules in general as *norms*. This usage not only corresponds roughly with similar (non-family) notions in the literature (7, 12, 15), but it also connotes some of the important characteristics of the concept:

I. That the norms are usually phenomenologically unique for each family observed. We thus keep our focus firmly centered on the family unit, with individual and broader social or cultural considerations remaining secondary, even though we assume that a given set of norms or relationship rules is more common in one culture than another.

II. That the norm is a setting or baseline on which family behavior is measured and around which it varies to a greater or lesser degree.

*Norm* thus implies both the focus and the mechanics of our theory. This might be represented schematically as in Figure 1, which can be seen to resemble a graph for a mechanical regulating device such as the household furnace thermostat, in which case the "range of behavior" would be the temperature scale and the "norm" the desired temperature setting.

One type of norm, described elsewhere, (9), is the marital *quid pro quo*. This term (literally "something for something") is a metaphorical statement of the marital relationship bargain; that is, how the couple has agreed to define themselves within this relationship.

Inseparable from our definition of norm would have to be a definition of *homeostatic mechanisms,* the means by which norms are delimited and enforced. The scowl the Martian observed on a bridge player when his competitor might have cheated indicated that the rules of the game had been or were about to be violated, or to put it another way, indicated that the class of behaviors in which the offending player has just indulged is to be excluded in their future dealing.[8]

[8] Most of us, as bridge players, would readily perceive that our opponents meant to exclude not only the specific cheating tactic just attempted but *any* cheating behavior at all. Further, few of us would interpret the specific behavior (e.g. the exchange of significant glances) to be excluded in subsequent *non-bridge* situations. But the classification of behavior is not always so self-evident. The problems of mutually understood generalizations from specific behaviors will be dealt with in detail in a later article.

Homeostatic mechanisms are therefore an extension, in an ongoing relationship, of the give and take of relationship definitions by which the original rules were worked out. It can be safely assumed, however, that the homeostatic mechanisms probably operate to restrict behavior to a much narrower range when the interactional system has stabilized into a family system than when the relationship was first being worked out. Couples, such as described earlier, who may engage in wondrously varied be-

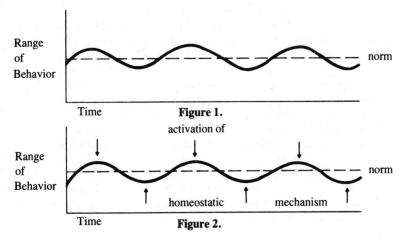

**Figure 1.**

**Figure 2.**

havioral ploys during courtship, undoubtedly achieve considerable economy after a while in terms of what is open to dispute, and how it is to be disputed. Consequently they seem both to have mutually excluded wide areas of behavior from their interactional repertoire (and never quibble further about them), *and* to have learned to cue each other homeostatically with a privately understood "code," so that little gestures may mean a lot. Such economy, of course, is inversely related to the effort required of the researching observer.

In terms of the schema just presented for norms (Figure 1 above), homeostatic mechanisms can be seen as behaviors which delimit the fluctuations of other behaviors along the particular range where the norm is relevant.[9] Again, the analogy with the household thermostat is useful:

---

[9] Again, homeostatic behaviors obviously belong to a higher level, logically, than the behaviors to which they refer. We might speculate that this higher range of behaviors also has norms and if so, that paradoxes might arise.

when the temperature deviates from a pre-set norm, this deviation is registered and counteracted by the homeostatic mechanism of the thermostat system. (See Figure 2.) Thus, if the norm of the family is that there be no disagreement, when trouble begins to brew, we might observe general uneasiness, a sudden tangentialization or change of topic, or even symptomatic behavior on the part of an identified patient, who may act out, talk crazy, or even become physically ill when family members begin to argue. The family is distracted and brought into coalition (frequently against the patient) and the norm holds until the next time.

It is significant in the development of family theory that it was the observation of homeostatic mechanisms in the families of psychiatric patients (11) that led to the hypothesis of the family as a homeostatic, and eventually specifically as a rule-governed, system. For norms become quickly apparent if one can observe the reaction to their abrogation and infer therefrom the rule which was broken. Tiresome long term observation of the beaten path, with careful noting of possible routes which were *not* taken, can eventually yield a fair guess about the rules of the game. But the observable counteraction of a single deviation is like a marker to our goal. Therefore, though it is still difficult to assess exactly the norms of the system the schizophrenic patient and his family maintain when the patient is "ill," one need only witness the immediate and frequently violent reaction to his recovery to be convinced that there are powerful family mechanisms for maintaining these norms.

*Norms and Values*

Norms as herein defined and discussed are not to be confused with the important sociological concept of *values*. Certainly both constructs represent guideposts which organize behavior, and both are enforced by observable sanctions. So one might be tempted to put the two in the same class and distinguish them on some minor ground, e.g., values are generally presumed to exist *a priori* and to result in ("cause") certain behavior patterns, while norms are inferred *from* behavior and are not seen to be causative; or, one might propose that values are overt and acknowledgeable while norms are covert, the two being analogous perhaps to laws, customs, respectively.

These apparent comparabilities are, however, superficial and misleading. *A norm describes interpersonal relations;* that is, they are interpersonal both in unit and subject matter. Values, on the other hand, are *nonpersonal* in subject matter and *individual* in unit. One person can value something or "have" a certain value, and several family members (in-

dividually) can value something, but a family *as a whole* cannot. Even
if all family members concur in a certain value the result is a summation
of individuals—and therefore remains in the domain of individual theory.

Where, then, do values fit into our scheme of family rules? Certainly
not in terms of specific injunctions for or against certain individual behaviors, or in the meaning of these behaviors for the individual (in terms
of dissonance, guilt, etc.). Behavior which may be guided by a presumed
value is not distinguishable from any other kind of behavior in our interactional framework. But values, or more precisely, the invocation of
values, can have interpersonal ramifications: values can be cited to demand, enforce, or justify a particular kind of behavior in a relationship.
If the family norm proscribes disagreement, when a family discussion begins to get out of order, almost any member can invoke the shared *value*
of democratic functioning (taking turns, etc.), and thus re-establish family order. In short, *values in this theory of the family are one kind of
homeostatic mechanism.* Because values represent an extra-familial coalition (with religion, society, culture, etc.), they exert leverage on relationships within the family. Thus, from our perspective, inside the family
looking out, so to speak, values are used as interpersonal tactics which
affirm or enforce a norm.[10]

Mother and infant, for example, have a strictly complementary relationship (that is, one based on differences which fit together), in which
the norm is that the infant is totally dependent on the mother for all
gratification. As the child grows older, he may engage in behaviors which
abrogate this norm, especially masturbation. Whatever else masturbation
may mean to either individual, in this ongoing relationship, it is an indication of self-sufficient pleasure on the part of the child (10) and as such
threatens the norm of their relationship, i.e., that the mother controls all
the child's needs and pleasures. If the mother is unwilling to accept this
change in the norm, she may punish the child, and/or she may invoke
strong moral injunctions against the "deviant" behavior. In this case, her
value judgment against his masturbation represents a forceful coalition
of mother and society, a coalition which may in fact succeed and perpetuate the complementary norm to absurdity.

As is readily apparent, values usually have recognizable origins in the
culture, subculture, ethnic background, or social group, but there are
idiosyncratic values as well. Some may be ignored, some espoused with

---

[10] This is not, of course, the same as saying that this is *all* a value is—the
student of value orientations cuts the pie quite another way and validly so—
but this is all a value can be within the theory here outlined if consistency is
to be maintained.

special fervor, as these values tend to fit into the enforcement of the family norms. Thus, while the psychoanalyst often sees values as rationalizations of intrapsychic phenomena, and the sociologist and anthropologist discuss them as idealized constructs somehow "possessed" by the individual, or on which many individuals concur, this family theory focuses on the communicative function of value-guided behavior and concludes that such behavior is tactical, within the family, where it serves as a homeostatic mechanism.

This use of the term "value" corresponds with that of others who have previously used "norm" as it is defined here. Thibaut and Kelley, in "The Social Psychology of Groups" (15), describe a norm as a behavioral rule that is accepted, at least to some degree, by both members of a (non-family) dyad. They state that the observer, after noting a regularity in behavior or regular routine shifts in the activities of the pair, can help explain this regularity by inferring that the behavior is organized around norms. They also note that if the regularity is disrupted, the "injured" person will often attempt to restore it by exercising his personal power to enforce the norm, or *by appealing to a supporting value.*

Garfinkle (7) discusses what he calls "constitutive rules"—rules which one is not aware of until they are broken or abrogated. "Constitutive rules" correspond, in some ways, to my use of the word "norm." For example, supermarket shoppers were disconcerted to observe a graduate student buy a package of cigarettes and then proceed to open the pack and count the cigarettes. This deliberately staged behavior called into question the norms of the relationship between shopper and producer which might be paraphrased as: "If I (shopper) buy a pack of cigarettes, I can count on you (producer) to put 20 cigarettes in the pack." Thus the shopper is spared the impossible task of verifying the size, weight, and number of everything he purchases; in other words, a certain level of trust is established. If some shopper discovered only 10 cigarettes in a package, he might or might not realize the exact nature of his trust in the producer, but he would probably write him a letter invoking values, even laws. (The effect on other shoppers produced by the psychology student's behavior is an indication that people react against discovering their own norms. It is similar to becoming aware of one's breathing—what once worked silently and smoothly is now a problem.)

*Rules versus Roles*

Probably the most generally accepted notion in family study is that of *roles,* which has wide currency among an unusually varied group of investigators—psychoanalysts, sociologists, learning theorists, to name a few.

A family role is a model abstracted from the legal, chronological, or sexual status of a family member (mother, husband, son, sister, etc.); this model describes certain expected, permitted, and forbidden behaviors for the person in that role. Several kinds of analysis follow from the family role concept: study of the process of learning the role behaviors, of the inevitable multiplicity of roles with which any given individual is labeled (spouse and parent, child and sibling, and so on), and of course of the integration of roles into a family structure.

This last field of study would seem, perhaps, to be very similar to our proposed theory of family rules, focusing as both do on the interlocking behaviors of family members. This is not true, for a number of reasons. Most important, in the role concept we again face a term which is basically *individual* in origin and orientation and which, therefore, is ill-suited for the discussion of family process. A role encases the individual as a separate unit of study so that the *relations between* two or more individuals must necessarily be secondary phenomena. If we would study relationship first, then we cannot, as will be illustrated shortly, base this study on individual constructs.

A second point of difference is the inseparability of the role concept from a culture-limited view of family structure. There is no clear line between the role as descriptive or as idealistic; that is, people are classified by conformity or non-conformity to predetermined categories which are products either of cultural stereotype or of theoretical bias. The implication is that a healthy family has Father in the father role, Mother in the mother role, Son in the male child role, etc. This neglects and even obscures the aspects of interactional process which may be significant, which may in fact be the more general phenomena of which role-taking is only a by-product.[11]

This leads to a more basic difference between rules and roles—the reliance on observation as opposed to *a priori* definitions. A role, with its theoretically concomitant behaviors, exists independently of behavioral data. That is, not only the general notion of role but the specifics of the various sorts of family roles are theoretical, not phenomenological. When observational data is involved, it is in relation to the theoretical role as a

---

[11] There is a growing body of theory on idiosyncratic family roles especially in relation to psychopathology, e.g., the notion of the identified patient as the family scapegoat (4), as well as Berne's (5) pungent descriptions of the many roles for many persons which comprise the interactional setting of various forms of symptomatic behavior. These certainly bring us much closer to interactional data, but there is a tendency to inject such formulations with individual motivational schemes (such as masochism), which detract from the originality of the descriptive approaches.

model ("inadequate performance of a role," "role breakdown," "role reversal"). It seems apparent that analysis of such discrepancies between model and reality only emphasizes further the gap between category and data.

To illustrate that rules and roles are two fundamentally different ways of looking at family data, let us consider a specific role theory—the sex-role view of marriage—and an alternative view which has been proposed in terms of family rules. (9) The incontrovertible and inevitable fact that marriages are composed of one man and one woman only has led to the belief that sex differences between spouses are highly significant in the nature of marriage. Men and women have certain fundamental differences at birth which are presumed to be amplified by social learning of a wide variety of sex-linked behaviors and attitudes; in short, each adult should have achieved a male or female role. The convergence of the two roles, as the only immediately obvious similarity between all marriages, is commonly assumed to be the key to marriage as an institution. Thus sexual compatibility is greatly stressed as vital to the success of a marriage (though this may be only a special case of the more general necessity for *collaboration* in marriage). Conformation by each spouse to the proper role stereotype is presumed to be basic, not only to sexual compatibility, but to the mental health of the spouses and their children and the permanence of the marriage.

There are, however, other characteristics true of marriage (and of almost no other relationships) which might therefore be just as reasonably considered basic to the nature of marriage as is its sexual composition. These are seldom considered, I feel, because they refer, not to individual spouses, but to the *relationship* of marriage and thus do not fit our usual language. Consider that the marriage (not the persons involved) is (a) a voluntary relationship, (b) a permanent or at least open-ended, non-time-bound relationship, (c) an exclusive relationship which is supposed to suffice for the partners in a great many areas of human functioning, and (d) a broadly and complexly goal-oriented relationship, with vital tasks covering not only a wide cross-section of human affairs, but extending indefinitely through time. This is a unique and by no means spurious, inconsequential combination of characteristics and must certainly be considered at least as important to the nature of marital relationships as individual sexual factors.

Thus, the marital *quid pro quo* (as defined earlier) has been proposed. The *quid pro quo* theory of marriage is used as an illustration here because it represents a full reversal of the role theory of marriage: *the individual differences which are unquestionably present in a marriage are*

*seen as results of the active process of working out this unique and diffi-
cult relationship, not as the primary cause of the relationship phenomena.*

Let us review the distinction we have made between rules and roles, in
terms of these two specific theories of marriage. First, sex-role constructs
are inevitably individual in orientation; any deductions about relationship
consequences must be greatly limited by the premises to which these individual notions are limited. Second, there are theoretical and cultural
preconceptions about "proper" sex roles, such that men are supposed to
work, be strong and not openly emotional, defend the home, etc., while
women are to keep house, stay inside it, be soft, loving, and maternal. No
allowance is made for the relationship which underlies this arrangement,
or for the possibility that this is a good way of working out rules for a
relationship *but not the only way.*

This brings us to point three, which is that real marriages may deviate
widely from these cultural stereotypes and be highly successful, because
an equally workable relationship agreement (*quid pro quo*) has been
maintained. There seems to be little question that difference *per se* is necessary in marriage: the specifics of such differences are much less important than the circularity of their evolution and maintenance. Therefore,
*a priori* categories of differences will only lead us astray.

Some of the problems of family theory and research have been considered, and general criteria have been suggested by which these problems
might be avoided. A theory of the family has been proposed, based on the
model of the family as a rule-governed, homeostatic system. A companion
paper to follow will discuss clinical and experimental applications of this
theory, with special emphasis on pathological family systems.

## REFERENCES

1. BATESON, G., "Information and Codification: A Philosophical Approach,"
   in Ruesch, J. and Bateson, G., *Communication: The Social Matrix of
   Psychiatry,* New York, Norton, 1951, pp. 168–211.
2. BATESON, G., "Social Planning and the Concept of 'Deutero-Learning',"
   *Science, Philosophy, and Religion,* Second symposium, New York,
   1942.
3. BATESON, G., JACKSON, D. D., HALEY, J. and WEAKLAND, J., "Toward a
   Theory of Schizophrenia," *Behav. Sci.,* 1, 251–264, 1956.
4. BELL, N. W. and VOGEL, E. F., "The Emotionally Disturbed Child as
   the Family Scapegoat," in Bell, N. W. and Vogel, E. F. (eds.) *The
   Family,* Glencoe, Ill., Free Press, 1960.
5. BERNE, E., *Transactional Analysis,* New York, Grove Press, 1961.

6. VON BERTALANFFY, L., "An Outline of General Systems Theory," *Brit. J. Philos. Sci.*, 1, 134–165, 1950.
7. GARFINKEL, H., "The Routine Grounds of Everyday Activities," *Soc. Prob.*, 11, 225–249, 1964.
8. HALEY, J., "Family Experiments: A New Type of Experimentation," *Fam. Proc.*, 1, 265–293, 1962, p. 279.
9. JACKSON, D. D., "Family Rules: The Marital *Quid Pro Quo*", reprinted on pp. 21–31 of this volume.
10. JACKSON, D. D., "Guilt and Control of Pleasure in Schizoid Personalities," *Brit. J. Med. Psychol.*, 31, 124–130, part 2, 1958.
11. JACKSON, D. D., "The Question of Family Homeostasis," *Psychiat. Quart. Supp.*, 31, 79–90, 1957.
12. LEARY, T., *Interpersonal Diagnosis of Personality,* New York, Ronald Press, 1957.
13. MARUYAMA, M., "The Second Cybernetics: Deviation-Amplifying Mutual Causal Processes" (unpublished manuscript, September 1962).
14. SHIBUTANI, T., *Society and Personality,* Prentice-Hall, Englewood Cliffs, New Jersey, 1961, pp. 20–23.
15. THIBAUT, J. W. and KELLEY, H. H., *The Social Psychology of Groups,* Wiley, New York, 1959.

*While Jackson was still working on this paper, he already had plans for another presentation dealing with the subject of rules as determinants of human behavior. This paper, published shortly after* The Study of the Family *and written with the help of Janet Beavin, goes much more systematically into the question of the emergence of rules and the typical pathologies of rule conflicts. The arena chosen for this study is the marital dyad which, as a result of its long-lasting and ubiquitous nature and its relatively limited complexity, is particularly well-suited for research into the superpersonal aspects of human relationships and of their conflicts. There are three main points in this paper: 1) The sexual aspects of a marital relationship are by no means the most important ones—even without them, this form of an exclusive, long-lasting human relationship would not be essentially different from what it is; 2) Many rules arising in this human context are the outcome of the partners' interaction and not of their individual decisions or actions, and they cannot, therefore, be reduced to the madness or badness of one of them; 3) Other rules are the outcome of something amounting to a bargain between the partners. The paper's title is "Family Rules: Marital Quid Pro Quo."[1] The theory of*

[1] The Roman law term *quid pro quo* means literally "something for something." To avoid a frequent misunderstanding it should be remembered that *quid* and *quo* are not two different words, but that the latter is merely the ablative form of the former, as required by the preposition *pro*.

*marriage, first proposed in this paper, appeared in much greater detail, shortly after Don D. Jackson's untimely death in 1968, in* The Mirages of Marriage.[2]

# FAMILY RULES: MARITAL QUID PRO QUO

## *Don D. Jackson, M.D.*

Because they are so obviously and invariably composed of only one man and one woman each, marriages in our society are usually described in terms of sexual differences, which are of course considered innate or at least fixed characteristics of the individuals involved. All manner of behaviors quite removed from primary sexual differences can be brought into the framework of male-female differences, which framework then becomes an explanatory model of marriage. This view pervades our popular mythology of sexual stereotypes, it influences marriage manuals and similar advisory accouterments, and it certainly guides our scientific study of the marital relationship, no matter how inconsistent or unspecific this theory proves to be. The rich variety of forms which anthropologists have shown us "masculinity" and "femininity" take in marriage across the world should indicate something is amiss with the assumption that absolute, specific sexual differences in marriage are of heuristic value. The function of such differences in organizing a special relationship is seldom considered; it may be that a shared belief in any difference at all would serve the same purpose. It is proposed here that the individual differences which are so evident in marital relationships may just as reasonably be a result of the nature of that relationship as of the nature of the individuals who compose the relationship.

Heterosexuality is not the only unique feature of marriage; there is another characteristic which, strangely enough, often goes unnoticed, but may be the most important aspect of marriage: it is the only well-known, *long-term collaborative relationship.* Thus there are several nonsexual aspects which must be considered in any analysis of marriage and marriage problems.

Reprinted from *Archives of General Psychiatry* 12:589–94, 1965, with permission. Copyright 1965, American Medical Association.

This work was supported by National Institute of Mental Health Grant No. MH–04916. The paper was written with the assistance of Janet H. Beavin.

[2] William J. Lederer and Don D. Jackson, *The Mirages of Marriage.* New York, W. W. Norton, 1969.

1. It is a *voluntary* relationship, even though undertaken in a culture which views marriage as almost compulsory.

2. It is a *permanent* relationship; that is, it is supposed to be a lifetime contract. ("Till death do us part.")

3. Marriage in the western world is an *exclusive* relationship, in which the parties are supposed to be virtually sufficient each unto the other, with a marked exclusion of third parties and outside relationships.

4. It is a broadly *goal-oriented* relationship with many vital mutual tasks to be carried out on a long-term basis and marked by time-bound eras—each with its special problems.

To describe these premises of marriage is not to imply that they are necessarily realized nor that the parties enter into marriage with such concepts in mind. These are shared beliefs about the nature of marriage as an institutionalized relationship, and the assets and liabilities of marriage as a legal arrangement stem, in large part, from the workability of these norms.

Unused as we are to thinking in terms of different kinds of relationships (rather than different kinds of individuals), still we can see that there are probably no other dyadic relationships which, *regardless of the sex of the partners,* can be similarly characterized. For instance, the assumption (not to say the reality) of permanency excludes most other volitional relationships which are not troubled by the curious paradox of "having to want to stay together." The *homosexual "marriage"* comes to mind immediately as a possible example of a relationship in which primary sexual differences are absent but the relationship problems as outlined above are more or less relevant. We might question whether being against the social grain—two against the world—has something to do with the durability of some such relationships. Yet, even in homosexual "marriages" there is the evolution of sex-role differences. Homosexuals may choose for their relatively permanent partners their opposites in terms of "masculinity" and "femininity," (and they often use a sex-role language for their relationship even when parent-child or sibling terms would seem more appropriate). While it can always be asserted that sex-role identification preceded the relationship (ie, one partner is "really" female), this cannot be proven; so, just as in heterosexual marriage, the differentiation of the individuals along sex lines can be seen as primary *or* as a means of working out the problems posed by the rules of the marital relationship, that is, as effect, not cause.

Other instances in which the same relationship problems seem to be posed are fairly easily distinguished. In the *roommate* arrangement, for instance, volition, relative permanence, and mutual tasks do frequently apply; but there is no expectation that the two will not engage in highly important, independent, third-party relationships. In fact, it would be unusual for each roommate *not* to maintain independence or external coalitions with regard to financial, sexual, intellectual, and even companionship needs. Lacking a premise of virtual self-sufficiency of the dyad, the roommate arrangement also avoids many of the problems which arise in marriage. *Business relationships* are oriented to an explicit and specific central goal, as opposed to marriage which cannot be said to have any single goal. In fact, for marriages we have to make up goals such as "the rearing of children" or "companionship" even when such functions can successfully be carried on without legal or secular blessings. Business relationships are also necessarily diluted by a wide variety of intrinsic factors, not the least of which are the time-defined working day and, again, the vital role of third parties such as customers, staff, even the stock market. There must be enduring, nonhomosexual relationships between, perhaps, unmarried possibly related women; here one thinks of the maiden aunts or old maid school teachers of our American mythology, and one begins to wonder how such relationships are worked out. Unfortunately for our research interests, these relationships seldom come to the attention of professionals. So it seems we are unable by means of counter-example to prove immediately whether marriage is the way it is because a man and a woman are involved, or because it is a unique kind of a relationship for any two people at all. *Thus, it is possible that one could outline marriage as a totally nonsexual affair, nearly excluding all sexual differences, or at least minimizing the causal role usually assigned such differences.*

The sex-role view of marriage is so widely accepted that the position just taken seems nearly impudent. It nevertheless seems important to reconsider some of our beliefs about marriage since our present knowledge of individual theory is quite exhaustive when contrasted with the paucity of systematic knowledge of relationship per se. In our traditional conceptual framework, the individual is held by the boundaries of his skin, and whatever transpires between two such captives—that which is neither clearly "I" nor clearly "thou"—is a mystery for which we have no language or understanding. Our thoughts, research efforts, and even what Benjamin Whorf called "our view of the cosmos" are limited or facilitated by the language which we use. Therefore, we must first have a language which enables, even forces, us to think interactionally. The necessity for a language with which to study interaction may lead to the abandonment of terms which belong to the study of the individual in favor of terms which focus on the relationship. The concept of "family rules"[1] represents one such tool. The observation of family interaction makes obvious certain *redundancies,* typical and repetitive patterns of interaction which characterize the family as a supraindividual entity. One of the simplest such rules is proposed in this paper: the marital quid pro quo, an alternative to the theory of individual differences in marriage.

To suggest that the individual, sex-aligned differences which we witness in marriages may not be due to individual sexual differences, or indeed have anything to do with biological sexual requirements, is not to say these differences do not exist. To the contrary, just such differences can be the basis of working out a relationship. The stresses and successes of marriage still need not be attributed to sexual or even individual personality differences, but could conceivably be expected to be true of any hypothetical relationship which is also voluntary, permanent, exclusive, and task-oriented. The actual differences between marriage partners are probably not nearly so important as the difficulty in collaborating; furthermore, any two people in these conditions have to work out rules based on differences or similarities. Sexual differences are readily available, but if there were no real differences to help define the relationship, differences would probably be made up. In this light, our present language of marriage imposes many encumbering myths about maleness and femaleness. For it seems that differences are inevitable in a relationship, especially in an ongoing, goal-oriented relationship such as marriage. Imagine two perfectly identical persons—not real-life identical twins who have long since become distinguishable to themselves and others—but a carbon-copy pair who are in fact the same person in two bodies. If such a pair were to live together, it is obvious they would have to evolve differences which did not before exist. The first time they approached a door that must be entered in single file, the die would be cast. Who is to go first? On what basis is this decision to be made? After it is made and effected, can things ever be the same again? If they fight, someone must win. If one precedes and the other forbears, it cannot then be said they are identical, since one would be aggressive, thoughtless, or "the one who takes the initiative," while the other would be passive, patient, or sluggish. In short, a relationship problem which has nothing to do with individual differences—for there were none in our hypothetical pair—has been solved by evolving differences which may be considered shorthand expressions of the definition of the relationship which was achieved. Later, these differences are available to handle other, similar circumstances wherein identical simultaneous actions are neither possible nor desirable. There is an old European tale of a detective posing as a lodger in a boarding house where a number of mysterious suicides have occurred. He notices across the courtyard from his window an old woman who is weaving. As he becomes entranced by her elaborate movements he begins to mimic them. Then with slow horror it becomes apparent to him that it is she who is following *his* movements, not he who is following hers. As the cause and effect become inextricably tangled, he throws himself out the window at the spinner.

When we consider the work to be done by marital partners—money-making, housekeeping, social life, love-making, and parenting—the tasks which must be attempted and to greater or lesser degree accomplished, then we are overwhelmed by the impossibility of sameness and the efficiency of differences. In the marital relationship, at least, two individuals are faced with the challenge of collaboration on a wide variety of tasks over an indefinite, but presumably long, period of time. In most of these areas—sexual, financial, occupational—no simple or nonpersonal division of labor is obvious. Cultural stereotypes are of some help, but even these appear to be fluid in middle-class America.

From research done on the parents of white, middle-class families observed at the Mental Research Institute, it seems that the way couples handle this crucial relationship problem is by a marital quid pro quo. When two people get together, they immediately exchange clues as to how they are defining the nature of the relationship; this set of behavioral tactics is modified by the other person by the manner in which he responds. The definition which is agreed to (and if the marriage is to work some sort of agreement must be reached), this definition of who each is in relation to the other can best be expressed as a quid pro quo. Quid pro quo (literally "something for something") is an expression of the legal nature of a bargain or contract, in which each party must receive something for what he gives and which, consequently, defines the rights and duties of the parties in the bargain. Marriage, too, can be likened to a bargain which defines the different rights and duties of the spouses, each of which can be said to do X if and because the other does Y. Quid pro quo, then, is a descriptive metaphor for a relationship based on differences, and expression of the redundancies which one observes in marital interaction. One of the most common quid pro quo's observed in white, middle-class, suburban families is the following arrangement: the husband is, broadly, an instrumental type who deals with matters logically and intellectually, and is considered the practical, realistic one; his wife is the more sensitive, affective or "feeling" sort of person who understands people better than things. This sort of quid pro quo is extremely utilitarian for the sort of life such a couple is likely to lead, since the exchange implies a fairly clear division of labor which defines the contribution made by each. Carried to the extreme, this quid pro quo could result in rigidity and misunderstanding, though it is probably not as prone to pathology as some other relationship agreements. That this arrangement has little to do with fixed "sex roles" as we ordinarily think of them has been confirmed by Robert Leik[2] who recently measured this mode of differentiation in actual families as well as "mock family" stranger groups (ie, stranger groups with the same sex and age composition as the real families tested). He found that:

The traditional male role (instrumental, non-emotional behavior) as well as the traditional female role (emotional, non-task behavior) appear when interaction takes place among strangers. *These emphases tend to disappear when subjects interact with their own families* (italics mine).

And he concluded that:

In general, *the relevance of instrumentality and emotionality is quite different for family interaction than for interaction among strangers.* This major finding poses new problems for the theoretical integration of family research with that based on ad hoc experimental groups. Such integration is possible only through recognition of the fact that the context of the interaction with strangers places a meaning on particular acts which is different from the meaning of those acts within the family group (italics mine).

Thus, though this quid pro quo is a common and culturally convenient arrangement, it is not intrinsic to sex roles in marriage. Quite the opposite —the ongoing family relationship apparently custom-tailors the marital bargain to its own particular situation.

Another type of quid pro quo is a "time-bound" relationship, that is, one in which the marital agreement is seriate. If A says to B, let us do X, spouse B assents because they have established a time-bound relationship in which the next move would be B's. The husband may suggest to his wife that they go to a movie; she says yes, and then she has the right to say, we can have a beer afterwards. Similarly, the wife may take certain rights which the husband will grant because he knows he will have a turn in the near future. This time-binding is finite, and while it may not always be a matter of minutes (as it is in sexual intercourse) or of days, it is probably not months or years. Flexibility in time-binding is probably another word for "trust" in relationship, and this may be the most workable of quid pro quo's.*

* Trust is obviously a key concept in marital and even national relationships. It is a belief that the other will do for you what you just did for him, and since you do not know when this will occur, trust appears not to be time-bound. But these are probably intervening signals which declare A's intent to repay B even though no specific date is ever set. I hope not to have my life insurance cashed, but that ad of the great Rock of Gibraltar constantly refurbishes my trust.

The phenomenon of time in relationships—especially marriage—needs study. Relationships that are not rigidly time-bound have great flexibility, while some of the crises of various periods of family life may relate to time. That is, the unspoken promise never kept may, with the passing of time, become more obviously unlikely to be kept, eg, that the husband will spend more time with the family as soon as his business gets on its feet becomes less believable as time goes by and the children grow up; at some point the "promise is broken" simply by the passage of time.*

There is then a peculiar relationship which can be observed in both marital and exploitative political situations, when the quid pro quo is not in fact time-bound but is treated as if it is. If A says to B, let us do X, B says yes because A indicates that eventually B will get his reward. B's day is allegedly coming, and though it never does, A keeps acting as if it is going to and B keeps acting as if he accepts this. These are often pathological relationships which in marriage are frequently characterized by depression and even suicide. The vicious cycle aspect of this relationship is apparent—the more B lets himself be conned, the more he has coming eventually and the less free he is to try another game, since he has so much already invested.

If the gist of these examples has been clear, it should not be necessary to point out that the quid pro quo is not overt, conscious, or the tangible result of real bargaining. Rather, this formulation is the pattern imposed by the observer on the significant redundancies of marital interaction, and should always be understood metaphorically, with the tacit preface, "It seems as if. . . ." The specifics of marital bargaining are not of interest to us. It is at the level of exchange of definitions of the relationship (and, therefore, of self-definition within the relationship) that we can usefully analyze in terms of quid pro quo. If we were to focus only on the content level of marital interaction, we might miss the probability that the so-called masochist does not like or need to suffer—he gets something out of the relationship by using the one-down position as a tactic.

Note, for instance, the following example:†

H: I wish you would fix yourself up. Take $50 and get a permanent, a facial —the works!

---

* So-called menopausal depression is often related by clinicians to the onset of woman's inability to have children. My own observations led me to seriously question this. Among other considerations is the fact that the wish for a child may help deny an unsatisfactory marriage.

† This is not a transcribed example but was reported in couple therapy.

W: I'm sorry, dear, but I don't think we ought to spend the money on me.

H: *! !æ*! I want to spend it on you!

W: I know, dear, but there's all the bills and things. . . .

Here the apparently one-down behavior of the wife is actually quite controlling. If we look beyond the particular $50 about which they are disputing, we can see the relationship they have worked out: the husband is allowed to complain about the wife and act in charge, but the wife indicates she does not intend to follow his orders, that in fact his orders are stupid and, since she sets no time conditions, we do not know if she will ever get a permanent or not. This is one clue to the quid pro quo. Rather than executing a piece of action, this couple is going through a repetitive exchange which defines and redefines the nature of their relationship. Thus on another occasion:

H: Hey, I can't find any white shirts!

W: I'm sorry, dear, they're not ironed yet.

H: Send them to the laundry! I don't care what it costs!

W: We spend so much on groceries and liquor, I felt I should try to save a few pennies here and there.

H: Listen for *!!æ*, I need shirts!

W: Yes, dear, we'll see about it.

Note that just as the wife does not specify *when,* nor whether she is really saying yes or no, the husband does not insist on clear, definite information. It would be misleading to ascribe motivation to this couple. To say he likes to bluster or she likes to frustrate him is senseless and yet irrefutable. What is important is their interactional system: once having established such a pattern of interaction, they are victims of blindness and reinforcement.* Further, their roles are defined not by "male aggressiveness" and "female passivity," but by the simple fact that wives are supposed to be pretty and to take charge of the laundry and husbands are affected by whether or not wives fulfill these expectations.

This is so obvious, yet we as researchers are victims of the sex-role propaganda, too. Most psychiatrists would probably doubt that a family in which the husband runs the house and the wife brings home the money could rear apparently healthy children. Yet in two such examples brought

---

* B. F. Skinner has stated that aperiodic negative reinforcement is the most potent conditioner. Because couples are apart a good deal and engage in a variety of contingencies some of their negative interactions take on an aperiodic aspect. This may make it difficult for A to label B in black and white and yet enhance B's vulnerability.

to our attention this appears to be the case. To understand why these couples function well, we would do much better to analyze their present relationship and seek to identify their particular quid pro quo than to seek the answer in their individual backgrounds and calculate the probabilities that such individuals would meet and marry.

It is becoming more accepted among clinicians that there are no marital relationships which are unbalanced or impoverished for *one* spouse. Observation of the interaction reveals the "bargain" struck between alcoholic and spouse, between wife-beater and wife. The quid pro quo reasoning, then, is still tautological and, within its own sphere of proof, just as irrefutable as notions of human instincts and sex roles. If one believes that marriage is a relationship bargain and is the judge of the terms of this bargain in any particular case, then he can prove his own hypothesis. Again it is important to restate that the concept of family rules in general and of the quid pro quo in particular is only a descriptive metaphor imposed by the observer on the redundancies he observes in interaction. This is not only *true* in the many important areas of the social sciences where the researcher must be both judge and jury, but it is also highly desirable as long as we avoid the pitfalls of reification and acknowledge the fictitious nature of all our constructs. This is a necessary first step if we are to devise a language which will elucidate and convey the process, not the property. Our goal is to do verbal justice to the phenomena in which we are avowedly interested. In our early attempts at interpersonal research, we are constantly limited by the only terminology we have—an ill-fitting bequest from theories of the individual. The notions of family rules and the marital quid pro quo are levers to force us away from the characteristics of individuals onto the nature of their interaction, and are at least somewhat more appropriate to describe the phenomena we will observe in interaction.

It is possible that the formulation of "rules" such as the quid pro quo has enormous predictive potential. If we are reasonably accurate in our formulation of a metaphor for a couple's relationship, we can forecast the likelihood of success or failure and even the fate of children in the family system. For instance:

The "Big Daddy-Baby Doll" arrangement is not likely to be a workable quid pro quo. While Baby Doll may be able to continue her half of the bargain for some time, the material offerings with which Big Daddy must be constantly forthcoming are, after all, finite in number. There are only so many countries to tour and so many jewels which can be bought and worn. No matter what his wealth, her satiation will probably eventually endanger the quid pro quo so that the marriage must terminate or find a new level of operation.

Other arrangements may survive the early period of marriage but cannot be expected to accommodate children. For instance:

A couple had a quid pro quo of total independence; each pursued his own career and was succeeding. They scorned the usual financial and housekeeping arrangements, basing all decisions on the maximization of the independence of both. Though one might wonder how it happened in an atmosphere of total independence, the wife became pregnant; her career and way of life were drastically limited. The marriage foundered because the original quid pro quo could not possibly be made to include maternity and motherhood. A new relationship had to be established.

Some parental relationships can survive the onslaught of a little stranger, but cannot accommodate his emotional health:

The family maxim seemed to be "People who live in glass houses shouldn't throw stones." Husband and wife scrupulously avoided even the mildest and— to us—vital criticism of each other, and in turn was not criticized by the spouse. This ban on information, however, provides a poor teaching context for children and is not likely to encourage healthy, spontaneous curiosity. The marriage lasts, but the brighter-than-average son was referred to therapy for marked academic underachievement.

These examples are, of course, retrospective. But our success in post-diction of psychopathology in children from the blind analysis of examples of marital interaction in terms of the quid pro quo leads us to hope that, with refinement, prediction and prophylaxis of pathological systems are possible.

### Summary

A theory of marriage is proposed which is based on the relationship rather than the individuals. Specifically, the quid pro quo formulation holds that the similarities and differences between spouses comprise the metaphorical "bargain" on which the marital relationship is based. The advantages of this scheme are that (1) we have a language which aids our observation of truly interactional phenomena, and (2) there is the promise of improved predictive power when the "rules" of the relationship are grasped.

## REFERENCES

1. JACKSON, D. D.: Study of the Family. Reprinted on pp. 2–20 of this volume.
2. LEIK, R. K.: Instrumentality and Emotionality in Family Interaction, Sociometry 26:131–145, 1963.

*In the next contribution, Haley presents the outline of a theory of pathological systems. Basing himself on the study of triadic relationships as his minimal unit of observation, he adds an additional order of complexity to the potential pathologies of dyads as described by Jackson in his* quid pro quo *paper. In these triangular relationships, Haley postulates, one member is usually of a different generation from the other two, and the triangle consists in a coalition of two members belonging to two different generations (in the case of family relations) or to two different hierarchical levels (as may be the case in an organizational system) against the second member's peer. In and by itself this constellation is not yet pathological although it is likely to be the cause of manifest friction, conflict, and jealousy. It begins to satisfy the accepted criteria of pathological involvement only if the existence of the coalition is* denied, *be it because it is tabooed, or because it violates the principle of equal rights and equal treatment for all concerned or any other, similar convention. Two things are of particular interest in this paper. The first is that it provides a new, interactional perspective of what is considered the focal point of intrapsychic pathology, i.e., the Oedipus conflict. The other is the fact that even in the average family, composed of two parents, two children, and two sets of grandparents, there potentially exist fifty-two triangles of the type just described, and that every member of such a three-generational family is involved in twenty-one triangles, every one of which may be a source of pathological complications—a complexity of truly staggering proportions which is all the more incisive as it remains largely outside the awareness of all concerned.*

# TOWARD A THEORY OF PATHOLOGICAL SYSTEMS

## Jay Haley, M.A.

At this time psychiatry would appear to be undergoing a basic change in orientation. Quite possibly the change is a discontinuous one, which

Reprinted by permission of the author, the editor and the publisher from J. Haley, "Toward a Theory of Pathological Systems," in *Family Therapy and Disturbed Families,* ed. G. Zuk and I. Boszormenyi-Nagy (Palo Alto, Science and Behavior Books, 1967), pp. 11–27.

can mean that the knowledge and training necessary for the previous orientation is not helpful in dealing with the developments yet to come. To describe a change of this kind while it is happening is difficult, but the emerging ideas are becoming sufficiently clear to be contrasted with the past point of view.

## Method

In the past it was assumed that a science of man could be developed by studying a man in isolation from his fellows, by examining him as he dealt with strangers in artificial group situations, or by analyzing the ideology of the society he inhabited. Primarily man as an individual has been the focus of study; the goal has been to describe and classify the individual in terms of his body type, character, personality, clinical diagnosis, and so on. The nature of this focus has severely limited the possible explanations about people and why they do what they do. Putting the individual person alone in a frame, the investigator attempted to explain all there was to know about him without including other people in the picture; to explain "why" someone did what he did, it was necessary to postulate something inside the person, such as instincts or drives or emotions. If a person behaved peculiarly, it had to follow that there was an internal defect or the person was experiencing conflicts within himself, such as conflicts between opposing drives or needs. If a person changed in psychotherapy, then something inside him must have changed, such as an increase in understanding or a shift in perception. When men of different cultures were compared, the individuals were contrasted on the basis of their ways of thinking or their values and beliefs. The influence of psychiatric ideology upon social theorists usually led them more in the direction of the individual and further from a social orientation. Within psychiatry there was an absolutely basic assumption that the problem was how to diagnose and treat the individual patient.

In the last decade in psychiatry the frame around the individual has been broken, and questions about "why" a man does what he does are being answered in terms of the context of relationships he creates and inhabits. The reasons for this change have been the continuing emphasis upon interpersonal relations over the years and the recent development of ideas about systems. The change is a shift in focus from the individual and his nature to the habitual and systematic patterns of behavior men develop when dealing with their intimates. The direct manifestation of this change is in the field of family research and family therapy.

In the last few years, for the first time in history, married couples and whole families are being brought under systematic observation. Family members are observed actually dealing with one another. The research problem is how to conceptualize the repeating, responsive behavior in this ongoing social network in such a way that statements about regularities in the interchange will hold true over time. The problem is no longer how to characterize and classify these individuals; it is how to describe and classify the habitual patterns of responsive behavior exchanged by intimates. Can one categorize the typical processes in the group, describe changes if they occur, and differentiate one organization from another? With this focus, the "cause" of why someone does what he does is shifting from inside him to the context in which he lives. The question of whether a family containing a psychiatric patient is a different type of organization from another family is a question of whether there is a system of inter- active behavior which provokes, or requires, one or more members of the system to behave in a way that could be classified as psychopathological. A similar question is whether there are discernable trends in relationships that predictably lead to violence or divorce and the dissolution of the fam- ily. These questions have relevance beyond the family research field. Inso- far as any group of men have a history and a future together (for exam- ple, research groups or business organizations), the type of exchanges generated in the system may determine whether there will be amiable relations and productive work or a disturbed and unhappy group of par- ticipants. In the larger social scene, the family of nations may develop patterns of exchange that predictably lead to disruption and war. For inquiry into these questions, the focus must be shifted to the exchange of acts in a relationship and away from the description of man as if he were autonomous. This means breaking new ground.

If we take seriously the accusation often made that the psychological and social sciences, as contrasted with the physical sciences, are still in the dark ages, there is an analogy between what is happening today and what happened in the physical sciences in the seventeenth century. What had survived from Greece at that time was an interest in the orbits of the planets and a theory that the planets moved in circular orbits around the earth, the center of the universe. In this period, certain men began to doubt the explanations of the ancients about these orbits, and yet they had few actual observations of planet movements and they were even un- certain whether such observations were necessary. They had no concep- tualization of physical laws as a framework for the observations available to them, and they were handicapped by a variety of past theories, includ- ing theories that the planets were propelled by angels. A further difficulty was the opposition to new points of view shown by an establishment of knowledgeable people who had an investment in the ancient theories. Yet within a relatively short time the orbits of the planets were accurately determined and from this effort came the laws of Newton, which had relevance far beyond this particular question and influenced the entire nature of scientific investigation.

Today in the field of social relations we appear to be in a remarkably similar situation. Some people have begun to doubt the past theories about human beings, such as the idea that men are driven by instincts, and yet there are few factual observations of people in "orbit" in their intimate relationships. Many people are even uncertain whether such observations are necessary. We also have no conceptualization of laws of social relationships, if such regularities exist, as a framework in which to place the few observations that we do have. In addition, our current establishment of knowledgeable people has a large investment in the past theories of the individual as an autonomous being.

In that earlier scientific endeavor, there were several steps necessary before the problem could be solved. First of all, it was necessary to make a bold shift in the focus of attention. Copernicus did this when he suggested that planets orbited around the sun rather than the earth. To take this necessary step, men had to revise basic assumptions about man and the universe. The current shift of focus in psychiatry from the individual to the social network he inhabits could be said to be comparable to the shift from the earth to the sun as the center of the universe. It is a bold step, and many people react almost religiously against the idea that man is not the focal point but is rather helplessly responding within his network of ongoing relationships. Those who protest say the importance of the individual is being overlooked and he is being made a mere element in the system, just as they said man was diminished if his planet was not the focal point of the universe.[1]

The natural scientists' second step was to begin to doubt the statements and observations of the ancients and to collect accurate observations of

[1] A similar response was made to Freud when he suggested that the idea of man's being unable to control his own mind was the third great blow (after a sun-oriented universe and a descent from animals). Freud argued that man was driven by unconscious forces within himself which he was helpless to control. The current family-oriented view in psychiatry would also argue that man is helplessly driven, but by the people around him in the system he inhabits. Perhaps this diminishes man even more, since the "cause" of his behavior is no longer even located within him but in the outer context. However, this point of view also implies that he participates in creating that context.

the movements of the planets. Kepler obtained these "facts," and after immersing himself in them was forced to abandon the ancient idea of circular orbits and to conclude that the planets moved in elliptical patterns. This discovery of the shape of the orbits made possible the formulation of a new set of causal explanations. Today we have begun to doubt the statements and observations of our own "ancients" but we have hardly begun the task of collecting our observations. Despite the large number of books on marriage and the family, which describe what families are supposed to be like, it is only in the last few years that investigators have actually begun to bring families together and to observe the members dealing with one another. We have a great many opinions, which are adaptable to any causal explanation, but we will need many years of observing and testing families in operation before we have sufficient observations to refute a theory.

The final step of the men of earlier times was to derive from their new observations new generalizations sufficiently broad to include the idea that what occurred in the heavens also occurred on earth. In this way they delineated laws of nature that had wide application in many fields of endeavor. Now we, too, are beginning to assume that the idea of a coalition between family members is relevant to coalition patterns in any ongoing social group and that patterns in a marriage could be relevant to those of international relations. That is, we are beginning to seek laws, or regularities, which hold true in any system of relationships with a past and a future. It is this possibility that makes research on the family appear potentially so rewarding.

We can hope that it will not take as long to develop a science of human relationships as it did to develop the physical sciences, because we have that vast attempt to guide us. However, we should also not assume that we can jump the preliminary steps necessary and have a sophisticated theory of human relationships appear full blown in all its grandeur. Over time, we will need the three factors necessary in any scientific endeavor: (1) we must have a collection of facts—observable events which either occur or do not occur, (2) we must be able to formulate those facts into patterned regularities, and (3) we must devise theories to account for these regularities and be willing to discard past ideas if they handicap us in our efforts.

Regarding the collection of facts, in family research it is not yet clear what the relevant "facts" are or what the best method is of collecting them. When studying families, if we confine ourselves to observable events we have only the behavior of family members as they respond to one another: their bodily movements and vocal intonations, their words and acts. If we extend our "facts" to include unobservable events, then we have the emotions, attitudes, expectations, and thought processes of the participating family members. Agreement has not yet been reached as to which of these types of data are most appropriate. Additionally, we face the problem that our "facts" are determined by the ways in which we collect them; there is not agreement about how to proceed in family research. There are three general methods of collecting data: (1) using the self-report of family members about their families obtained either by questionnaire or by interview, (2) bringing family members together to study them in operation, with the data consisting of observations by human observers who attempt to reach agreement on what they see happening, and (3) placing families in communication networks where their behavior is recorded on instruments. These three different schools of family research are obviously going to collect different "facts" about families.

A further difficulty in family research is the problem of formulating some sort of theory as a guide for the type of observations to make and the kind of methodology to use. We need to conceptualize formal patterns of human relations in such a way that we can ultimately collect data which will verify whether or not certain patterns actually occur. At this time we must conceptualize with only a minimum number of observations of families in operation. Yet we must speculate on the basis of what we have and then decide what sort of approach might support or refute our speculations. A speculation will be offered here about a characteristic pattern which appears evident in pathological systems.

Although men have not focused upon the systematic study of relationships, they have observed each other in action for many years and we might assume that if some aspect of ongoing relationships was truly important it would be emphasized in past literature. There exists a formal pattern that has been noted so often that it has been given a name, "The Eternal Triangle," and has been the focus of man's attention to psychiatry, religion, and politics, as well as in the fiction he has created to express his life experiences. It seems, in fact, to be the only relationship pattern that has been named in folk speech. Perhaps its importance is based on the fact that the essential learning context of the human being is triangular: in the usual biological family unit, two people unite to create and rear a third.

In the family research of the last decade there has been a progression from descriptions of individuals to descriptions of dyads (such as mother and child) to triadic descriptions (such as parents and disturbed child). Larger family groupings, for example a quadrad, have not been emphasized, despite a move toward studying the entire family network. The extended family is usually discussed in terms of the smaller units. For example, the influence of the grandparent generation is usually discussed in terms of the influence on a parent of *his* mother and father. This focus on a maximum unit of three people would seem to be partly because of the complexity of larger units and partly because the triangle appears to be a "natural" unit.

## The Perverse Triangle

If we take the triangle as our unit of study in a family or in any on-going social system, we can raise the question of what sort of triangular arrangement will generate what could be called a pathological system. In this case "pathological" means a system that will lead to the dissolution of itself or to violence among the elements, or indicates elements which behave in ways that appear peculiar and inappropriate. In terms of the family, a pathological system is one resulting in continual conflict, in divorce, or in the kind of symptomatic distress in one or more family members that requires community attention. If we examine the past literature and activities of man, we find that there is a triangle of this sort —it can be called a perverse triangle—that has long been taken for granted without being made explicit. These are its characteristics:

1. The people responding to each other in the triangle are not peers, but one of them is of a different generation from the other two. By "generation" is meant a different order in the power hierarchy, as in a human generation of parent and child or in an administrative hierarchy such as manager and employee.

2. In the process of their interaction together, the person of one generation forms a coalition with the person of the other generation against his peer. By "coalition" is meant a process of joint action which is *against* the third person (in contrast to an alliance, in which two people might get together in a common interest independent of the third person).

3. The coalition between the two persons is denied. That is, there is certain behavior which indicates a coalition which, when it is queried, will be denied as a coalition. More formally, the behavior at one level which indicates that there is a coalition is qualified by metacommunicative behavior indicating there is not.

In essence, the perverse triangle is one in which the separation between generations is breached in a covert way. When this occurs as a repetitive pattern, the system will be pathological. This concept is not being offered as something new but rather as a more precise formulation of what is becoming commonly assumed in the literature on pathology and the family.

As an illustration, in the area of administration it has been taken for granted that a breach of generations will make difficulty in an organization. It is said if a manager "plays favorites" among his employees the organization will be in distress. Put in terms of a triangle, the manager in such a case is forming a coalition across generation lines with one person against his peer. If he merely forms an alliance with an employee, the problem does not necessarily arise, but at the moment he sides with one *against* another while simultaneously denying that this is happening, the system will become pathological.[2]

This illustration is a rephrasing of a point made in most administrative manuals: the administrative levels in the hierarchy must be kept separate for the proper functioning of an organization. There is one other point assumed in good administrative procedure: communication should not jump levels. That is, an employee should not be allowed to "go over the head" of his immediate superior and contact a higher superior. Once again, this idea can be rephased in terms of a breaching of generations: a coalition between a higher and a lower level against a middle level in the power hierarchy. It is assumed that such breaching should not take place and that if it occurs secretly as a consistent pattern, the organization will be in distress.

One would expect that if this perverse triangle were causal to pathological systems it would not only be avoided in organizations but it would be assumed to be important in the field of psychopathology, and this is obviously so. In psychiatry, one finds the perverse triangle, slightly rephrased, as the central thesis in psychodynamic theory. In psychoanalytic theory and in much of psychiatry it is argued that the Oedipal conflict is a focal point in the cause of psychiatric distress. The origin of this idea is particularly pertinent here. Sigmund Freud at one time proposed that

---

[2] If one seeks a "cause" of the distress in terms of the individual, it could be put in terms of an unresolvable conflict, or paradox, for the person coalesced against. A generation line or administrative level is implicitly a coalition among peers; employers are in coalition with others on their level and employees are in coalition with others on their level. Within that framework, if an employer and employee form a coalition against another, the other is faced with two conflicting definitions of the situation: (a) his fellow employee is in coalition with him as part of the natural framework of administration, but within that framework (b) his fellow employee is siding with the employer against him. Being forced to respond when there is a conflict between these two different orders of coalition creates distress.

hysteria was the result of a sexual assault on the patient by an older relative. In this sense he proposed that there was a breaching of generations which should not have occurred and, insofar as it was a secret act, could be considered a covert coalition across generations. However, he then discovered that in certain cases the sexual incident could not actually have happened, and he shifted from the idea of a familial cause of this malady to an intrapsychic cause—a fantasied wish for the sexual act. This was the birth of the Oedipal conflict, the wish of the boy to have sexual relations with his mother and the consequent fear that his father would not take this coalition kindly and would castrate him. The Oedipal conflict became a universal explanation of the neurosis.

In essence, this conflict, as in the play from which Freud drew the name, can be seen as a coalition across generation lines which is covert or denied. The action of the play *Oedipus* consists of the lifting of the secrecy of this breaching of generations. Thanks to Freud, one can discover this pattern in most of the drama and fiction man enjoys. If one analyzes the content of popular moving pictures, one notes that the theme of the younger man coalescing with a woman against an older or more powerful man is so common that it is standard procedure. The outcome of this triangle seems to vary with different decades, perhaps reflecting changes in the authority structure of the culture. As another of the endless variations, we have *Lolita,* where the older man secretly coalesces with the girl against her mother. One might expect that the essence of dramatic conflict resides in the secret coalition across generations, perhaps because the audience recognizes the danger of it. It could be argued that this pattern is portrayed symbolically as a reflection of the incest tabu, but one could also argue that the incest tabu is a product of the recognition that cross-generation coalitions result in distress for all participants in the family network.

In the psychiatry of the past, which focused upon the individual, the triangle was considered of basic importance, and when we turn to the newer approach of the relation of pathology to the family we find a similar emphasis common in the literature. Many family descriptions are cast in a framework of individual description, but implicit in them is a view of pathology nestling in a perverse triangle. For example, it has long been suggested that a disturbed child is a product of parents who are in conflict: the child is caught between them by being in coalition with one or the other. When the mother is described as overprotective and the father as passive, the implication is that mother is siding with child against father, who remains withdrawn. The mirror picture is presented, where father and child are in covert coalition against a difficult mother. Generally, the inability of parents of a disturbed child to maintain a common front to enforce discipline is a reflection of their inability to maintain a separation between the generations. A similar breach of generations appears in the case of the disturbed child who associates with his parents but avoids his peers.

It is also becoming more common to read in the descriptions of the extended family a similar pattern occurring in the next generation in disturbed families. It is often pointed out that there is a cross-generational coalition by a parent with a grandparent, usually phrased in terms of an excessively dependent relationship. For example, the husband's mother is said to be constantly in the picture, and while the wife pushes him to assert himself and keep his mother in her place the husband indicates that his mother isn't really a problem (thereby denying the coalition against his wife). Commonly, too, in the disturbed family a wife is said to be excessively involved with her mother in a coalition against her husband. In folk speech we find the situation a problem sufficient to produce the "mother-in-law jokes."

The existence of a coalition between a disturbed child and a parent occurs so often in conjunction with a coalition of one of his parents with a grandparent that one might suggest they are inseparable. That is, it could be stated as a hypothesis that a breaching of generations with the child will coincide with a breaching at the next generational level. (Often, too, it will coincide with a coalition of child and grandparent against parent.) If such a triangle at one generation always accompanies a similar one at the next generational level, we can suspect a regularity in networks of family relations where the patterns in any one part of the family are formally the same as those in some other part.

Anyone who has observed or treated abnormal families assumes that the ways the parents form coalitions with the child against one another appears "causal" to the disturbance in the child. The idea is also present, with a slight translation, in the studies of the hospitals where patients are sent for treatment. Some years ago Stanton and Schwartz noted in their study of the mental hospital (Stanton and Schwartz, 1954) that a conflict between an administrator and a therapist was a "cause" of a patient erupting in a disturbance. This result can also be seen when one staff member sides with a patient against another staff member in a perverse triangle.

If we use the triangle as a unit of study and break down a family network into its triangular components, a rather awesome complexity appears. In an average-size family where there are two parents and two children, and each parent has two parents, this group of eight people composes 56 triangles. Any one person in the family is involved in 21 family triangles simultaneously (and this does not include aunts and uncles, neighbors and employers). Every one of the 21 triangles in which parents and children are involved carries the possibility of a coalition across generations. If the occurrence of a secret coalition across generations is indeed pathological, the potentiality for disturbance is exceedingly high in any family.

An analysis of a family network in terms of triangles also reveals that any one person in the family is at the nexus of a large number of these triangles. He is also the *only* person at this particular nexus. The fact that no two people are in the same position in a context, even in the same family, raises profound questions about whether individuals can be compared. To say that a neurotic is different from a psychotic implies that the context in which they live is comparable. If it is not, the two people cannot be compared. All attempts to classify individuals into types have assumed that they face essentially the same situations and that therefore differences must be *within* them. This assumption was made without any investigation to determine whether different individuals face the same situations. The family evidence being gathered indicates that different individuals live in quite different worlds.

If we assume that an individual's behavior is adaptive to his intimate relationships, it follows that he must not behave in one triangular group in a way which will disrupt another triangular grouping in which he is involved. For example, his behavior in the triangle with his parents will have repercussions in the triangle with his grandparents. In fact, the way a person relates to any one pair in the network will influence the response to him of any other pair. In a family where all the triangular groups consist of amiable members, the situation does not appear complex. But let us suppose that a child is at the nexus of two triangles, or groups, which are in conflict. Suppose, for example, that if he pleases his mother and her mother he will disturb his relationship with his father and his mother because the two groups are in conflict. To behave adaptively, the child must maneuver in such a way that his behavior in one group does not disrupt the other. If one imagines that all 21 of the triangles the child inhabits are in conflict with each other, and if the child is at the nexus of all these conflicting groups, then to adapt and survive in such a network he must exhibit strange and conflictual behavior. It is possible to explain the symptoms of schizophrenia as adaptive to this kind of conflicting set of groups. In fact, it appears that this way of looking at the family system could ultimately lead to a social description of any symptomatic behavior —a translation of psychopathology into the language of social behavior.

### Schizophrenia as a Conflict of Groups

A way of explaining schizophrenia was offered some years ago by a research group in which I participated. It was noted that schizophrenia could be described as a disorder of levels of communication: the patient qualified what he said or did with an indication that he was saying or doing something else, and then qualified this meta-message with yet another which conflicted (Haley, 1959). That is, schizophrenic behavior was described as a disorder of Logical Types in the Russellian sense. It was hypothesized at that time by Gregory Bateson that the patient must have been raised in a learning context of conflicting levels of communication. This context was labeled a double-bind situation (Bateson et al., 1956). The idea proposed was that the schizophrenic had been raised in a situation where he faced conflicting levels of message from a parent or a combination of both parents with an injunction against commenting on this conflict or leaving the field.

At that time I was particularly interested in attempting to correlate more precisely the behavior of the schizophrenic with his situation in his family to investigate whether schizophrenia was a form of adaptable, responsive behavior. To collect data on this point, it was necessary to accept the reports of the family members about what had happened in the past during a psychotic episode. Alternatively, one can observe the occurrence of psychotic symptoms in the patient during the course of family therapy and examine the situation in which the symptoms erupted. Such an incident can be used here to illustrate the familial context of a schizophrenic.

A schizophrenic daughter improved sufficiently to be sent home from the hospital on a trial visit, and her parents responded to this situation by separating. Mother left father (but called him and told him where she was going) and she asked her daughter to go with her (even though at the time she was saying she could not tolerate her daughter's company). When her mother made this request, the daughter faced a situation in which she had to choose between her parents and either stay with father or go with mother. The daughter's solution was rather complex. She went with her mother, but when they arrived at their destination, her grandmother's home, she called her father. The mother then protested that this meant she was siding with the father against her, and the girl said she had only called the father because when she said goodbye to him she had given him an odd look. A characteristic symptom of this daughter was her "odd looks" and the question was whether this behavior was irrational or adaptive, given this situation. The girl's behavior became more extreme when the father came and reclaimed the mother. The girl was asked by her mother to go to the store, and declined. The grandmother did the errand, and while the mother and father were in the other room discussing the girl's refusal, the girl began to scream. She was then rehospitalized.

At one time, the daughter's behavior might have been explained as adaptive to a situation where there was a conflict of family rules. The rule was that the daughter was not to form an open coalition with either father or mother, and yet the separation forced her to break her rule. She could not merely do nothing because that would have meant staying with her father. Her solution was to have a symptom—the odd look—which solved the problem of how to avoid siding with either parent.

In terms of the larger family context, it is possible to see a family "rule" in a somewhat new way. Repetitive behavior between two people can be seen as not merely the following of an arbitrary rule that has developed between them but as a product of responses in other parts of the family. That is, a rule not to have an open coalition with mother or father can be seen as a response to the consequences among other family members if the coalition occurs.

Examining the larger context in which this girl was living, and focusing upon only the most important people in her life—her parents and two grandmothers—we see that she was involved in a group of ten cross-generational triangles. It would be possible that none of these triangles would involve cross-generational coalitions. The grandmothers might keep out of the parental difficulties, the parents might maintain a separation between themselves and the daughter, and the daughter might not attempt a coalition with either parents or grandparents but would confine her associations to her peers. Quite the opposite extreme was apparent in this situation. Impressions from family interviews indicated that all family members were involved in a consistent pattern of perverse triangles. The two grandmothers bid against each other for the daughter, the father's mother sided with him against the wife (she had once offered the wife a cash bribe to leave her son because she could take better care of him), and the daughter was constantly siding with her mother's mother against her mother and staying with her on visits home from the hospital. The most apparent and persistent cross-generation coalitions occurred in the triangle of the girl with her parents. Father accused mother and daughter of being against him, which they denied. Mother accused daughter of being in coalition with father against her and cited sexual play between them, among other activities, as proof of this. Generally the parents behaved as if there were no generational differences with the daughter.

The amount of struggle and conflict between the different family triangles appeared extraordinary and was complicated even further by the mother's sisters, who were also continually intervening in the family affair. When the girl was forced by this physical separation to choose between her parents, her response carried repercussions throughout the wider network of family triangles. If she went with her mother or if she did not, she was faced with a situation where her response would not only be condemned but she would provoke open disruption in the extended family. For example, to go with her mother also meant joining the mother's family against the father's family, joining one grandmother against another, and joining grandmother against father. At the nexus of warring family factions, what would be an "appropriate and normal" response to this situation? It would seem to be one in which the girl should behave in one way to satisfy one faction and another way to satisfy another, and then disqualify both ways by indicating she was not responsible for what happened in any case. Such conflicting communication would be diagnosed as schizophrenic behavior.

### Persisting Triangles

Assuming for the moment that a pathological family system consists of a network of perverse triangles, questions arise about how a family got that way, why the members persist in behavior that is disturbing, and how one may go about changing such a system. It seems doubtful that the "cause" can be sought in the behavior of any single individual or even that of a set of parents. The pattern undoubtedly is passed down over many generations. However, the pattern must be continually reinforced if it is to continue. At a minimum, two people each of a different generation must cooperate to perpetuate it.

One might look upon the situation as one in which at least two people are dissatisfied with the status quo. If a wife is pleased with her association with her husband she is not likely to attempt to join child or parent against him. In a sense, such a coalition is an attempt at a change. Yet there is a perduring quality even in this attempt at change, because to breach generations in an attempt to change continues the family situation which leads to dissatisfaction. However, if one examines the question of "cause" in terms of dissatisfaction, he is focusing once again upon the individual. Such a focus usually indicates an avoidance of looking at the larger context. When one shifts to the larger view, alternative explanations appear that make "cause" appear more complex. For example, it is possible that the wife joins child against husband not merely because of internal dissatisfaction but as an adaptive response to her relationship with her parents. To maintain stability in relation to her parents, she may find it necessary to join child against husband because an amiable relationship with her husband would have repercussions in the way she is dealing with her parents and the way they are dealing with each other. In this sense, "cause" is a statement about regularities in larger networks.[3]

The argument that the extended family has less influence today because many generations do not live under the same roof is not necessarily valid. Young people may marry and settle in their little box in the suburbs, but they are not out of contact with their extended families. Anyone who has dealt with disturbed couples or families knows that communication takes place and repercussions occur in the extended family no matter how geographically distant the members may be.

When one examines an idea of this sort and thinks about how to verify it with more than impressionistic data, the basic problems of family research arise. Suppose we wished to test the hypothesis that families which exhibit violence, dissolve in divorce, or produce members suffering from psychopathology all characteristically exhibit covert cross-generational coalitions. In the past we might have assumed that we need only ask the family members the right sort of questions in order to determine whether the perverse triangle is more frequent in "abnormal" than in "normal" families. Now it is becoming more accepted that the self-report of family members can be used, at most, as an indicator of an area of research and not as a means of validating a hypothesis. (This is particularly so when one is concerned with levels of behavior that involve denials.) It seems necessary to bring the family members together and study the network in operation. One must precisely define "coalition" and "generation," and devise a context that will generate an opportunity for coalitions while providing a means of denying their existence. Then one must place family members in this context to determine whether or not such coalitions occur in a variety of family triangular groupings, and do this with a sufficiently large sample of families to be able to make statements about differences at some designated level of significance. If one uses human observers to observe families and guess whether coalitions are occurring there is always the possibility of bias. If one does not use observers, he must devise a situation where instruments will record the results—and the use of instru-

[3] It would seem superfluous to bring to the question of "cause" of psychopathological behavior anything about the person's history, past conditioning, or internalized images. An adequate description of the present family network should be sufficient.

mentation to record multiple levels of communication is difficult. Yet ultimately if we are to bring rigor to this sort of study we must provide the opportunity for covert coalitions as they are defined in that context (Haley, 1962). Devising such an experimental procedure and testing an adequate sample is, let us say, a challenging task.

Granting the complexity of the data in the field of ongoing relationships, we have on our side the fact that such relationships appear to contain enormous redundancies. If we can describe and test a systematic pattern in one segment of a family, we should find echoes of that pattern throughout the other parts of the system. We appear to be dealing with networks as tightly organized in repetitious patterns as the orbits of planets.

### Family Therapy

The tightness and rigidity of the family network become particularly evident to therapists attempting to bring about change in whole families. As with individuals, family studies indicate that flexibility is synonymous with normalcy and rigidity with pathology. It would seem to follow naturally that the more severe the disturbance, the more rigid the family pattern; change appears to be brought about more easily with minor pathologies than with families of schizophrenics. Had we more elaborate theories of the technique of family therapy, we might have more success with severely disturbed families. It would appear, however, that such theory will only be built over time.

The various methods of family therapy that have appeared would seem to have one factor in common: a focus on the problem of coalition both within the family and between therapist and family members. It is generally assumed that it is unwise for a therapist to join one member of a family against another. Yet it also appears that members of disturbed families are exasperatingly skillful at provoking a therapist to side with them and at antagonizing him to side against them. In terms of the point being made here, a therapist is causing rather than resolving a disturbed system if he joins in such coalitions while denying that he is doing so. Insofar as the parents consult him as an expert, he is of a different generation, a different order in the authority hierarchy. Should he join the child against the parents, as many novice therapists are tempted to do for reasons of sympathy and individual orientation, he is instituting a pathological system and repeating the usual patterns of the family.[4] The danger that the coalition will be a secret one is particularly present with those therapists who side with the child but deny it because they know they should focus upon the whole family. One way to analyze family therapy is in terms of a process of the therapist constantly disinvolving himself from coalitions with family members as these occur in all their subtle variations. The art of family therapy seems to be that of developing ways of siding with all family members at once, or of clearly taking sides with different factions at different times while acknowledging this, or of leaving the coalition situation ambiguous so that family members are uncertain where the therapist stands. Family therapists seem to recognize, either consciously or by intuition, that generations should not be breached, and that denial should not take place if a breach does occur.

The tightness of organization in the disturbed family also indicates new possibilities in family therapy appearing on the horizon. If all parts of a family network are responsive to change in any one part because of the tightness of the organization, then a certain freedom appears with regard to which set of family relationships to focus upon in family treatment. Certain factions of a family might be more accessible to change than others. In schizophrenia, for example, the parents and schizophrenic child might be the triangle most resistant to change so that treatment of another section of the family could produce better results. Yet to suggest this possibility indicates how rapid a change has been taking place in psychiatry. Not many years ago, it was thought a waste of time to attempt psychotherapy with a schizophrenic. More recently, it has seemed pointless to treat *only* the schizophrenic, because of his involvement with his parents (and the hospital staff), who should also enter treatment. Now it is conceivable that the schizophrenic could be treated without ever entering therapy since a change in him is assumed to be brought about if another part of the extended family in which he lives is changed. Although such an idea might appear extreme, there is a recent precedent for it. Disturbed children were once treated as *the* problem; then the parents were given individual treatment in addition; and finally, parents and child were treated as a group. Recently it has been so taken for granted that the dis-

---

[4] A similar danger occurs with individual therapy where the therapist declines to see the family members of his patient. A spouse may find himself faced with a coalition between an authority and the relative (with all information about the relationship funneled through the relative). A disturbance in the family system can be perpetuated by this secret cross-generation coalition.

turbed child is a "product" of the marital problems of the parents that the child is excluded and only the parents treated. This shift toward assuming that the "cause" of an individual's behavior resides in the context in which he is living reflects the extensive changes that have taken place in the basic orientation of psychiatry in less than a decade. Only that long ago was it suggested that the symptoms of a patient are a product of, and serve a current function in, a unique type of family. If families with abnormal members have a special type of organization, as family research is now attempting to document, then the argument that symptoms are responsive behavior to a particular context is supported (in contrast to the past view that psychopathology is only a product of something askew inside the individual). The consequences of this different point of view must inevitably permeate psychiatric thinking. In diagnosis, the change will be toward including more than one person in the diagnostic category. In treatment, the assumption is developing that one person cannot change unless the context of a relationship in which he lives also changes, which leads to more treatment of marital pairs and whole families as a natural consequence. It is possible that individual theory can be extended to include the relationship, but the current confusion in the field when attempts are made to bridge between the two points of view indicate that this is doubtfully possible and that future developments in psychiatry will represent a discontinuous change from the past.

## REFERENCES

BATESON, G., et al. Toward a theory of schizophrenia. *Behav. Sci.,* 1956, *1,* 251–264.

HALEY, J. An interactional description of schizophrenia. *Psychiatry,* 1959, *22,* 321–332.

HALEY, J. Family experiments: a new type of experimentation. *Fam. Proc.,* 1962, *1,* 265–293.

STANTON, A. H. & SCHWARTZ, M. S. *The mental hospital.* New York: Basic Books, 1954.

*The elements of denial and mutual make-believe, as well as the attribution of madness or badness to the family member who breaks an important family rule and points to the lie, is also the core element of Ferreira's article on family myths. But while Haley, in his preceding paper, deals mainly with conflicts and struggles arising out of covert coalitions of two family members against a third, Ferreira's concept of the family myth refers primarily to patterns of reality distortions shared by all family members involved—and even by outside observers. The amazing plausibility of the make-believe, subscribed to by the family and convincingly presented to the outside world, is presented here on the strength of evidence from Ferreira's extensive experimental research on family interaction and decision-making.*[1] *It goes to show once again how difficult it is to free one's own thinking from the monadic, linear, and unidirectional model of "somebody does something," imposed on our thought processes by the structure of all Indo-European languages, and shift to the circular causality of systems interaction in which every event causes a response which through its very occurrence then feeds back upon its cause, thus becoming itself a cause of further interaction, and so on* ad infinitum.

*As the reader will appreciate, Ferreira's paper is thus not only a further elucidation of the concept of family rules and of "mental" disturbances as the outcome of disturbed interaction, it is also a seminal contribution to the understanding of the pathologies of larger social systems (e.g., corporations, political systems, and international relations).*

[1] Antonio J. Ferreira and William D. Winter, "Family Interaction and Decision-Making," *Archives of General Psychiatry* 13:214–23, 1965. William D. Winter and Antonio J. Ferreira, "Interaction Process Analysis in Family Decision-Making," *Family Process* 6:155–72, 1967.

# FAMILY MYTHS

## Antonio J. Ferreira, M.D.

In the course of a research project on family decision-making, we came across a family whose behavior in the testing situation was such a contradiction of the cherished image they had of themselves as to excite our curiosity and attention. The family had been in conjoint therapy for several months, and the family therapist as well as a number of other investigators happened to have unanimous opinions as to the roles played by the three family members. The mother, who described herself as "bossy and domineering" had, for all appearances, the ruling hand in the family: very animated, she talked all the time, asked questions, gave opinions, took direction. The father, a former hospitalized "schizophrenic," was, by contrast, a very passive and aloof individual, who hardly participated in the conversation, soft-spoken, unassuming, and unobtrusive almost to the point of self-effacement. The child, a thirteen year old boy who was said to be making a poor school adjustment and to be given to temper tantrums, was obviously anxious and ill-at-ease, laughing often (with the mother) and at times somewhat inappropriately. On the request of their therapist, they accepted the idea of participating in our family project, and being tested.

The testing procedure consisted of two steps. First, the individual family members were placed in separate rooms, in complete isolation from each other, with instructions to fill out a questionnaire which described several hypothetical situations of a rather neutral content. For each situation there were a number of choices. The individual was then to indicate the choices he liked the most were he to find himself in that situation. Upon completion of this first step, the three family members were brought together and requested to fill out the same questionnaire again, but this time *as a family,* i.e., with the understanding that the choices were now to be regarded as stemming from and affecting all three family members.

As they gathered around a table to decide on their choices as a family, the mother immediately took over. With the gaudiness of spirit her therapist had led us to imagine, she handled the questionnaire, read the questions, and voiced her wants. She gave every indication of being the absolute boss of the family. With the apparent support of her son, who tended to follow her manic-like behavior, she conveyed to everyone observing behind the screen of the one-way vision room the unmistakble impression of her "domination." In fact, "domination" was perhaps the least that anyone could have said about her forceful behavior, her conviction, and her undisputed power. In contrast, her husband rarely said a word or moved a muscle. Smoking a cigarette, he seemed to be concentrating exclusively upon the spirals of smoke which slowly rose to the ceiling. But for an occasional grunt or murmur barely audible through the microphone, he hardly seemed to participate in the family decisions. It was, therefore, with only academic interest that we looked for the test results on the relative "dominance" of the family members, as measured by the number of times where the choices of the individual member, expressed by the individually answered questionnaire, coincided with the choices later adopted by the family group. From the point of view of every expert behind the one-way vision room, it was obvious that the mother—who had been the one writing down the family choices—had scored the highest "dominance," perhaps even the theoretical maximum of 21 fulfilled wishes. But, to our amazement, the findings were incredibly different. The mother had scored a modest 12 (in fact, 1 below the average), and the son, our second suspect for the highest "dominance," had scored an 11. In contrast, the father —by means we could hardly surmise—came up with a score of 17, one of the highest scores among all families tested. Very likely, then, mother's "domination" was only a myth, a *family myth*.

The notion of family myth[2] refers here to a number of well-systematized beliefs, shared by all family members, about their mutual roles in the family, and the nature of their relationship. These family myths contain many of the covert rules of the relationship, rules that are kept hidden from view, embedded in the triviality of home cliches and routines. As may be apparent from their smooth operation, some of these myths are so integrated in the every day living as to become an inseparable part of the perceptual context within which family members draw their lives together. Although to an outsider they may appear as blatant misstatements of the facts in the family, these organized beliefs—in the name of which the family initiates, maintains, and justifies many interactional patterns—are beliefs shared and supported by all family members as if they were some sort of ultimate truths beyond challenge or inquiry. Consider:

In Family A, the husband has to drive the wife wherever she may need to go, oftentimes to the detriment of his business activities, since she does not know how to drive a car, nor does she care to learn. Although this pattern has been in operation since they were married some sixteen years ago, she explains it in terms of not being "mechanically inclined," a statement which the husband immediately endorses and corroborates.

In Family B, no friend is ever invited to the house since no one quite knows when father is going to be drunk. The mother, who pointedly "does not drink," not only provides most of the family income (part of which goes, of course, for the father's liquor), but also stands vigil over who comes in the house lest someone will think that "he is almost an alcoholic."

In Family C, the delinquency of a teen-age son is becoming the increasing concern of the local Juvenile Authorities. The parents profess total bewilderment on how to direct their son on a less troublesome path. They consider themselves a "very happy" family, with a "happiness" marred only by their son's encounters with the law. In this regard, the parents claim that they are constantly out-argued by their son, who happens to be, in the mother's proud and public statement, "the legal mind in the family."

In these families, like in many others, it is obvious that important interactional patterns operate under rules not openly stated. Although, by their regularity and consistency, these patterns may be characteristic of the respective families, the determining rules are not easy to visualize or formulate. In fact, most of these rules are known only by inference, and to the extent to which they are translated into family myths, *i.e.*, the beliefs and expectations which the family members entertain about each other and the relationship.

In terms of the relationship, family myths are of a very definite economic value. Since they are shared unquestionably by all family members, family myths promote ritual and provide some restful areas of automatic agreement. In their implicit statements, they are blue-prints for action that dispenses with further thought or elaboration. For instance, in the situation of Family A mentioned above, the myth that "mother is not mechanically inclined" was not only shared by everyone involved, but corroborated by the father, who, with a patronizing smile, explained that "even around the house she is always letting things fall from her hands . . . that's the way she is . . . she has always been like that . . ."; consequently, he had to be the driver in the family. "Besides," he added, with her nodding approval, "she doesn't trust cab drivers." In its content, the family myth may appear to refer only to an individual, or to a particular twosome, but it is important to realize that in fact it always refers to the whole family. In Family A, the myth that "mother is not mechanically inclined" was a myth about mother, but a *myth that determined the behavior of all family members,* and defined some important aspects of their relationship. The family myth defined some of the rules of the relationship by ascribing a role to each family member. But the emphasis here, it must be noted, is on the complementarity of these roles.[1,3] For instance, in the myth that the mother was not mechanically inclined, there was the implied statement that, in fact, someone else in the family *was.* And a balance between these two roles must have had to be established for the relationship to remain stable. If, as we say in Family C, someone is defined as "the legal mind," it is implicitly assumed that there must be someone else in the family to whom the counter-definition of having "not-a-legal-mind" applies. In fact, it is apparent that in the context of the family relationship, for any individually defined role there is to be found a *counter-role* in the person of one, or more, other family member. When a family awards to one of its members the title of "patient," it automatically confers to one or more other family members the contrasting label of "not-a-patient." And as much as the former implies a role, so does the latter imply what we may call a counter-role which sets off and complements the other. Whether to emphasize the role, or the counter-role (whether, in the example of Family B, to say that the father was an "alcoholic," or that the mother was "the wife of an alcoholic") may be a matter of taste or tradition, for the statements are equivalent. Thus, the "alcoholic" husband may require the careful tendering of the counter-alcoholic wife; the "delinquent" youngster may be contrasted with antithetical behavior of the counter-delinquent member or members; and, at least in some instances, the "psychotic" behavior of a family member may be paired off, or better, intertwined with the counter-psychotic behavior of some other family member or members.

Family myths are not, of course, the exclusive possession of pathologic families. They are probably present in all families, and it seems likely that a certain amount of mythology may be necessary to the smooth operation of even the healthiest family relationship. However, it seems that family myths are more obvious and unalterable, perhaps more numerous and pervasive, in pathologic relationships. In fact, pathologic families are often conspicuous for their myths. In some of these families, we often gain the impression that almost all of the rules that define the relationship are covert, and inferred only from family myths. Such families, often schizophrenia-producing, have relationships of the type that Wynne[4] called pseudo-mutual; seemingly over-burdened with their own mythology they retain very little freedom for unrehearsed action, and suffer much in their inability to deal with new situations or unexpected events.

The origin of most family myths is usually lost in the cradle of the relationship. Some myths seemed to have been passed on from generation to generation; it is conceivable that a certain similarity in role assignment as implied in the family myths may play some part in the choice and acceptance of a mate. But, be that as it may, once the myth becomes operative it is likely to stay as an integral aspect of the relationship where it functions as an ordering force, a buffer against sudden changes or alterations. In this sense, the family myth is to the family what the defenses are to the individual. For in its function as a *group defense,* the family myth promotes homeostasis, and the stability of the relationship. Even in the extreme cases of *folie à famille,* where the family myths reach psychotic proportions, the homeostatic and defense function of the myth is well evidenced in the fact that it is the family myth, the *folie,* which permits the relationship to remain unchanged in its nature although at the price of severe disruption with outsiders. Thus, the family myth is promoted to become part of *the inner image* of the family, expressing the way in which the family is seen, not so much by outsiders, but by its members from the inside. To the therapist, as to any other outsider, the family myth may appear irrational and unrealistic; but to family members, it is perceived not only as emotionally indispensable, but as an integral part of their reality. When, for instance, a mother says about her infant daughter that "this is the pretty one, that one is the smart one," a myth may be in the making. However, to the growing girls, the myth is their reality. It is reality in two ways: first, it is the way in which the world is presented to them in description and experience; second, even if the truth of the statement should be challenged by future events, the message had already been forcefully conveyed that "this is the way in which things are to be looked upon and reacted to." In a family myth, questions of fact and of opinion —*quid facti, quid juris*—are one and the same.

To the therapist, the notion of family myths carries some rather important implications. Of particular interest here is the realization that many families seek psychiatric assistance *in order not to change, i.e.,* as part of the effort to maintain the *status quo* in the relationship. This seems to be particularly so in families where there is the myth of the "happiness" of the family life. Sometimes, as illustrated in Family C, the myth is taken to the extreme of affirming that "we have always been very happy together until lately when our son got into trouble with the juvenile authorities . . . even so, we are quite congenial . . .". And although it is abundantly clear that the son was more than a fly in the parents' honey, the myth of their being a happy family in spite of the son's "little difficulty," as they called it, remained unabated throughout the brief attempt they made at psychiatric help. It is worth noting that in instances of this sort, the psychiatrist's consultation comes about, often, only as a means to strengthen an old, perhaps now inoperative, family myth. Indeed, with such families, the psychiatrist may be easily led on a predetermined path; by prescribing a pill, hospitalizing, or even speaking euphemistically about the "illness," he often strengthens the family myth that someone is a "patient" whereas someone else is not.

In this respect, the question of unveiling a family myth is of no less interest to the therapist. Since the family myth functions towards the maintenance of the relationship and the preservation of its nature, the subject is a particularly sensitive one to all family members. On this point the greatest gentleness and discretion may be required of the therapist. For an otherwise insistent attempt to unveil the truth behind the myth is bound to produce some surprising developments. As in the story of the Emperor's new and invisible clothes, where a small child's voice told the truth of his nakedness, the truth-bent therapist may be confronted with an unexpected sight: that of all family members banding together in a ferocious unanimity of opinion that could easily lead to the dissolution of the incipient therapist-family relationship.

Thus, the notion of family myth raises a number of speculative ideas of possible importance in the practice of family therapy. As to theory, its greatest relevance seems to be in the transition ground that lies between the individual and the group, between psychiatry and sociology. For, on the one hand, the family myth finds an extension into individual's myths, such as described in "neurotic" or "psychotic" fantasies, while, on the other, it continues and often affiliates into the larger social myths, such as racial myths (the "inferiority" of the Negro), national myths (the French *"toujours, l'amour"*), religious myths ("mine is the only true God"), and others. As a concept that stands in the threshold of both individual and group dynamics, the family myth poses some intriguing theoretical questions about families and about individuals—questions that seem to be leading to a serious challenge of the traditional views on the nature of psychopathology.

## REFERENCES

1. HALEY, J. 1963. Marriage therapy. Arch. Gen. Psych. 8:213–234.
2. FERREIRA, A. J. 1963. Family myth and homeostasis. Arch. Gen. Psych. 9:457–463.
3. JACKSON, D. D. 1957. The question of family homeostasis. Psychiat. Quart. 31 (suppl): 79–90.
4. WYNNE, L. C., RYCKOFF, I. M., DAY, J., and HIRSCH, S. I. 1958. Pseudo-mutuality in the family relations of schizophrenics. Psychiat. 21:205–220.

*By the mid-sixties the work of MRI had progressed from its clinical, empirical origins to a point where it seemed feasible to attempt a formalization of its basic, theoretical assumptions—mainly of its relationship to the dimly perceived outline of a comprehensive theory of human communication. In 1967, Watzlawick, Beavin, and Jackson published a book, entitled* Pragmatics of Human Communication;[1] *in which they examined the behavioral (pragmatic) effects of communication.*

*There are two principal ways in which the phenomena of human communication can be studied. The first consists in a detailed investigation of these phenomena in an attempt to capture them in all their natural richness. The difficulty with this approach lies in the enormous complexity of communication which imposes on the researcher the inevitable need for limitation, for the time-honored scientific procedure of isolating variables. But in view of the uncertainty as to what may be assumed to be significant and, therefore, worth isolating, correlating and analyzing, one can never be sure if after years of hard work the variables chosen for isolation may not turn out to be noise rather than signals in an information-theoretical sense—to say nothing of the far more likely possibility of having destroyed the complexity of the phenomena under study precisely by the isolation of these arbitrarily chosen variables.*

*The other possible approach is a diametrically different one. It is based on the assumption that human communication and, therefore, interaction*

[1] Paul Watzlawick, Janet Helmick Beavin, and Don D. Jackson, *Pragmatics of Human Communication. A Study of Interactional Patterns, Pathologies, and Paradoxes* (New York, W. W. Norton, 1967).

*must be based on a code, or something similar to a grammar, a calculus
or an algorithm, to make sense at all, and that all participants in interaction
are bound to obey (to a greater or lesser degree) this body of rules of
communication. And as Jackson already pointed out in the first two papers
of this chapter, these rules are very likely to be outside the awareness of
all concerned. Just as it is possible to speak a language correctly and
fluently and yet have no knowledge whatsoever of its grammar, we all are
obeying the rules of communication, but the rules themselves, the "grammar" of communication, is something we are unaware of.* Pragmatics of
Human Communication *is an attempt to formulate some of the basic
axioms of this presumed calculus of communication, to show how they
determine human interaction and to describe the types of pathology that
arise when these axioms are violated.*

*The following description by Watzlawick and Beavin of some formal
aspects of communication is a synopsis of the material presented in detail in* Pragmatics.

# SOME FORMAL ASPECTS OF COMMUNICATION

*Paul Watzlawick and Janet Beavin*

This paper will describe an approach to the study of human interaction
which is based on the assumption that *communication* is synonymous with
what is observable in such interaction. That is, communication is seen
not as just the vehicle, not as just the manifestation, but as a better conception of what is often loosely gathered under the rubric "interaction."

We have, of course, no complete or formal theory. We will, rather,
present what appear to be very simple and obvious premises which, however, *followed through to their necessary conclusions,* seem to yield a
fundamentally new and quite productive outlook.

Before this, however, some general comments about the "obviousness"
of these points should be made. First of all, it is often the intimately important, especially in our own behavior, which is overlooked or difficult
to see, precisely because it is, like breathing, largely out of awareness until
drawn to our attention. Second, and more important, while few would
flatly exclude in theory the ubiquity and importance of the social context,
actual research and application too frequently stop at lip service, so that

Reprinted from *American Behavioral Scientist,* Vol. 10, No. 8 (April 1967),
pp. 4–8, by permission of the Publisher, Sage Publications, Inc.

involvement with a particular (monadic) subject of investigation results, in practice, in the neglect of the interactional perspective. That is, communicational factors are often regarded as random, or potentially excludable, sources of variance, This problem arises both in the definition of *what* is to be studied and—since the behavioral sciences are ultimately self-reflexive and all research by humans on other humans is social—to the strategy and analysis of *how* the data are studied; that is, to methodology as well as to content. In either case, even when the interactional context is thus, in effect, ignored, it does not go away; there always remains a valid *communicational* interpretation of the data. The latter is, unfortunately, often in conflict, or at least difficult to integrate with the investigator's intended, more monadic interpretation (e.g., 1, 2). Third, and perhaps most important, these basic notions may be obvious, yet they still are neither systematized into an adequate theory of communication, nor consistently utilized in research.

But such considerations take us beyond the aims of this paper. For the present, we will primarily identify the subject matter of the problem.

### Pragmatics as Reciprocal Process

Morris (3) proposed that semiotic (the general theory of signs and languages) could be divided into three main areas. We suggest that these can, analogously, describe three levels of analysis of human communication: *syntactics* as the study of the formal relations of signs to one another; *semantics* as the study of the relations of signs to the objects to which the signs refer, i.e. the study of meaning; and *pragmatics* as the study of the relation of signs to their users. The last, the pragmatics of human communication, encompasses our interest, which is the behavioral effects of human interaction. However, it is necessary to make at least one important qualification of the above framework, which may be said to be not so much about communication, as about signs, senders, and receivers and, thus, still primarily concerned with individuals in isolation. We would prefer to use the term pragmatics to refer not to any sendersign or sign-receiver relation but rather to an *interpersonal* relation. We would not even say "sender-receiver" relation, if this could be avoided in our language, in order to be able to focus on a *reciprocal process* in which both (or all) persons act and react, "receive" and "send," in such detail and complexity that these terms lose their meaning as verbs of individual action. As Birdwhistell has put it:

An individual does not communicate; he engages in or becomes part of communication. He may move, or make noises . . . but he does not communicate. In a parallel fashion, he may see, he may hear, smell, taste, or feel—but he does not communicate. In other words, he does not originate communication; he participates in it. Communication as a system, then, is not to be understood on a simple model of action and reaction, however complexly stated. As a system, it is to be comprehended on the transactional level. (4, p. 104)

Herein our focus will be on dyadic, in-person communication, in which the cues exchanged emanate directly from the voice, the body, or the immediate context. Such communication is clearly amenable to analysis in terms of the principles to be outlined below. However, only further study will prove whether these principles might not be fruitfully applied to the study of, for instance, the mass media, international communication, the psychoanalytic concept of communication with one's introjects, or animal communication, though we would expect that this is so.

### In the Presence of Another, All Behavior Is Communicative

Our case for the generality of such phenomena as will be described rests primarily on an assumption of the inevitability of communication in social situations (which certainly include more than those defined by mere physical presence—the above premise states a minimum whose upper limit is yet to be defined). It is first of all necessary to remember that the scope of "communication" is by no means limited to verbal productions. Communications are exchanged through many channels and combinations of these channels, and certainly also through the context in which an interaction takes place. Indeed, it can be summarily stated that *all* behavior, not only the use of words, is communication (which is not the same as saying that behavior is *only* communication), and since there is no such thing as non-behavior, it is impossible *not* to communicate. Recent animal studies show, for instance, that certain monkeys will seat themselves during their rest periods in a forest clearing so that no animal looks at any other while staring straight ahead into the forest. This is not only in order to keep watch but also for the purpose of resting. They seem to find it necessary to avoid even the communication inherent in a glance, very much as a man in a waiting room may stare at the floor if he wants to be left alone by other persons present. But this behavior itself amounts to the message "Leave me alone" and is normally understood by the others as such.

All behavior is communication: this is true but not trivial. All behavior has an effect as communication, an often very powerful effect which may be one of the most proven assertions of social science—though not always deliberately proven. That is, it is quite common that experiments with a variety of independent variables, including pharmacological agents, show significant changes in human behavior which are, however, not replicable *with that variable.* However, the original effect did in fact occur, and is usually construed as a "placebo" effect. We concur with those who interpret each such case as a demonstration of powerful though as yet unspecified communicational effects.

At the present state of knowledge there is no ultimate evidence whether all behavior is really completely free of "noise" in the information-theoretical sense. However, to date, explorations of the problem of noise (randomness) versus redundancy (order, patterning) in behavior seen as communication have shown so consistently an almost unbelievable degree of order and structure behind the protean manifestations that it becomes more and more plausible that communication in the widest sense is at least as rule-governed as natural language is determined by its grammar and syntax (e.g. 5, 6). And, just as in learning a natural language, the ability to communicate is based on the acquisition of a very abstract structure or code which is never formalized and, in this sense, is never truly conscious.

The suggestion that there is virtually no sender-originated noise in human communication almost immediately raises the related issues of "conscious," "intentional," or "successful" communication. Many communicational events are routinely excluded from, or differently classified within, theory based on a simpler "information" model because they were either not *intended* to be communication or did not succeed in communicating what was intended. To take an extreme position, one which rests precariously on the edge of infinite regress, any measure of intention is ultimately, garnered in a communicational setting. Thus, I may *say* that I did not (consciously) intend to ignore you, or you may yourself label my behavior in this manner. But this labelling procedure is no more and no less than further information in our ongoing communication. This, of course, has nothing to do with whether the unconscious really exists or whether people really have intentions. Seen as *labels of the participants,* such information is only communication—valid as such but not complete.

The issue of successful or unsuccessful (and, therefore, implicitly meaningless) communication obviously rests in part on the same sort of judgment of participant or observer. But again, to take an extreme counter-example, verbal or nonverbal nonsense is communicative: information, especially at the relationship level (discussed immediately below) *is* conveyed to the receiver; this point has been especially well taken in regard to schizophrenic behavior, e.g. Haley (7), which may be seen *positively,* as occurring and meaningful, rather than as gibberish outside the pale of human communication.

### There Are Many Levels of Information in Every Communication, and One Always Pertains to the Relationship in Which the Communication Occurs

A prisoner is held by two guards in a room with two doors. He knows that one door is locked, the other unlocked, but does not know which. He also knows one of the guards always tells the truth, the other always lies, but again the prisoner does not know which. Finally, he has been told that the only way to regain his freedom is to identify the unlocked door by asking *one* question of *one* of the guards. For a long time the prisoner ponders this seemingly unsolvable problem, but eventually asks the correct question: he points to one of the doors and asks one of the guards (it does not matter which door or which guard), "If I asked your comrade whether this door is open, what would he say?" If the answer is yes, then that door is locked, and, vice versa, if no, then it is open.

The charm of this unlikely story lies not only in the fact that a problem with two unknowns (the door and the guards) is elegantly solved through the discovery of a simple decision procedure, but in that a fundamental property of communication is involved in the solution. The prisoner has been given two quite distinct orders of information to work with. One has to do with impersonal objects (the doors), the other with human beings as senders of information, and both are indispensable for the solution. If the prisoner could investigate the doors himself, he would not need to communicate with anyone about them, he would merely have to rely on the information supplied by his own senses. Since he cannot, he has to include the information he has about the guards and their habitual ways of relating to others, i.e. truthfully or mendaciously. Therefore, what the prisoner does is to deduce correctly the objective state of the doors through the medium of the specific relationship between the guards and himself, and, thus, eventually arrives at a correct understanding of the situation by using *information about objects* (the doors and their state of being locked or unlocked) together with *information about this information* (the guards and their typical ways of relating—specifically, conveying object information—to others).

Not only in the abstraction of this story, but in real life as well, these two orders of information are present in all communication. They are called the *content* and the *relationship* aspects of message material; and while the one or the other may have greater relative importance in a given piece of communication, communication composed of only the one or the other are impossible, just as a computer needs data (information) and a program (information about this information), and cannot function with only one of these inputs. The relationship as well as the content aspect is a basic, ever present property of communication.

To exemplify: if woman A points to woman B's necklace and asks, "Are those real pearls?", the content of her question is a request for information about an object. But at the same time she also gives—indeed, cannot *not* give—her definition of their relationship. How she asks (especially, in this case, the tone and stress of voice, facial expression, and context) would indicate comfortable friendliness, competitiveness, formal business relations, etc. B can accept, reject or redefine but cannot under any circumstances—even by silence—not respond to A's message. A's definition may, for instance, be a catty, condescending one; B, on the other hand, may react to it with aplomb or defensiveness. It should be noticed that this part of their interaction has nothing to do with the genuineness of pearls or with pearls at all, but with respective definitions of the nature of their relationship, although they may continue to talk about pearls.

Whether or not communicational closure is reached on the content level will produce agreement or disagreement between the communicants; on the relationship level, it will result in understanding or misunderstanding between them—two phenomena that are essentially different, even though the ordinary terms we must use for labels do not reflect the distinction with complete precision. (The many levels and vicissitudes of communication in this area have recently been the subject of an excellent study by Laing *et al.* [8]). Thus, it is possible for two communicants to disagree about an objective issue but understand each other as human beings, to agree but fail to understand each other as human beings, or, to agree *and* to understand each other; by the same token, of course, two communicants may fail at both levels and, thus, both disagree with and misunderstand one another. A particularly frequent and clinically very important type of communication occurs when the two levels are confused, in the sense that the communicants attempt to resolve a relationship problem on the content level—e.g. argue about a specific issue in order to establish who is the better. Another situation of particular clinical importance arises when a person is somehow coerced into denying his own correct perceptions (on the object level) in order to maintain the *status quo* on the relationship level. Asch's experiments on independence and submission to group pressures (9) provide an excellent example and so do, of course, all double bind (10) situations.

From the above it appears that it is easiest to illustrate the relationship aspect of communication with pathological examples in which incongruency of definition occurs. But, of course, in those relationships where there is understanding, or congruency of definitions, omnipresent though often very subtle cues support and reinforce this state of affairs. Pathological examples may be helpfully clear, but they also mistakenly promote a common notion about "breakdown" of communication which misses the generality of the underlying principles. This formal aspect of communication, then, is presented here not to divide "good" and "bad" communication, but to define an inevitable property of all communication.

Thus, stated more strongly à la Heisenberg, there are no objective facts outside the relationship context in which they are experienced. Even—perhaps, especially—the interpersonal situations in which scientific data is gathered about human behavior should be examined in this light. For example, a young medical student was assigned an exercise in epidemiology as a summer project in which he was to make a survey of the incidence of suicide in a particular area. Candid coroners informed him that this was not strictly possible, as a verdict of suicide versus natural or accidental causes of death was based on social as well as medical facts—delicacy, the testimony of involved survivors, the context in which death occurred, and other considerations routinely entered into the final verdict. Indeed, Rosenthal's studies of "experimenter bias" examine what might in our language be called effects stemming from the relationship level of communication between experimenter and subject, while Turner considers this same kind of relationship context more broadly:

Human behavior is so organized that subjects can and do enter experiments with conceptions as to what behavior is appropriate to produce, what degree of compliance is desirable, and what one owes to the experimenter. I suggest that these remarks, which merely draw upon the commonplaces of the role conception of social action, would be utterly trivial if made in reference to almost any other role relationship; and yet with regard to the lab situation of subject and experimenter they are likely to seem merely nihilistic. . . . Like job interviews, courtroom proceedings, therapy sessions and card games—experiments are social situations, possessing a complex structure in their own right. One man's experiment is another man's *in situ* social situation . . . (11, pp. 2–3)

### A Stream of Communicational Events Consists in a Series of Overlapping Stimulus-Response-Reinforcement Triads

In pointing to the relationship aspect of communication and to the fact that all behavior must be considered communication, some necessary corrections of a purely verbal-information model of communication may have been achieved, but the result is still not different from the standard sender-receiver model in its individual focus. In order to step from the emanations of participants to communicational process, a model of this process is needed.

If A and B are interacting, that is, exchanging behaviors, these behaviors can be seen as a stream of alternating communicational events, and this stream may be represented as

$$a_1\, b_1\, a_2\, b_2\, a_3\, b_3\, \ldots\, b_{76}\, a_{77}\, b_{77}\, a_{78}\, \ldots\, a_n\, b_n$$

Let us consider some of the ways the observer may *punctuate* this stream of events, that is, what conception of what "really" occurs is imposed on it.

One of the most common formats (indeed, nearly impossible to aovid in our language) is that of individual actions, so that the events are seen as

$$a_1\, a_2\, a_3\, \ldots\ldots\, a_{77} \qquad a_{78}\, \ldots\, a_n$$
$$b_1\, b_2\, b_3\, \ldots\, b_{76} \qquad b_{77}\, \ldots\ldots\, b_n$$

And especially if one of the participants, say A, is the subject of study (for example, a psychiatric patient or an experimental subject), then only items $a_1$, $a_2$, $a_3$, etc. are examined. The behavioral events are divided and isolated on the basis of whether they are ascribed to A or B. Laing *et al.* have focussed sharply on these "banal and unproductive errors":

> The failure to see the behavior of one person as a function of the behavior of the other has led to some extraordinary perceptual and conceptual aberrations that are still with us. For instance, in a sequence of moves in a social interaction between person A and person B, $a_1 \rightarrow b_1 \rightarrow a_2 \rightarrow b_2 \rightarrow a_3 \rightarrow b_3$, the sequence $a_1 \rightarrow a_2 \rightarrow a_3$ is extrapolated. Direct links are made between $a_1 \rightarrow a_2 \rightarrow a_3$, and this artificially derived sequence is taken as the entity or process under study. (8, p. 8)

Often this sequence is further collapsed into an overall statement about A, the actor. That is, the static sum of these behaviors

$$a_1 + a_2 + a_3 \ldots\ldots + a_n = A'$$

is seen as a characteristic of A—e.g. incomplete sentences, literality, hostility, etc., depending on the level of abstraction at which a statement is made about A. In such cases, any "explanation" of A's behavior must be *intra*personal, attributable to some intrapsychic structure or process which then becomes the primary object of analysis. A less extreme, quasi-interactional approach is to include the behavior of the other but in the same form as above. That is, $b_1 + b_2 + b_3 \ldots + b_n$ becomes B′ which is then somehow related to A′—for example, the concept of sadomasochistic symbiosis for a sequence of behaviors between two persons.

In the above cases, either the individual is conceptually isolated from the behavior of those around him, or his behaviors are seen as time- and order-free "properties" of him as an individual, or both. The alternative has been illustrated by Scheflen:

> We notice three people standing on a corner facing each other and talking. A number of abstractions is possible. Each has on a brown suit. Thus, browness is abstractable. So is humanness, or standing-ness, or two-leggedness. But it is also possible to make another kind of abstraction. We can abstract *relatedness,* e.g. proximity, kinship, cooperation, and so on. *Once we abstract relatedness we no longer have organismic wholeness or individuality.* We have a concept. There are only qualities or behavioral arrangements in a concept; there are no people. (5, p. 58)

One scheme which includes both parties in a dyadic relation and which also takes note of the *relation between* events and the order in which they occur is the stimulus-response-reinforcement format from psychology. Thus, $a_1$ is called the stimulus, $b_1$ the response, and $a_2$ the reinforcement. However, probably as old as studies of this kind is the joke about the laboratory rat who boasts to another rat, "I have trained my experimenter so that every time I press the lever he gives me a piece of cheese." What this rat does is simply to impose a different punctuation on the stream of events: what to the experimenter is the rat's response, the rat considers its stimulus to the experimenter; what he then does and calls a reinforcement, the rat sees as a response, and so forth. What we are proposing, following Bateson (e.g. 12) is essentially to extend this conception of things to encompass both the experimenter's and the rat's positions. That is, any behavioral event in a sequence is a stimulus for the event which follows it, and both response and reinforcement to the one which preceded it:

$$
\begin{array}{ccccccccc}
& & & \ldots & a_{16} & b_{16} & a_{17} & b_{17} & \ldots \\
S & R & Rf & & & & & & \\
& S & R & Rf & & & & & \\
& & S & R & Rf & & & & \\
& & & S & R & Rf & & & \\
& & & & S & R & Rf & & \\
& & & & & S & R & Rf & \\
\end{array}
$$

Just as all behavior in interpersonal sequences is communication, so all such behavior has this triple aspect, being "simultaneously a stimulus, a response, and a reinforcement, according to how we slide our identification of the triad up and down the series." (12, p.4) We propose this as the minimum complexity of any interchange.

Far from being spurious, however, the *punctuation of the sequence of events* is a highly significant corollary to the premise of an essentially unpunctuated stream. As philosophers of science, e.g. Popper (13), have pointed out, man is born with a propensity to look for regularities in the constant stream of events surrounding and involving him. The Berkeleyan question whether these regularities exist in actual fact or are merely introduced by the observer, will be of no concern here. (There is no reason why the day should be divided into 24 hours, but this arbitrary division is a very useful one). The fact remains that the same principle is at work in human communication: man tends to pattern the stream of communicational events into an order which to him is familiar and predictable. This, however, presupposes selection and the criteria applied to this process of selection are anything but simple and obvious. In particular, these criteria need not be obvious to, or shared by, the other communicants. Discrepancies in the punctuation of jointly experienced events are in fact at the root of many conflicts in most areas of human interaction, and the ever present blindness for the other's punctuation, coupled with the naive conviction that reality is the way *I* see (punctuate) these events, almost inevitably leads to the mutual charges of badness or madness.

Thus, for instance, nation A may arm to protect itself against a real or imaginary threat by nation B. Nation B considers *this* a threat and increases its armaments, justifying this step as a purely defensive measure, made necessary by nation A's threatening attitude; nation A now has further "proof" of nation B's aggressive designs, etc. etc., a mechanism extensively studied by Richardson (14). A paranoid patient suspects the motives of others; this prompts the others to prove to him the honesty and sincerity of their intentions, which not only confirms but increases his suspicions, for, he argues, if they were not out to hurt him they would not be trying so hard to make him believe that they meant well. A depressed patient withdraws; his withdrawal worries those close to him; they try to help him by increasing their attention; on perceiving their concern and anxiety he feels doubly guilty for causing them emotional pain; on seeing his depression thus increase they try harder and at the same time feel more desperate for being unable to help him; which in turn compounds his depression to the point of considering suicide for being so "bad" to those who love him.

These examples of vicious circles can be multiplied almost indefinitely. The point is that when the model of overlapping stimulus-response-reinforcement triads is adopted, no one participant's behavior can be said to *cause* the other's: each is both cause and effect of the behavior of the other. In most ongoing relationships, it becomes obvious on examination that the behavior of each participant is predicated on that of the other. The exact nature of these relationship links and the more abstract rules which govern them emerge as a new, virtually unexplored area of human behavior.

One final, very general point derives from such considerations. In the communicational perspective, the question whether there is such a thing as an objective reality of which some people are more clearly aware than others is of relatively little importance compared to the significance of different *views* of reality due to different punctuations. However, awareness of how one punctuates is extremely difficult owing to another basic property of communication. Like all other complex conceptual systems which attempt to make assertions about themselves (e.g. language, logic, mathematics) communication typically encounters the paradoxes of self-reflexivity when trying to apply itself to itself. What this amounts to is that the patterns of communication existing between oneself and others cannot be fully understood, for it is simply impossible to be both involved *in* a relationship (which is indispensable in order to be related) *and* at the same time stand *outside* it as a detached, uninvolved observer (which would be necessary in order to encompass and to be aware of the relationship in its entirety). This is essentially similar to the impossibility of obtaining full visual awareness of one's own body, since the eyes, as the perceiving organs, are themselves part of the body to be perceived.

As Russell, Gödel and Tarski have shown once and for all, no system complex enough to include arithmetic can achieve its own fully consistent formalization within its own framework and its own language. Whether or not human communication is a comparable system and, therefore, beset by the same problem of ultimate undecidability, is not yet clear at all. There is much that speaks in support of this assumption, mainly the above mentioned problem of subjective awareness, or the fact that to communicate (or even to think) about communication itself is itself communication. In this sense both one's subjective experience of communicative processes with others as well as the study of communication as such has to employ concepts whose range includes themselves and, thus, lead into Russellian paradoxes of self-reflexiveness, into an infinite regress of assertions about assertions, and into the problem of undecidability in Gödel's sense (15). Bronowski, in a lucid study of this vexing problem (16), has shown precisely that on the one hand "any description in our present formalisms must be incomplete, not because of the obduracy of nature, but because of the limitation of language as we use it," (p. 5) but that on the other hand it is obvious that the mind somehow solves these problems in a highly typical way for which mathematics or logic offer no analogies.

It seems to us that in the field of human communication the main evidence for the correctness of this assumption is supplied by the phenomenon of growth and change in relationships which are the equivalent of Baron Munchhausen's feat of pulling himself from the quagmire by his own pigtail. The paradox of change has occupied the human mind since the days of the Presocratics, and it will not be solved here. But it remains a question of the greatest importance, especially in the light of communicational patterns and the question of their changeability which, after all, is the main factor in psychotherapy, in conflict resolution on a personal as well as on an international scale, and ultimately in man's awareness of reality.

## REFERENCES

1. DON D. JACKSON and JAY HALEY, "Transference Revisited," *Journal of Nervous and Mental Disease,* 137 (1963) 363–371.
2. ROBERT ROSENTHAL, *Experimenter Effects in Behavioral Research* (New York: Appleton-Century-Crofts, 1966).
3. CHARLES W. MORRIS, "Foundations of the Theory of Signs," in Otto Neurath, Rudolf Carnap, and Charles W. Morris (eds.), *International Encyclopedia of Unified Science* (Chicago: University of Chicago Press, 1938) I, No. 2, 77–137.
4. RAY L. BIRDWHISTELL, "Contribution of Linguistic-Kinesic Studies to the Understanding of Schizophrenia," in Alfred Auerback (ed.), *Schizophrenia. An Integrated Approach* (New York: Ronald Press, 1959) pp. 99–123.
5. ALBERT E. SCHEFLEN, *Stream and Structure of Communicational Behavior, Context Analysis of a Psychotherapy Session* (Behavioral Studies Monograph no. 1, Eastern Pennsylvania Psychiatric Institute Philadelphia, 1965).
6. R. E. PITTENGER, CHARLES F. HOCKETT, and J. J. DANEHY, *The First Five Minutes* (Ithaca: Paul Martineau Publisher, 1960).
7. JAY HALEY, "An Interactional Description of Schizophrenia," *Psychiatry,* 22 (1959) 321–332.
8. R. D. LAING, H. PHILLIPSON, and A. R. LEE, *Interpersonal Perception* (New York: Springer Publishing Company, 1966).
9. S. E. ASCH, "Studies of Independence and Submission to Group Pressures," *Psychological Monograph,* 70, No. 416 (1956).
10. GREGORY BATESON, DON D. JACKSON, JAY HALEY, and JOHN WEAKLAND,

"Toward a Theory of Schizophrenia," *Behavioral Science* 1 (1956) 251–264.

11.  ROY TURNER, "Problems in the Study of Interaction," (Paper read at the Pacific Sociological Association Meetings, Vancouver, April, 1966).

12.  GREGORY BATESON, "Exchange of Information about Patterns of Human Behavior," in William S. Fields and Walter Abbott (eds.), *Information Storage and Neural Control* (Springfield: Thomas, 1963).

13.  KARL POPPER, *Conjectures and Refutations* (New York: Basic Books, 1962).

14.  LEWIS FRY RICHARDSON, "Mathematics of War and Foreign Politics," in James R. Newman (ed.), *The World of Mathematics* (New York: Simon & Schuster, 1956) II, 1240–1253.

15.  ERNST NAGEL, and JAMES R. NEWMAN, *Gödel's Proof* (New York: New York University Press, 1958).

16.  J. BRONOWSKI, "The Logic of the Mind," *American Scientist* 54 (1966) 1–14.

# CHAPTER 2

# Research

*Theory-building and research are interdependent; in traditional scientific procedure they should derive impetus and confirmation from each other.*

*The papers included in this chapter report on some of the research projects carried out at MRI during the period under review.*

*The ideal goal of clinical family research would appear to be an instrument capable of scoring and measuring family interaction with such precision and economy that its results would provide the following:*

*a) a method of classifying families on the basis of their specific patterns of interaction;*

*b) a correlation of family interaction patterns with clinical diagnostic criteria, i.e., the identification of "typical" interactive behaviors in families with, for instance, a member who is schizophrenic, delinquent, suffering from a psychosomatic disorder, etc.;*

*c) as a corollary of b) an objective definition of family "health" or "normality";*

*d) a method of identifying and measuring family change, e.g., after therapy.*

*Since the foundation of MRI, an enormous amount of work has been spent in various attempts to approach this goal. However, even before shortage of funds for basic research limited our activities in this area, detailed studies of families with a psychiatrically disturbed member had led to an important, though negative, tentative conclusion. It is that—reasonable as it may appear on the surface—the hope of finding clear correspondencies between family interaction patterns and established criteria of clinical diagnosis was not just premature but most probably unrealistic. After all, clinical diagnosis is based on the monadic, intrapsychic model of psychopathology; the attempt to apply it to the pathology of systems must perforce lead to the language confusion briefly mentioned in the Introduction.*

*But as soon as one attempts to take a system-oriented approach, yet another problem—one more easily ignored in atomistic approaches—becomes clear, namely, the inverse relation between economy and relevance. What we mean by this is that the simpler, less inferential and more readily obtainable the data that a researcher may decide to cull from the fantastic richness of human interaction, the less relevant they are for his grasp of this richness. To use a deliberately trivial example: To establish the average age of all members of a family can be done quickly, cheaply and reliably, but the relevance of this measurement will be virtually zero. Conversely, the occurrence of particular patterns of paradoxical communication may be highly meaningful, but their identification may pose almost unsurmountable conceptual and technical difficulties. In the face of these difficulties, researchers then tend to impose some restrictions on the complexity of the phenomena, thereby running the risk of falling back into the other extreme of manageable but perhaps irrelevant data.*[1]

*The papers reproduced in this chapter try to circumvent this difficulty in different ways. The first, by Sluzki and Beavin, follows the approach mentioned in the commentary to Chapter 1: It utilizes two basic, relatively noninferential properties of communication and shows their elegant usefulness for the classification of dyadic interchanges. The properties in question are Bateson's concepts of* symmetry *and* complementarity *which distinguish themselves by the fact that they denote patterns of relationship rather than monadic, static, "mental" qualities.*

*It should also be noticed that Sluzki and Beavin succeeded in ridding the symmetry-complementarity duality of a considerable flaw, inherent in its early formulation, i.e., the vexing concepts of pseudosymmetry (when the partner in the one-up position allows the other to appear as an equal) and of meta-complementarity (when both partners agree, symmetrically, that one of them shall be in the one-up, complementary, position).*

[1] A typical example of this dilemma is provided by the work of Jaffe and Feldstein at the William Alanson White Institute in New York, who set out to study the richness of dyadic interaction, but had to settle for sequences of speech and silence: "Our initial interest was the study of dyadic interaction in the framework of psychotherapy research. This application dictated a focus upon certain interpersonal or *system* features of conversation, that might be relevant to the communication of mood, to the phenomenon of 'empathy' and to the breakdown of effective dialogue. Investigations of such problems are confronted with a mass of clinical interview material which, in all its richness, is largely unmanageable. *Expediency, therefore, led us to concentrate on the on-off patterns of vocal signals in face-to-face conversations.* (Italics ours.) (Joseph Jaffe and Stanley Feldstein, *Rhythms of Dialogue* [New York: Academic Press, 1970], p. 2.)

*Although this article is published here for the first time in English (it was originally published in Argentina), it has served as the basis of a number of secondary research projects as well as dissertations in this country and abroad.*

# SYMMETRY AND COMPLEMENTARITY: AN OPERATIONAL DEFINITION AND A TYPOLOGY OF DYADS

*Carlos E. Sluzki and Janet Beavin*

## Introduction

The communicational approach has aided the study of psychopathological and normal behavior through the description and comprehension of various characteristics of the distorted communication patterns of disturbed persons. These features have been studied either impressionistically, or as based on objective traits which permit the formal conceptualization of communication patterning. Among the latter, the authors find of particular value the concepts of interactional symmetry and complementarity on which the present work is based. The object of this paper is to present a dyadic typology which results from a review of the concepts of symmetry and complementarity and to describe a frame of reference for this typology and some operational tools developed for its application to interpersonal data.

Symmetry and complementarity were introduced by George Bateson in 1936 when in *Naven* (2) he described a theory of human interaction based primarily on his anthropological observations of the Iatmul tribe of New Guinea. Bateson asserted that

. . . many systems of relationship, either between individuals or groups of individuals, contain a tendency towards progressive change. If, for example, one of the patterns of cultural behavior, considered appropriate in individual *A,* is culturally labelled as an assertive pattern, while *B* is expected to reply

This work was supported by National Institute of Mental Health grant No. MH—1136201 to MRI.

Originally published in *Acta psiquiátrica y psicológica de América Latina* 11: 321–30, 1965.

to this with what is culturally regarded as submission, it is likely that this sub-mission will encourage a further assertion, and that this assertion will demand still further submission. We have thus a potentially progressive state of affairs, and unless other factors are present to restrain the excesses of assertive and submissive behavior, *A* must necessarily become more and more assertive, while *B* will become more and more submissive.

Progressive changes of this sort we may describe as *complementary* schis-mogenesis. But there is another pattern of relationships between individuals or groups of individuals which equally contains the germs of progressive change. If, for example, we find boasting as the cultural pattern of behavior in one group, and that the other group replies to this with boasting, a competitive situation may develop in which boasting leads to more boasting, and so on. This type of progressive change we may call *symmetrical* schismogenesis. (2. pp. 176–177)

Note that there are two separate aspects of the above theory: first, a conceptualization of change or development in a relationship, a process which Bateson entitled "schismogenesis"; and second, the introduction of two basic forms which relationship may take: symmetry and comple-mentarity. Later, he referred to each of these as a "genus of interaction patterns," defining symmetrical as

. . . the behavior in rivalries and other relationships, where *A* is stimulated to do something because *B* has done this same thing; and where *B* does more of this because *A* did some of it; and *A* does more of it because *B* did some, and so on. This is the sort of symmetry characteristic of keeping up with the Joneses, some armaments races, and so forth. . . . The complementary side of interactive behavior [is that] in which what *A* does fits, in some sense, with what *B* does but is essentially different from it. This category of complementary interaction includes, for example, dominance and submission, exhibitionism and spectatorship, succoring and dependence, and so forth—a series of patterns where there is mutual fitting between *A*'s behavior and that of *B*. (4, p. 270)

These concepts were subsequently used by Bateson's research group and that of the Mental Research Institute (e.g., 4,6,7,10,12). Jackson and Haley, for instance, used these terms in the context of what they called "control theory," that is

. . . the belief that all persons implicitly or explicitly are constantly attempting to define the nature of their relationships. . . . The communicative behavior that [is viewed] as an attempt to define the nature of the relationship consists of labelling a relationship or aspect of a relationship in one of two ways: complementary or symmetrical. . . . In a complementary relationship the two people are of unequal status in the sense that one appears to be in the superior position, meaning that he initiates action and the other appears to follow that action. Thus two individuals fit together or complement each other. . . . The most obvious and basic complementary relationship would be the mother and infant. A symmetrical relationship is one between two people who behave as if they have equal status. Each person exhibits the right to initiate action, criticize the other, offer advice, and so on. . . . The most obvious symmetrical relationship is a pre-adolescent peer relationship. (7, p. 126–127)

In this usage, Haley (e.g., 6) especially has distinguished two "positions" of complementary behavior: "one-up," who is in control or in charge, and "one-down," who is accepting or being taken care of. Haley then goes on to identify various "ploys" or maneuvers made by individuals in order to define the relationship in a particular way. E.g., a "one-up" maneuver by $A$ would define the relationship as one in which $B$ should submit to $A$. $B$ may, however, respond with a symmetrical definition of the relationship by which he indicates that they are equals, and so forth.

Watzlawick has synthesized these various usages as follows:

. . . in the first pattern the emphasis lies on attempts to establish and maintain equality. It is, therefore, called symmetrical. The other pattern is based on the acceptance and enjoyment of difference. It is referred to as complementary. . . .

In [this] context . . . the term equality refers to the fact that the partners exchange the same sort of behavior, or, in other words, they *demand* equality through the message character of their behavior. In this connection, it is quite irrelevant what precisely they are doing; what *does* matter is that as $A$ relates to $B$, so $B$ relates to $A$. If $A$ offers to give, $B$ also offers to give; if $A$ wants to receive, $B$ also want to receive. If one occupies a position of strength, so does the other, and if one claims helplessness, so does the other. . . .

In a complementary relationship, on the other hand, people exchange behavior which together forms the same sort of Gestalt as day and night, inside and otuside, mountain and valley, etc. What this means is that in a complementary relationship $B$'s behavior presupposes $A$'s while at the same time it provides reasons and purpose for $A$'s behavior and vice versa. . . . In past publications of the two aforementioned groups these positions have been variously described as primary, superior or "one-up" on the one hand, and secondary, inferior or "one-down" on the other. . . . They shall be used here with this understanding: primary, superior or "one-up" refer to the position of that partner in a complementary relationship who defines the nature of this relationship, while secondary, inferior or "one-down" refer to the other partner who accepts and goes along with this definition. As can be seen, this has nothing to do with the respective strength or weakness of the partners *per se*. Indeed, one partner's weakness can easily be the very element by which *he* defines the relationship as one in which the other is to protect him. (12, pp. 7–8)

Despite a fundamental core of common meaning, it should be obvious from the foregoing that these terms have come to have a variety of definitions and connotations, depending on the frame of reference in which they are used. These variations are often subtle and implicit, making the actual application of symmetry and complementarity to concrete interactional data all the less clear. In order to achieve an operational definition, it is necessary to make explicit our theoretical premises and the precise unit and level of analysis to which the study is directed.

### Initial Assumptions

Before we become more specific, certain premises about the interactional processes of communication within stable systems such as the family should be stated:

1. The focus herein will be on two-person interaction, mainly because the *dyad* is the simplest interpersonal system which can be considered as a unit of analysis. Triads, tetrads, and so forth, are far more complicated systems which we would attempt to deal with only after thorough analysis of dyadic interaction.

2. The study will be further limited to *long-lasting* (dyadic) relationships, the primary examples of which are marriage couples, siblings, some international relationships—and very few others. We assume that these long-lasting dyads behave—along certain parameters, one of which may be symmetry/complementarity—like homeostatic systems (8), tending constantly towards an equilibrium both within the dyad and with the ambient.

3. This equilibrium is attained and maintained through certain chains of interactive behaviors which interlock in patterns peculiar for each stable dyad. That is, the dyad does not present a random variety of behaviors but tends to act within a repetitive pattern of types of interactions; *it is probable that each dyad shows mainly one type of interaction as an expression of its peculiar homeostatic system.* This leads to the conclusion that, if a comprehensive and mutually exclusive systematization of the field of interaction could be made, each dyad could be classified according to its main (more repetitive) type of interaction.

4. If every message of an interaction is understood as the definition, reinforcement, or redefinition of the nature of the relationship (1,9) then it is probable that in every exchange of messages, we will find clues that will permit us to determine which is the prototypical interaction of any

particular dyad. That is, even in brief interaction there will be indicators accurate enough to infer long-lasting patterns of interaction.

These premises permit the clarification of a frequent connotation of symmetry and complementarity which arises when the relationship is not considered as a whole; these categories viewed as power positions, can lead to the erroneous idea that *one* person defines the nature of the relationship while the other cannot but accept that definition. This is especially the case when the power structure of the complementary relationship is considered autocratic, as if only in the democratic (isocratic) relationship do both partners define the nature of the relationship.*

Within the theoretical framework previously stated and according to variables which will be detailed below, it is possible to operationally define symmetry and complementarity according to the *structural similarity or dissimilarity (respectively) of the reciprocal communicative behaviors of the members of a dyadic system.* These terms are further defined to be contemporaneously mutually exclusive and exhaustive, i.e., an interaction cannot be but symmetrical or complementary. In the case of complementarity, the existence of two relative "positions" is implied: one-up and one-down.

In order to fix more clearly the operational application of this definition, some comments will now be made on the various possible *levels* and *units* of analysis to which these concepts can be applied.

### Level of Analysis

Human communication occurs simultaneously at several different levels, along various channels, all of which carry information. These levels have been classified as I. Audible-linguistic; II. Audible-paralinguistic; III. Nonaudible-paralinguistic (kinesics); and IV. Contextual (11). When, in a dialogue, each person transmits at all levels, the field of the meaningful messages is so wide and so complexly interrelated that a choice must be made of the level to be studied in order to avoid being drowned by the amount of data. Previous examples in the literature on symmetry and complementarity seem not to distinguish among these levels but rather

* A by-product of the lack of a strict definition of complementarity and symmetry from the interactional point of view has been the creation of other terms such as "meta-complementarity" (i.e., one-down "lets" one-up be one-up and is thus really in charge) and "pseudosymmetry" (i.e., one-up defines the situation as symmetrical). In our framework such terms (which could go on in infinite regress) cannot exist, since they refer the definition of the relationship to the intentions of one individual in this relationship.

to refer to them interchangeably and in combination. (Only Bateson and Jackson [4] specify that a level which corresponds to II and III above is sufficient when the verbal language of another culture is unknown to the observer.) We propose a limitation of the analysis to the *audible-linguistic* level for three reasons: our belief that, while the four levels differ in many respects and may even be simultaneously incongruent,* structural relations (perhaps an isomorphy) are likely to exist between these various levels, i.e., that the structure of the system composed by the elements of each level is likely to be a function of the other levels; second, that therefore a study of patterns within one level is a justifiable circumscription of the data; and finally, because the description and systematization of the other three levels is decidedly incomplete in comparison with the first.

A further distinction must be made between the kinds of messages sent within the audible-linguistic level. As in every digital message, they provide referential information as well as information *about* the way the data are handled by the source, that is, not only *what* is told but also *how* it is told. We choose for our study both types of information, placing a heavy emphasis on the second, the so-called structural characteristics.

## Unit of Analysis

The following units of observation have been used as the source of data for the assessment of symmetry and complementarity:

1. A *single message*† or "maneuver," defining the nature of the relationship as symmetrical or complementary (e.g., 6). This unit is especially of interest when the subsequent redefinition of the relationship by the other is studied.

Still, it seems clear that while certain information can be obtained from a single message, a judgment as to symmetry or complementarity cannot be made without reference to preceding or succeeding messages (10). Thus this unit of analysis is only apparently elemental because it is in operation inseparable from a bi-message perspective:

* An objection that may arise here is the fact that the messages simultaneously sent at different levels can be not congruent but contradictory. In fact, the "double bind" hypothesis proposed by Bateson and coworkers (5) is based on the observation that a patterned mode of contradictory messages—mainly at different levels—may redundantly occur in special contextual relations. But the present object of study is not the patterned relations *between* levels but the patterned structures *within* a level.

† Within the level of analysis just identified as audible-linguistic, a single message can be understood simply as a single speech of an (alternating) dialogue.

There is, strictly speaking, no such thing as a complementary piece of "behavior." To drop a brick may be either complementary or symmetrical; and which it is depends upon *how the piece of behavior is related to preceding and subsequent behaviors of the vis-à-vis.* (Bateson and Jackson, 4, p. 273, italics added)

A second objection to the single message unit being termed symmetrical or complementary is that such an assessment ultimately rests on the imputed motivation or intention of the speaker, i.e., how he is "trying to define" the nature of the relationship. This information, as it is not directly available to the observer, remains impressionistic or inferential and will not satisfy our criterion for an operational unit.

2. A *transaction,* which is the relation between two contiguous messages, i.e., a "link" between one message and the one which precedes it, and also between the same message and the one which follows it, and so on. In a sequence of speeches between individuals $A$ and $B,$ the transaction units would be A1/B1, B1/A2, A2/B2, etc. A determination of symmetry and complementarity can be made on the basis of the study of the structural relation of the two messages.

Since symmetry and complementarity are herein intended as strictly interactional, describing *relative* positions, a transaction seems to be the smallest possible analytical unit for these terms.*

3. *Three-message unit.* It has also been suggested that the study of the relation between three consecutive messages (of a two-party interaction)

---

* Having chosen the transaction for our microscopic, independent unit, a question arises whether these are really all summatively equal, even in theory. That is, one transaction (especially a complementary one) may "frame" subsequent transactions, as Bateson (3) has implied. If a husband, for instance, tells his wife to keep her voice down and she accedes, then no matter how symmetrical or even converse complementary their subsequent interaction may appear, as long as she spoke softly we cannot ignore the persistent after-effect of the original complementarity. There is a reason for choosing to disregard —for the moment at least—the observation of this phenomenon: our agreement with Bateson and Jackson (4) that every message is not only a stimulus and a response but also a *reinforcement.* Observation, in fact, confirms that even in established relationships such as marriage, cues are constantly exchanged which reinforce or modify the definition of the relationship, with a very high amount of redundancy, both in the same and in different levels of communication. Even when strong contextual factors operate (in institutions, military life, etc.), cues are still repetitively exchanged to reaffirm the nature of relationships. We must admit, though, that the practical difficulties of assessing exactly the extent of the "influence" of one transaction over subsequent transactions strongly supports this choice.

is necessary for the assessment of symmetry or complementarity, on the grounds that

> . . . every item in the sequence is simultaneously stimulus, response, and re-inforcement. A given item of *A*'s behavior is a stimulus insofar as it is fol-lowed by an item contributed by *B* and that by another item contributed by *A*. But insofar as *A*'s item is sandwiched between two items contributed by *B,* it is a response. Similarly *A*'s item is a reinforcement insofar as it follows an item contributed by *B*. The ongoing interchanges, then, which we are here discussing, constitute a chain of overlapping triadic links, each of which is comparable to a stimulus-response-reinforcement sequence. (Bateson and Jack-son, 4, p. 274)

In fact, this three-message unit can be reduced to two consecutive *trans-actions* with little or no loss of information, provided that a search is sub-sequently made of patterns of consecutive transactions.

4. *Overall interactional unit.* Finally, the overall configuration of the dyadic relationship, considered as an ongoing interactional process, can be studied as a whole. When Bateson introduced the terms symmetry and complementarity (2), they were subordinated categories which described the two possible directions of the process called "schisomogenesis." We assume that this process occurs whenever a new relationship is established, and only very seldom and in regard to basic changes, in a stable relation-ship. We probably will not actually observe it in our usual studies because we mainly work with stable dyads and also perhaps because of the rela-tively short period of these observations. Still, the overall patterning of the ongoing interactional process can be seen as the most general and en-compassing unit of analysis for symmetry and complementarity.

These various units should be understood as not exclusive, but rather as interdependently related, and to be studied in conjunction; in fact, taken in cumulative sequence, transactions tend to appear in long-lasting pat-terned fashion for the overall relationship. Even more, we assume that all perduring dyads can be described as patterned combinations of symmetri-cal and/or complementary interactions, and we believe that a finite typol-ogy of dyadic interaction can be established based on all the possible com-binations which might comprise these patterns.

### Scoring Procedures

Having framed the level and units of analysis, the next operational step is to apply the definition to this specific field through scoring instruments which rely on objectifiable variables, and to study the patterns which present themselves from the logically possible alternatives.

*Transaction analysis.* For reasons outlined above, the transaction seems to be the most desirable basic interactional scoring unit because, as will be recalled, it is the smallest unit which permits behaviors to be scored *relative to each other* and without regard to the presumed or imputed intentions of the participants. Since our chosen level of analysis is that of the *structuring of the content* (the "how" more than the "what") of the conjoint speeches of every transaction, the transactions will be scored according to whether they comprise similar or dissimilar (but fitted) elements at this level. To be more specific, content may be structured as question, referential statement, instruction, or order, negation, agreement or acceptance, etc. These are general forms in which specific information is exchanged. As can be seen, they correspond more or less to the basic grammatical forms (interrogative, declarative, imperative), with the addition of some metacommunicational categories (agreement and negation). So, disregarding *what* is said, it is possible to schematize *how* a dialogue proceeds via these forms. For example:

| A1: | What do you think? | (Question) |
| B2: | I think X . . . | (Referential statement) |
| A2: | Yes, I agree. | (Agreement) |
| B2: | And, furthermore, I think X' . . . | (Referential Statement) |
| A3: | Now let's talk about X and Y. | (Instruction) |
| B3: | No, let's talk about Z. | (Negation + Instruction) |
| A4: | Yes, I think Z is . . . | (Acceptance + Referential) |
| B4: | Z is also . . . | (Referential Statement) |

The transaction is *symmetrical* if the second message is like the first, *complementary* if the second message is unlike the first, with the type of message culturally labelled as "in charge" designated one-up and the other message which accepts or invites that charge, one-down. Some generalized examples of symmetrical and complementary transactions according to this scheme are

giving/taking instructions = complementary (giving = one-up, taking = one-down)
asking/answering = complementary (asking = one-down, answering = one-up)
asserting/agreeing = complementary (asserting = one-up, agreeing = one-down)
referential statement/referential statement = symmetrical

agreeing/agreeing = symmetrical
giving instructions/countering with instructions = symmetrical.

Note that the form of the individual statement is not what determines symmetry or complementarity, but the pair of statements considered together. E.g., instructions which are accepted form a complementary transaction, but instructions which are countered form a symmetrical one. The example above may thus be scored as follows:

A1:   Question ⎫
B2:   Answer   ⎭ Complementary

A3:   Instruction ⎫
B3:   Counter-     ⎬ Symmetrical
      Instructions ⎭

B1:   Assertion  ⎫
A2:   Agreement  ⎭ Complementary

B3:   Instruction ⎫
A4:   Acceptance  ⎭ Complementary

A2:   Agreement ⎫
B2:   Extension  ⎭ Complementary

A4:   Assertion ⎫
B4:   Assertion ⎭ Symmetrical

B2:   Assertion  ⎫
A3:   Counter-   ⎬ Symmetrical
      Assertion  ⎭

*Speech score assignment.* Once the transaction has been scored, post factum individual speech scores can be assigned, based on whether that member was engaged in a symmetrical or complementary transaction (and if complementary, in which position* he stood), for example:

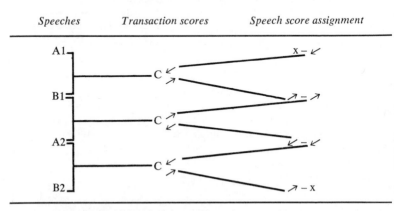

| *Speeches* | *Transaction scores* | *Speech score assignment* |

(That is, in complementary transaction A1/B1, *B* was in the one-up position, and in complementary transaction B1/A2, *B* was in the one-up position, so his score for speech B1 is ↗ – ↗.)

* ↗ denotes one-up, ↙ one-down.

Since it is the second speech which, when compared with the first, "defines" the transaction, these speech scores can be seen as the member's definition of his interactional position (by his speech) followed by his partner's redefinition of that same speech by the partner's subsequent contribution. In speech B1 of the example above, $B$ defined his position as complementary one-up with regard to the just previous A1; $A$ redefined (reinforced) $B$'s position in B1 as complementary one-up in relation to the immediately following speech A2. Again, it is important to note that the terms "define" and "redefine" do not refer to motivations or purposes of the individuals involved, but rather to valences mechanically assigned to each speech strictly on the basis of *relative behaviors*.

## A Typology of Dyads

When the assigned individual speech scores are observed in sequence (according to the consecutive order of the speeches of the dyad), their distribution can be seen to be not random but limited to certain logical possibilities. When the transaction is complementary, for instance, any speech score of $A$'s which ends in ↗ can only be followed by an initial ↙ in the speech score of $B$'s next speech. This fact reduces $B$'s possible speech scores to three (↙↙, ↙s, ↙↗), each of which in turn determines three possibilities for the next speech of $A$. Further, if one individual's speech scores are stereotypic (mainly one type), then, since these scores are based on relative positions as just described, the partner's scores must also be stereotypic in correspondence, as they are interdetermined. (A summary of the possibilities after any particular speech score is presented in *Figure 1*, where corresponding stereotypic pairings are also indicated).

*This interdetermination leads to the possibility of establishing a consistent typology for those dyads which exhibit a stereotyped pattern of interaction,* based on the rigidity of their mutual relative positions. Such patterns are also expressed in the patterning of assigned speech scores, as follows:

I. ss:           $A$ defines his position as symmetrical and is so redefined by $B$ and vice versa. A preponderance of such scores will indicate that a dyad could be typed as *Stable Symmetry*.

II. ↗↗ and ↙↙:   $A$ defines his position as ↗ and is so redefined by $B$, who thereby defines his own position as ↙ and is so redefined by $A$. A preponderance of such scores will indicate that a dyad could be typed as *Stable Complementary*.

III. ↗↙ :    *A* defines his position as ↗ and is redefined as ↙ by *B*, who thereby defines himself as ↗, etc. A preponderance of such scores will indicate that a dyad could be typed as *Symmetrical Competition toward One-Up*.

IV. ↙↗ :    *A* defines his position as ↙ and is redefined as ↗ by *B*, who thereby defines himself as ↙, etc. A preponderance of such scores will indicate that a dyad could be typed as *Symmetrical Competition toward One-Down*.

V. ↗s and s↙ :    *A* defines his position as ↗ and is redefined as symmetrical by *B*, who thereby defines his own position as symmetrical and is in turn redefined as ↙ by *A*, etc. A preponderance of such scores will indicate that a dyad could be typed as *Asymmetrical Competition toward One-Up and Symmetry*.

VI. ↙s and s↗ :    *A* defines his position as ↙ and is redefined as symmetrical by *B*, who thereby defines his own position as symmetrical and is in turn redefined as ↗ by *A*, etc. A preponderance of such scores will indicate that a dyad could be typed as *Asymmetrical Competition toward One-Down and Symmetry*.

The term "Stable" as used to describe two of the six deducted types is meant to imply consistency of the partners' relative positions according to the symmetry/complementarity paradigm as, for instance, originally described by Bateson. "Competition" means that the partners' overall interactional positions deviate from the paradigm; this inconsistency does *not* imply instability or the imminent dissolution of the dyad.

The six previously described types encompass dyads with a high degree of stereotypy in their configuration; it is also possible that some dyads may not have one predominant configuration but, on the contrary, fluctuate from one to another. Such a dyad will be called "Fluid."*

Thus we have a final typology of seven configurations:

   I. Stable Symmetry
  II. Stable Complementarity
 III. Symmetrical Competition toward One-Up
 IV. Symmetrical Competition toward One-Down

---

* It is further possible that this Fluid type could be divided into two subtypes according to whether the fluidity is adaptive or merely chaotic, that is, whether the flexibility is meaningfully related to intradyadic changes or environmental contingencies (7), or it is not apparently so related. In either case, the behavior of the dyad is not random but, we assume, diachronically patterned in its fluctuations.

V. Asymmetrical Competition toward One-Up and Symmetry
VI. Asymmetrical Competition toward One-Down and Symmetry
VII. Fluid

## Methods of Analysis

From this basic operational procedure, several manipulations of the data so obtained suggest themselves as worthy of detailed study and trial on a large sample.

A. The summation over speech scores which determined the dyadic type could be handled at least two ways: arithmetically, that is, a simple summation yielding the distribution and preponderance (if any) of score categories. Or, stochastically, a summation procedure which calculates the relative occurrence of logically possible sequences of scores, i.e., the *probability* that, given one specified score, the next will be another specified score. For instance, when any score ending in $\nearrow$ has occurred, the next score must be either $\swarrow\swarrow$, $\swarrow\nearrow$, or $\swarrow$s, each of which can be found to occur a certain percentage of times after x$\nearrow$; such a percentage can be interpreted, predictively, as the probability that such a score will occur after any x$\nearrow$. If the x is made specific and the probabilities recast, further refinement of patterning is possible.

B. Another analysis can be made of the diachronic patterning of relative positions of the members according to their speech scores. Having assigned to each consecutive speech a number corresponding to its order in the total dialogue, we can graph simultaneously both members' relative positions at any given moment of the interaction, as shown in *Figure 2*. This technique is presented simply as the prototype of an analytic tool, for only a large sample would provide data for the establishment of those stable patterns which might be expected to be shown by such a graph. E.g.: (1) Stereotypy vs. fluidity—the flatness of the traces would correspond to stereotypy of the pattern, while undulation would indicate fluidity; (2) "Fit" of the partners' patterns—when appropriate pairings (according to the typology) share a common horizontal plane, the relative identity of the partners' traces would indicate their fit within a particular class of symmetrical/complementary interaction; (3) Changes over time or task-subject—such a chart could also provide a vivid representation of such progressive changes as might be related to the establishment of a pattern of interaction or a change in the interactional situation; (4) Relations between interactional structure and content—when a change (adoption of or deviation from a given pattern) appears in the relative positions on the graph of the interaction, a study of the content of the previous and immediate speeches can be made, observing the correlation between these two levels of analysis in many different contingencies. In general, such analyses, as well as the stochastical method mentioned earlier, would seem to tap the stimulus-response-reinforcement information described in connection with the three-message unit and which could be lost with the choice of the smaller, transaction unit.

C. Other transactional variables, such as the flow of speech (mechanics of successive utterances) and some formal relations between the contents of consecutive speeches, have been devised in the course of this study. While their specific description is not within the scope of the present article, these and other transactional variables might be combined with the basic symmetrical/complementary variable for further refinement of the general typology.

## Suggestions for Further Study

Given the theoretical framework and specific instrument outlined herein, the following directions of further research suggest themselves:

1. Mass application and analysis—to test the instrument and the family typology scheme, using (a) different interactional task-situations; (b) different kinds of couples (e.g., according to age, psychopathology,* culture); and (c) other types of dyads (international, siblings, industrial, etc.).

2. Measurement of change—(a) before, during, and after therapy; (b) spontaneous and long-lasting, as for instance in a couple from early in their marriage.

3. Addition of a third person to the present analysis of dyads, with a concomitant study of coalitions.

## Summary

After a review of the concepts of interactional symmetry and complementarity, a delimitation of the unit and level of communication to which

* Preliminary analysis of eight couples shows suggestive correspondences of the parental typology with the psychopathology of their child. That is, parents of psychosomatically ill children exhibited markedly fixed symmetry (I), parents of psychotics were "fluid" (VII), while the parents of a less homogeneous neurotic group combined symmetry with asymmetrical competition (V or VI).

they can refer is suggested in order to formalize their application to specific data. A typology of characteristic family patterns based on these dimensions is presented, and some research directions proposed.

**Figure 1.** Interdetermination of Speech Scores.

B

| A | ↗↗ | S↗ | ↗S | SS | S↙ | ↙S | ↙↙ | ↗↙ | ↙↗ |
|---|----|----|----|----|----|----|----|----|----|
| ↗↗ |  |  |  |  |  | X | X |  | X |
| S↗ |  |  |  |  |  | X | X |  | X |
| ↗S |  | X |  | X | X |  |  |  |  |
| SS |  | X |  | X | X |  |  |  |  |
| S↙ | X |  | X |  |  |  |  | X |  |
| ↙S |  | X |  | X | X |  |  |  |  |
| ↙↙ | X |  | X |  |  |  |  | X |  |
| ↗↙ | X |  | X |  |  |  |  | X |  |
| ↙↗ |  |  |  |  |  | X | X |  | X |

B's three possible speech scores after a given speech score of A's are indicated, with the stereotypic response shaded.

## REFERENCES

1. BATESON, GREGORY, "Information and Codification: A Philosophical Approach," in Ruesch, J., and Bateson, G., *Communication: The Social Matrix of Psychiatry,* New York, W. W. Norton, 1951. Pp. 168–211.
2. BATESON, GREGORY, *Naven* (2nd ed.), Stanford (California), Stanford University Press, 1958.

**Figure 2.**   Diachronic Graph of (Fitted) Speech Scores.

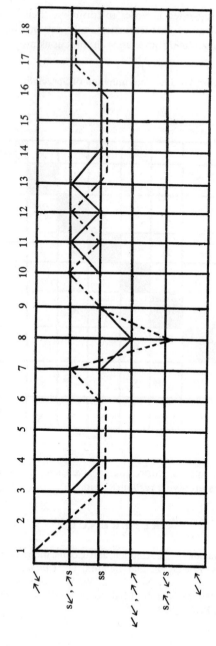

Husband (broken line) and wife (solid line) are discussing the meaning of the proverb, "A rolling stone gathers no moss."

3. BATESON, GREGORY, "A Theory of Play and Fantasy," *Psychiat. Res. Rep.* 2: 39–51, 1955.

4. BATESON, GREGORY, and JACKSON, DON D., "Some Varieties of Pathogenic Organization," in Rioch, David McK. (ed.) *Disorders of Communication* 42: 270–283, Research Publications A.R.N.M.D., 1964.

5. BATESON, GREGORY, JACKSON, DON D., HALEY, JAY, and WEAKLAND, JOHN, "Toward a Theory of Schizophrenia," *Behav. Sci.* 1: 251–264, 1956.

6. HALEY, JAY, *Strategies of Psychotherapy,* New York, Grune & Stratton, 1963.

7. JACKSON, DON D., "Family Interaction, Family Homeostasis, and Some Implications for Conjoint Family Psychotherapy," in Masserman, Jules H. (ed.) *Individual and Familial Dynamics,* New York, Grune & Stratton, 1959. Pp. 122–141.

8. JACKSON, DON D., "The Question of Family Homeostasis," *Psychiat. Quart. Supp.* 31: 79–90, 1957.

9. JACKSON, DON D., "The Study of the Family," reprinted on pp. 2–20 of this volume.

10. JACKSON, DON D., RISKIN, JULES, and SATIR, VIRGINIA, "A Method of Analysis of a Family Interview," *Arch. Gen. Psychiat.* 5: 321–339, 1961.

11. VERON, ELISEO, "Communicación y trastornos mentales: El aprendizaje de estructuras" (Communication and mental disorders: the learning of structures), *Acta psiquiát.psicol.Amér.lat.* 10: 77–85, 1964.

12. WATZLAWICK, PAUL, *An Anthology of Human Communication,* Palo Alto (California), Science and Behavior Books, 1964.

*Another way of reducing the complexity of human communication to manageable proportions lies in the expedient of limiting the interchanges to a particular subject or framework. This is the basis of all so-called Structured Interviews, in which the family is confronted with a particular communication task. A middle course is thus steered between the Scylla of overwhelming complexity and the Charybdis of irrelevant detail. The following report deals with one aspect of a Structured Interview, i.e., the attribution of blame, and shows that there exist significant differences in the handling of blame in various types of families, although it would certainly be an exaggeration to say that these differences in themselves could serve as reliable criteria of differential family diagnosis.*

# PROTECTION AND SCAPEGOATING
# IN PATHOLOGICAL FAMILIES

*Paul Watzlawick, Ph.D., Janet Beavin, M.A.,*
*Linda Sikorski, M.A., and Betty Mecia, A.B.*

In 1966 the principal investigator reported on the development of a structured family interview technique, composed of several tasks and designed to elicit specific family interaction patterns for the purpose of diagnosis and the planning of the most appropriate therapeutic interventions (4). The present paper reports on further research done on one of the tasks, the so-called "blame" part, which aims to uncover patterns of scapegoating and defense. Originally, this task was designed for work with families of schizophrenics. Since in these families the mothers are hardly ever blamed for anything (and at best blame themselves for something they could not possibly be held responsible for), it seemed worthwhile to devise a communications context in which the mothers had perforce to be blamed. Only subsequently did we find that this task was useful also with other kinds of families as an instrument to elicit complementary patterns of protection and scapegoating.

*The Task.* To recapitulate briefly, the family are seated around a table with the father to the left of the interviewer, the mother to the father's left, followed by the children in clockwise direction from the oldest to the youngest. Each family member is asked to write down the *main fault* of the person sitting on his left. The family are assured that the interviewer will not reveal the author of any statement. In addition, they are told that the interviewer will himself add two statements to the ones written by them. (These statements are always "too good" and "too weak." They are added to increase the degree of freedom available to the family and are hopefully ambiguous enough to be applicable to anyone.) It is further explained to them that the interviewer's statements are made about any two family members and not necessarily about the father (who sits at the interviewer's left). After writing his statements, the interviewer shuffles the cards and begins to read them out, one after the other, to the family. After reading each card he asks all family members in turn, beginning with the

The work described in this report was made possible by grants from the National Association for Mental Health.

Originally published in *Family Process* 9:27–39 (1970). Reprinted with permission.

father and finishing with the youngest child: "To whom do *you* think this applies?" However, although he shuffles the cards in plain sight of the family, the interviewer always starts with his own two statements ("too good" and "too weak") and only then reads out the family's statements in the random order produced by the shuffling. If necessary, the interviewer will not accept responses like "This applies to both our children" or "This does not apply to anybody in our family." Each family member is thus forced to blame somebody, and by so doing implies automatically that in his opinion this criticism\* was levelled by the person sitting on the right of the "victim."

*The Sample.* This report is based on data obtained from 48 white, middle-class families, with patients falling into the following categories:

| | | | |
|---|---|---|---|
| delinquency | 10 | cystic fibrosis | 4 |
| psychosis | 4 | marital problems | 1 |
| school underachieving | 9 | non-specific pathology | 1 |
| ulcerative-colitis | 19 | | |

They were composed of 48 pairs of biological parents and 129 children, ranging in age from 8–20 years. There was a total of 51 identified patients, only three of whom were parents; one colitis and two fibrosis families had two children suffering from the same condition. No "normal" families were included in the sample, at least in part because they are difficult to define operationally. It can be seen from the above that the sample is heavily loaded towards conditions which permit a relatively non-inferential diagnosis.

## Results

The relatively simple task of attributing one blame statement to each family member yields a rather large number of data. They can be ap-

---

\* It should be noted that such terms as "criticism" or "blame" have a special meaning in this context. Ordinarily, the connotation of "criticism" includes the possibility of *not* criticizing; that is, we say someone is highly critical and mean that he could be less so, or not at all. In this case, not being critical was not an alternative open to our subjects. They were, all equally, required to write and then to verbalize only faults about each other. Insofar as we are interested in this end of the spectrum, this a valid procedure. But it does lead to qualifications when we are tempted to generalize to the more global meaning of "criticism" on the total spectrum, which normally includes the option to be silent or even complimentary.

proached from different angles and we shall next describe these different approaches, including the results obtained through each of them.

*The Individual Family Profile.* The most obvious use of the data obtained from a given family is to establish the protection/scapegoating patterns of *that* family. This approach yields what may best be called the Individual Family Profile. The following example is that of a family composed of the parents and three sons. The identified patient is the second son (S2), who is underachieving at school, owing to frequent gastrointestinal disturbances for which no physical causes had been found. Their "Blame" profile is the following:

|  | F | M | S1 | S2 | S3 |
|---|---|---|---|---|---|
|  |  |  |  |  | S2 |
|  | S1 |  |  |  | S2 |
| Protection | S1 |  |  | F | S2 |
|  | S1 | S1 |  | S1 | S2 |
|  | S1 | S1 | S2 | S3 | S2 |
|  | S2 |  | F | S1 | S2 |
|  |  |  | F | S3 |  |
| Scapegoating |  |  | F | S3 |  |
|  |  |  | F | S3 |  |
|  |  |  | M | S3 |  |
|  |  |  | M | S3 |  |
|  |  |  | S2 |  |  |

**Figure 1.**

Since this is a family of five, five blame statements were written (disregarding the two statements, "too good" and "too weak," contributed by the interviewer). Since every family member has to state to whom each of the five blame statements applies, 25 such attributions are made. The profile shows only those blames which were attributed to the *wrong* person.

All entries above the horizontal line refer to attributions *away from* the person about whom the blame was actually written. Thus, the father (first column) was protected by all four other family members in the sense that they all attributed the blame actually written about him to the first son. (We therefore find four "S1" entries in that column.) In the case of the third son (S3, the fifth column), the attributions are even more striking: he is completely protected at the expense of the identified patient (S2) in that all five attributions (therefore including *his own*) are heaped on S2.

All entries below the horizontal line are the complement of those above it. They therefore show to what extent the family member in question is scapegoated and in favor of whom. It can, for instance, be seen that S1 (third column below the line) is the most scapegoated family member; he received four attributions that should have gone to father, two of mother's and one of the second brother. The brunt of the third son's total protection is carried exclusively by the identified patient (S2) who wrongly receives all of S3's blame and in addition one of S1's.

These family profiles are useful since they show the general degree of protection and scapegoating. The fewer incorrect attributions made, the fewer entries will be found above and below the horizontal (zero) line. We have, for instance, a delinquent family whose attributions are 100% correct; their profile thus has no entries whatsoever above or below the horizontal. The usefulness of this tool is marred by an obvious drawback. The evidence for the validity and the reliability of the blame profiles can only be established by the long-term observation of the family during treatment, which means that the relatively "hard," objective data supplied by the profile can only be judged against the relatively "soft," impressionistic data of clinical observation. Within this limitation, however, we found that the two types of data correlate well, i.e. that the blame profile gives a very clear, concise picture of the protection and scapegoating mechanisms actually found in the interaction of a family over a longer period of observation and therapy.

The other approaches to the data all make use of the entire sample of 48 families, grouping the data in various ways for comparative evaluation. These comparisons require the construction of standardized scores of performance, weighted for family size, which will be explained below.

*The Identified Patient.* An important question is how do identified patients fare in such a situation, compared to the other members of their family? Specifically, are they perceived more or less accurately, or protected or scapegoated; do they themselves perceive the others more or less accurately?

For this purpose, each individual family member's behavior was condensed into several indices which reflect the accuracy of receiving and attributing negative characteristics among each other. It is this accuracy or inaccuracy which we imply when we use such global terms as "protection" of a family member from criticism, or "scapegoating" (being blamed instead of someone else). We may also speak of the relative accuracy or honesty with which any particular member will speak negatively of the others. (We will not be concerned with other possible approaches to the data, such as the content of the items, or the subsequent fate of the writer of the item.)

As implied above, every criticism involves two persons—the attributor of the fault and the one to whom it is attributed. Every time a fault is assigned, data is produced on both these persons. Therefore, the first, obvious distinction in scoring was between whether the individual was being seen in his role as the target or as the critic. The basic nature of the data, in either case, is whether it was accurate or not—accurate in the sense that it coincided with the intention of the person who wrote the item.

When it is one's turn to assign a particular item, one can be accurate or inaccurate in placing the statement on the person about whom it was actually written. More specifically, each critic can be (a) accurate—actually, honest—about the item he wrote himself, and (b) accurate in guessing the intended target of items he did not write.

As the target of items, each individual can be (a) accurately assigned the item which was in fact written about him; (b) inaccurately assigned other items, not actually written about him; he may also receive the interviewer's items, which cannot be described as accurately attributed, but which contribute to the total of faults heaped upon any particular individual.

Of course, since family sizes, and therefore the number of items written, varied, the raw scores in terms of numbers of items are meaningless for inter-family comparisons. It is necessary for all scores to be weighted by family size, as follows: the score is the number of items actually received or attributed in such and such a way, divided by the potential number, given $n$ = the size of the family. The bases used below may be clearer if one recalls the experimental situation: After the $n$ items (one about each family member) have been written, 2 extrafamilial items are added, and the total $n + 2$ items are read in turn. For each item read, each of the $n$ family members must make an attribution of the item. These $n$ attributions of $n + 2$ items are the data points. So, for example, we see that any individual can receive the item written about himself a maximum of $n$ times; there is only one such item, and each member must assign it to someone. There are $n-1$ items written about someone else, and each of these must be assigned $n$ times—potentially to him.

In summary, we have the following indices of performance in this situation:

INDIVIDUAL SCORE

I. *Receiving*
   a. Receiving the item actually written about oneself       $a/n$
   (range: $0$ = maximum inaccuracy, to $1.0$ = accurately assigned by all family members)

b. Receiving other items not actually written about oneself (range: $0 =$ total accuracy, to $1.0 =$ maximum possible inaccuracy)   $b/n(n-1)$

c. Overall accuracy of fault attribution, i.e., receiving the items actually written about him *and not* others (range: $-1.0 =$ maximum inaccuracy where an individual would receive none of his items and all of the others, to $+1.0$ for total accuracy)   $(a/n) - b/(n^2-n)$

d. Total intrafamilial attributions received (range: $0 =$ none, to $1.0 =$ received all of them)   $(a+b)/n^2$

e. Total extrafamilial items received—"Too good" and "Too weak" (range: same as d)   $e/2n$

f. Total criticism received (range: same as d)   $(d+e)/(n^2+2n)$

II. *Attributing* (intrafamilial items only)

g. Correct attributions of fault-statements written by others (range: $0 =$ maximum inaccuracy, to $1.0 =$ total accuracy)   $g/(n-1)$

h. Written by self and correctly assigned   0 or 1

i. Overall accuracy of attribution (range: same as g)   $(g+h)/n$

We compared the patient's score with the mean of all his family members. The mean of all IP's compared to the mean of all others gives a quantitative summary of the result. However, for statistical tests, these means cannot be compared directly. The patient's and his family members' scores were obviously not sampled independently of each other, nor are they usually independent statistically (the more one person is scapegoated, for instance, the less the others can be). So, for tests of significance, the "sign test" was used.*

For the sake of readability of this report we have omitted a good deal of the statistical details in the following presentation of the results obtained from items I-a to II-i. The results are:

---

* This test treats a family as a single observation and asks only: Was the IP's score greater or less than the mean of the scores of the other members of his family? If the patient is essentially a randomly drawn member of his family (the null hypothesis), then, by chance, his scores will be distributed half of the time above and half below the others. If not, then they will show a consistent direction ($+$ or $-$), to a degree which we can say is likely to be "chance" only such and such a percentage of the time. This is a two-tailed test [1].

I-a: In general, the patient is less protected than others in his family. That is, everyone else tended to accurately assign the item written about the patient. In delinquent families, the IP is less protected than other family members. The IP's "receiving" score exceeded the average of his family's other members 8 of 10 times. The same is true of colitis families where the patient was less protected than the average of others in his family 12 out of 19 times. Over all types of families, the patient mean was only slightly higher than that of other (.66 vs. .60), but the sign test is very significant, since the IPs exceeded the rest of their family's average 30 of 46 times (P < .002).

As noted earlier, the equally likely alternative to concluding that the IPs are less "protected" is that they are more accurately perceived. That is, the items written about them might be clearer to all family members than items written about the others. If so, this was *not* for the obvious reason that the IPs' items referred to their symptoms, which they, perhaps surprisingly, very rarely did.

I-b: There was no significant difference in the scores of patients and others on this scale. In fact, the numerical scores of the others tended to exceed those of the IPs. For the families of delinquents, this difference was more marked but not statistically significant.

If I-b is interpreted as a measure of scapegoating, there is a resounding lack of support for the common notion that the patient is his family's scapegoat. He does not particularly receive the others' critical items for them; he is accurately omitted from these "blames."

I-c: Overall, there is no significant difference between IP and Others. Since this score reflects the combined accuracy in the two previous scores, the delinquents come out as significantly more accurately perceived (and thus neither more protected nor scapegoated) than their family members. Their average score is .71, compared to .53, and 8 of 10 times they exceeded their family average (P = .055). There is a considerable difference in overall accuracy between delinquent and other families:

|  | IP | | Others | | Combined averages | |
|---|---|---|---|---|---|---|
| 10 Delinquent families | .71 | (10)* | .53 | (36) | .58 | (46) |
| 38 Other families | .27 | (41) | .35 | (136) | .33 | (177) |
| 48 Total families | .36 | (51) | .39 | (172) | .38 | (223) |

* Number of persons.

I-d: There is a slight tendency for IPs to receive more intrafamilial blame. It probably reflects their above-mentioned tendency to get their *own* item accurately (I-a), which is, of course, a component of this score.

I-e: The patterns for extrafamilial blame are rather interesting. Both the delinquents and underachievers (IPs with school problems) received these items significantly *less* than their family members. Further inspection reveals that the patients in both these groups received very few of the "too good" items—reasonable enough for behavior-problem patients. The 10 delinquents were called "too good" only twice; none of the underachievers were called "too good." Their "too weak" attributions were received approximately as chance would predict.

The colitis patients are treated in the opposite manner: they tend to receive more of the extrafamilial items, although not significantly so. This trend stems from a disproportionate share of the "too weak" items (20 IPs received this attribution a total of 32 times). Their "too good" distribution is a little less than might be expected (13 times).

In other words, by chance, each extrafamilial item would be distributed over IPs in proportion to their representation in the subpopulation being considered. These figures for the three major diagnostic sub-groups are summarized below:

|  | IP | Others |
|---|---|---|
| *Delinquent* (10 families) | | |
| number of persons | 10 | 36 |
| number of "too good" received | 2 | 44 |
| number of "too weak" received | 6 | 40 |
| *School Problem* (9 families) | | |
| number of persons | 9 | 34 |
| number of "too good" received | 0 | 43 |
| number of "too weak" received | 10 | 33 |
| *Ulcerative Colitis* (19 families) | | |
| number of persons | 20* | 68 |
| number of "too good" received | 13 | 75 |
| number of "too weak" received | 32 | 56 |

* Recall that one family had two children with colitis.

The overall total for all families combines these two opposite trends and is therefore not significant.

I-f: These results seem to echo the I-e component, with delinquents tending slightly to receive *less* total blame. Similarly, the colitis patients tend to receive *more* total blame. The total effect is that patients receive more total blame than others. This is due to the I-d effect already mentioned, plus the influence of the larger number of colitis patients receiving "too weak" attributions.

Turning to the accuracy with which IPs and others attribute items, we would have to give honors to the patients:

II-g: Patients tended to be more accurate in attributing items written by others to their actual targets than were the other members of their families (.60 vs .56), although not significantly so. One might conjecture that perhaps the difference lay in some difficulty of attributing the item written by the patient. But the patients' items were not missed more than the average of their family members'.

II-h: In about half the families (26), everyone in the family accurately attributed his own item. In the remaining cases, the IPs were overwhelmingly more honest about the items they had written than the others were about those which they had written.

II-i: In this summary scale, the patients remain the most accurate perceivers and attributers of the fault items.

### Delinquent vs. Ulcerative Colitis Families

One of the sub-goals of the present study was to establish as sharp as possible a contrast between at least two types of families with very different diagnoses. Delinquency and ulcerative colitis, two conditions of obviously very different etiologies, were chosen for this purpose. This is the reason why the sample is heavily loaded towards these two diagnoses.

Several differences were already noted in the discussion of the IP above. Especially the delinquent IPs seemed to be quite different from the others, including the colitis patients.

For comparing whole families, different codes which summarize all the members' behavior are needed. Those constructed are very similar in focus to the individual scoring described above. We shall again present here these codes in simplified form.

In the following, we speak of *self-blame* whenever a person (accurately or inaccurately) attributes an item to himself. The special case of self-blame which consists in wrongly attributing an item to oneself we shall call *self-scapegoating,* since by doing this the person takes upon himself a blame which refers to someone else. *Self-protection* means, of course, the attribution of an item written about oneself away from oneself to another family member. *Scapegoating of others* consists in the attribution of an item written about someone else away from that person to another family member (excluding, of course, oneself), and *protection of others* is its converse.

Comparing the families of delinquents, colitis patients and the remaining sample, we find the following results:

|  | Delinquency | Ulcerative Colitis | Others |
|---|---|---|---|
| Self-blame | high | low | high |
| Self-scapegoating | low | high | equally high & low |
| Self-protection | low | high | high |
| Scapegoating of others | low | medium | high |
| Protection of others | low | low | high |

From the above, it can be seen that the common denominator of the families of delinquents is a high degree of accuracy of their interpersonal perception. (As already noted, one of these families was 100% correct.) This finding is consistent with the clinical impressions derived from working with families of delinquents.

The colitis families, on the other hand, distinguish themselves by a generally low accuracy of interpersonal perception. This is quite in keeping with the results of clinical studies (e.g. 2), according to which these families are restricted both as far as their range of permissible behaviors and the expression of feelings about self and others are concerned. The above data suggest that their contradictory behavior (e.g. low self-blame *and* high self-scapegoating *and* high self-protection) is not the result of some specific pattern of interaction, but rather of the random nature of their blame attributions due to their inaccurate perceptions of self and others.

*Families as A Whole*

Finally, all the above family total variables were cross-tabulated over all families, and we found the following correlations to be of interest:

In the larger families (five or more members), the IP is more likely to be a middle child, i.e. neither oldest nor youngest. Notice that this amounts to the obvious fact that the statistical probability of the IP being a middle child increases with the number of middle children. We mention this because it seems to indicate that, contrary to a prevalent belief, there is *no* systematic relation in this study between sibling position and mental health.

The larger the family, the less they tend to use self-blame. Since all these variables were weighted by family-size, this finding is more than an obvious artifact of the availability of more persons besides oneself to blame.

Protection of others increases as family size increases from small (3–4 members) to medium (5 members), but not beyond medium. That is, the smaller families divert blame from the real target onto a scapegoat *less* than do medium- or large-sized families.

Scapegoating in general is low when the IP is the youngest child, medium to high when the IP is another (parent, oldest or middle child, or when there is more than one IP).

Self-protection tends to be at the expense of the IP's siblings. That is, they receive the items which others will not attribute to themselves, when they were in fact written about them, and not about these siblings.

Not surprisingly, high overall protection in families is highly correlated with dishonesty in the attribution of the item written by oneself.

Protection of other family members tends least frequently to be at the expense of the IP's siblings.

*Theoretical Considerations*

There are some important questions regarding the inferential meaning of these data. It is very tempting to say, simply, that one is measuring "protection," "scapegoating," etc. But the validity of these conceptual inferences depends on their justification in the operations performed. Basically, the problem is that in order for a family member to assign an item accurately, he had to (1) perceive the intended target, and then (2) state this overtly. His inaccuracy, therefore, may originate at either of these stages—he did not recognize about whom it was written *or* he did not wish to say this but rather gave it to someone else. The important point is that our method does not permit us to distinguish which is the cause of the inaccuracy, and so our conceptual conclusions must be equivocal to this degree.

The reason the two processes cited above cannot be distinguished is obvious, although its solution is not. To remove any doubt about the first would mean assuring that each person knew exactly to whom each item applied. This, however, would virtually assure that everyone would be accurate. That is, to the degree that the actual target is made clear by the interviewer (even if privately to each individual), to the same degree is any distortion from this target made a very implausible alternative for the subject. The situation then demands that one simply report what one is told. Even "pathological" families would probably respond to the demand characteristics of this situation.

Another possibility might be the use of all arbitrary items, so that they could not be "accurately" perceived, only assigned. There are several faults with this procedure: (1) it eliminates information about specific distortions; (2) there are serious questions of what to tell the family about where the items came from—whether to have them also write items and then substitute these in deception, or tell them they are an arbitrary pool. Most important, (3) the unambiguity of this system is dubious, since what the experimenter intends as arbitrary and equiprobable need not be so for the family. Consider the extrafamilial items injected here. They were intended to increase the degrees of freedom available, so that the last item would not have to be assigned to the last remaining individual—i.e. to make inaccuracy plausible in the sense discussed above. Their vagueness was intended to make them general. But who, outside the family, can assure that the item could not have been written about a particular member more than another? As was noted above, the delinquent patient very seldom received the attribution "too good."

So it seems that we are stuck with measuring both interpersonal perception and intentional distortion as one. Further reflection makes it clear that the two are not really ever conceptually distinct in the usual clinical discussions of "scapegoating" or "defense." Only more recently, in work such as Laing's *et al.* [3], has the issue of interpersonal perception in families been formally considered. We may now ask more subtle questions, such as (1) how accurately do family members perceive each other? (2) how accurately will they verbalize this perception? (3) where inaccurate perception exists, does it take a particular form? (4) is the verbalization aimed wrongly because the perception is wrong, or despite the accurate perception, or because the perception is ambiguous and such ambiguity is typically resolved in favor of certain individuals and at the expense of others?

Such questions take us far beyond our present methodological ingenuity. We go to such lengths to pursue them in order to avoid oversimplified conclusions from our data. We learned some things with a fair degree of certainty; but within that, there is a conceptual bivalence which haunts this area of family research.

## Summary

Data are presented from a part of a structured family interview in which each family member is required to write a blame statement about the person sitting on his left. They are all then asked to state to whom they think each item applies. The sample consists of 48 pairs of biological parents and 129 children ranging in age from 8 to 20 years; the three main diagnostic groups composing the sample are ulcerative colitis, delinquency and school underachieving. If examined separately for each family, the task performance yields a Family Profile (showing the specific uses of protective and scapegoating mechanisms in that family); if used for inter-family comparisons, the data show statistical significance in several areas, the most important being: a) The patients are in general less protected, but also less scapegoated, than other family members. b) Patients tend to be more accurate in correctly attributing items written by others; they were overwhelmingly more honest about the item they had written. c) A great difference in accuracy of interpersonal perception exists between delinquent families (high accuracy) and colitis families (low). d) There is no systematic relation between sibling positions and being a patient.

## REFERENCES

1. DIXON, W. J. and MASSEY, F. J., JR., *Introduction to Statistical Analysis*, 2nd Edition, McGraw-Hill, New York, 1957.
2. JACKSON, D. D. and YALOM, I., "Family Research on the Problem of Ulcerative Colitis," reprinted on pp. 335–351 of this volume.
3. LAING, R. D., PHILLIPSON, H. and LEE, A. R., *Interpersonal Perception*, Springer Publishing Co., New York, 1966.
4. WATZLAWICK, P., "A Structured Family Interview," *Fam. Proc.*, 5, 256–271, 1966.

*Yet another way of approaching the complexity of interactional phenomena and of formalizing data is represented by Jules Riskin and Elaine Faunce's work on Family Interaction Scales. They developed a scoring procedure based on observable (and therefore low-inferential) variables, derived empirically from the observation of family behavior in a semi-structured interview situation, i.e., the response to the interviewer's request "Plan something together."*

*In a sense, then, this work is the opposite of Sluzki and Beavin's article at the beginning of this chapter. They applied an existing theoretical formulation (Bateson's symmetry-complementarity concept) to dyadic interchanges, while Riskin and Faunce used the interplay between clinical assumptions and the raw material of interchanges.*

*The Family Interaction Scales permit the classification of families into five different types (including "normal" families). As the reader will see, this system supports the premise—mentioned in the Introduction—that there is no one-to-one correspondence between the nomenclature used for individual, monadic diagnosis and the systemic aspects of family interaction and pathology.*

*The original work was published in three separate articles. They are here presented in abbreviated and unified form.*

# FAMILY INTERACTION SCALES

*Jules Riskin, M.D., and Elaine E. Faunce*

## I. Theoretical Framework and Method

This paper reports on the research project, "Evaluation of Family Interaction Scales," a method developed by the senior author for studying whole family interaction. The paper first reviews the theoretical framework and describes the research design and method. It then summarizes the research findings. It concludes with a discussion of the substantive aspects of the project and its significance.

Psychiatric interest in the family has expanded tremendously in the last 15 years. This is evident both in the growth of the family-therapy field[4] and in the increased focus of developing methodologies for studying families independently of immediate treatment implications. Wynne and Singer, for example, have published several papers describing their methodology for relating the parental interaction to certain behavior patterns in the child.[16,17,20,21] Mishler and Waxler[11] have recently published a monograph reporting their five-year project on a methodology for studying family interaction. Also, Haley,[5,6] Ferreira and Winter,[3,19] Cheek,[1,2] Lennard et al,[9,10] and Reiss,[12] to mention but a few, have all been doing related work.

Originally published as three separate articles in *Archives of General Psychiatry* 22: 504–512, 513–526, 527–537 (1970). Copyright 1970, American Medical Association. Reprinted with permission.

This study was funded by grant No. 11534 from the National Institute of Mental Health.

Arthur M. Bodin, PhD, and Shirley MacIntosh, PhD, administered the Structured Family Interview. Connie Hansen, MSW, and Joan Herrick, MSW, interviewed the families at home. Barbara McLachlan and Gloria Vannatter observed and transcribed the Structured Family Interviews. The Palo Alto school system assisted in obtaining families.

Lincoln Moses, PhD, Arthur M. Bodin, PhD, Harris Clemes, PhD, and James Ware, PhD, provided statistical consultation. Kathy Lambourne and William Patrick McDowell assisted with the statistical computations.

A common aim in all these approaches has been to move beyond the clinically based, impressionistic observations and inferences (which have proven essential in providing the initial hypotheses) and to develop more objective, operational methodologies for assessing family interaction. These studies, in general, have tended to focus primarily on the formal aspects of communication rather than on the specific content of the interaction. A commonly shared assumption is that the family is the immediate and central matrix in which the child's personality development must be viewed. Also, many of the researchers in the field, including us, share the conviction that longitudinal predictive studies must be done eventually in order to test theoretical formulations relating family interaction to the behavior of the children. Such projects are tremendously complex and arduous, and clearly require more sophisticated methods and instruments than have been available.

The research project to be described here is in line with the work referred to above. There are some important similarities, for example, in the belief that more operational methodologies need to be developed and in the overlap of some of the variables used. There are, however, also significant differences, a major one being that in this project the unit of observation was the *whole family,* as contrasted with dyads, triads, or other family subgroups.

*Theoretical Frame*

The theoretical frame of reference for this study was influenced by the work of Jackson[8] and Satir.[14] We view the family as providing the basic environment in which the child's personality develops. The parents influence the children by direct interaction with them. Also, the parental interaction in itself serves as a model for the children to observe and identify with and/or react against. Each child in turn influences his parents and siblings, and, thus, a mutually interactive process goes on. A related premise is that the whole family as a unit is greater than the sum of its parts.

To understand individual personality development, then, we believe it is essential to include the whole family as a major unit of study. It is, therefore, necessary to develop instruments for assessing whole family interaction, including methods and operational concepts which will enable us to relate our theoretical concepts about family interaction to the observable behavior of the family unit and its members.

The primary goal of this project was to develop and evaluate the validity and reliability of a method for investigating significant aspects of whole family interaction. We attempted to construct an instrument which would utilize concepts that had both theoretical and empirical relevance. Towards this end, several scales were developed to assess family interaction and the behavior of its members. Basically, these scales are composed of simple dichotomous categories which require low-inferential ratings about observable behavior. They are related to the process and style of interaction rather than to content, though in part they are derived from content. The emphasis on process is based on the assumption that repetitive, formal patterns of family interaction, and not just the ongoing verbal content, influence the children's personalities.

Brief definitions of the Family Interaction Scales categories are as follows: (1) Clarity: Whether the family members speak clearly to each other. (2) The topic continuity: Whether family members stay on the same topic with each other and how they shift topics. (3) Commitment: Whether the family members take direct stands on issues and feelings with one another. (4) Agreement and disagreement: Whether family members explicitly agree or disagree with one another. (5) The affective intensity: Whether family members show variations in affect as they communicate with one another. (6) The quality of relationship: Whether family members are friendly or attacking with one another.

We also looked at the patterns of who-speaks-to-whom and who-interrupts-whom. (See Riskin[13] for a more elaborated series of definitions with examples. That paper contains an earlier form, but essentially the same group of scales. Also, a highly detailed manual for the entire scoring procedure is available at cost [$6.00] from us.)

From the six main scale categories and the patterns of who-speaks-to-whom and interruptions a series of subcategories was derived. Descriptions of these variables follow.

*Clarity Categories* (1) Clarity: The speech is explicit, unambiguous, completely clear to the observer. (2) Unclarity: This includes incongruencies (eg, irony and sarcasm), bizarre or incongruent laughter, and linear disqualifications (self-contradictory comments). (3) Laughter: The speech includes laughter or is laughter only. (4) Nonscorable: The speech cannot be judged as being either clear or unclear because it was spoken too softly, too fast; overlapped someone else's speech; was interrupted before enough words could be heard to make a judgment; or had no verbal aspects (eg, a sigh).

*Topic Categories* (1) Same topic: The speech is on the same topic as the immediately preceding speech. (2) Total topic change: Includes 3, 4, and 5 below. (3) Appropriate topic change: There is a change of topic on the preceding speech, and it is a change appropriate to the context.

(4) Behavior-focused topic change: Comments relating to deportment of "behave yourself," eg, "John, don't pull at the microphones." (5) Inappropriate topic change: Change of topic inappropriate to the context, eg, "Let's go to the beach" followed by "The Johnsons bought a new car." (6) Jokes: Any speech the family clearly responds to as a joke. (May respond to same topic or topic change.) (7) Intrusiveness: One person speaks after another person has explicitly been invited to say something, eg, "Johnny, what do you want to do?" and Mary answers, "Let's go to the mountains." (May be same topic or topic change.)

*Commitment Categories* (1) Commitment: All speeches explicitly asserting the speaker's wishes, desires, feelings, wants, opinions, suggestions, ie, the speaker clearly takes a stand. (2) Request commitment: One person asks another to commit himself, eg, "What would you like to do?" (3) Nonapplicable: Informational statements or questions, eg, "What time is it?" or "I'll be getting two weeks vacation this year." ("Nonapplicable" does not mean an irrelevant statement or question. The speech gives or asks for information or clarification and "does not apply," or fit into, categories 1 and 2.)

*Agree—Disagree Categories* (1) Agreement: Explicit agreement, eg, "I agree with you"; "Yes, that's right." (2) Disagreement: Explicit disagreement, eg, "Let's go to the beach" followed by "No, let's not." (3) Nonapplicable: The speech is neither agreement nor disagreement.

*Intensity Categories* (1) Intensity up: Much affect in the speech; enthusiastic, strong feeling. (2) Intensity down: Little affect, withdrawn, depressed-sounding, flat. (3) Normal: Ordinary conversational tone; neither up nor down.

*Relationship Categories* (1) Positive relationship: A speech which in tone of voice or words, or both, is friendly to the person spoken to. (2) Negative relationship: A speech which in tone of voice or words, or both, is critical or attacking of the person spoken to. (3) Neutral: A speech which is neither friendly nor attacking.

*Who-Speaks-to-Whom Categories* (1) parent-to-parent interaction: Parent speaks directly to the other parent. (2) Child-to-child interaction: Child speaks directly to another child. (3) Child-to-parent interaction: Child speaks directly to a parent. (4) Parent-to-child interaction: Parent speaks directly to a child.

*Interruption Category* Interruptions: One person interrupts another person.

These categories are related to conditions, which, it is often assumed, the family environment must provide if the child is to develop into a "normal" adult. Also, specific quantitative and qualitative variations in these conditions are assumed to be associated with pathological states. In the present study, we have attempted to demonstrate the validity of these categories by making across-group comparisons with certain current behavioral patterns in the families.

In order to facilitate the reader's understanding of the theoretical bases of these scales we will present, in summary form, our underlying theoretical notions about them (Table 1). *We wish to stress that in the present work there has been no attempt to investigate formally any of the possible etiological hypotheses which might be inferred from Table 1. Table 1 is presented only to clarify the theoretical bases from which the scale categories were derived.*

*Research Design and Method*

Table 2 summarizes the research design. It will be elaborated upon in subsequent paragraphs.

*Families* All families that participated in the project were required to meet the following criteria: white; suburban middle and upper-middle class; at least second-generation American; biological family intact; at least three children, none younger than 6 or older than 21; and all members living at home. These criteria limit the generality of the findings, but it was necessary to control for certain socioeconomic and demographic variables which we were not attempting to study in this project.

Forty-four families were studied. A variety of families, ranging from "normal" to various kinds of "abnormal," were included in the sample population in order to determine how the scale categories were distributed and how they differentiated among the different types of families. All diagnoses were made by experienced therapists not associated with this project or by official community agencies, or both.

(Brief working definitions of the terms "normal" and "abnormal" are as follows: A "normal" family is one in which no family member manifests clinical psychiatric symptoms, as defined by the American Psychiatric Association's nomenclature manual. An "abnormal" family is one in which one or more members manifest any of the major categories of symptoms as defined by the APA manual, including functional psychotic, neurotic, psychophysiological, and acting-out character disorders. Marital problems and school problems were also included in the "abnormal" category.)

The families came from two sources. One group, consisting of 29 families, was obtained through a local high school. The presence or absence of psychiatric symptoms was *not* a selection criterion. (It was later learned that some of these families had official psychiatric labels.) The other group, composed of 15 families, was referred by local therapists, and contained *only* families with a labeled pathological disturbance.

The families, whether from the school or the therapists, were explicitly informed, before agreeing to participate, about the strictly research nature of the project. They were offered no inducement other than the opportunity to be involved in "a research project studying the important field of family interaction, of how family members communicate with one another."

School Families Ninety-four families were randomly selected from a list of 10th and 11th graders of a local high school. Letters were sent to these families on the school stationery informing them of the project and asking their cooperation. They were then contacted by telephone by a project staff member who set up an appointment with the families to visit them in their homes and to explain the project in more detail. At this stage, four families were dropped from the list because they had moved and could not be located. Of the remaining 90 families, 36 were ineligible because they did not meet all of the selection criteria (mainly, an intact family living together). Of the 54 eligible families from the school sample, 31 (57%) accepted and were interviewed and 23 (43%) refused for various reasons (mainly "too busy" or "not interested"). Two of the families that accepted and were interviewed had to be dropped from the project because their tape-recordings were mechanically too poor to be used. This left 29 families from the original school sample that participated fully in the study.

Therapist Families Twenty-five families were referred by local therapists and agencies. Of these families, two refused the invitation to participate, saying that they were not interested, and 23 accepted and were interviewed. Eight of these families were subsequently dropped from the project because they did not meet all of the selection criteria or because their tape-recordings were mechanically too poor to be used. This left 15 therapist families, including a family with a labeled schizophrenic, families with serious behavior problems, and families with serious neurotics. Except for the deliberate inclusion of family members with labeled pathological disturbance, these families met the same criteria of those from the school.

*Standard, Semistructured Interview* All 44 families were administered a standardized, semistructured interview. The interview was a modified version of the one described by Watzlawick.[18] It lasted about 90 minutes and contained a series of nonthreatening, nonpathology-oriented questions. The families were interviewed by an experienced interviewer at the Mental Research Institute in a room with microphones and a one-way viewing mirror. Two assistants observed from behind the mirror, with the family's knowledge. The families also knew that they were being taped. Neither the interviewer nor the observers had any prior knowledge about the families, ie, whether they were referred by the school route or via therapists, in order to avoid being biased by any expectations as to either normality or pathological disturbance.

This project focused primarily on one part of the interview, during which the whole family was asked, "Plan something you could all do together as a family; all of you please participate in the planning." The interviewer left the room and the family had about ten minutes to deal with the task.

*Transcripts* Highly accurate transcripts were prepared, requiring a minimum of 15 hours for preparation of approximately four to five minutes of the family discussion of the "plan something" task. The transcribers had no knowledge of the families, other than names, ages, and the sex of each person. Body movement, an extremely complex dimension, was not studied except to help in determining "to whom" a speech was addressed.

**Table 1.**—*Relationship Between Scale Dimensions and the Child's Personality*

| | LEVELS* | | |
|---|---|---|---|
| Dimensions | High (Too High) | Medium (Optimal) | Low (Too Low) |
| Clarity | Compulsive; intellectualized; humorless | Good reality testing; direct expression of wishes and feelings; sense of identity; value rationality; express humor | Distrusts own perceptions; poor reality testing |
| Topic continuity | Lacks spontaneity; compulsive defenses; passivity | Controls impulsive behavior; learns cooperation; takes initiative | Impulsive; competitive; acting-out |
| Total topic change | Highly competitive; lack of cooperation; acting-out | Spontaneity; assertiveness; initiative | Lacking in spontaneity; compulsive defenses; passivity |

**Table 1.**—*Relationship Between Scale Dimensions and the Child's Personality* (*Continued*)

| Dimensions | LEVELS* High (Too High) | Medium (Optimal) | Low (Too Low) |
|---|---|---|---|
| Inappropriate topic change | Impulsive; fragmented thinking and behaving | Expresses humor; not overly rigid | Compulsive defenses |
| Intrusiveness | Impedes sense of autonomy | . . . | . . . |
| Commitment | Acting-out; stubborn | Sense of identity and autonomy; be assertive; takes responsibility for self | Passive; depressive |
| Request commitment | (Indirect means of avoiding commitment) | Learns to explore limits | Lacks initiative |
| Avoid commitment | Assertiveness is bad; learns passive resistance | . . . | . . . |
| Agreement | Conflict is dangerous; dissension is bad | Open positive coalitions permissible; learns cooperation | Does not learn how to cooperate or compromise |
| Disagreement | Does not learn how to cooperate or compromise | Sense of individuality and independence; assertiveness and aggressiveness are permissible | Uniqueness is bad; assertiveness is bad; conflict is dangerous |
| Intensity | Problems with impulse control | Emotional spontaneity is good; learns how to express tension openly | Compulsive, depressive defenses; neurotic constriction; psychosomatic symptoms |

| Positive relationship | Reaction-formation against anger; relationship with parents too seductive | Sense of self-esteem; trust in others | Low self-esteem |
|---|---|---|---|
| Negative relationship | Feelings of worthlessness; self-hate | Learns to express anger | Neurotic constriction; pathological defenses against anger |
| Interruptions | Highly competitive; acting-out | Spontaneity; competitiveness permissible | Lacks spontaneity; neurotic constriction |
| Nonscorable | (Neurotic tension in family) | . . . | . . . |
| Who-speaks-to-whom | . . . | (No scapegoats; all get fair share) | . . . |

* The terms "high," "medium," and "low" are defined statistically. "Too high," "optimal," and "too low" are clinical terms. It might help to conceptualize these dimensions in terms of extremes, eg, a *totally* clear family vs a *totally* unclear one.

*Scoring* The transcripts for the two groups, school families and therapists-referred families, were pooled and scored in random sequence. The scoring procedure was in effect a "microanalysis" of the family discussion. The basic unit which was scored was the "speech," defined essentially as all the sounds one person uttered until someone else made a sound, verbal or simply vocal but without distinguishable words. Each speech was scored in terms of *all* the scale dimensions, that is: (1) speaker and spoken to were assigned; (2) interruptions were noted; (3) a speech was judged as "clear" or "unclear"; (4) on the "same topic" or "different topic"; (5) whether it was a commitment or not; (6) whether an agreement or disagreement; (7) whether of high or low intensity; and (8) whether it was friendly or attacking. Each speech, therefore, was assigned eight scores. The first 80 speeches and the third block of 80 speeches, representing approximately the first two minutes and the fifth and sixth minutes of the "plan something" discussion, were scored. Previous work had suggested that four to five minutes of family discussion did contain enough information on which to do a meaningful anlaysis.[13]

The scorers were the principal investigator and the research assistant, each of whom, with no prior knowledge of the families, independently scored one half of the transcripts. The written transcript alone was first used to score the "agree—disagree" category; then the tape-recording was used along with the transcript to score the other categories, since we were particularly concerned with the tone of voice and other nonverbal, vocal

**Table 2.**—*Research Design*

Recruitment of 44 families:
"Normals" and "abnormals"
↓
Participation in standard interview
(Interviewer has no prior knowledge of family)*
↓
Transcription of portion of interview
(Transcribers have no prior knowledge of family)*
↓
Scoring of transcribed portion of interview
(Scorers—different from transcribers—have no
prior knowledge of family)*
↓
Data analysis ⟵——— "Independently-assessed characteristics"
(Interviewer has no prior knowledge of
family)*

* The project was designed to minimize the chances that bias due to information about a family learned at any one stage would influence any later judgments.

**Table 3.**—*"Plan Something" Transcript**

| SPEECH NO. | WHO | TO WHOM | SPEECH |
|---|---|---|---|
| 1 | Mother | Children | "Well, what would you girls like to plan?" |
| 2 | Daughter 1 | Mother | "Go to the beach." (High-pitched laugh) |
| 3 | Mother | Daughter 1 | (laughs) |
| 4 | Daughter 3 | Mother | "I want. . . . . ." |
| 4A† | Son 1 | Mother | (Interrupts) "I want to go to the beach." |
| 5 | Mother | Son 1 | "You do too?" |
| 6 | Son 1 | Mother | (very softly) "Yeah." |

| 7 | Father | Daughter 2 | "How about you, Mary? Huh?" |
| 8 | Daughter 2 | Father | "Yeah." |
| 9 | Father | Daughter 2 | "You're going to the beach too?" |
| 10 | Daughter 2 | Father | "Uh huh." |
| 11 | Mother | Daughter 3 | "And you, Julie?" |
| 12 | Daughter 2 | Mother | "And John?" |
| 13 | Daughter 3 | Mother | "Uh humn." |
| 14 | Father | Children | "Well, when do you want to go?" |

* The family is asked to "plan something together" and the interviewer leaves the room.

† Indicates an interrupting speech.

qualities in all of the other scales. It required three to four hours to score the 160 speeches on all categories for each transcript.

Table 3 contains an example of a brief section of the "plan something" discussion and Table 4 contains the scores for that section.

*Reliability* The basic scoring unit of this study was the speech; reliability was defined, therefore, as speech-by-speech agreement between the two raters (inter-rater) and between a rater's original scoring and his rescoring of the same family (intra-rater). Speech-by-speech reliability data were obtained for the clarity, topic, commitment, and agree-disagree scales; it was not computed for the intensity and relationship scales because the frequency of real scores (nonneutral) on these two scales was so low as to make the computation of speech-by-speech agreement meaningless. (An on-going check of total use of categories by the two raters was, however, made on these two scales while the scoring was in progress.)

Three types of reliability data were computed: (1) ongoing inter-rater reliability; (2) inter-rater reliability over time (six months); and (3) intra-rater reliability over time (six months). Ongoing inter-rater reliability checks were made throughout the scoring of the entire group of 44 families to ensure that the two raters did not "drift apart" from each other in the baselines they were using in their scoring. Eleven families were jointly scored, ie, both raters scored these families independently and inter-rater reliability figures were obtained. The scorers then conferred about their differences and came to a mutual agreement on the final scores. These reliability checks were systematized so that the joint scoring was done on every fourth family that each rater scored. For those families

**Table 4.—Scoring of the "Plan Something" Transcript**

| NO. | WHO* | TO WHOM* | CLARITY† 1 | CLARITY† 2 | CLARITY† NS | TOPIC† 1 | TOPIC† 2-1 | TOPIC† 2-2 | TOPIC† NS | COMMITMENT† 1 | COMMITMENT† 2 | COMMITMENT† RC | COMMITMENT† NA | COMMITMENT† NS | AGREE-DISAGREE† 1 | AGREE-DISAGREE† 2 | AGREE-DISAGREE† NA | AGREE-DISAGREE† NS | INTENSITY† 1 | INTENSITY† 3 | INTENSITY† 5 | INTENSITY† NS | RELATIONSHIP† 1 | RELATIONSHIP† 3 | RELATIONSHIP† 5 | RELATIONSHIP† NS |
|---|---|---|---|---|---|---|---|---|---|---|---|---|---|---|---|---|---|---|---|---|---|---|---|---|---|---|
| 1 | M | Children | 1 | | | 1 | | | | | | RC | | | | | NA | | | 3 | | | | 3 | | |
| 2 | D1 | M | | 2-I-L | | 1 | | | | 1r | | | | | | | NA | | | | 5 | | | 3 | | |
| 3 | M | D1 | | | NS-L | | | | NS | | | | | NS | | | NA | | | 3 | | | | 3 | | |
| 4 | D3 | M | | | NS-In | 1 | | | NS | | | | | NS | | | NA | | | 3 | | | | 3 | | |
| 4A | S1 | M | 1 | | | 1 | | | | 1r | | | | | | | NA | | | 3 | | | | 3 | | |
| 5 | M | S1 | 1 | | | 1 | | | | | | | NA | | | | NA | | | 3 | | | | 3 | | |
| 6 | S1 | M | 1 | | | 1 | | | | | | | NA | | | | NA | | 1 | | | | | 3 | | |
| 7 | F | D2 | 1 | | | 1 | | | | | | RC | | | | | NA | | | 3 | | | | | 5 | |
| 8 | D2 | F | 1 | | | 1 | | | | 1r | | | | | | | NA | | | 3 | | | | 3 | | |
| 9 | F | D2 | 1 | | | 1 | | | | | | RC | | | | | NA | | | 3 | | | | 3 | | |
| 10 | D2 | F | 1 | | | 1 | | | | 1r | | | | | | | NA | | | 3 | | | | 3 | | |
| 11 | M | D3 | 1 | | | 1 | | | | | | RC | | | | | NA | | | 3 | | | | 3 | | |
| 12 | D2 | M | 1 | | | | 1-I | | | | | | NA | | | | NA | | | 3 | | | | 3 | | |
| 13 | D3 | M | 1 | | | 1 | | | | 1r | | | | | | | NA | | | 3 | | | | 3 | | |
| 14 | F | Children | 1 | | | | 2-1 | | | | | RC | | | | | NA | | | 3 | | | | 3 | | |

* M = mother; D = daughter; S = son; F = father.

† Clarity: 1 = clear; 2 = unclear; I = incongruent; L = laughter; NS = nonscorable.

Topic: 1 = same topic; I = intrusiveness; 2-1 = appropriate topic change; 2-2 = inappropriate topic change; NS = nonscorable.

Commitment: 1 = spontaneous commitment; 1r = requested commitment; 2 = avoids commitment; RC = requests commitment; NA = nonapplicable; NS = nonscorable.

Agree-Disagree: 1 = agreement; 2 = disagreement; NA = nonapplicable; NS = nonscorable.

Intensity: 1 = intensity down; 3 = normal; 5 = intensity up; NS = nonscorable.

that were not jointly scored, reliability figures were obtained on two or three of the coding scales per family. The data for the ongoing, inter-rater reliability are presented in Table 5.

Six months after the scoring of all 44 families had been completed, a random sample of families were rescored. Seven families were rescored by the original rater and six families were rescored by the rater who had not done the original scoring. Again, speech-by-speech agreement was computed only on the clarity, topic, commitment, and agree—disagree scales. Table 6 presents the inter-rater and intra-rater reliability over time.

*"Independently Assessed Characteristics" Interview* Socioeconomic and demographic data about each family were collected by an interviewer (an experienced family therapist) who was unfamiliar with the specific hypotheses and also had no prior knowledge of the families. Using considerable skill, tact, dogged persistence, and persuasion, she was able to interview every one of the 44 families who had participated in the standard interview. During a joint interview with both parents in their home, she elicited factual information such as their educational background, the psychiatric and medical history of each family member, any police contacts and the reason, and history of labeled marital problems and school problems. In addition, she made impressionistic observations, such as how the parents related to her and how they interacted with each other. When necessary, she obtained additional information from the therapists who had worked with family members.

A five-way classification of families was derived from the information about psychiatric problems, marital problems, school labeling, and police contact. All 44 families were then assigned to one of the five family groups. Definitions of these five groups plus a composite description of a typical family in the first three groups are given below.

GROUP A This group contains the multi-problem families. These families have three or more labeled problems including neurotic and/or psychotic, and/or psychosomatic, and/or acting-out, and/or underachieving, and/or the "marriage," ie, they are the most troubled families. There are ten families in this group. A typical group A family would have the following diagnoses: marital problem; father has been labeled as a schizoid personality; mother has been labeled as depressed; two children have been labeled as underachievers, and one child has an acting-out label, either from the school or the police.

GROUP B This group contains families that have two or three labeled problems. These families are basically seen as "constricted" and usually have one labeled neurotic member plus a marital problem and/or an underachiever. There are five families in this group. A typical group B family would have the following diagnoses: the parents are in therapy for a marital problem and one of the children has a neurotic-reaction label.

GROUP C This group contains families that have child-labeled problems only, either acting-out (delinquency) or underachieving in one or more children, or both. There are 12 families in the group. A typical group C family would have the following problems: one of the children has been picked up by the police for shoplifting or setting fires and another child has been labeled by the school as an underachiever.

GROUP D This group contains families that were from the school sample and were originally part of group E. These families have no official labels of any kind, but all the interviewers agreed that there seemed to be significant problems in the family, either between the parents, or with the children, or between the parents and the children. There are eight families in this group.

**Table 5.**—*Ongoing Inter-rater Reliability*

| SCALE | RANGE (%) | MEAN (%) |
|---|---|---|
| Clarity | 98.7–83.1 | 94.5 |
| Topic | 95.6–79.3 | 85.3 |
| Commitment | 88.7–65.6 | 80.6 |
| Agree-Disagree | 96.8–75.6 | 89.1 |

**Table 6.**—*Inter-rater and Intra-rater Reliability Over Time*

| SCALE | RANGE (%) | | MEAN (%) | |
|---|---|---|---|---|
| | Inter | Intra | Inter | Intra |
| Clarity | 98.1–90.6 | 98.8–95.0 | 95.0 | 96.6 |
| Topic | 95.6–81.9 | 99.4–83.3 | 87.4 | 90.7 |
| Commitment | 88.8–75.0 | 98.8–83.1 | 80.3 | 89.8 |
| Agree-Disagree | 91.9–85.6 | 96.3–91.3 | 88.6 | 94.5 |

GROUP E This group contains families that have no labels and the interviewers all agreed that they were functioning well ("normally"). There are nine families in this group.

In summary, group A contains 10 families; group B contains 5 families;

group C contains 12 families; group D contains 8 families; and group E contains 9 families.

An analysis of the socioeconomic data on these five groups of families revealed that they are basically homogeneous. Table 7 contains these data.

**Table 7.**—*Socioeconomic Data*

| DATA | FAMILY GROUPS | | | | |
|------|---|---|---|---|---|
| | A | B | C | D | E |
| Mean age | | | | | |
| Father | 42.7 | 45.8 | 44.5 | 44.4 | 44.0 |
| Mother | 41.3 | 43.2 | 41.8 | 41.1 | 40.7 |
| Children | 16-10 | 16-9 | 16-9 | 16-8 | 16-9 |
| Mean No. of children | 3.6 | 3.4 | 3.7 | 3.7 | 3.4 |
| Education* | | | | | |
| Father | C† | C | C | C | C |
| Mother | C | C | C | C | C |
| Occupation* | | | | | |
| Father | P† | P | P | P | P |
| Mother | HW† | HW | HW | HW | HW |
| Mean No. of community activities‡ | | | | | |
| Father | 2-3 | 4 | 2-3 | 2 | 3 |
| Mother | 1-2 | 2 | 3 | 3 | 4 |
| Children | 1-2 | 2 | 3 | 2 | 4 |
| Moves since children | Many§ | Many | Many | Many | Many |
| Religion | Pr† | Pr | Pr | Pr | Pr |

* Hollingshead's *Two Factor Index of Social Position.*
† C = college;  P = professional;  HW = housewife;
Pr = Protestant.
‡ No. of contacts per week outside of family.
§ Many = more than three.

*Data Analysis* Finally, the interactional scores for all 44 families were reduced by computer techniques and comparisons across the five groups of families were made, using standard nonparametric statistical tests. The results of this analysis will be reported in the second paper of this series.

*Summary*

This section has presented the theoretical framework and method used in evaluating the instrument, the "Family Interaction Scales," developed for measuring whole family interaction. Forty-four families were obtained through a local high school and local therapists. The families were administered a standard semistructured interview and a five-minute segment was scored using the "Family Interaction Scales." The families were subsequently interviewed at home and certain socioeconomic and demographic data were obtained. The 44 families were then divided into five groups and their interaction scores were compared across groups. In essence, the procedure involved a "microanalysis" of the whole family interacting together in a standardized interview setting. Subsequent sections will present the research findings, a discussion of the methodology, and some of the implications of the findings for future research.

## II. Summary of Data Analysis and Findings

[The details of findings have been omitted from this edited version.]

In reviewing the findings, four general points are apparent: (1) many of the variables yield significant discriminations among the five family groups; (2) there is a wide range of their ability to do so; (3) there are clear patterns among several of the groups of variables, even though any given variable, by itself, might be only weakly discriminating or even nonsignificant; and (4) in general, the variables composed of ratios tend to be more sensitive than the simple percentage variables, and reinforce the findings for the latter.

To summarize the findings for the main groups of variables:

The *clarity* variables discriminate, especially between family groups A and E and between groups A and B. Groups E and B have significantly more clarity than group A, and group A has significantly more unclarity than groups E and B.

The *topic* variables, considered individually, do not yield significant differences beyond the chance level. Patterns, however, stand out, especially differences between family groups A and E, with group A high on topic change and group E high on same topic. Groups B and C tend to be high on topic change and group D is high on same topic.

The *commitment* variables strongly differentiate, most noticeably between groups A and E, and groups C and E. Groups A and C are high on commitment and request commitment. Group E is unexpectedly low on commitment but is high on informational statements and questions.

The *agree:disagree* variables show a range of discriminatory sensitivity. Agreement is weakly discriminating; disagreement is stronger, and the ratios of agree—disagree are most discriminating. Differences are particularly clear on the agree variables between groups E and C and on the disagree variables between groups B and C. Group E is high on agreement and group C is low. For disagreement, group C is high and group B is low.

The *intensity* variables yield no significant differences (with one exception) among the family groups. The marked depressive pattern for group B, however, stands out.

The *relationship* variables, especially negative relationship, are strongly discriminating among the family groups. The patterns reveal that groups E and D tend to be high on positive relationship with group C being low, and groups A, D, and B are high on negative relationship with groups E and C being low. The low negative relationship for group C was a major unexpected finding.

The *who-speaks-to-whom* variables are nondiscriminating.

The *interruption* variables are only weakly discriminating. In terms of patterns, the contrast between family groups B and E is especially notable, with group E consistently high and group B being consistently low on interruptions.

The *relationship:disagree* variables, in general, strongly discriminate among the family groups and support the findings for the relationship and disagreement percentage variables.

The *commitment:agree—disagree* variables strongly discriminate among the five groups of families but in the direction opposite from that predicted.

The group of *miscellaneous* complex ratios, along with the other complex ratios, contains several variables which discriminate well and which essentially reinforce the findings for the simple percentage variables.

A considerable number of variables, then, do discriminate among the groups of families, both in terms of significance and also in terms of several consistent and meaningful patterns which emerged from considering groups of variables. As was expected, the over-all strongest differences were between the two family groups most sharply differentiated clinically, namely groups A and E. Important general differences can also be seen between groups C and E, and groups B and E. Several specific differences are also present between groups C and B, groups A and C, and groups A and B. Also, the clinically observed constricted behavior of group B was borne out in the patterns of its scale scores.

Some findings were quite unexpected, particularly the very low commitment for group E and the very low amount of negative relationship for group C. (It is difficult to evaluate the findings for group D, the "questionable" families, and its differences from the other groups were only minimally discussed in this paper.)

### Conclusion

The primary goal of this project was to develop and evaluate a method for assessing whole family interaction. We believe that the results have demonstrated that the "Family Interaction Scales" instrument taps meaningful areas of family interaction and that several of the scale categories have statistical significance. We, therefore, conclude that the method is a useful one for investigating whole family interaction and for discriminating among different types of families.

The emphasis in this section was on presenting findings. The final section will be more directly concerned with a discussion of the methodology, with some of the implications of the substantive findings, and with possible applications and future directions for this kind of research.

### III. Discussion of Substantive Findings and Significance

[The discussion of methodology has been omitted from this edited version.]

### Substantive Aspects

Up to this point we have been discussing methodological problems involved in the development of the Family Interaction Scales. We will now shift the emphasis and start with the premise that the scales are valid and reliable and do assess meaningful areas of family interaction. (We have, in fact, some evidence that the scores for the variables, derived from the scales, convey clinically meaningful information about the families. Eleven people, working individually, were asked to match blindly four groupings of variable scores against the descriptions of the five family groups. These matchings were accurate to a degree far greater than chance by Kendall's coefficient of concordance ($P < 0.0005$). In addition, we have been able to construct a clinical description for a single family, confirmed by the therapist, solely on the basis of a detailed study of that family's scores on the 125 variables.) Using the mean rank values for the family groups on the individual variables, we will present a tentative sketch of a typical "profile" for the family groups, recognizing of course that these family groups are not pure type. We will also offer speculations concerning some of the clinical implications of these family profiles. Note that the comments for each family should be understood as being relative to the *other* family groups. We will not be concerned in this section with whether the findings for any given variable are statistically significant or not.

*Group A: The Multiproblem Families* These families were the most unclear on the clarity variables, including a high amount of irony, sarcasm, and laughter. They had the highest amount of total topic change, indicating much competing and cutting each other off. They were high on inappropriate topic change (but not the highest as originally expected), and highest on "behave yourself" comments. That is, though they are chaotic, they also set limits, at least verbally. They were the most intrusive group, and they also had most of the "mind-reading" comments, ie, those in which one person speaks for another. For example, Johnny says, "Mary would like to go to the mountains." (There were so few of this type of comment that "mind-reading" was not included as a formal variable.) They were the highest on total commitment and high on spontaneous commitment, suggesting they are very opinionated and assertive of their own personal wishes and feelings. There was very little information-sharing and seeking (categories NA and NA? on the commitment scale), but they were highest on request commitment, suggesting that people tended to put others on the spot. They were also highest on parrying and avoiding of commitment when requested. They tended to disagree slightly more than they agreed (note this in conjunction with their being highly unclear and highly opinionated). They tended to express slightly more affect outward than holding it inward. On relationship, there was, in general, an absence of support, especially from child to parent. And there was a very high amount of attack across all the who-to-whom categories. The atmosphere, then, was distinctly the most unfriendly one. Their communication network was characterized by high child-to-child interaction with minimal parent-to-parent interaction. The child-to-parent interaction was also minimal. They were in the middle on interruptions. Their many disagreements were not balanced by friendly statements, suggesting that the absence of support concurrent with high disagreement could lead to quite explosive situations. They are strongly opinionated without much cooperation (the latter manifested by low agreement), which suggests power struggles without resolution of differences. They are opinionated without being on the same topic, which suggests a collection of isolated people talking past each other. One particular person in each family stands out as both strongly agreeing and disagreeing while at the same time speaking quite unclearly.

To summarize, these families are very unclear, with very many shifts of topic. They are strongly opinionated and are also frequently asked for their opinions. They disagree more than they agree; there is a slightly intensity-outward direction to their affect; the atmosphere is strongly unfriendly. There is much potential for explosive behavior. They are highly assertive, unfriendly, competitive, and chaotic.

In terms of personality development (ie, etiological hypotheses), we would speculate that this kind of family would not provide a climate for the development of high self-esteem or respect for others as individuals, nor would it provide models for learning clear modes of communicating or effective cooperation. In terms of their observable behavior, this picture is, in general, consistent with clinical impressions of these families.

*Group B: The Constricted Families* These families are extremely, even compulsively, clear. They speak in complete sentences; their speeches are not fragmented, nor do they laugh much. Unexpectedly, they shift a great deal on topic, relatively more on inappropriate topic change than on appropriate topic change. This aspect of their interaction is the only crack in their otherwise highly controlled behavior, and perhaps serves them as a safety valve. The manifestations of the inappropriate topic changes in the interview room are that the children tend to "goof off" and the parents do not set limits (they are lowest on "behave yourself" comments). There are a moderate number of jokes (without laughter, though), and they are highly intrusive. They are quite low on spontaneous commitment, but are asked rather frequently for opinions and do respond when asked. They are medium on information-exchanging. They agree very little and are the lowest on disagreement. There is, therefore, slightly more agreement than disagreement, although both are quantitatively low. There also is one target person who is disagreed with frequently. In terms of intensity of affect, there is both a marked absence of enthusiasm and a strong presence of a depressive tone. The atmosphere is generally a somewhat unfriendly one. The parents are critical of the children, without balancing supportive comments. The children are unfriendly with one another and with their parents. Quite unexpected was the finding that the parents are quite friendly to each other (as well as talking a great deal to each other). There is at least one scapegoat in each family who is very strongly attacked. The parents talk highly with each other, and the children speak to the parents. Parents tend not to talk to the children (but are critical when they do), nor do the children talk with one another. This group of families is the lowest on all the interruption variables, which is consistent with the marked absence of spontaneity in these families. There is a relatively large amount of attacking without much open disagreeing, which suggests a quality of covert bickering. They tend to be in the middle for commitment relative to agree plus disagree, with quite wide differences among members within the families. They are also very clear relative to their agreeing and disagreeing.

To summarize, these families are compulsively clear. There is much shifting of topic, with the children misbehaving and the parents not setting limits. There is a lack of spontaneous commitment, and there is little agreement or disagreement. The mood is depressive and unfriendly, with the parents critical of the children, yet supportive of each other. There is a marked inhibition of affective expression and spontaneity.

The picture is, in general, consistent with clinically constricted families with, however, a few surprising contradictions. The high appropriate and inappropriate topic change, without limit-setting, seems to be their primary way of releasing tension. It also may be a way of setting up covert messages that later acting-out by the children will be permissible. The high amount of friendliness between the parents may, in part, be accounted for by their attempting to put on a "good front" for the interviewer. It is quite unexpected in the light of how these families often behave clinically. To speculate etiologically, the children are being brought up in an unfriendly, depressive, compulsive atmosphere with a stress on tight control of spontaneous behavior (with perhaps a covert message to act out). This would seem to be the kind of atmosphere which might produce compulsive, controlled children.

*Group C: The Families With Official Child-Labeled Problems* These families do not speak clearly, not so much because they actually speak unclearly but rather because there is much fragmenting and interrupting of their talking. They tend to be in the middle on same topic, appropriate topic change, and inappropriate topic change. One person in each family, though, is quite high on topic change. They are the second highest on "behave yourself" comments. They do make an effort to set limits on inappropriate behavior, a somewhat unexpected finding which may in part be because of their attempting to perform well in public. They are very low on jokes. They are moderately opinionated. They are, however, the highest on requested commitment (as contrasted with spontaneous commitment), and there tends to be one target person who is frequently asked for his opinion. They are also the highest on requested commitment in relation to request commitment, suggesting there is much "yes-sirring" occurring, but this is coupled with a high degree of parrying and avoiding of commitment. They very strongly disagree without balancing this with agreement. This suggests an argumentative, noncollaborative atmosphere, all rather low-keyed emotionally. One person is very strongly disagreed with, suggesting a possible scapegoat role. They are affectively constricted, with little intensity-up and much intensity-down, which suggests a depressive tinge. There is an absence of positive support (which was expected) but also a striking absence of attacks (which was totally unexpected). That is, the "relationship" atmosphere is bland, neutral—they do not give clear relationship messages. In terms of who-speaks-to-whom, they have the most generalized participation of all the groups. They have medium intragenerational interaction with slightly more intergenerational interaction. One person tends to stand out as speaking much more than being spoken to. They are medium-to-high on interruptions, indicating that they are somewhat spontaneous in spite of some indications of constriction. There is a great deal of disagreement without positive, friendly statements to balance it. This supports the impression of low-keyed bickering, which could become explosive. They are fairly assertive in relation to very low agreement, which again suggests open power struggles, and this impression is reinforced by the high disagreeing. But these power struggles seem muted, as if they might be quite fearful of their potential violence. They are very high on same topic relative to agreement, suggesting no resolutions of differences; and they are very low on same topic relative to disagreement, which reinforces the notion of much argumentation.

To summarize, there is a low-keyed, sullen, argumentative, non-cooperative atmosphere in these families. They are muted, with a slight depressive tinge, and with many hints of underlying power struggles—not displaying much affect, but with very much disagreement. They are not very clear, primarily because of a great deal of fragmenting in their speaking. There is a moderate degree of inappropriate behavior, with a considerable show of limit-setting. They are assertive without being cooperative. There are also signs of one person being a scapegoat.

This picture is fairly consistent with much of the clinical behavior of families who label their problems as residing in the children. The principal contradictory finding is the striking absence of attacks. Two possible (not incompatible) explanations are that they have learned the dangers of letting the anger get too open and that they are trying to present a reasonable front to the interviewer. Etiologically, the pattern would be consient with children growing up in an atmosphere which is both tense and encourages acting-out.

*Group D: The "Questionable" Families* Group D has the fewest significant differences of all groups when compared with the other groups of families. Also, it follows no consistent pattern in the way in which it differs from the other groups. This finding probably reflects the nature of group D (and, incidentally, reinforces an earlier point about averaging together a heterogeneous group of "abnormals"). Group D is a "group" only by virtue of having been separated from group E because of some question concerning the "normality" of these families. It is quite heterogeneous and includes, for example, one family with a brain-damaged child, another family with a deaf father, and another family which has a daughter with an illegitimate child. In other words, in each case the interviewers had some question or suspicion that (unlabeled) significant problems were present, even though none of the members of these families bore official psychiatric labels.

Because of the varied nature of this group and the absence of significant findings, we believe it would be meaningless to make substantive comments about it as a composite "type."

*Group E: The Normal Families* These families tend to be in the high-medium range on clarity and in the middle on unclarity. They are low as a family on nonscorable, although one person in each family is high. The unclarity is partly because of irony and sarcasm and partly because of laughter. Their falling in the middle range was expected. Their communication is neither compulsively clear nor confused, and they use a good deal of humor.

They tend to stay on the same topic, and this applies to everybody in the family. They are fairly low on topic change, both appropriate and inappropriate. That is, they seem to continue one topic until it is resolved before moving onto another one, and there is minimal "goofing off." They are the highest on jokes, which is congruent with several other measures of spontaneity (eg, intensity outward, friendliness, considerable laughter, and interruptions). They are the lowest on intrusiveness. In general, their tendency is to stay on the same topic rather than to make topic shifts, and to shift topic appropriately rather than inappropriately. They are unexpectedly very low both on spontaneous and requested commitment and on request commitment. (This low amount of spontaneous commitment, however, seems to be counterbalanced by the other expressions of spontaneity, noted above.) But they are very high on information-asking and giving. That is, there is minimal expression of opinions or putting people on the spot and maximal amount of interacting on a factual level. They agree very highly (this is quite compatible with their being high on same topic and having high information-sharing) and are in the middle range for disagreements. This suggests that it is not dangerous to disagree, nor is the high agreement simply a reaction formation. There are no target scapegoats. They seem to be able to cooperate without being intimidated by differences.

They display a wide range of intensity of feelings, both up and down, with a tendency for outward-directed (intensity up) feelings to predominate. They have by far the friendliest atmosphere. There is much positive support, including parent-to-parent, parent-to-child, and child-to-parent. There is a relative absence of attack (as well as the absence of any one specific target for attacks), but they can show some anger (they are not as low as group C), mostly between children and from children to parents. There is a relative absence of attack from parent to child. It would seem that the friendly atmosphere is not simply a defense against angry feelings. No one person dominates the communication network. There is slightly more intragenerational interaction than intergenerational. They have the most interruptions but with no one person either being strongly interrupted or highly interrupting. They are able to disagree in a friendly, nonattacking atmosphere, which suggests a respect for the individuality of the other person. They tend to agree without much forcefulness (both because of the high agreement and the low commitment). They tend, however, to disagree with somewhat more forcefulness. One person per family is particularly high in this respect, and another person is particularly low. They are very high on agreement relative to clarity. This is because they are in the medium range for clarity and the highest for agreement. They are low on disagreement relative to clarity. For agreement-plus-disagreement relative to clarity, they are very high, and this is generally true of all family members.

To summarize, these families are moderately clear. They are not compulsively rationalistic, chaotic, or fragmented. They freely laugh and use some sarcasm and irony. Humor is distinctly present. They tend to stay on the assigned task, with minimal misbehaving and limits are invoked when appropriate. They are spontaneous (laughter, jokes, intensity-up, and interruptions all high). There is very little intrusiveness. There is much information-sharing with minimal expression of strong opinions. They are able to progress with the planning of a task without getting caught up in defensive power struggles. They are able to cooperate but are also free to express differences in a nonthreatening manner. There is no evidence of scapegoating. The atmosphere is friendly and supporting. Differences are respected and nonthreatening. There is particular support by the parents for the children, and they manifest a wide range of affectivity, with the emphasis on expressing their feelings openly.

The principal unexpected finding was their low commitment. A possible reason is that they have a large reserve of good will, shared consensus, and understanding and can, therefore, be more concerned with focusing on the task without the matter of individual autonomy becoming an issue of contention. The very high agreement and the fairly low amount of attack were also somewhat unexpected, although in retrospect these findings do not appear especially inconsistent, in view of their ability to disagree and to do some attacking.

The normal families appear to provide a supportive atmosphere in which a child's self-esteem is able to develop adequately. The family provides models for cooperation. They express themselves fairly directly without being compulsive about speaking clearly. Respect for differentness is permitted and encouraged. Individuality is valued. Defensive power struggles are shown not to be necessary in important, intimate relationships. (A detailed write-up of extended home visits to two of the normal families has been done [C. Hansen, unpublished data].)

*Significance of this Research*

The major emphasis and significance of this project has been in developing an operational methodology for studying the family as an interactive unit rather than as a collection of individuals or of subgroups of the family. We believe we have been able to progress beyond the stage of clinical impressionistic observations of family interaction with the methodology we have developed. This method may also be applicable to families in other contexts, eg, as a possible means of evaluating change in therapy or as a means of evaluating families during longterm, longitudinal studies; it could also be used for investigating other small groups.

We have suggested a way of classifying families other than by the application of traditional psychiatric individual nomenclature. In our system, we emphasized the effectiveness of the family interaction, and characterized families by their predominant "atmosphere."

The study has yielded some substantive findings, even though methodology was the primary aim. Perhaps most importantly, it offers some clues on normal family functioning—objective descriptions that may have more reliability than personal, subjective observations. It also provides objective checks on certain pet notions held by some students of family interaction. We found, for example, that unclear communication does seem to be associated with extreme pathological disturbance (but not necessarily psychosis).

Both the substantive aspects and the methodology may be useful tools in attempting to clarify the extremely complex problem of the relationship between the family as a unit and the individual as a unit.

**126** THE INTERACTIONAL VIEW

## REFERENCES

1. CHEEK, F. E. The father of the schizophrenic. *Archives of General Psychiatry* 13:336–345, 1965.
2. CHEEK, F. E. The schizophrenogenic mother in "word and deed." *Family Process* 3:155–177, 1964.
3. FERREIRA, A. J. and WINTER, W. D. Decision-making in normal and abnormal two-child families. *Family Process* 7:17–36, 1968.
4. GAP REPORT. *The Field of Family Therapy.* New York: Group for the Advancement of Psychiatry, 1970.
5. HALEY, J. Research on family patterns: An instrument measurement. *Family Process* 3:41–65, 1964.
6. HALEY, J. Speech sequences of normal and abnormal families with two children present. *Family Process* 6:81–97, 1967.
7. HOLLINGSHEAD, A. B. *Two Factor Index of Social Position* (printed privately), New Haven, 1957.
8. JACKSON, D. D. The question of family homeostasis. *Psychiatric Quarterly* 1(suppl. 31):79–90, 1957.
9. LENNARD, H. L., BEAULIEU, M. R., and EMBRY, N. Interaction in families with a schizophrenic child. *Archives of General Psychiatry* 12:166–184, 1965.
10. LENNARD, H. L. and BERNSTEIN, A. *Patterns in Human Interaction.* San Francisco: Jossey-Bass, Inc., 1969.
11. MISHLER, E. G. and WAXLER, N. E. *Interaction in Families: An Experimental Study of Family Processes and Schizophrenia.* New York: John Wiley and Sons, Inc., 1968.
12. REISS, D. Individual thinking and family interaction. *Archives of General Psychiatry* 16:80–93, 1967.
13. RISKIN, J. Family interaction scales: A preliminary report. *Archives of General Psychiatry* 11:484–494, 1964.
14. SATIR, V. *Conjoint Family Therapy.* Palo Alto: Science and Behavior Books, 1964.
15. SIEGEL, S. *Non-parametric Statistics.* New York: McGraw-Hill Book Co., 1956.
16. SINGER, M. T. and WYNNE, L. C. Thought disorder and family relations of schizophrenics: III. Methodology using projective techniques. *Archives of General Psychiatry* 12:187–200, 1965.
17. SINGER, M. T. and WYNNE, L. C. Thought disorder and family relations of schizophrenics: IV. Results and implications. *Archives of General Psychiatry* 12:201–212, 1965.
18. WATZLAWICK, P. A structured family interview. *Family Process* 5:256–271, 1966.
19. WINTER, W. D. and FERREIRA, A. J. (eds.) *Research in Family Interaction: Readings and Commentary.* Palo Alto: Science and Behavior Books, 1969.

20. WYNNE, L. C. and SINGER, M. T. Thought disorder and family relations of schizophrenics: I. Research strategy. *Archives of General Psychiatry* 9:191–198, 1963.

21. WYNNE, L. C. and SINGER, M. T. Thought disorder and family relations of schizophrenics: II. A classification of forms of thinking. *Archives of General Psychiatry* 9:199–206, 1963.

# CHAPTER 3

# Training

*Formal training was initiated at MRI as early as 1959, at a time when even the term conjoint family psychotherapy was known to only relatively few professionals in the mental health field. The following decade saw a rapid proliferation of training programs, the introduction of family therapy courses for psychiatric residents at many medical centers and the foundation of other family institutes in many parts of the country.*

*It is not surprising that together with this rapid growth of family therapy as a method in its own right, the training methods have also undergone an evolution since those early days. But in retrospect it is, for instance, difficult to appreciate how profoundly research in interaction (and therefore also training in interactional therapy) was changed through the introduction of such devices as the tape recorder and sound-film equipment. Prior to their advent, all interaction was evanescent, was "real" only the moment it occurred and was then immediately and irretrievably lost. With no way of recording the basic raw data, the verbal and kinesic behavior of subjects and experimenters or therapists, detailed and repeated study of actual interaction was not possible. Both research and training depended on clumsy, incomplete, and unreliable memories and impressionistic descriptions.*

*Sound-recordings provided an initial breakthrough, but they are limited to the purely acoustic parts of an interchange, and sound-filming requires complicated equipment and expensive processing. A further breakthrough occurred with the introduction of the video-recorder. This instrument, requiring no special lighting and permitting immediate, repeated playback, is one of the grestest modern aids in training and research.*

*In the following paper, Arthur Bodin describes some uses which video-recording offers in the training of family therapists.*

# VIDEOTAPE APPLICATIONS IN TRAINING FAMILY THERAPISTS

*Arthur M. Bodin, Ph.D.*

The advent of videotape has opened new avenues of development in therapy, training and research, some of which will be described as they have been evolving at the Mental Research Institute (MRI).

## The Context

Since the context is as important in using videotape techniques as it is in using other techniques in training and therapy, some relevant features of the MRI setting will be described. The MRI is a multidisciplinary, nonprofit institute which was initiated in 1959. Since then it has focused its research efforts on the exploration of communication and the nature of interaction in families and other social systems. Parallel with these concerns a training program has evolved, focusing at first on conjoint family therapy and continuing now to broaden its scope to communication and human systems.

## The Spectrum of Uses

The videotape uses discussed here relate to training and therapy applications, but not necessarily to research applications. Training applications presented here include: 1) taping prior to particular courses, 2) tape libraries, 3) splitting audio and visual channels, 4) "on line" feedback, 5) self-presentation exercises and 6) comparative analysis of an individual's on- and off-stage performance in order to gain perspective on what constitutes authenticity.

Therapy applications presented are: 1) early uses, 2) overt rather than covert use of the video controls, 3) temporal variations in the duration and timing of videotape recording and replay in relation to certain purposes, such as recapturing previous moods and consolidating the participants' grasp of change and stability evidenced across the sweep of therapy,

This paper relates in part to work supported by Training Grants MH-10001 and MH-10829 from the National Institute of Mental Health.

Originally published in *The Journal of Nervous and Mental Disease* 148: 251–61 (1969). Reprinted by permission.

4) some examples of what patients learn by watching post-session replays and 5) some generalizations about what the therapist may learn from patients' reactions to themselves.

## Equipment

### The Man-Machine System

Any discussion of videotape equipment must take into account the intimate relationships between the machine setup and the people and purposes connected with its use. These factors, inextricably linked, comprise a man-machine system. The optimal installation and operation of such a system requires attention to its human and nonhuman elements, as well as an understanding of the inevitably mutual effects they have on each other. The spectrum of desired applications must be defined; the machine best suited to the technical demands of the situation must be selected; and personnel must be trained adequately to make good use of the equipment. For instance, home visit or field work applications demand portability and thus dictate selection of one of the lighter machines recording on half-inch tape. The advantages of portability and both initial and subsequent economies are accompanied by some loss in resolving power, so that the finer features of facial expression are less faithfully rendered. Where on-line feedback is desired, a monitor screen is needed in the same room with the camera along with relatively simple controls, or a skilled cameraman who might even double as co-therapist.[1] In addition, the configuration of camera(s) in relation to the seating arrangement must be considered. The choice in height of the camera mounting(s), the focal length of the lens(es), the availability of remote controlled zoom, and pan and tilt capabilities must all be related properly to the room size, number of people to be squeezed onto the frame (or split-frame), the amount of money available, and the accessibility of patients and therapists who will not be paralyzed by visible and audible paraphernalia.

## Description

A significant new range of therapy training at the Mental Research Institute was opened up in 1963 by the acquisition of a videotape recorder.

[1] This technique is being explored at the Family Therapy Center in San Francisco by its directors, Ben Handelman and Dr. Alan Leveton. Todd Bryant is serving as cameraman/co-therapist.

The total setup during the past half year (the period discussed in this report) consisted of a GE television camera equipped with a wide angle as well as a standard lens, a TV monitor, and an Ampex VR–7000 tape recorder, which takes tapes 1 inch wide that last 1 hour and cost about $60 each.

Several options for improving our stationary one-camera video setup became available this summer. One option was to purchase a second video camera and install a corner shelf for it diagonally across from the one already in use. Another was to forego the coverage afforded by two cameras in favor of the flexible focusing afforded by a remote control zoom lens. This latter alternative would have permitted individual faces to be brought into sharp focus when particular facial expressions were apparently revealing for more than a few seconds at a time; and dyadic, triadic and whole group kinesic patterns could be brought within the video frame when gross bodily movements or positions might be revealing. Instead, however, we chose a third configuration: a fixed camera on a tripod, equiped with a wide angle lens (12.5 mm) to take in the whole family and the therapist, plus a movable camera with a close up lens (50 mm), mounted on the wall still higher and equipped with remote controlled pan and tilt functions. The therapist has an on/off switch at his elbow during therapy sessions, and in training situations the co-teacher in the observation room has another switch. Either switch can override the other.

## Developing Uses in Training

The developing uses in training fall into an order determined by two factors: an historical or evolutionary sequence, and a continuum in terms of subtlety-complexity. Fortunately, these factors display considerable congruence.

### Precourse Taping

An innovation designed for a 10-week Intermediate Course in Family Therapy at MRI consists of videotaping a family's initial therapy session about a month before the first class session, when the tape is played and discussed. This provides a basis for noting changes which occur by the time of the family's fifth session, which the trainees observe in their second class period as a "live" demonstration.[2] The family's intervening sessions might be skipped, unless the total sequence seemed particularly valuable. Subsequent demonstration sessions would continue to show what

[2] This innovation was conceived by Dr. Sheldon Starr.

changes take place over the period of the course (though some assessment-focused sessions with other families might be interpolated for the sake of variety; this does not interfere with the trainees' ability to comprehend the sweep of therapy with their main demonstration family).

The precourse taping of a demonstration family's therapy achieves an obvious advantage for the class. It permits a relatively short-term class to see family therapy changes over a longer time period than that spanned by the course itself without "tying up" many valuable blank tapes which can be used for library development. This advantage is a particularly vital one in teaching short courses, such as 2-week family therapy summer workshops.

### Library Possibilities and Problems

*Possibilities.* An obvious extrapolation of the precourse taping idea is the development of a library containing several families' therapy sessions videotaped at some appropriate intervals, such as every 5 weeks, from the initial session through termination and even follow-up.

The value of such library materials will undoubtedly increase as we continue to accumulate, refine and codify our liberary materials, and as publishing companies, professional associations and other centers offer an increasing variety of similar materials on a purchase, rental or loan basis.

*Problems.* Although library plans of this kind have considerable merit, they also have distinct drawbacks. One such drawback is their enormous expense. Because of the high cost of videotape, it is extremely important to formulate an overall plan for deciding which material to discard. Perhaps the most essential step is to take the time immediately after each recorded session to write down just what seems worth saving in terms of what points of theory or technique are highlighted, and approximately where these occur on the tape. If the recorder is in another room and a knowledgeable observer is on hand, the digital counter may be used to good advantage. The on/off switch permits a certain amount of on-line editing.

Another drawback in videotape library materials is that no matter how well they are used, they cannot give the trainees quite the same "feel" for family therapy which they can get by "live" observation. The latter can be rendered still more valuable by inviting the family to join the trainees for some post-session review. We have found this procedure effective both as an additional aspect of therapy for the family, and as a powerful way of having trainees experience at first hand what it feels like to deal with the family system. They learn how easy it is to overestimate (and thus foster) the fragility of individuals and of families, while underestimating their strengths, including their ability to cope with therapists as fellow human beings. Bringing families and trainees together creates a context which often permits the *families* to give useful, growth-producing feedback which they might not otherwise feel free to offer, particularly within the context of a demonstration session. Thus, for our purposes, the use of videotape *library* materials is an important but supplementary aspect of training.

*Channel Splitting*

A training application of our videotape system which we plan to try soon will have half the trainees watch a family therapy session through a one-way mirror with the sound turned off, while the other trainees will listen to the same session in the other observation room with the curtain drawn across their one-way mirror. Each subgroup will be given a few minutes after the session to consolidate individual notes into a group account of the highlights of what happened and how. Then the whole class will meet together again, each subgroup reporting its impressions to the other. After some discussion of the differences in subgroup impressions (which will probably include greater emphasis on process by the seeing-without-hearing group, and greater emphasis on content by the hearing-without-seeing group), the video monitor will be used to present all the trainees with the full audiovisual replay of the session. In a subsequent meeting the two subgroups may be asked to reverse roles.

Another way of achieving this reversal—though without the advantage of approaching the material "cold"—is to precede group reporting and combined channel audiovisual replay with the use of a standard audio recording of the first session. This will permit the initial vision-only group to hear without seeing, while in another room the original sound-only group will view the videotape with the sound turned off. This procedure has the advantage of letting each group experience each condition for the same therapy session. Following this reversal step, a second report based on the added cues might prove enlightening.

We shall need some experience with the various logistic possibilities of such audio-visual channel separation exercises before we can learn how to use them best, but we expect that one or more variations will demonstrate vividly the importance of attending to nonverbal communication, per se and in relation to verbal communication, as a means of understanding the processes of family interaction and therapy.

### In Situ *Feedback to Patients, Therapists and Supervisors*

The phrase *"in situ* feedback" is here to connote any feedback given within the context of the actual situation, whether or not it is genuine on-line feedback. Thus, *in situ* feedback in the context of training is not limited to continuous or instantaneous feedback to those in the therapy room. Since the training situation extends beyond the therapy hour, *in situ* feedback could consist of prompt post-session replay with participation of the family therapy trainee, and perhaps even the patients, in the viewing and discussion. This feedback process is well suited to aid in illuminating countertransference; it can be further enhanced by the exercise of good judgment in selecting segments of the tape to be viewed and in deciding when to stop for discussion or back up for another look. These procedures often provide helpful learning experiences for the patients as well as the therapist.

The use of such procedures in relation to observed interviews conducted by the trainees is designed to provide feedback *for* the supervisory process which follows immediately after each interview; however, this supervisory process *itself* is not videotaped. Using videotape for feedback in relation to various supervisory roles would therefore be one of the interesting possibilities for further exploiting this equipment in our program. The co-teachers of the Intensive Course would not be the only ones to receive such feedback, inasmuch as the trainees are paired so that each trainee gives feedback to his partner after observing him. Thus this supervisory application of videotape would provide a rare opportunity for our family therapy trainees to receive direct audiovisual feedback as a feature of their supervised experience in conducting family therapy.

### *Presentation of the Self*

Planned feedback demonstrations outside the context of therapy have several advantages. One is that the demonstrations which have evolved here often focus on the full face image of just one trainee at a time—an important feature of this particular equipment, inasmuch as the resolving power of the monitor does not permit *detailed* observation of facial expressions of a whole group "taken" with the wide angle lens. Secondly, the use of videotape outside the therapeutic context permits teacher-trainers to set up tailor-made situations that highlight the particular issues at hand, such as creating a self-disclosure task in order to have the trainee see how he comes across in a context calling for openness.

A particularly interesting use of the video equipment for self-presentation has been evolved in which the teacher outlines to the class a number of salient features which they may wish to observe when they view themselves on the video monitor; then he widens the discussion to include such features suggested by the class members themselves.[3] Each trainee is advised to specify in advance which facets of feedback he will be most interested in receiving. Then the trainees go before the video camera one at a time for a 5-minute individual self-presentation. The task is structured in such a way that it calls for a certain amount of self-disclosure. For example, the trainees might be asked to cover several topics: "Where are you in your professional and personal life right now?" "Where do you expect to be in your professional and personal life 6 months from now?"

When the trainees subsequently view themselves answering these questions, they are asked to deal with questions such as: 1) "What did you see and hear?" 2) "What sense did you make out of what you saw and heard?" 3) "How did you feel about it?" 4) "What, if anything, are you going to do with the information provided by this exercise?" The value of this exercise may be enhanced by doing it once at the beginning of the course and again at the end of the course. The use made of the material at that time would then include enhancing the trainee's ability to see what growth he had made and how he now presents himself to others. The material might also be useful in a research evaluation of training programs.

The technique of videotape feedback for training that has just been described was seen by the author as it was used with 34 individuals, including himself. Since these were personal experiences, I will shift for a moment to a more personal point of view to report that I noticed the anticipatory excitement and joking which most individuals displayed before being videotaped. Some handled their anxiety by commenting on it immediately upon going "on camera." These people later reported that their comment had put them at ease by removing their anxiety from the category of things unspeakable. My own moment of greatest anxiety was that immediately preceding the group feedback when we all watched the replay of my videotape. I experienced relief and a little surprise at the consensus that I came across as calm and self-assured, particularly since I had been experiencing some anxiety while watching my replay. The others in the group seemed relieved when I expressed these feelings. They said it made them feel better to know that everyone participating had experienced anxiety in this situation.

A particularly common occurrence—quickly noted by the group members with mirthful self-recognition—was the opening self-introduction fol-

[3] This innovation was developed by Dr. Frederick Ford.

lowed by licking the lips, gulping, clearing the throat, tilting the head or some combination of these. Each expressed surprise at seeing himself perform one or more of the superfluous gestures. All three training groups in which this occurred (courses in Communication and Human Systems for nurses, and for male professionals who work with people) expressed strong feelings that these gestures were self-depreciating and distracting. The group memibers felt that such gestures were the equivalent of saying something like, "I'm Joe Smith (though I don't expect any of you to have heard of me, and I don't really know why you should listen to me). . . ." The trainees generally felt that becoming aware of this and other mannerisms was a helpful experience.

*Separating Acting from Authentic Being*

In one course an incident occurred that closely paralleled a development in our therapeutic application of videotape feedback. One of the trainees handled her 5-minute presentation of herself with a string of fictitious names and past nicknames, adding, "I don't know who I am; you may call me anything." Inasmuch as this same trainee had created quite a stir several weeks earlier by screaming suddenly in apparent panic during a stressful encounter group situation, I felt that her videotape self-presentation afforded an opportunity to deal with her now familiar histrionics. Therefore, instead of letting the next trainee proceed, I entered the room with the video camera and asked the trainee who had just finished to take another turn before the camera. I explained that I felt she had presented herself in a manner that was simultaneously somewhat poetic, self-consciously artistic and exaggeratedly theatrical. Then I presented her with a paradoxical request: that this time she exert every effort to *act* undramatic.

She re-presented herself in a manner which no longer prompted her teachers and fellow trainees to engage in clinical speculations about her. More specifically, she began by introducing herself with her real name—which she had totally omitted from her earlier string of aliases—and proceeded without further ado to describe some relevant feelings about herself before the course, during the course and as she expected to feel after the course. The observers concurred, in their post-replay discussion with the trainee, that they had been far more comfortable during her second turn. They stuck to their guns even in the face of her protestations that she had been not only uncomfortable, but damned angry at having been double-bound into acting untheatrical. Nevertheless, the group insisted that she had seemed far more natural, even though she maintained that her *apparent* unaffectedness had been achieved only by the greatest affectation. She soon became more popular in the group, and her supervisor began making more glowing reports from her field work placement setting.

The general principle inherent in the example given above can be put very simply. There is a special use of videotape with people who are acting in a way which strikes others as somehow "unreal," or who are complaining that they themselves are troubled by not being able to distinguish clearly between when they are in some sense "on stage" and when they are "being themselves," if ever. This application consists of placing the person in a situation clearly calling for a "performance." When the person subsequently watches his own performance on the video monitor, the change of context imposes a powerful demand characteristic, "pulling" for authenticity, now that he has shifted his "set" from the role of the actor to the role of the critic viewing the actor.

## Developing Uses in Therapy

### Early Uses

Until recently our use of the videotape equipment as a treatment tool in the course of training family therapists has been somewhat limited; its main early application consisted of experimental use of therapeutic videotape feedback.[4] Realistic time limitations comprise one of the barriers to applying it further for this purpose on a routine basis in the Intensive Course in Family Therapy. Another factor discouraging the routine use of videotape as a therapeutic modality in our training courses has been its relative scarcity as a tool readily available to those who complete our courses. This situation, however, is changing at an apparently accelerating rate; there are now at least two other groups in our local area which own their own videotape recorder setups and use them in combinations of practicing, studying and teaching family therapy.

### Use of the Obvious: Don't Hide the Controls

A technical question arises in regard to the use of our on/off videotape recording switch in the therapy room itself. From the start, we envisioned the use of this switch as an integral part of the therapy, since both ethical and rapport factors counseled against the use of any concealed switching

---

[4] This experimental work was conceived and conducted by Dr. Robert Spitzer, formerly Director of Training at MRI.

device, such as a floor pedal. In deciding to keep the switch literally right out on the table in full view, we realized that its use would inevitably come to be interpreted by family members—"on" meaning, "This interests the therapist," and "off" meaning, "Oh, oh, why did he just tune out?" Of course, in time the families would probably learn that turning the recorder off is *not* the same as the therapist turning *himself* off.

Bowing to the inevitable, we decided to try to use the switch in the therapy room as a therapeutic modality or at least an adjunct, by self-consciously using its social reinforcing potential: that is, by doling out precoded signals of therapist approval or disapproval, according to whether the behavior seems to fall within some prespecified category. We shall need much experience to learn how best to do this, but an example may convey the underlying concept. The father of an underachieving junior high school student was given to long-winded sermonizing. His daughter's poor performance in school was due in part to her tuning out the teacher, including the time when homework assignments were made. Had the therapist been able literally to tune out the father every time he went into one of his sermons, the point would have been made quite powerfully, particularly since this father demanded a *show* of attention.

Switching to the "on" position need not be a signal of mere interest or approval. Let us suppose there is a couple with this pattern: the wife constantly interrupts her husband, while the husband looks down and pauses, as though inviting interruption. Both spouses have complained of the pattern as they see it, but despite further discussion, it has not changed. The therapist might announce that he sees a particular interaction pattern which he believes is dysfunctional or upsetting to both of them, and which he suspects they are unable to perceive—at least, so far as their individual contributions to it are concerned.

Next he could tell them that he was going to get that pattern down on the videotape for them with many illustrations, so they could study them later. Each time the therapist pushed the switch to the "on" position, both husband and wife would soon be asking themselves what they had just done to deserve it. Perhaps, however, each would attribute the switching to the action of the other spouse. The therapist could state that he was going to get a number of video shots which—whatever else they included—would definitely show what the husband was doing that was lousing things up. After perhaps 5 or 10 minutes of this, or some appropriate behavior change on the husband's part, the therapist would announce a shift in his focus to the wife's behavior.

Such a procedure might prove *less* distracting than a further interruption from the therapist to tell the wife when she is interrupting, and to tell the husband that he has once again invited interruption. Moreover, the procedure places considerable pressure on the patients to become more actively engaged in the process of monitoring their own behavior rather than being told about it by the therapist each time. Of course, many other pertinent signals go on all the time in therapy without the benefit of an electrical switch, but having such a switch at hand may help make the therapist more aware of how and when to use all such signals.

Another possible use of the switch became evident to the author when he heard that all the participants in some marathon groups get early practice in using the video camera—partly as a means of facilitating attitudinal change in those who are timid about overtly calling attention to specific features of another person's behavior.[5] The author was struck with the possibility of offering the use of the on/off switch to *any* member of the family after having each member practice it a couple of times. One potentially popular use may be to call attention to some irritating habit of someone else in the family. In other words, a wife may turn on the machine as a way of saying, "Now my husband's doing that thing of his, only this time I'm going to get it recorded so you'll all be able to see how inconsiderate he is, and even he will have to admit it this time!" If family members do experience such "between the lines" meaning in their own and each other's utilization of the on/off switch, the desire to deprive the others of self-incriminating evidence may constitute a powerful motive to abandon annoying behaviors. Even struggles over who is to control the on/off switch may prove extremely productive as interaction process material in therapy.

*Time Considerations*

*Duration of taping and replay.* The applications just presented raise a pair of interesting technical questions: How long should the videotaping session last, and how long should the replay segment last? These are related questions, of course, and probably in most instances they will have to be thought through together. Outlining some of the probable considerations may help. For example, if the session is to be limited to 1 hour, and if there is to be immediate total replay and some discussion with the family, then 25 minutes would be about the upper limit of the videotaped session per se. This assumes that the equipment is all ready at the start of the session, and that there is to be little or no stopping and starting of the tape during the replay.

A shorter segment should be selected or a longer total session should be arranged if there is to be much opportunity for stopping and starting the

---

[5] This innovation was developed and described by Dr. Frederick Stoller.

tape, and for perhaps repeating some portions several times as various viewers express their reactions *during* the replay. Replaying a full 50-minute session may be too taxing unless each viewer has some specific and active task, such as to note (perhaps even in writing) some type of interaction or to comment right away when feeling surprise or some other strong emotion. The therapist must come to terms with some compromise solution if the monitor he works with is not in the therapy room itself, since moving a family back and forth for immediate viewing of several brief segments is not feasible under these conditions.

*Timing of taping and replay.* Dr. Frederick Stoller (see footnote 6) manages not to compromise, since he uses highly portable equipment rather than a permanent two-room installation with the monitor outside the therapy room. Thus, in his marathon groups, he can immediately play back short segments at will, blending these into the flow of the total session. With the MRI setup already described, a possible solution may be to provide a monitor mounting in the therapy room—with, of course, a provision for turning it off at times when it might otherwise prove distracting.

*Recreating lost opportunities.* A third possible application of the replaying of videotape from an earlier session has been suggested by Dr. Robert Spitzer (see footnote 5). This technique entails showing the family a selected segment of a particularly meaningful moment of breakthrough. Dr. Spitzer's example was an over-controlled, tyrannical father who cried in one session for the first time in the memory of anyone else in the family. They responded with acceptance and even with relief at his belated show of humanity, and he himself spoke of the tremendous burden he had been carrying needlessly by fearing to show that sometimes he feels sorry for himself, is frightened and needs to depend on others as well as to have others lean on him. Despite some verbal priming in later sessions, however, the magic of that moment's mood was never quite recaptured. What if the therapist had had a videotape of the father's "breakthrough" session and had replayed to the family the most moving moments? Might not that have recaptured the magic mood, thus catalyzing the arrested process of its consolidation by all as a new aspect of father? With that, the family might have moved on to new and more comfortable ways of interacting.

The therapeutic gains of this technique will, of course, be associated with some corresponding costs in terms of the therapist's time; one cannot recreate the past without sacrificing something in the present.

*Recognizing gain and gaps.* Extrapolating from Dr. Starr's (see footnote 3) idea of precourse videotaping as an aid to trainees in noting changes over time during family therapy, we realized that the families themselves might benefit directly from viewing earlier tapes of themselves. Though we have not yet made much use of this idea, we mention it in order to share our current thinking about some likely areas for exploration. When families (or groups or individuals) feel at an impasse, or when the therapist wishes to get moving again after a plateau seems to have lasted long enough for whatever consolidation was needed, it might prove helpful to replay and discuss with the family tapes made early in their therapy. Gains might be noticed which were not otherwise evident to the family or the therapist or both. The tapes might encourage the family to make further progress by demonstrating that they are capable of change, and that they have already made some changes they feel good about without having fallen apart. In addition to the encouragement derived from their own pleasure at recognizing progress already made, they might also be motivated by reminders of old patterns which they still want to change.

Another use of early session replays may be in the termination phase, as an aid to consolidating what has happened. Going backwards in time momentarily in order to highlight changes may increase the family members' sense of control and hence decrease their fear of undergoing spontaneous irreversible retrogressions.

*Reactions to Replay*

*What is learned.* A number of families, couples and individuals in therapy with the author have viewed and discussed one or more of their videotaped sessions. The author asked that each person write down on a card immediately after viewing the replay whatever he could to shed light on the following three questions: 1) What did you learn about yourself from watching the replay? 2) What did you learn about anyone else in the family? 3) What did you learn about how you interact or relate to one another in terms of the whole family functioning together?

Some examples of what people claimed to have learned from videotape replay *prior to further discussion* may be helpful in appreciating some of the potential of even this crude technique for the therapeutic application of videotape. A husband who had been complaining of his wife's aloofness and reluctance to express warmth wrote that he saw himself spending a good deal of his time leaning away from her, looking out the window when she was talking. Another husband wrote that his wife ". . . was pretty much left out. I cursed a lot. She was not involved, smoked a lot. This shows my inattention." In other words, he saw that she lighted a cigarette (he detests her smoking) as a signal to recapture his attention when he had been talking purely about himself.

One daughter wrote that her father should be given a chance to talk about anything at length, since he usually does not. She added, "Mother needs to gesture more and talk less. [Younger brother] should quit interrupting, even if it's for the truth that no one else will speak. . . . He just doesn't pay attention. Maybe we haven't paid attention to him when he talks about his interests, but when someone doesn't pay attention, he just goes deeper into the subject matter."

In another family, a daughter who had been acting like her younger sister in order to draw attention (which the parents gave promptly, though disapprovingly) wrote, "I learned that I sounded more sulky than I felt, and I looked and sounded like I was being real stubborn. Hm . . . come to think of it, I guess I *was* stubborn." With this family, the function of replay was largely to remind them how much they had enjoyed a three-phase role-taking sequence we had just completed. At first the author took the daughter's role in such a way as to include rather than belittle her younger sister, then the father's role in such a way as to notice and appreciate the older sister's new behavior, while she now took over her own new role. Finally, both the father and the older daughter took their own roles, grinning with obvious relish at having affected a transition, at least momentarily, to new and more mutually appreciative roles.[6]

*Some generalizations.* In order to generalize from the collected feedback cards which patients had written about the experience of seeing themselves, the author reviewed these cases. Only two generalizations emerged: 1) Those people who had made the least progress in therapy had written no comments that showed that they had learned anything about themselves. Moreover, they had written only something negative or else nothing at all about their spouse. 2) It was only among these people that a second bad sign was noted: not being able to take a more self-distanced position during the replay. This was evidenced by such running comments as, "Yeah! I said it before, and I'll say it again, 'cause I agree with every word I'm saying there!"

It seems, then, that one of the uses of video confrontation may be as a prognostic aid, and that a particularly vital aspect to observe is each person's reaction to seeing himself in interaction with others. Then such observations can be used in the therapy.

[6] A related use is envisioned by the author and Dr. Stanley Clemes in connection with human relations training at a local police academy. To train police in "keeping their cool," they may be asked to participate in a series of difficult confrontations in which actual blacks or radical students will take increasingly provocative roles, but only after each confrontation scene is viewed and discussed with the police before proceeding to the next and more difficult confrontation.

## Conclusion

A subtle, yet significant, feature implicit in the videotape applications described above is that the trainees themselves may be exposed to a wide variety of ways of using videotape. Increasingly, we are making *explicit* to the trainees, as part of their courses, our thinking thus far about the uses of videotape in training and therapy. We feel that paying some attention to this area and opening it up as a worthy topic for discussion and demonstration will add to our own understanding of how to use videotape and will better equip and encourage our trainees to use this powerful medium for therapy and training in their own work settings.

*With the growing demand for service, increased attention is of necessity paid to the complex problem of training adequate numbers of personnel to fulfill the existing needs. The reader is probably aware of recent trends towards the use of so-called paraprofessionals, that is, of people trained specifically in certain key areas of the helping professions, rather than following the traditional method of educating professionals along very broad lines, which often not only cover virtually all areas of possible future activity but even include much that is not likely to be directly utilized.*

*A report by Mosher, Reifman, and Menn describes their experiences with the training of young, relatively inexperienced nonprofessionals to assist schizophrenic patients in living through their psychotic experiences. The two treatment facilities, Soteria House (opened in 1971) and Emanon House (functioning since 1974), follow some of the ideas of the famous Kingsley Hall project in London, but at the same time are careful to avoid the complications which Laing and his associates encountered in their pioneering efforts with this form of treatment.*

# CHARACTERISTICS OF NONPROFESSIONALS
# SERVING AS PRIMARY THERAPISTS

*Loren R. Mosher, M.D.,*
*Ann Reifman, B.A., and Alma Menn, A.C.S.W.*

The solution to a problem is often interwoven with the manner in which the problem is defined. According to legend, Alexander the Great cut the Gordian knot with a sword, thus defining the problem not as how to untie the rope, but how to separate the cart from the yoke. The legend is analogous to the current problem of schizophrenia. How the knot of schizophrenia is untied is linked to how the problem is defined: the selection of the type of treatment to be given, and the individuals best suited to deliver it, is determined in large part by the theories and definitions applied to the disorder.

Since Kraepelin's time, schizophrenia has been considered a disease and as such has fallen under the purview of medicine. To this day, most individuals diagnosed as schizophrenic continue to be treated in hospitals, offered drugs with expectations of cure, and treated by medical doctors and nurses—despite the fact that no specific organic lesion has ever been found in schizophrenics, and that drugs, while helpful, have not proven to be curative.

Schizophrenia remains our most recalcitrant mental health problem. Its scope is reflected in the disappointingly low levels of psychosocial functioning achieved by the majority of discharged schizophrenic patients, in their high readmission rates (about 50 per cent within two years), and in the relatively large population (more than 200,000) of currently hospitalized patients.[1] These figures reveal the inadequacies of our present treatment of schizophrenics and serve as powerful justification for continuing to seek new concepts for the delivery of services to them.

In the belief that a fresh approach to the treatment of schizophrenia is needed, we have attempted to redefine the problem by looking at the psychotic episode as a crisis in development with potential for positive growth, rather than as an outbreak of disease that portends slow, inevitable deterioration.

Accordingly, in the combined research and services program described here, we do not follow the guidelines of the traditional medical model. Because existing treatment facilities are often resistant to change, our project's setting is a house in the community. It is modeled in many ways after Kingsley Hall in London, which was created by the Philadelphia Association, a group of therapists whose members included Ronald Laing and David Cooper. Thus we have moved the problem of schizophrenia out of the hospital and into the community, and out of the hands of medical doctors into those of specially trained paraprofessionals.

Originally published in *Hospital & Community Psychiatry* 24:391–96 (1973). Reprinted with permission.

[1] L. R. Mosher and D. B. Feinsilver, *Special Report: Schizophrenia.* National Institute of Mental Health, Rockville, Maryland, 1971.

In describing this approach more fully, we will focus primarily on the characteristics of the people who constitute the treatment staff and the types of therapeutic relationships they establish with schizophrenic individuals.

The project was started in May 1971. Its design is a comparative outcome study of two matched cohorts of first-break, unmarried schizophrenic patients between 15 and 30 years of age, deemed in need of hospitalization; they are to be followed for two years after discharge. Both experimental and control patients are obtained from a large screening facility, processing 600 new patients a month, that is part of a community mental health center. Patients who meet the research criteria are assigned consecutively, as space is available, to the experimental or the control group.

Control patients are admitted to the wards of the community mental health center, where they receive the usual treatment, including drugs. Experimental patients are treated (ordinarily without medication) in a comfortable 16-room house in the San Francisco Bay area; its name, Soteria House, comes from a Greek term for deliverance. Six patients at a time can be accommodated in the house, and up to four staff members can live in.

A battery of measures is used to assess both groups of patients from several aspects: psychiatric data on diagnosis, type of onset, presence of paranoia, and symptom pattern; ward and house staff ratings of behavior and improvement; family's perception of behavior and personality characteristics; and self-ratings of such areas as social and work functioning and attitude toward illness. Patients will be followed at six-month intervals for two years after discharge through psychiatric and family ratings and self-ratings. Changes reflected in the assessments over time will be measured by analysis of variance and covariance. A fuller exposition of the research design was published earlier.[2]

### Theory of Schizophrenia

What is central and crucial to our mode of treatment is our view of schizophrenia and the individuals we have selected as therapists. At Soteria House, the schizophrenic reaction is viewed as an altered state of consciousness in an individual who is experiencing a major crisis in living.

[2] L. R. Mosher, "A Research Design for Evaluating a Psychosocial Treatment of Schizophrenia," *Hospital & Community Psychiatry,* Vol. 23, August 1972, pp. 229–234.

This altered state involves personality fragmentation with the loss of sense of self. Experiences merge, the inner and outer worlds become difficult to distinguish, and mystical sensations are experienced.

Most clinicians would agree that psychosis evolves as a process of fragmentation-disintegration. But at Soteria House, the disruptive psychotic experience is also believed to have unique potential for reintegration and growth. Our treatment milieu, by guiding the patient through his altered state of consciousness rather than repressing it, is designed to help him emerge from his life crisis a stronger, better integrated person with the capacity to pursue a life that he himself will view as a success.

Such a view of schizophrenia implies a number of therapeutic attitudes. Soteria House staff members take all manifestations of the psychotic experience as real. Irrationality, terror, and mystical experiences are seen as extremes of basic human qualities that can be related to as valid experiences. Too often the psychotic person's experiences have been repeatedly negated by his family and associates, a process that appears to have contributed to the development of madness in the first place. In our view, the process of fragmentation and regression is not only valid but perhaps necessary for psychological growth. We instruct our staff that their therapeutic role is analogous to that of the LSD-trip guide.

We believe that relatively untrained, psychologically unsophisticated persons can work within this theoretical framework more easily than highly trained ones because they have learned no theory of schizophrenia, whether psychodynamic, organic, or a combination of both. This allows them freedom to be themselves, to follow their visceral responses, to adopt a phenomenological stance, and to be a "person" with the psychotic individual.

Highly trained mental health professionals tend to lose this freedom in favor of a more cognitive, theory-based, learned response that may invalidate the patient's experience. Professionals also tend to use their theoretical knowledge for defensive purposes when confronted, in an unstructured setting, with the potentially threatening behaviors of acute psychotics. This pattern of response is not available to our unsophisticated nonprofessional therapists.

## Staff Selection

Our project director (AM) had previously worked on an experimental ward in a local state hospital where some of the notions of psychosis as a potentially positive, growth-inducing experience had been put into practice. There were a number of psychiatric technicians and volunteers in the hospital project who were interested in working in a community setting. In addition, our project had gotten word-of-mouth publicity. Thus when we announced our interest in hiring individuals to work intensively with unmedicated acutely psychotic persons, there were about 20 applicants for four full-time positions.

The final selection was a complex process. Applicants were asked to work in tandem with an experienced person on the experimental ward at the state hopsital. The way in which they handled themselves was then discussed and evaluated in terms of their ability to tune into the psychotic person's "space," and to provide a constantly reassuring presence, without being intrusive or demanding or "laying their trip" on the psychotic person.

From the resulting pool of 15 candidates, six were selected, two as full-time workers and four as half-time workers. They were chosen to provide a balance of experience, sex, age, and talents additional to their ability to work with acute psychotics. For example, a man and a woman were selected because of their stable, affectionate relationship and because they were excellent craftsmen. Two of the six had previously worked as psychiatric technicians, another had worked in a VISTA psychiatric rehabilitation program, and one had taken a one-year course in community psychiatry.

Because our project raises questions about a number of traditional mental health practices, it is potentially threatening to the Establishment. Therefore, we felt it wise not to select politically radical staff who might be in active conflict with the existing order. Our staff are not pro-Establishment; rather, they are basically apolitical. Their work in the house dominates their lives. They may feel strongly about various aspects of the existing order, but they are not devoting significant amounts of time and energy to acting on those feelings.

We believe that an apolitical staff is important for two reasons. First, the work in the house is so draining that it would be an unusual person who could both work with psychotics and actively pursue anti-Establishment activities. Second, because we are located in the community, it is not possible for us to be insulated from the existing order; it must be dealt with every day. If our staff were to set themselves up in an adversary role, the community would soon make it impossible for us to operate. We felt that problems with our neighbors would be difficult enough without adding unnecessary conflict. The decision seems to have been a wise one, as our relationships with the community have been relatively smooth.

## On-the-Job Training

The first six months of Soteria House's existence served as a training period for staff. The training was not formal; no readings were assigned, no lectures given. Rather, inexperienced staff members worked alongside those who had experience in treating psychotic individuals. Throughout and after each therapeutic session, the staff discussed their feelings and reactions among themselves or with the project director or a consulting psychiatrist. (At Soteria, a therapeutic session can last anywhere from ten minutes to three weeks, since, in our experience, psychosis does not fit very well into 50-minute hours.) Together they probed all the feelings engendered—the doubts and uncertainties, hopes and fears, and insights about which techniques were helpful and which were compromising or mechanizing.

Thus we use a fairly traditional apprenticeship model for training. In the sessions and discussions we focus major attention on the need to "be with" and not to "do to" the psychotic person. The abilities to tolerate, support, and be emphatically involved with the patient, without becoming overwhelmed by fear, are stressed. Although our nonprofessional therapists do not use the various intellectualizing devices employed by more highly trained persons, they still may feel a need to manipulate, distance, categorize, and be demanding in difficult situations. Feelings that seem to cause the staff to shift from the "being with" to the "doing to" mode are explored in detail.

A brief account of an early experience illustrates the way training is conducted and the role of our consulting psychiatrist. A new patient, Paul, had a history of violent outbursts, but since admission he had been quietly trailing after one of the staff, Stan, helping him with household chores and errands. On his third day in the house, Paul became extremely quiet during lunch, began to weep silently, and retreated to his bed. After about a half hour, Stan wanted to do something but was unsure what it should be. He telephoned the consulting psychiatrist and described what was going on. The psychiatrist asked him what he wanted to do. Stan said he wanted to go into Paul's room. The psychiatrist told him to go ahead and that he would come along soon to help.

By the time the psychiatrist got to the house an hour later, Stan was well into the session with Paul. The psychiatrist notified Stan that he was in the house, but stayed in another room. It was clear that Stan no longer needed any help. He stayed with Paul all afternoon and late into evening. The next day Stan discussed the experience with the psychiatrist in detail, and later related it to the entire staff. The session had been a kind of breakthrough—the first time Paul had been able to express to anyone some of his terrifying thoughts.

By not responding immediately to Stan's call for help, the psychiatrist acknowledged his belief that Stan was capable both of understanding Paul and of dealing with any extreme hostility that he might express. His self-confidence enhanced, Stan continued to feel he could rely on the psychiatrist at times of uncertainty.

## Personal Characteristics of Staff

Data were collected on the ten staff members who were employed between May 1971 and June 1972. (Two of the original six resigned after six months because they found the work too draining and the salary too low; they were replaced by three part-time workers. The tenth member studied was the project director.) There were five men and five women, aged 21 to 40, with a mean age of 27.6 years. Seven were single, two married, and one divorced. All were rated superior on the vocabulary test of the Wechsler Adult Intelligence Scale. Their education ranged from 11 to 18 years, with a mean of 14.6 years, and they were predominantly from the middle and lower-middle social classes, as defined by the Hollingshead scales for the father's occupation. Their previous experience in mental health work ranged from none to eight years, and averaged three and a half years.

Additional, in-depth information on their backgrounds was taken from written autobiographies, a social-history form, and informal discussions. From all this information we can present a composite description of our staff.

The kinds of people who choose to work at Soteria are those who want neither to become part of the 9-to-5 business world nor to drop out and become part of the hippie scene. They are young and bright; most have attended college, but few have formal education in psychology. They can be characterized as having led very long lives in relatively few years, and as being tough but tolerant, hard-working, energetic, and well-integrated individuals.

The degree of their toughness and integration (ego strength) came as a surprise to us, because we had expected that more would report having experienced crises of psychotic proportions. None of the crises they did experience were labeled and treated. We also expected that many would have extensive experience with psychedelic drugs, but that also was not the case. Like most California youth, they have tried various drugs, but none have adopted drugs as a life style. Their current use of intoxicants of any type is minimal.

In exploring the reasons for those two unexpected findings, we found a very interesting pattern: all but one of their families of origin were problem families, sometimes including an alcoholic father or a psychotic mother. Psychiatrists reading the staff's autobiographies might well predict serious psychological problems for many of them. Instead, our staff seem to be examples of invulnerable children raised in difficult situations.

In attempting to discern the reasons for their invulnerability, we found that they had not been so intimately intertwined with the psychopathologic parent as was a sibling, usually older. (Significantly, none of our staff are first-born or only children.) Although our data are incomplete on this point, the siblings of several staff members appear to be significantly psychologically impaired.

Interestingly, the role most often played by our staff members in their problem families was that of a somewhat neutral caretaker for the parent. That may have something to do with their having chosen to work at Soteria, since a similar pattern of family life has been noted by Henry[3] for healers and by Burton[4] for psychotherapists. Stone has also noted similar phenomena in psychotherapists who had unexpected success with schizophrenic patients.[5]

## Test Data

Although we have focused thus far on relatively "soft" descriptions of the staff and their relationships with patients, we have also collected data from the following hard measures: the A/B Therapist Scale,[6] California Psychological Inventory (CPI),[7] Myers-Briggs Type Indicator,[8] As's Tol-

[3] W. E. Henry, "Some Observations on the Lives of Healers," *Human Development,* Vol. 9, 1966, pp. 47–56.

[4] A. Burton, "The Adoration of the Patient and Its Disillusionment," *American Journal of Psychoanalysis,* Vol. 29, November 1969, pp. 194–204.

[5] M. H. Stone, "Therapists' Personalities and Unexpected Success With Schizophrenic Patients," *American Journal of Psychotherapy,* Vol. 25, October 1971, pp. 543–552.

[6] J. C. Whitehorn and B. J. Betz, "A Study of Psychotherapeutic Relationships Between Physicians and Schizophrenic Patients," *American Journal of Psychiatry,* Vol. 111, November 1954, pp. 321–331.

[7] H. G. Gough, *California Psychological Inventory,* Consulting Psychologists Press, Palo Alto, California, 1956.

[8] B. Myers, *Manual: The Myers-Briggs Type Indicator,* Educational Testing Service, Princeton, New Jersey, 1962.

erance for Experience Inventory,[9] FIRO-B,[10] Welsh-Barron Figure Preference Test,[11] and the verbal portion of the Wechsler Adult Intelligence Scale. Staff members are tested on hiring, at three-month intervals, and on leaving the project. The measures were selected in an attempt to relate our staff's characteristics to those of professionals who treat schizophrenia, to study changes in our staff over time, and to help others screen candidates for similar work in other settings.

The usefulness and generalizability of the data are limited by our small sample and a lack of similar data on a comparison group. (We are now collecting such data on our own control ward and on a psychiatric research ward of a university hospital.) We will restrict this report mainly to descriptive profiles (omitting the CPI because of incomplete data analysis) and some negative findings.

• *A/B Therapist Scale.* Ever since Whitehorn and Betz reported this scale's usefulness in distinguishing successful from unsuccessful therapists of schizophrenics, it has been the subject of many studies with conflicting results.[12] We included it because it is so widely used to characterize therapists. Based on the 23-item form of Whitehorn and Betz, our staff's mean was 11.1 (SD, 1.52), with a range of 9 to 13. Because the data lack a bimodal distribution, we have not dichotomized our therapists into A and B types. In addition, we cannot yet relate the scores to outcome or compare our staff to other groups.

The number of difficulties we encountered with this scale makes us seriously question its usefulness, at least in our circumstancees. First, the form is probably not appropriate for women, as it is based on the Strong vocational interest test for men. Second, four or five different versions have been used in different studies, making it difficult to compare results. Third, the A/B categorization is determined differently by different investigators, also making comparisons difficult.

• *As experience inventory.* This self-report measure was developed to relate subjective experiences to hypnotizability. It is designed to tap the degree to which a subject reports experiencing altered states of consciousness and states theoretically related to the ability to be hypnotized. We

[9] A. As, J. W. O'Hara, and M. P. Munger, "The Measurement of Subjective Experiences Presumably Related to Hypnotic Susceptibility," *Scandinavian Journal of Psychology.* Vol. 3, No. 1, 1962, pp. 47–64.

[10] W. C. Schutz, *FIRO Scales Manual.* Consulting Psychologists Press, Palo Alto, California, 1967.

[11] G. S. Welsh, *Welsh Figure Preference Test: Preliminary Manual.* Consulting Psychologists Press, Palo Alto, California, 1959.

[12] A. M. Razin, "A-B Variables in Psychotherapy: A Critical Review," *Psychological Bulletin,* Vol. 75, January 1971, pp. 1–21.

used the test in an attempt to quantify the degree to which our staff had experienced states of consciousness related to those they would be dealing with in the residents. Two sub-scales, for example, are "altered state— fading of reality orientation" and "tolerance for logical inconsistencies."

Our staff scored very high over-all on this measure (mean, 37.9; SD, .63). Only five per cent of the college students reported by As had higher mean scores. Interestingly, despite high scores on eight of the subscales, our staff scored significantly lower (as compared with their other subscale scores) on the "willingness to relinquish ego control" subscale. That finding fits with our description of them as being tolerant but tough; that is, any peak experiences or dissociative states they had were under their control. It also is reminiscent of many descriptions of creative persons as able to experience unusual states, such as primary process thinking, while maintaining control over them.

• *Welsh-Barron Figure Preference Test (RA form)*. This 86-item figure-preference test was originally devised to measure artistic ability or creativity. A higher score indicates a preference for complex figures, which has been shown to correlate with artistic ability. Our staff's mean score of 36 is nearly that achieved by artists (40). Taken in conjunction with their histories and the As data, this measure indicates that our staff share a number of characteristics found among creative persons.

• *Myers-Briggs Type Indicator*. This measure was originally devised to tap certain personality qualities as reflected in a series of four basic dichotomous preferences: extraversion or introversion, sensing or intuition, thinking or feeling, and judgment or perception.

Our staff were evenly split between extraversion and introversion. On the other three variables, all ten members showed a remarkably consistent pattern indicating their reliance on intuition (indirect perception by way of the unconscious), on feeling (discriminating between the valued and nonvalued rather than impersonally between true and false), and on a perceptive, intuitive process in their dealings with the outer world. This pattern is interpreted as their preference for and effectiveness in using intuition to perceive possibilities, form judgments, and adapt to the environment. These qualities seem especially well suited to the tasks they are asked to perform.

• *FIRO-B*. The behavior scale of Schutz's Fundamental Interpersonal Relations Orientation Test measures three fundamental dimensions of interpersonal relationships—inclusion, control, and affection. Each dimension is rated for expressed or manifest behavior and for wanted behavior, grading from 0 to 9.

Our staff scored low on expressed and wanted inclusion, low on expressed control and middle on wanted control, and middle on expressed and wanted affection. For both control and affection, the staff wanted more than they expressed, revealing a somewhat rebellious nature. Otherwise, the staff's scores are so mid-range (2.7 to 5.1) as to make clear interpretation hazardous. The lack of extreme scores is striking. The average size of the standard deviations (1.8 to 2.9) clearly indicates the heterogeneity of scores on these variables. The heterogeneity may result from our selection procedure, and may be necessary if a relatively small number of people are to form relationships with a wide variety of psychotic individuals.

To study changes in our staff members over time, we administered our battery of tests at three-month intervals. We had anticipated significant changes because of the intensity of the staff's experiences and their relative inexperience with psychotic individuals, but after one year we have been unable to identify a significant change on any measure.

When we interviewed seven current staff members to see how they felt they had changed during their experience at Soteria, all but one felt they had changed significantly. They expressed an increased sense of who and what they are, including their limits; a greater tolerance and acceptance of themselves and others; and greater self-confidence. It appears that the tests do not tap the aspects the staff describe as having changed. Perhaps the As, Welsh-Barron, Myers-Briggs, and A/B Therapist scales address staff's well-formed, relatively unchangeable character, which we have described as tough or reflecting high ego strength, or possibly the interviews simply failed to elicit evidence of areas that did not change. The former possibility appears most likely at this time.

Our staff seem to share relevant characteristics with two groups, artists (creative people) and psychotherapists of schizophrenics. The association with artists is based principally on the high scores on the As experience inventory and the figure-preference test, and the remarkably consistent Myers-Briggs type preferences for intuition, feeling, and perception. The relationship to psychotherapists is based on descriptions of the staff's families of origin; that is, they came from difficult situations that seem to have made them into very sturdy characters and to have taught them a caring role. These similarities must not be overdrawn until we have more comparison data on staffs of other facilities. In addition, the problems with anecdotal, retrospective family-history data are well known. Nonetheless we believe the various commonalities we have identified between our staff and the other two groups are sufficiently suggestive to warrant further empirical study.

·

# CHAPTER 4

# Normality, Neurosis, Psychosis

*"There is no such animal as the normal person," submits Don D. Jackson in the first paper included in this chapter, in which we have put together several representative articles, all dealing with the relativity of the three terms that make up its title. For as soon as the monadic, intrapsychic perspective is abandoned and the observer's field of vision expanded to include not only the individual, but his significant others and the social context in which their interaction takes place, our traditional views of both normality and madness are severely challenged. This shift, which Haley (p. 33–4) quite plausibly compares to the conceptual step of our thinking from the earth to the sun as the center of the universe, while certainly not generally accepted, is not a new idea. Enough has been said in the foregoing about its clashes with more traditional views of human problems and conflicts. But we must not lose sight of the fact that even this idea has its historic forerunners. Some of them certainly merit brief mention:*

*There is, first of all, Lasègue and Falret's famous study "La folie à deux, ou folie communiquée," published in 1877, in which these two French psychiatrists put forth the surprisingly modern thesis that "the problem is not only to examine the influence of the insane on the supposedly sane man, but also the opposite, the influence of the rational on the deluded one, and to show how through mutual compromises the differences are eliminated."[1] But the time was not ripe for this view of madness, and the idea of insanity as an outcome of communication remained merely an odd boulder in the mainstream of psychiatry.*

*Some twenty-five years later the scientific world was electrified by re-*

---

[1] Ch. Lasègue and J. Falret, "La folie à deux, ou folie communiquée," *Annales Médico-Psychologiques*, vol. 18, November 1877. (English translation by Richard Michaud, *American Journal of Psychiatry*, supplement to vol. 121, 4:2–18, 1964.)

*ports that a retired schoolteacher in Berlin had taught his horse, appropriately named Clever Hans, the most astonishing mental feats: arithmetic, telling time, recognizing photographs of people whom the horse had met on previous occasions, and much more. The horse and its master were subjected to the most painstaking scientific investigations, but they all showed that no deception was involved and that the horse had indeed developed these remarkable abilities. The euphoria went on for a while, until a graduate student of psychology and medicine discovered that the horse, who tapped out the results with his hoof, had simply learned to start tapping as soon as everybody expectantly looked at his foot and to stop tapping as soon as a wave of ill-concealed excitement ran through the humans surrounding him and many of them looked up—which was, of course, the moment when the horse had arrived at the right number of taps. But in those days, the idea of such a simple, unintentional, and nonverbal interaction was completely alien to the prevailing paradigm of science and the entire phenomenon therefore had to be considered a property of the monad—in this case, the horse.*

*The reason for mentioning this seemingly irrelevant case is that at about the same time the division of psychoses into exogenous and endogenous ones was gaining increasing acceptance. Exogenous psychoses, it will be remembered, are those caused by factors outside the central nervous system, while endogenous disturbances are thought to originate from within it. In retrospect it is not difficult to appreciate that in those days it must have been much easier to diagnose and describe those mental disturbances which are in fact caused by identifiable outside factors (such as physical or emotional traumata, poisoning, infections, etc.), but that on the other hand no equally solid, identifiable evidence for the causes of the endogenous disturbances could be found. Especially as far as the schizophrenias and the manic-depressive disease entities were concerned, "endogenous" really and simply came to mean "not exogenous" and thus inadvertently gained the questionable status of a* definitio per exclusionem *(a definition arrived at the exclusion rather than by the presence of the crucial factors). But with the tyranny of words being what it is, the mere existence of a name seems to be evidence of the existence of the thing thus named—and so we have "endogenous" psychoses not because they have been shown to exist, but because there exists a name for them. Essentially the same semantic somersault underlies the case of Clever Hans: His "genius" was, and could not not be, considered "endogenous" (and, incidentally, was solemnly certified by a panel of thirteen sober-minded and eminent scientists), until a graduate student, approaching the phenomenon with an entirely different scientific paradigm, was able to show that it was "exogenous"—albeit exogenous in a sense that was alien to the sci-*

*entific thinking of that time. The paradigm in question was that of* communication *as a determinant of behavior. (The interested reader is referred to Rosenthal's presentation of the Clever Hans case[2] and in general to his work at Harvard University on experimenter influence.[3]*

*One more particularly glaring historic example comes to mind in this connection. It is the famous Schreber case. Schreber, a German judge, born in 1842, became insane at age forty-two and died in a mental hospital in 1911. He is the author of an autobiographical account, published in English under the title* Memoirs of My Nervous Illness,[4] *which Freud, who never met Schreber, utilized for a detailed study of the psychodynamics of paranoia.[5] As a result of Freud's analysis, it is believed that "Schreber is now the most frequently quoted patient in psychiatry."[6] In 1959 the psychoanalyst William Niederland published the first of a series of papers, eventually followed up by a book,[7] in which he drew attention to certain astonishing similarities between Schreber's delusions and his father's child-rearing methods. A comparison between many passages from the son's* Memoirs *and the father's sadistic "educational" techniques, described in his numerous books on education and discipline,[8] reveals almost literal correspondencies. It is thus evident that the son's delusions did not originate from within his central nervous system, but were truly exogenous in the most frighteningly concrete sense of this term. That he did not, or could not, refer to their origin literally, but couched them into metaphorical (religious) language, hardly changes the fact that his delusions were as little endogenous as Clever Hans' genius. However, interaction did not yet*

---

[2] Oskar Pfungst, *Clever Hans,* edited by Robert Rosenthal (New York: Holt, Rinehart and Winston, 1965).

[3] Robert Rosenthal, *Experimenter Effects in Behavioral Research* (New York: Appleton-Century-Crofts, 1966).

[4] Daniel Paul Schreber, *Memoirs of My Nervous Illness,* translated and edited by Ida Macalpine and Robert A. Hunter (London: Dawson & Son, 1955).

[5] Sigmund Freud, "Psycho-analytic Notes upon a Autobiographical Account of a Case of Paranoia (Dementia paranoides)," in *Collected Papers,* vol. III, pp. 385–470 (New York: Basic Books, 1959).

[6] Schreber, op. cit., p. 8.

[7] William G. Niederland, *The Schreber Case: Psychoanalytic Profile of a Paranoid Personality* (New York: Quadrangle Books, 1974).

[8] The father, Daniel Gottlieb Moritz Schreber (1801–1861), was a physician and recognized authority on pedagogy and child-rearing. Further detailed comparisons between the *Memoirs* of the son and his father's works can be found in Morton Schatzman, *Soul Murder: Persecution in the Family* (New York: Random House, 1973).

*"exist"—not because it did not take place, but because it had no place in the scientific paradigm of that era, and the attribution of endogeny was the only possible explanation.*

*But if madness be a myth, so then is its opposite—normality. Don D. Jackson's paper examines the relativity of this concept, giving a panoramic overview of many facts and figures contradicting this myth.*

# THE MYTH OF NORMALITY

## Don D. Jackson, M.D.

Again and again, psychiatrists, psychologists, and others concerned with mental health are called upon to decide how "sick" a person is. Their ability to arrive at anything that resembles a sound judgment is hampered because there is no standard of psychological "normality" or "good health."

In somatic medicine, physicians know that the normal systolic blood pressure will range from 110 to 130. When the reading is 160, the physician can readily label it deviant and recommend treatment for high blood pressure. But researchers in the mental health fields have been so engrossed with the study and treatment of people who are labeled "sick," they have had neither the opportunity nor the interest to study people who are "well."

One tragic result of the failure to develop a reliable yardstick is the appalling hit-or-miss process by which people are sent to mental institutions. A sociologist recently evaluated one hundred and sixty cases in a state known for relatively high standards in its mental hospitals. The psychiatric interviews to determine sanity were sometimes as brief as one and a half minutes and averaged only nine minutes each. A direct observer of twenty-five of them rated the persons interviewed as follows: seven met the criteria of insanity as postulated by the law; eleven might have done so in time; seven definitely did not. Yet the psychiatrist recommended freedom for only two. It appeared obvious to the observer that the psychiatrist tended to search for error or pathology. For example, there was a patient who answered a number of very difficult questions, including complicated arithmetical problems, but on the basis of a single wrong answer was adjudged suitable for commitment. One psychiatrist stated,

Originally published in *Medical Opinion and Review* vol. 3, no. 5, pp. 28–33 (1967). Reprinted with permission.

"If the patient's own family wants to get rid of him, you know there has to be something wrong." It brings to mind a jingle that might fit most state hospitals: "When in doubt, don't leave them out."

The myth of normality has an insidious influence, not only for those unfortunates who are judged insane, but on the lives and attitudes of us all. Both the experts and the public are trapped by propaganda and by historical and psychological forces (fear being one of the most paralyzing) that lead to the dichotomization of mankind in the normal and the abnormal. We now live in an era of classification in which labels are sought for all human activities. This kind of classification is part of our attempt to simplify life and build reassuring fences around the perimeters of experience. The more common the experience, the more comfortable it makes us; it is easy to classify and can thus be called a known fact.

Anything occurring outside common experience stimulates fear and is labeled "freak," "accidental," "miraculous," "crazy," lest we need admit *we simply don't understand.* People are most anxious to classify behavior and observations about the human personality because the unknown forces operating inside each man, and among men, are the most frightening of all—hence the most uncontrollable. However, the few extreme cases at the end of the mental health continuum, those which are fairly obvious and more readily classifiable, represent only a small portion of mankind; the bulk falls somewhere in the "normal" range. How crazy a particular person appears to you depends on your own frame of reference and the limits of your own experience.

Since pre-Biblical days, classifications have been used to support ethno-political ideas of racial or national superiority. The Nazi belief that a super race could be evolved through control of heredity differs only in degree from the attribution of mass personality traits to entire nationalities, as the "hot-blooded" Spanish or the "emotional" Italians. These meaningless generalizations serve to maintain the comfortable fiction of our own national personality traits, which are, of course, admirable in our eyes.

Such reductionist thinking is common even among experts and well-educated professionals. For instance, the discovery in medicine that traumas cause disease was picked up rather uncritically by psychiatrists. On the one hand, psychic traumas are alleged to cause neuroses and psychoses; on the other, the absence of obvious trauma (especially in childhood) in a mentally disturbed person is assumed to mean that he has a weak constitution. A trauma, moreover, is seen as some kind of horrendous occurrence, such as rape, severe beating, the death of a mother while a child is very young, and so on, so that the complexities and subtleties of human interaction are lost. One could postulate that lesser traumas too insidious and too constant to be noticed are far more damaging to the human personality than are the more dramatic occurrences that are easier to label and to understand.

Just as psychiatrists lifted the trauma theory from physical medicine as a piece, they also base assumptions about the human personality and its relation to heredity on the results of animal experiments. The leap from animal to human is made with astonishing ease by some theorists who ignore the greater subtlety and complexity of human experience.

One of the most deeply entrenched belief systems in our culture today holds that the measure of man's intelligence is directly related to inheritance and brain-cell functioning, and that intelligence tests can produce a valid estimate of a human being's total potential. Although *no* personality trait has been established as hereditarily determined, and although behavioral scientists agree little on which aspects of personality they would label as traits, the intelligence quotient model as applied to personality still remains very much in vogue.

The differentiation of normal and abnormal personalities, which reflects in the rigid notion that individual limitations are fixed or inherent, is expedient for mankind and is used unabashedly for the most mercenary, cruel, and inhumane purposes. If one assumes that the truly abnormal is produced by pathological cells, one need have little guilt about man's inhumanity to man. In the South, those who support inferior schools for Negroes frequently defend their economies by stating that Negroes are unable to learn as rapidly as Caucasians, so better facilities would be wasted. Similarly, if the mentally ill are completely different from all the rest of us, it makes sense for us to isolate them miles from town in stone and brick mausoleums euphemistically called state hospitals. It makes things nice and tidy to have the two groups: one that is crazy and belongs in isolation, and one that is sane and is free.

Most psychiatrists, however, will admit that hospitalization generally depends much more on the family's attitudes than it does on the patient's. Recent statistical evidence comes from a follow-up study of all Canadian war veterans who suffered schizophrenia during World War II. There was little difference in the symptoms (including hallucinations and delusions) displayed by those who were in and those who were out of the hospital, but a great deal of difference was found between the families of the two groups. Those veterans who were not hospitalized had families that were more optimistic and supportive.

It has been assumed that a certain percentage of people suffer nervous breakdowns or are admitted each year to state hospitals, and that this constitutes the mentally abnormal group. The rest of us are considered to be in quite a different category. However, a recent study of a midtown section of New York City yielded some staggering statistics. A carefully selected representative sample of sixteen hundred persons was interviewed. According to the ratings of several experienced psychiatrists, 81.5 percent of the sample suffered from some type of emotional disorder: 2.7 percent were incapacitated by their symptoms; 7.5 percent had severe, 13.2 percent had marked, 21.8 percent had moderate, and 36.3 percent had mild psychiatric symptoms. Only 18.5 percent were considered to be well. Many persons outside hospitals, perhaps even the majority, make their way through life with symptoms (especially during particular periods) that would be labeled pathological if diagnosed by a psychiatrist. Fortunately, most of these persons cannot afford psychiatrists, so do not get labeled.

The importance of such block-by-block surveys of "normal" persons can hardly be overestimated. When the relatives of a patient in a mental hospital are interviewed, of course, a certain degree of emotional disturbance can be found; this is the foundation for the belief that psychiatric disorders are hereditary. But such conclusions about heredity become meaningless if the incidence of emotional disorder in the general population is high, as indicated by the New York City study. One could begin equally well with the patient's psychiatrist, or with the hospital staff, and come up with a sizable degree of emotional disorder.

If one reviews the few studies available on ordinary people, there is little safety in clinging to a normal-abnormal dichotomy. In one study, psychiatrists interviewed a hundred men whose functioning could be considered above average by most standards. Of these men, three-fourths had childhoods affected by appreciable tension and conflict between their parents and often by parental separation and divorce. Ten men claimed that their parents lived blissfully together, yet gave family histories of serious psychosomatic disorders. The authors further stated that if these hundred men had been interviewed because of alleged asthma, headaches, or other psychosomatic disorders, the amount of psychic trauma that they reported occurring in their childhood would have been considered sufficient to account for their symptoms. Instead, this was a group of symptom-free, successful men.

It is a well-known fact that five of our Nobel laureates in literature were very friendly with the bottle, and several had psychotic relatives. Many of the most important contributors of original scientific ideas have had nervous breakdowns, and the incidence of psychosomatic disorders in gifted actors and artists is impressive. Case histories, biographies, and autobiographies of outstanding persons demonstrate repeatedly that "out of the mud grows the lotus."

If someone overcomes a particularly sordid, squalid background, geneticists attribute his achievement to superior genes rather than to the accidents of rearing that abound in most of our lives. That is, they ignore the adult friend, the school teacher, or the lucky break that may represent the turning point in a person's life and help produce a Superior Court Justice rather than a criminal. Many studies have been made of gifted children, comparing noncreative and extremely creative children with comparable IQs. It has been found repeatedly that the families of the creative children were generally less happy and evidenced greater conflict and tension. In short, it took anxiety plus IQ to make the child superior.

Genetic theories about what is normal and what is not normal rely on the assumption of the "thingness" of pathology, labeling human traits or characteristics as if they were tangible realities, when, in fact, such "traits" are only ideals and remain undefined and unobserved in any scientific sense.

As a student of the family for many years, I think it is safe to say that there is no such thing as a normal family any more than there is a normal individual. There are parents who appear to live in extreme harmony together but have nervous children, and parents who get along miserably but whose children appear to be functioning well. When one hears the expression, "Gee, they're a normal family," the speaker is usually referring to some facet of family living and not to the total familial interaction, which is unknown to the casual observer. Such statements are usually made by persons who value conformity and see this family as one that lives up to all the ideals of the ladies' magazines, including the cardinal principle of "togetherness." Truly, such behavior has little to do with mental health. There are cultures and families within our own culture, in which the family structure is very different from what is commonly considered normal. Yet the individuals therein are creative and productive.

It should be clear by now that I strongly believe psychologists and psychiatrists should stop asking, "What is normality?" It seems to me that for purposes of scientific theory formulation, and also for practical clinical purposes, a different and more fruitful approach can be taken. One that would incorporate the views that human beings possess a variety of potentialities, that the achievement of certain potentialities may entail certain limitations, and that achievement and limitation vary with conditions. Thomas Szasz says that mental illness is a myth, whose function is to disguise, and thus render more palatable, the bitter pill of the moral conflicts in human relations. He states that what we have are problems in living together, and not poor mental health. These problems are biological, economic, political and sociopsychological.

What can replace the concept of normality? Obviously, for purposes of scientific study, we need to categorize in some fashion. It is possible to rate the members of a family, for example, on their level of ability to function in various areas of living. Thus, a man who earns ten thousand dollars a year has a certain degree of economic functioning; whether he has any friends or any sex life will be judged separately. This rating does not imply good or bad, since a high level of functioning does not necessarily indicate happiness or good moral character, or vice versa. There is also no implication that a person *should* function well in all areas. It is unlikely or impossible that he will, yet he can be compared with other persons in those areas in which he appears to function well or poorly. The advantage to be gained is that of evaluating each person in a wide variety of activities and contexts; our bias, while not eliminated, is apt to be less blinding than it is within the current concept of mental health.

An illustration will clarify this conceptualization. During World War II psychiatrists examined thousands of draftees and rejected many of them on the grounds of emotional instability. In recent years, the Army has come to reject virtually no one for emotional disorders. Even those who have had a schizophrenic breakdown are not necessarily rejected. The reason is quite simple. There are all kinds of jobs in the Army and many can be adequately performed by soldiers who don't impress interviewers as potential heroes. The liberal (compared to World War II) attitude toward selection during the Korean campaign did not result in increased psychiatric casualties among combat heroes. As a matter of record, casualties were reduced by putting psychiatrists to work on combat troop morale instead of letting them sit back at a General Hospital waiting for patients.

I submit that there is no such animal as the normal person. Instead there is a wide variance in adaptive patterns and behavioral repertoires. How a person acts varies with the culture, the subculture, the ethnic group, and the family group in which he lives. We tend to forget that values change, because we are so often uplifting the new and forgetting the old. At one point in our history, blushing was considered to be lady-like and was rewarded socially. Later it was considered cause for treatment by a psychoanalyst. Today the art of blushing seems virtually to have disappeared—is it, or was it, normal or abnormal?

If we recognize that normality is a myth that carries with it false genetic implications and dubious judgments about who is better than whom, we might be in a better position to undertake research about various kinds of functioning and techniques of problem-solving. We might also be in a better position to recognize that *most* people contribute something to the human condition and that man is fantastically adaptable. Those people or nations unlike ourselves are *not* inferior—just different. It is time to give up the false security born of labeling what we are doing as "right" or "normal" instead of using the more accurate but less reassuring term "conventional." It is going to be tough on some physicians to not label their unusual, anxious, or irritating patients—but think of the challenge!

*As mentioned already, the idea that behavior depends on communication and interaction is not new. In addition to its occasional scientific recognition, it is the stuff of everyday experience. But such common knowledge or specific insight has remained limited and is especially rare where layman and specialist alike would most need it; that is, in looking at and dealing with unusually difficult behavior—badness and madness.*

*The next article offers a case in point. In it John H. Weakland considers sociocultural investigations of schizophrenia—the epitome of madness. It has been said in science "a significant difference is a difference that makes a difference." This article illustrates how significantly different the evaluation of past studies and the planning of future ones becomes, if one takes a thoroughly interactional viewpoint, rather than one which, even while aiming to relate them, views schizophrenia and social living quite separately and in disparate frameworks.*

# SCHIZOPHRENIA: BASIC PROBLEMS IN SOCIOCULTURAL INVESTIGATION

*John H. Weakland*

This article represents an attempt to develop and convey a fresh picture of the significant general problems presently inherent in investigating various aspects of schizophrenia (for example, its nature, etiology, prevalence) in relation to its sociocultural environment, and to outline some approaches to effective handling of these problems. This is to be done by bringing into view the general aims, premises, and problems exemplified but not made explicit in much of the existing work in this area, and contrasting these with a different viewpoint developed in the course of firsthand studies of schizophrenia in the family context—a kind of sociocultural environment in miniature.

Originally published in *Changing Perspectives in Mental Illness,* ed. Stanley C. Plog and Robert B. Edgerton (New York: Holt, Rinehart and Winston, 1969). Reprinted with permission.

Accordingly, there is here no comprehensive review of past work in this area, nor critique of specific aspects of such work within its own frame of reference. Instead, I shall only sketch certain main outlines of such work, neglecting details to clarify the broad fundamental picture, and emphasizing what is amiss more than acknowledging accomplishments. A more inclusive and balanced view of this already sizable field, for other purposes, is readily obtainable by reference to various bibliographies (Baldwin et al., 1962; Clausen, 1956; Driver, 1965) and conventional reviews (Clausen, 1959; Benedict, 1958; Benedict & Jacks, 1954; Dunham, 1961; Hunt, 1959; Leacock, 1957; Lemkau & Crocetti, 1958). Particular mention should be made of Mishler and Scotch (1965) who review the field at length, citing original work, other reviews, and methodological discussions, and themselves consider from another viewpoint some of the main issues raised here.

### Schizophrenia in Society: Traditional Approaches

Some selective examination of existing work on sociocultural factors and schizophrenia (including some related material on society and mental illness more generally) is necessary here to provide a concrete basis for discussion. For this purpose, I shall rely on two articles that already report on large areas of the field in brief and orderly fashion. These will be used to formulate a description of typical studies, largely in their own terms, and a summary characterization of them. Then, by further examination based on the family viewpoint to be described, it will be shown: (1) that these studies involve a common, but largely implicit, structure of aims and premises as well as procedures; (2) that this structure fits poorly with the inherent nature of the subject matter; and (3) that these studies themselves indicate some awareness of this discrepancy but fail to meet it directly and take it seriously.

The two sample articles are, in the main, representative of two closely related yet significantly different groups of studies. One group deals with schizophrenia within a given society—most commonly the United States. The other is concerned with schizophrenia in other kinds of societies; these studies are therefore at least implicitly cross-cultural. Aims and approaches correspondingly differ somewhat between these groups.

*Intrasocietal Studies*

Hunt's (1959) review provides a well-organized descriptive sample of studies of the first type, and some pertinent discussion. Hunt first mentions demographic studies as the oldest and crudest type of investigation in this field. These studies relate rates of incidence of mental disorder to such variables as age, sex, marital status, and race. It is noted from more extensive reviews by Felix and Kramer (1953) and Rose and Stub (1955) that schizophrenia in males is more frequent among foreign-born and Negro groups than native whites, and its onset is concentrated in the 20–35 age range.

Ecological studies are characterized as explorations of relationships between mental disorders and a variety of environmental factors such as high population density, poverty, and high delinquency rates, in defined urban districts. These studies are correctly noted as having been a very influential type since the pioneer study by Faris and Dunham (1939); they have been reviewed extensively by Queen (1940) and Dunham (1955). Workers in this area have, interestingly, exhibited a clear concern about possible *causal* relationships between the factors studied and schizophrenia, but at the same time have maintained a certain caution and distance from this question. That is, none of the factors studied were necessarily presumed to be causally significant, and the possible causal means or connections were largely left undiscussed. The findings have indicated higher rates for schizophrenia in geographical districts characterized by the factors mentioned.

Social stratification studies, examining relationships between mental disorders and various indices of socioeconomic status, appear as a development and refinement of the prior ecological studies. Chief among these, and typical of problems and methods, is the extensive study headed by Hollingshead and Redlich (1958) at Yale. These investigators devised a scheme for assessing individuals studied to one of five social class strata, defined in terms of occupation, education, and area of residence. They were careful to use a normal control sample and to control for population distribution of class membership. Perhaps even more carefully, "The investigators take pains to point out that their results have reference only to diagnosed or treated and not 'true' rates [Hunt, 1959, p. 98]." They found that, on this basis, schizophrenia is more common among lower status groups (Hollingshead & Redlich, 1954a, 1954b, 1958). Similar findings are cited from the work of Tietze, Lemkau, and Cooper (1942a), Frumkin (1955), and Clark (1949). Hunt (1959) himself already points toward the need for a critical overview of such findings: "It may be that whether a given patient is classified as . . . schizophrenic when diagnosis is uncertain, will be in some measure a function of his social status. If this is true the studies reviewed . . . would, at least in part, refer only to status factors in the *diagnosis* of mental disorder [p. 99–100]."

A number of studies attempting to relate rates of mental disorder to social mobility also are largely a development from earlier ecological studies. Work of this kind is found in Tietze, Lemkau, and Cooper (1942b), in parts of Hollingshead and Redlich (1954a, 1954b), and in Hollingshead, Ellis, and Kirby (1954). A study by Ellis (1952) is of special interest, since in attempting to test the hypothesis that mobility is often partly inspired by emotional drives resulting from unsatisfactory primary group relations, but then leads to further deteriorations of these relations with accompanying neurotic symptoms, she took a step beyond the usual studies by suggesting a possible mechanism—disturbances in primary group relations—as relating mobility and mental disorder. In general, these studies showed no clear results concerning spatial mobility, but indicated that patient groups, especially schizophrenics, tend to be more mobile in status than nonpatients—but mobile *upward,* contrary to certain expectations.

A final group of studies is concerned with relations between social variables and treatment of mental disorders; that is, how much therapy of what sort (for example, psychoanalysis, other psychotherapy, organic therapy, custodial care), and by whom (for example, psychiatrists, psychiatric residents, social workers) is received by patients of various classes. The work of Hollingshead and Redlich (1954a, 1954b, 1958) was important in this area also, along with work by Robinson, Redlich, and Myers (1954), Myers and Schaffer (1954), Auld and Myers (1954), Winder and Hersko (1955), and Hunt, Gursslin, and Roach (1958). These studies suggest that the likelihood of treatment, its extent and intensity, and the status both of the form of therapy and of its practitioner all increase with higher class status.

Hunt also points out (1959, p. 103) that differential treatment according to class status could influence the interpretation of studies relating social class and incidence rates of schizophrenia, since observed incidence may, in complex ways, depend also on the treatment situation—the two may be measured separately without being independent.

Finally, Hunt discusses explicitly the strong yet largely implicit interest of these studies in causal or etiological connections between the social factors and related mental disorders. Three main kinds of hypotheses have been put forth. The first is the "drift" hypothesis, which argues that schizophrenics, especially, will be unable to function effectively in a society because of their disorder, and will "drift" downward in status and residential area. The second is the "social isolation" hypothesis of Jaco (1954). This proposed that social isolation, "the cutting off or minimizing of contact and communication with others" (measured by such variables as number of acquaintances, membership in fraternal organizations, visits with friends) is an etiological "precipitating variable" specific for schizophrenia, and that "those communities having high rates of schizophrenia will have a concomitantly high degree of social isolation." The third hypothesis is that of "culture contact," that experiencing sociocultural conflict or disorganization from immigration, assimilation of new cultural influences, or cultural complexity would provoke mental illness. Various studies already cited bear on this, as does the work of Goldhamer and Marshall (1953) on social change over a period of time and mental illness, by studying rates of first admissions to hospital for psychosis in Massachusetts over 100 years. In Hunt's judgment, none of these hypotheses has been confirmed. Yet whether such hypotheses result from the studies in question or merely underlie them, they help to fill out our view of their general nature.

## "Cross-cultural" Studies

We may now consider the group of studies concerned with mental illness in other societies. This group differs from the first, not only in studying various foreign or primitive societies different from our own, but also in their concern with a wider range of "cultural" problems; for example, the possible variation in nature or manifestation of mental illness, or in rates of incidence, in relation to specific or general characteristics of a given culture. Such studies especially tend to give more consideration to various theoretical and methodological problems, including some that also inhere in studies of the first group but receive little explicit attention there.

The valuable article by Lin (1953), which combines a report of an empirical study, a review of much related work, and significant consideration of a number of issues general to such research, is mainly drawn upon here to illustrate the nature of such studies. Lin first notes some prior general predictions about the probable incidence of various types of mental illness in China, based on deductions from conceptions of the nature of Chinese culture and character, and a few very limited, or unclear surveys. He then discusses various possible methods for measuring incidence of mental disorders of the population of a given geographical unit. The more common general method is based on hospital admission statistics, which may miss many cases, particularly where hospital facilities are not well developed. The other general method is investigation of a sample taken to represent the total population. Of several possible kinds of samples, all have evident serious flaws, except the census method, based on examination of all inhabitants of one area taken as a sample of a larger geographical unit.

This method was used by Lin, since hospital facilities were minimal in

Formosa, the site of his study, and tolerance of Chinese families in regard to abnormal behavior is rather high, and a large proportion of mental cases would therefore remain in the community even if hospital facilities were sufficient (1953, pp. 315–316). Also the method gave an opportunity to collect demographic and ecological data along with that on mental disorders. First, inquiries were made, using local census records and official personnel, to gather information about all inhabitants and suspected mental cases. Next, the investigators questioned family members or neighbors to get detailed accounts of these cases, and interviewed these persons where feasible. Finally, a confirmation visit was made, by teams which visited every house, checked the information from local records, briefly interviewed each family member, and interviewed in detail all reported cases plus anyone showing any sign of abnormal conduct.

Lin reports the incidence of schizophrenia and other mental disorders thus found, tabulated against the areas studied, and against his demographic and ecological data on age, occupation, and socioeconomic status. Lin also surveyed studies of the incidence of mental disorder in a dozen other societies, and compares them with his own findings. The Formosa rates for the major psychoses and epilepsy did not differ appreciably from those of other countries, but reliable comparison could not be made for nonpsychotic mental disorders, as the problems related to differences in sampling, intensity of study, criteria of mental illnesses, and data handling were too great. Lin also indicates awareness of other important empirical and theoretical complexities in such studies. "It must be re-emphasized that contemporary psychiatry lacks adequate data regarding incidence of types of mental disorders in different cultures. . . . Most European authors on this subject have emphasized hereditary and constitutional factors, and have made little of the cultural and environmental side of mental illness. But modern anthropologists . . . are making contributions to the study of relationships between psychological and cultural patterns frequently at the cost of oversimplification and generalization of hypotheses obtained through observation of primitive societies [1953, p. 335]." Even if these opposing difficulties about data are met, there are basic problems in interpretation, and therefore in the development of a theoretical framework for effective organization of data. For example, Lin's study indicated an absence of obsessive-compulsive neurosis, and this is consistent with other observations. However, "LaBarre (1946) noted the low incidence of obsessive-compulsive neuroses, and thought that the poorly developed 'sphincter-morality' in Chinese character might account for it; thus this lack in Chinese character structure might be related to the lack of strictness in the early training of children. Carothers (1947), on the other hand, attributed the absence of obsessional neurosis in Kenya Negroes to the fact that their culture itself was essentially obsessive-compulsive. In Chinese culture, the rituals connected with ancestor worship may provide an outlet for compulsive tendencies" (Lin, 1953, p. 334).

Hunt's limited consideration of "cross-cultural studies" has little factual to report. He does suggest, on the basis of the reports of Carothers (1953), Stainbrook (1952), and Linton (1956), that the fundamental types of psychosis recognized by Western medicine all appear in other societies, although rates and symptoms may vary considerably, and that specific localized types of psychosis seem very rare, but the situation is more variable for neuroses. Also he reports the assertion by Weinberg (1952) and others that schizophrenia is less frequent in cultures that are homogeneous and have intimate contacts than in cultures which are heterogeneous and have impersonal and hostile contacts, but concludes that, as with Jaco's similar isolation theory, there is as yet no adequate proof or disproof of this sweeping proposition. Hunt's review puts more emphasis on the severity of methodological and interpretative problems in cross-cultural studies, including conflicting tendencies that are likely to exist. The lack of hospitals interferes with usual survey methods, but census methods may also be biased; in one way by the difficulties of survival in primitive societies for anyone seriously psychotic, or in the opposite by acceptance of less serious cases merely as part of the society, not as "mental cases." Diagnoses are also apt to be vague or arbitrary in such studies.

### Summary

In summarizing the foregoing, we may say that the intersocietal studies in form are rather simple and repetitive typical sociological investigations except for their specific focus on mental illness. They are fundamentally concerned with collecting data on the incidence of schizophrenia, based on hospital admission records for cases diagnosed as schizophrenia, or less often based on some sort of census survey of a selected population sample, all the members of which are examined psychiatrically, although perhaps quite briefly, to see if this diagnosis could be applied. The resulting raw figures on numbers of cases are converted into rates by relating them to the total population of whatever social or geographical unit is presumed to have been sampled. Such overall rates are then often broken down by tabulation of incidence of various stock sociological categories, differentiated according to simple demographic variables. Data on the handling of schizophrenia or other mental illness may be gathered and utilized similarly; such work especially has included studies of the kind of treatment given various classes of patients. Rather separately, there has also been some concern with outcomes of mental illness, although such studies have mainly been clinically and individually aimed except for work concerned with the "therapeutic community," and with social attitudes toward the mentally ill (see reference in Baldwin et al., 1962, Ch. 18; and Driver, 1965, Chs. 7–8).

It is striking that although most of this work is only empirical or parametric, an interest in causal connections or wider theoretical problems is repeatedly evidenced; but such questions are very seldom brought into the center of the stage for explicit and careful examination. Instead, there is usually only some rather vague postulation of mechanisms connecting mental illness and social factors, or of similarities which interrelate them—as in suggesting "isolation" as common to the individual and social aspects of schizophrenia without much critical scrutiny of either the concept or the phenomena it is so freely used to characterize.

Two significant points characterize the cross-cultural studies. First, they bring up a number of important wider issues. They are concerned with the possibility of different manifestations of mental illness in different cultures, and different handling of it. There is more concern with methodological problems—for example, it is noted more that to determine the incidence of schizophrenia is itself no simple task. And there is more direct attention to issues about theory or about connecting mechanisms between cultural factors and mental illness. This is not to say that care is always exercised in these matters, however. An example to the contrary is the rather casual pronouncement of sweeping and conflicting statements about *the* nature of "primitive" society. When actually observed, primitive society is more like the stock market as characterized by J. P. Morgan. That is, it is hard to make any general statement with certainty, except "It fluctuates"; different cultures are remarkably different. Nevertheless, and perhaps largely because of this fact (it is hard to proceed with scientific "business as usual" in other cultures, as the evident differences in social facilities, practices, and attitudes force one to stop and consider, in research as in other areas of life, ideas and procedures taken for granted in our culture), the cross-cultural studies do tend to exhibit somewhat greater scientific sophistication, if they less readily produce neat quantitative tabulations. But, second, it is generally evident that these studies still want to produce these tabulations; they are basically concerned with the same kind of questions and aims as the intrasocietal studies. The methodological and theoretical problems they notice (are perhaps forced to notice) are seen as obstacles to these aims, not as suggestive of reorientation to a different, broader, and more connected viewing of culture and mental illness.

## Schizophrenia in the Family: An Interactional Approach

In contrast to this persistent orientation, under rather similar influences the research work of my colleagues and myself on schizophrenia and family interaction (Bateson, Jackson, Haley, & Weakland, 1956, 1963; Haley, 1959a, 1959b; Jackson, 1957a, 1957b; Jackson & Weakland, 1959, 1961; Weakland, 1960, 1962; Weakland & Fry, 1962; Weakland & Jackson, 1958) became increasingly oriented toward investigating the nature of schizophrenia, its social contexts, and their interrelation, all viewed similarly in terms of communication.[1] This work itself in important senses was a study of "cultural factors in schizophrenia." That is, although our research group included people trained in psychiatry and communications analysis as well as anthropology, and dealt with schizophrenia and families in our own society, it considered these matters as if they were new and foreign, and as if the family were a small society, so that this work could be viewed largely as an anthropological study of the culture of schizophrenic families. Thus, certain fundamental features of our theoretical or even epistemological orientation and research procedure also seem pertinent for extrapolation to the examination of schizophrenia in larger social contexts, and the basic scientific viewpoint they embody appears useful as an analytic tool for obtaining a new view of the usual work on schizophrenia and culture, by comparison and contrast.

It is significant that our present focus of study and our accompanying set of basic orientations largely developed, or became clearer and more explicit, jointly during the course of our research. Our interest in schizophrenia was at first only an outcome of Bateson's prior interest in the general nature of communication, especially the paradoxes and conflicting messages that may arise because human communication does not involve single, isolated messages, but always proceeds via multiple messages on different levels and different channels. Our research on these matters was being carried on in a mental hospital, and, urged on by Haley, we became interested in interrelations between the obviously disturbed communication of schizophrenics and our wider theoretical interests. The schizophrenic's "inappropriate affect," for example, in communicational terms stands out as an extreme case of conflict or incongruence between two messages, often one verbal and the other via facial expression, about one situation. The general value of examining the extreme or pathological to

---

[1] The account of our work and its bases presented here is my own formulation; although it often depends on observations and ideas from my colleagues, they might view and describe our joint work differently in various respects.

illuminate the usual or normal is well known—and quite different from a focus on the "abnormal" alone in the studies considered above.

Therefore we began to study the communicative behavior of schizophrenics. Since we conceived of communication as interaction, and there was then almost no verbatim interview material available even in transcript, let alone the tape or film records required to give nonverbal messages, we became involved in conducting our own interviews with the patients and recording them for detailed study. We were less interested in content than in the *formal* aspects of communication; study of our interview records at this level led us to see the presence of certain confusions in discriminating the logical types of messages as characteristic of the schizophrenics we studied. We then considered how such a failure of discrimination might have been learned; that is, what sort of formal pattern of communication directed to the child would produce this pattern in return? From this arose our concept of the double bind—a communication involving two conflicting, incongruent messages, at different levels—as a message pattern that should have such an effect. We therefore began to observe and record schizophrenics and their parents communicating in joint interviews. At this point in our alternations between theorizing and observation, we were into "family anthropology"; the only remaining development was partially to enter "applied anthropology," that is, to explore ways and means of family therapy with such families. This final state is relevant here not because of its practical significance, but because some aspects of a family or other social system become clear only when changes in functioning are attempted.

*Family Studies of Schizophrenia: The Basic Framework*

From the summary above, our work might seem not just varied, but diffuse. Yet one body of interrelated fundamental principles and premises can be discerned as underlying all this work and defining our general approach. These may be stated, proceeding from the general toward the more specific, as follows:

1. Our viewpoint was fundamentally interactional rather than atomistic. In particular, we aimed to understand and explain any selected item of behavior by viewing it in relation to its wider context of social interaction, as part of a related larger whole, rather than attempting to correlate two "separate" items.

2. We were especially concerned with ongoing systems of interaction, in which the system is more than and different from the sum of individual parts that may be distinguished within it. The family was viewed as a social system in this sense.

3. Systems are both characterized and maintained by the existence of recurrent patterns of interaction—for example, typical styles of relationships among the members in a family, or cultural patterns in a given society. Such patterns, and their significance, can only be found by close observation; they may not be foreknown or obvious.

4. Homeostasis—the ways interaction of elements within the system contribute to the correction of deviations, so as to maintain its ongoing existence—is a fundamental aspect of system functioning.

5. Emphasis on systems and interaction implies a primary interest in "contemporary causality"; that is, how existing behaviors are reciprocally stimulating and reinforcing, and contribute to the total pattern. This contrasts with a more linear-temporal view which seeks root causes of present behavior in the past, and also with a noncausal focus on empirically observed association alone.

6. *Communication* is seen as the key means of interaction. In human social systems, communication in this sense must be understood, and examined, as involving various kinds of messages—verbal and nonverbal, overt and covert, congruent and incongruent, at various levels—and as involving both report and command aspects—that is, influence as well as information. The concept of communication also provides a single framework for viewing both individual and group behavior.

7. The schizophrenic is viewed primarily as a member of his family— part of this social system, not primarily as isolated or outside of it.

8. "Schizophrenia," correspondingly, is taken as the behavior of that family member labeled as the patient or the crazy one (although other members may by certain standards seem equally "sick"). This behavior, like the behavior of family members generally, is examined first and foremost in terms of its observable nature as communication, and the significance of such communication in the overall family patterns and the maintenance of this functioning system.

9. This view also requires consideration of the patient's "saner" behavior together with his "crazy" behavior, rather than separating these elements of his overall individual pattern of communication—and equally, consideration of any "crazy" aspects of the behavior of other family members.

In work along such lines, it can be rather difficult to discriminate neatly between theoretical or epistemological orientations and general considerations of methodological approach; they are too closely interconnected. However, four other interrelated points from our work may be mentioned as being closer to the empirical pole:

1. Our research was based, not on a thorough grounding in past work on schizophrenia, but rather on the existence or assumption of a relatively

naïve observational stance, as if we knew little of schizophrenia and of families, or as if members of families of schizophrenics were the natives of some newly discovered tribe. The purpose of this is to maximize prospects of seeing something new and significant. In any area where major problems remain in spite of a history of extensive and intensive study, it is only reasonable to suspect that traditional observations and conceptions are inadequate or inappropriate in important respects, so that reliance on them prejudices research at its very foundations.

2. Therefore, apart from our very broad theoretical orientations, our basic work was heavily concentrated on close observation and description of raw data—the actual behavior of schizophrenics and their families, or at least on comprehensive recordings of such behavior on tape or film—carried on by our senior research personnel.

3. Fresh observation must be accompanied by *positive* description and definition. We aimed, at all levels of behavioral observation, to state what something is or is like, rather than what it differs from or is not. This is, in fact, a correlate of our general emphasis on studying interaction and systems, which focuses on inclusion rather than exclusion. The opposite position is all too prevalent, especially in fields concerned with deviant behavior; witness the common use of such terms as "illogical," "disorganized," or "word-salad," which characterize something negatively by contrast, by exclusion, or by labeling as a "mish-mash"—that is, there is heavy use of residual categories and labels for the very matters of central interest. Such characterizations may express well a negative evaluation or a sense of frustration, but are of little scientific use; even a rough or partial characterization in positive terms is much more informative, although harder to make.

4. In dealing with interaction and systems, from primary observation and description right through building up concepts and theories, to get too simple makes matters more complex. True simplicity, to whatever extent it is possible, can only be achieved by taking all the essential interrelated elements in a system into consideration *together*. If $C$ is a resultant of $A$ and $B$ interacting, then we may find much by studying these factors all together, but despite the apparent simplicity of minimizing the factors to be handled, we may find *nothing at all* by studying $A$ and $C$, or $B$ and $C$. If Occam's razor is used too forcefully, it will only cut up units. This principle seems plain, but it is so readily neglected in practice that two more concrete examples will be given. (a) Communication always involves a multiplicity of messages; if a communication includes the message "Do that" and also the message "Don't do that," observation and analysis of the behavioral effects of the communication based on half of the com-

munication—either half—will only be confusing, and averaging the two messages will be even worse. (b) If schizophrenia has to do with family interaction, it may be simpler—more informative and efficient—to study the schizophrenic even in the apparent chaos of his family than in "simple" isolation (if that were really possible—there is always interaction with the researcher to consider).

## Reviewing the Traditional Approach

In now utilizing this point of view to reexamine the traditional kind of sociocultural studies of schizophrenia (and other mental illness), there is no intention to criticize the ability, care, time, and effort expended in them in terms of their own premises and orientations. This is rather a viewing from a different angle of the kinds of problems they selected for study, the observations made, the concepts involved, and the interrelations between these. Any body of work, including our own research, could similarly be examined from some outside viewpoint; the results would probably always be both painful and profitable.

This examination will first show how these traditional studies, although manifestly only concerned with empirical correlations, implicitly involve a coherent epistemological position which we here point out and criticize. Next, certain further comments will be made concerning these studies' handling of their inherent major foci. Finally, an explanation of the occurrence and nature of many of these features will be proffered.

In this examination, it is naturally postulated from the very existence and labeling of these studies that they assume (1) that mental illness has some relationship with social life, and (2) that significant aspects of these factors or their relationships are unknown and problematic. Nevertheless, to begin with, these studies appear to take too much as known, or at least as simply and easily knowable, in several respects. They proceed as if schizophrenia were clearly recognizable and comprehensible, and as if there were a good list of the social factors that might be significant for it, so that the only problem is to tabulate a variety of these factors against rates of schizophrenia, in order to pick out the proper ones from the existing list. In our view, it is highly doubtful if such knowledge existed, or even exists yet. And as Mark Twain said, "It's not so much what people don't know that makes trouble; it's what they know that isn't so." Despite this danger, the usual studies do not appear to observe their subject matter sufficiently, meaning sufficiently in terms of quality, intensity, and openness. They do include a sizable *quantity* of observations, but these observations largely are based on existing records, and cannot excel these in quality or scope; even where census surveys have been made, the time devoted to direct observation of any one situation or person, normal or schizophrenic, is quite brief. Related considerations hold for description or labeling in these studies. Standard sociological and psychiatric terms and categories are applied extensively and rather routinely; their relevance and adequacy are not questioned, although various terms used appear to be overly simplistic or to involve constructs quite remote from directly observed data. Such use of standard variables facilitates data collection and recording by assistants; but from another standpoint, this means facilitation of *nonobservation* of basic raw data by the presumably most competent research personnel.

A different aspect of the same overall orientation is manifested in these studies' strong antitheoretical, and even antirelational, stance. These studies say little about either a general or a specific theoretical orientation. Although their basic aim is to investigate relationships between social and psychosocial variables, this investigation is highly restricted by almost exclusive reliance on empirical correlation. There is little consideration given to the *nature* of possible relationships between these spheres, in either theory or observation, so that even when there is some empirical evidence of association there is no basis for meaningful or logical connections, causal or otherwise. As an example, we may again consider the concept of "isolation." This is, in fact, fundamentally a relational concept. It might be used heuristically to promote further observation and exploration of what kinds of social interaction schizophrenics do engage in, and this might be useful in clarifying and connecting individual and social aspects of schizophrenia. But in the rush to use it quantitatively—that is, to move at once to a more abstract and narrow level of relationship—these possibilities are largely neglected. Also, even when various social factors are recognized (especially in cross-cultural studies) as being of interest and as necessarily interrelated—such as varying manifestations of mental illness, social recognition and attitudes, and treatment or other handling—the fact of significant relationship is not followed up. It is noted in a cautionary way ("This must be considered") and quickly set aside to get on with more specific and delimited tasks. If such an antirelational approach worked well, criticism might be inappropriate. But the studies themselves indicate an inadequacy in this respect; considerations of theory, causal connections, and other relationships keep cropping up, late in the game and in *ad hoc* fashion. The picture, overall, is one of determination and effort to cast out any theorizing, and its recurrent reappearance, rather surreptitiously. The whole matter resembles struggling with sin and temptation, and the proscribed relational thinking, correspondingly, enters these studies only through the back door and in varying disguises. This hardly seems as good as open and direct consideration of such important matters.

Furthermore, this antirelational, atomistic framework appears to operate strongly not only at this general level, but also at more specific levels, where its isolating effects are invidiously reinforced by marked tendencies to approach "mental illness" in negative or residual-catgory terms. The outstanding example of this is so common as ordinarily to be taken completely for granted. Again and again these studies, in their titles and in their texts, refer to "mental disorders." That this is a stock term means only that its use is prevalent and habitual, not that it is necessarily appropriate. Like any other "disorder" or "disorganization" reference (including both explicit and implicit references to "social disorganization" in these studies) it characterizes, isolates, and stigmatizes by negation and exclusion. Its use thus obstructs needed inquiry into what kinds of positive characteristics and organization the "disorder" exhibits, as it necessarily must if it identifiably exists at all, and how it is related to anything else. It is also quite consonant with such an emphasis that in these studies there is almost no positive functional view of mental illness either at a general social level (although the cross-cultural studies at least should recognize that deviant behavior, including behavior resembling that of our mental patients, is often clearly important for overall social functioning—for example, the role of the shaman) or at an individual level. The patient is seen as isolated, if he is seen at all, and not as actively involved in any social functioning. Even in relation to a diagnostician, he tends to disappear behind his symptoms, as if these had independent existence.

Indeed, a great deal of the foregoing is exemplified in condensed form in the concept of schizophrenia as a "syndrome" or "disease entity," which is basic to these studies. A syndrome is not behavior; it is an isolable (and isolating) fixed, distinct, and separate existent; it tends somehow to be more real than the patient himself. Perhaps this is because it appears simpler to deal with. Yet even in medical work on schizophrenia, this "reality" appears to exist mainly as an ideal; particular cases, or even cases generally, have a distressing tendency to conflict with the neat textbook picture of a fixed entity—even when any more normal behavior by patients is quietly ignored.

These studies are necessarily concerned with three main foci, namely *relationships* between certain *social variables* and *mental illness*—primarily its incidence, and secondarily its handling. Yet the social variables or categories in these studies are hardly ever social in the senses that seem crucially important. The groupings constructed by the investigators, presumably because they should be environmentally influential in producing schizophrenia, have little or no relevance to actual social interaction systems, which might be significant in the etiology of such a condition. (In some instances they have some relevance to this negatively, to situations conceived as lacking social interaction.) At best, they may imply some concern for groupings that might have certain common social attitudes or definitions of life situations, but what these may be or their supposed significance for schizophrenia is little considered. The categories, in short, appear to reflect a "fishing expedition" approach, but at the same time they are such stock categories of social research that their relevance as bait for hooking the elusive determinants of mental illness is already suspect.

Also, as mentioned above, these studies in many significant respects turn their attention and efforts away from rather than toward considering possible interrelations among the factors with which they are concerned. It might only be added here that although they pronounce their identity as social studies, the approach to interrelating variables that is used—that is, establishing empirically correlations between factors that are partially on a social level, partially on a psychological level, and even partially on a biological level (for example, the factors of age and sex)—does nothing toward providing some common framework relevant to social interaction, within which the various factors of interest can be viewed together. It is perhaps no wonder that investigators in this area seem impelled repeatedly to step out of the framework they have themselves originally set up and seek for some kind of connective concepts. But this is better done earlier and more deliberately.

Then there is the matter central to all this work, concern with determining the incidence of mental illness, especially schizophrenia. There have been specific misgivings on this score (for example, awareness of certain kinds of diagnostic difficulties), but quite regularly these have been noted in passing, as it were, only to be overridden in the need to get on with the research. Moreover, they have not only not been taken seriously enough, but critical consideration of the whole question of incidence has not been sufficiently wide and deep. In the first place, when schizophrenia is taken as an isolable syndrome (the studies allow that there may be certain problems of diagnosis because of different standards of psychiatric training and so on, but these are seen as only unfortunate but specific practical difficulties, beyond which lies a definite knowable entity), then these studies, although they are seeking significant connections between schizophrenia and social factors, begin with an attempt to radically separate schizophrenic behavior from its social context, and even to separate schizophrenic behavior from any other behavior of the same individual.

Two more specific problems are promoted by such a conception of schizophrenia. First, different indexes are used to identify cases without adequate consideration of what is being done differently. As noted earlier, the cases on which incidence figures are based are selected in two main ways—by making a diagnostic census, or by collecting records of hospital admissions. These methods may differ not only in completeness, which is often recognized, but, at least in part, in *what* they measure. A census, whatever the nature of reliability of its criteria and procedures, is based on judgment of symptoms in an interview situation within the general context of daily life. Thus, inclusion in a count of cases by this method is based on what are at least seen as purely psychological criteria (since the social relationship with the diagnostician, although necessarily present, is ignored), and ordinarily leads to no practical social consequences. Hospitalization, however, even where a similar diagnosis is made, is always subsequent to and partially dependent upon some kind of gross disturbance in the relationships of the patient-to-be with other people; an individual may have symptoms and not be hospitalized so long as he does not bother other people too much with them (see Goffmann, 1959). There are therefore "cases" of schizophrenia in hospitals less "sick" in terms of psychological or psychiatric diagnostic criteria than some "noncases" in the outer society; all this requires is that they be less disturbed but more disturbing. In short, in addition to its other vagueness and complexities, the category "schizophrenic" in practice always involves an element of social judgment of behavior in relation to others, and an element of psychological judgment of "symptoms," conceived as purely individual in nature. This problem can be seen as another consequence of an atomistic rather than an interactive viewpoint, as the latter would view symptoms as just one part of individual behavior, and individual behavior generally as something to be considered in relation to its environing social system. But even disregarding this more general view, it is evident that in the usual studies, data on incidence rest on two conflicting bases.

Second, the tendency to consider schizophrenia as if it were a known phenomenon also has unfortunate influences in attempts to relate its incidence to other variables. It is true enough that the present state of diagnosis and nosology is adequate to achieve consensus on the identification and even description of many or even most cases, by the psychiatrically trained and indoctrinated. But identification is not equivalent to scientific characterization; to know a case is $X$ is not necessarily to know what $X$ is, in any basic sense—not even if there are stock labels for bits of symptomatic behavior. And it is the essential, basic elements of any phenomenon that need knowing more than ever when the aim is to investigate its significant relationships with other phenomena of a different sort. Viewing "isolation" or "withdrawal from reality" as characterizing schizophrenia may be of some descriptive or communicative value in a context of hospital administration but still be of little value in any attempt to relate schizophrenia to social factors; in fact, assuming such characterization as sufficient blocks further examination and understanding.

Many of the points of criticism mentioned above have been made before, but they have not been seen as interrelated and pervasive aspects of a general approach common to these studies, nor has the extent of their implications been recognized. In sum, it appears that the traditional sociocultural studies of schizophrenia recurrently rely upon existing, standard psychiatric labels and methods of observation, standard sociological categories, numerical procedures and measures of association as if all these are both appropriate and sufficient to the objects of investigation, and consonant among themselves—even in the face of repeated evidence to the contrary in these studies themselves.

There are, as usual, rather compelling if not really good reasons for the recurrent appearance of such difficulties, and for the recurrent tendency of the studies to ignore or override them. Quite simply, the nature of studies of schizophrenia, like their object, is very much enmeshed in and influenced by practical rather than scientific considerations. People acting in crazy ways, and methods of labeling and dealing with them (that is, conceptions of mental disease, diagnosis, hospitals and record keeping, and so on) are urgent practical matters of social life, for individuals and for the social system. Correspondingly, these are deeply entwined with systems that are highly ordered but not scientifically ordered; that is, with the administrative, legal, and medical systems in our society, or their analogues in customary behavior elsewhere. Such systems, quite expectably, are normative; they are geared and ordered toward handling certain selected problems within established social frameworks and limits, not toward the clarification and understanding of basic general relationships among social phenomena. There is a natural tendency in research work toward utilizing the ordering represented in these established categories and procedures—but it is done at a scientific price, which rises rapidly if the nature and inherent limitations of this approach are ignored.

Moreover, although science itself is not a practical matter in basic principle, even science is a social activity, and it seems that the general scientific approach used in these studies also has probably been affected by similar practical biases and limitations. Given the social prestige of science (it knows all, or is just about to) and the prestige of atomistic discriminations, hard data, and quantitative methods in its enterprises at present, there are natural difficulties in recognizing openly that we really know little about schizophrenia and related social factors, and that a more deeply and frankly exploratory approach, based on observation and thinking, guided by a broad interest in interaction, may be more appropriate now and for some time yet than the piling up of empirical correlations of this with that, in hope of finding some important relationship.

Our own studies, however, in contrast to the traditional ones, did proceed along such lines, and this approach can be defended as scientific in the most fundamental sense, and as ultimately more productive. Some of the premises and principles described earlier were fairly clear and definite early in our research. Others became so only as we looked at schizophrenics from a communicational view and in a family context, first in idea and later in actuality. And in particular, our work began, largely, without initial specific definition or assumption of what is essential in schizophrenia, in families, or in their systematic study. These matters were left to become progressively clearer, within the framework of our most general orientations, during and in relation to the course of our research. This was realistic because it constituted an acknowledgement and acceptance of a basic general ignorance about these matters. This was possible because practical, official, or traditional criteria can suffice initially to identify and select objects for observation and description while still being quite inadequate to characterize them well. And, moreover, this was positively desirable, since the looseness and flexibility of this approach, in combination with a general framework and much empirical observation, promoted the gradual development of a new but unified and interrelated set of observations, methods, and concepts, all adapted to the objects of study and to each other. Such mutual adaptation of its various aspects, although seldom discussed, seems essential for penetrating and productive research.

This is, obviously, a procedure based on successive approximation, with repeated revision and increasing refinement of all aspects of the research. Research necessarily always involves such successive approximation, since we can never know adequately in advance what is relevant, and how, for a problematic situation. The more problematic the situation (and schizophrenia is an excellent example), the more this approach is fundamentally appropriate to all aspects of a study, yet the more difficult it may be to accept and use. To begin with so little definition may, very understandably, seem uncertain or threatening, yet it does offer a fundamental promise of gradually discovering research means appropriate to a largely unknown situation, which will progressively bring order out of chaos—or more accurately, will allow us to perceive and describe inherent order not seen before.

### Future Directions

After all the foregoing criticism, what constructive views can be offered? As just indicated, our approach is not one that promises too much in the way of quick results (although our family studies have rapidly become useful both in understanding and in treating schizophrenia), but it seems possible at least to outline positively some significant factors for the sociocultural study of schizophrenia and make suggestions toward their investigation from our standpoint.

#### Factors for Study

In fact, the very studies criticized have a quite positive contribution to make in this respect. As a group they have demonstrated that social factors are significant, and shown the basic elements that must remain central to this area: studies in this field are and will be concerned generally with *interrelating* information about the *occurrence* (or possibly absence) of schizophrenia, as behavior necessarily manifested by an individual or a number of individuals, with information about the *social contexts* of such behavior.

More particularly, as to occurrence, information must be gathered on the observable manifestations for each individual case, or set of cases, in a social group. In a framework that bears in mind that schizophrenic behavior is a mixed resultant of psychological and social organization and influence, and may be a different mixture in different societies, we should then look at relevant examples to see their general nature and any special characteristics, variations in such behavior, its severity or intensity, and (although perhaps finally rather than initially) its prevalence in the society or social group. That is, the question of rate of incidence should not be abandoned, but also it should not be put first in such investigations either in time or emphasis. Such overall incidence rates, although apparently a simple variable because of the high level of abstraction, may actually be more complex and less rewarding to study than examination of other aspects of schizophrenic behavior. Indeed, rough indications or estimates of incidence might for many purposes be preferable to concentration of effort on achieving precision that may be misleading, or even inherently impossible to obtain.

As to the social contexts of schizophrenia, to facilitate linking this broad concept with factors that in past work have been noted on a more separate basis, we may broadly discriminate between social factors concerning the *circumstances* of schizophrenic behavior and those concerning its *hand-*

*ling.* Among the circumstances that need investigation would be the general cultural patterns of the social group, characteristic styles of social interaction, and family and child rearing patterns. More specific factors would include social conceptions of the nature and etiology of mental illness, and related evaluations. For example, is schizophrenic behavior socially classified or labeled as an entity, and if so, as a disease, as spirit possession, as bad behavior, as a special personality type, or what? Such labels can be most important for the manifestation and outcome of schizophrenic behavior, since they strongly influence social judgments as to the existence and nature of certain behavioral phenomena, and also influence responsibility for and social reaction to them (witness the extent of efforts in our own society in recent years to label certain "delinquent" behavior, or alcoholism, as diseases and thus as involuntary). Such social conceptualization must be inquired about, as its nature can never be safely assumed or guessed. For example, it is reported that in Timbuctu syphilis, which is ubiquitous in the population, is considered a minor disease to be caught and got over with as soon as possible—about the way we view measles (Miner, 1965).

With regard to the social handling of schizophrenia much more may need investigation than the matter of psychiatric treatment, although this is an example within this category, and is of major importance in our society. In other social groups there may be other forms of treatment, or handling that is not conceived as treatment—for example, the person whose behavior would here put him in the role of patient may elsewhere move into a quite different role—a high status as a shaman, a feared one as a witch, or perhaps some tolerated but menial role. The roles that persons behaving in schizophrenic ways are apt to assume may vary not only in status, but also in the extent and nature of their integration with the rest of the social system. Changes of role with onset of schizophrenia, and then subsequent changes—whether toward "cure" and thus reversion to the former social role, or toward further development in a new role, and general social expectations about the temporal course of behavior and eventual outcome of schizophrenia, all need careful inquiry. The social fate of persons whose behavior we would call "schizophrenic" may be very different in different societies.

Such conceptions and expectations about social handling and outcomes of schizophrenia evidently may also be significant for its development and characteristics. Thus, in fact, sharp discrimination of circumstances and handling as if one were simply antecedent and the other consequent is fundamentally inappropriate. The two must ultimately be considered together, keeping in mind that in a social system, because of interaction and feedback, all factors must be seen as having both these aspects. The usual social consequences of any behavior are also a part of the circumstances of its occurrence.

### An Approach to These Factors

It is perhaps evident already from the discussion above that the main positive suggestion here is that some basic aspects of our family studies' viewpoint be tried out on a larger social scale, with a focus on the particular kinds of factors cited. In broad terms, it is proposed that the behavior patterns of schizophrenic individuals, including both normal and "crazy" aspects, be closely examined within and in relation to their particular sociocultural settings. The criteria for and definition of schizophrenia could be rather loose initially, so long as actual behavior was observed and described carefully in each case. Such observation and description should explicitly focus on schizophrenia as communicative behavior, and within this frame, on its general features, especially at a formal level (that is, such aspects as the recurrent combination of incongruent messages). Limited attention might be given to the content of schizophrenic communication as related to cultural themes. This has been a topic of interest in previous cross-culural studies, but, while finding such connections provides evidence for social influence on the manifestations of schizophrenic behavior, it also may draw attention away from the more important general features of structure and relationship, as has occurred before in the psychological study of symbolic and personal-history aspects of schizophrenic productions.

The use of such loose initial criteria is allowable because such studies would assume that in any event this cateogry "schizophrenia" is unclear and needs investigation, and also because the research emphasis would be more on viewing clearly social contexts and associated behaviors than on these behaviors as such. The main emphasis throughout, in fact, would be on investigating the social system from an interactional viewpoint, and schizophrenic behavior as a sector within this—that is, less on "pathology" and more on social science. Such investigation and interrelation is facilitated by focusing on communication, which refers to observable behavior, is directly concerned with interaction (since communication is the main vehicle for the transmission of influence as well as information among human beings), and is a concept applicable to descriptions of behavioral phenomena at the level of the social system, the family system, and the individual, so that these may all be examined within one common framework.

At the societal and family levels, attention would again be focused first on recurrent general patterns. On both anthropological and psychiatric grounds it appears that such general and formal patterns are of much more fundamental significance for determining the nature of individual behavior of members of a social system than are specific and unusual events. Although these may be more dramatic, and in some instances quite influential, even such influences can only be predicted or understood if the more pervasive context has first been seen (see Jackson, 1957b). This holds whether causality is considered with a historical emphasis, in which case general contexts are crucial to more specific learning and change, or with a more contemporary, circular view emphasizing reciprocal reinforcements of behavior patterns within an interactive system. The latter is the primary viewpoint proposed here; attention in theorizing, observation, and description (which themselves are highly interconnected) would be concentrated on any society or social group as an ongoing system, on its homeostatic nature, and on seeing the interactive and homeostatic functioning of behavior. This needs stressing especially for deviant behavior such as schizophrenia, since just these functional relations are apt to be overlooked or overshadowed by the factors of difference and distance apparent in such behavior, which have led to views emphasizing "isolation," "broken homes," "deterioration of primary group relations," and the like, which emphasize the overt and neglect covert organization and functioning. In our family studies, an emphasis on function and interaction has been revealing and rewarding; it leads to a picture of tightly intermingled contact *and* isolation of the schizophrenic and other members of the family system, which serves importantly in the maintenance of the typical behaviors of other members and the nature of the system as a whole. Not only is this visible on observing the interaction of family groups where the patient is present; even if a patient has long been hospitalized and his family far away it is often easy to see that they still affect each other strongly—perhaps by correspondence (Weakland & Fry, 1962), or in its absence (itself a message), by their recollection of unfinished business with each other. It seems probable that a similar approach to schizophrenia and a wider social system would also be valuable, and there is evidence of this in anthropological studies, which often show how the deviant individual and his behavior fill social roles that are of importance as part of the total cultural system.

Consistent with the foregoing emphasis on interaction within a social system, it may be suggested that work in this area should for some time focus on case studies, at a social level, using comparative information only as an aid to clearer observation of the main target. General cross-cultural comparison is a more complex task which should be deferred for some time.

### Schizophrenia and Culture: Some Broad Problems

The suggestions above obviously are quite general; they certainly do not provide any specific research design. This is appropriate to our view of the field as one that most needs exploration, so that guidance must be based on stating general principles to be used in connection with careful and intensive examination of relevant data. To be more specific would limit and bias study more than assist it. However, it is possible in conclusion also to consider certain particular problems related to any such studies as proposed.

These problems are chiefly concerned with broad aspects of the relationship of schizophrenia and culture. A relatively simple one, for a starter, is embodied in speculations as to the possible existence of a "schizophrenic society." From the standpoint taken here, the answer is "yes and no, but mostly no." Its basis may be seen by considering, first whether a pattern of individual psychological organization identifiable as schizophrenic might independently exist. This is very dubious, because the organization of individual behavior is so highly interrelated with social organization and interaction. But even if this were possible, there are only two possibilities at the social level. Either no functioning society could exist based only on such individuals, or some kind of cultural patterns involving such individual organization, such that an ongoing social system would result, could exist. But in this case, the term schizophrenic, without serious qualification, would really not be applicable for either the individuals or the society, because, as noted earlier, our usual concept of schizophrenia fundamentally involves certain elements of social deviance and malfunctioning, which by definition are absent in this case.

In other words, our "schizophrenic society" or more general "sick society" ideas are rough and mixed concepts usually used, for some given society, to point toward the presumed existence either of a predominance of individuals with schizoid (or other "pathological") personality organization, or of a social organization we see as undesirable and somehow analogous to schizoid patterns. Although these terms are poor, there is some evidence of reference to significant social realities. According to Fortune (1932), the people of Dobu were generally paranoid in personality make-up, yet they had a society which, although to our eyes it was riddled with hostility, suspicion, and black magic, nevertheless functioned. And the character structure of the Balinese, as described by Bateson and

Mead (1942), appears highly schizoid in terms of our psychological standards, yet, in connection with cultural patterns and social mechanisms which they describe, an extensive and considerable culture flourished.

Indeed, many features of the Balinese patterns of culture and personality organization seem to have parallels in several important Oriental societies, and it is worth considering how social and personal levels of organization seem to be geared together in such instances. Speaking broadly (as a basis for further investigation rather than as a definite account) sociocultural systems that strongly involve schizoid personality types appear correspondingly to involve distant rather than intimate social relationships. Such distance may not be obvious, as it is with many schizophrenics. On the contrary, the dominant impression, as in Bali, or in China or India, may be of a great deal of social activity and interaction, at close quarters. These two apparently opposed views are not really incompatible, but complementary. In such cultures there is much social interaction in large groups and in close physical proximity, but much less in terms of one-to-one relationships and emotional intimacy. And social relationships are largely carried on, not in terms of interaction whose nature is worked out between participant individuals, but in terms of extensive impersonal rules and standards of behavior and interaction that are given, known in advance. Such a system obviously can best exist in a traditional society, although the necessary rules could conceivably come into play otherwise—for example, as part of a social movement joined by true believers; it is certainly adequate to serve as a basis for even large and complex societies.

The implications of such a system for psychological functioning or malfunctioning (it seems almost impossible yet to avoid negative or residual categorizations) are interesting here, especially in their dualistic functioning. It is likely that individuals of schizoid character ordinarily would function well in such a social system, since its patterns are congruent with their relationship tendencies; indeed, these tendencies might well be rewarded and promoted more than other possible types of psychological organization. Thus, if surveys are possible, one might expect in such a society to find considerable schizophrenia or near-schizophrenia with a test delineating deep psychological patterns, but little schizophrenia if evaluation were based more on social functioning (as with hospitalization). As a further complication, however, it seems likely that the few cases that would thus be found (those that somehow exceeded such a social system's functional limits) might be very severe ones.[2] These considerations, taken

[2] For the development of this line of thinking I am indebted to discussions with John W. Gittinger.

together with the possible existence of positive social roles even for quite deviant schizophrenics, give some view of the relational complexities that may lie behind the deceptively simple concept of the "rate of incidence" of schizophrenia, and how little such rates may indicate directly about the "mental healthiness" of either the social system or of the population involved.

Culture-contact may also be considered in a related light, as another important situation that has suffered from over-simplified viewing, largely in relation to ideas about conflict and "disorganization." There has been little real study of culture contact—what changes, restructurings and developments occur and how, which must vary with the nature of the two cultures in each instance; it has only been noted in a few studies that schizophrenia does not appear to be associated with immigration. If one has a more positive conception of schizophrenia, as embodying a characteristic organization of its own, it is not so surprising that it should not regularly arise out of the many different ways in which customary behaviors might be rather randomly blocked or frustrated in various kinds of cultural contacts.

But if schizophrenia is both positively organized behavior and largely a matter of social interaction and influence, how can one conceivably explain the apparent fact of its occurrence in a vast variety of cultures? (This may not be established for all cultures, but the evidence still is considerable, and our experience with several quite different cultures also indicates a widespread core of similar behavior.) Certainly no definite answer to this problem is at hand, but a conceivable answer is. We view schizophrenia—both in nature and in etiology—as based essentially on certain formal patterns of communication involving incongruence between related messages of different levels, and the behavioral influence of such communication (Bateson et al., 1956). To illustrate these matters with examples requires bringing in some content, but the essence of schizophrenia depends on the structuring of certain universal factors of human communication and social interaction into patterns that, although distinctive, are of such high abstraction and generality as to be relatively independent of any lower-level cultural phenomena; thus schizophrenia can be supra-cultural to a considerable extent without being an organic illness. Furthermore, this view still allows room for the possible existence of partial interrelation of schizophrenia with factors within a given culture: (1) The content of a culture, being at a relatively specific level, may be reflected in the content of schizophrenia. (2) At a somewhat higher level, it is possible at least to imagine a society (one version of the psychiatric utopia often sought) in which cultural patterns would somehow encourage a minimal production of incongruent messages, with resulting influences on schizophrenia in the society. (3) And, at a yet higher level of cultural learning and patterning of interaction, societies may well vary in the extent to which congruence, as against incongruence, in communications is normal or expected; this should affect responses to otherwise schizophrenogenic communications in complex and fascinating ways.

Finally, what can be said of the most central problem in the study of schizophrenia when approached as suggested here—the interrelations of the individual, family, and social system? Perhaps not too much, beyond pointing out how badly this topic needs investigation, in a variety of societies (for example, would the family seem of equal importance for schizophrenia if our own work were repeated in a different society, or even in this society with more attention given to the wider social system?), and that the concept of communication provides a common framework for such investigation. Yet two further observations may suggest the kind of relationships that need looking into. On one hand, it has been suggested earlier that schizoid character structure, here seen tentatively as primarily a resultant of the family interaction system, could be the basis of a viable society (rather than the basis of deviance and pathology), given interaction patterns in the culture generally that would fit such character organization without undue strain, and thus simultaneously reinforce it. This in fact implies that the family and the social system are apt to have patterns that are parallel or similar to a large extent. On the other hand, in our own family work and related work by others, there is evidence suggesting that individuals may be very schizoid, yet be functioning and not labeled as sick, in their own family settings, which presumably foster such behavior but are also adapted to contain it. Such families also are often marked by the limited extent their members interact outside the family—they are closed systems to an unusual degree—but as children grow older, even in such families opportunities and pressures for extrafamilial contacts increase markedly (for example, school, work, military service, sexual relationships). And a schizophrenic break—the rapid appearance of overt psychosis—often seems to be related to such an individual's developing increased contact with some world of social interaction outside the family, although this outer world appears much "healthier" than that in the family. That is, there is here some indication of overt schizophrenic behavior as being related to certain incongruences between the *systems* of interaction at the family level and a wider social level, contrasting with the previous example of viable functioning where therre is congruence between these systems of interaction. Such considerations may provide that sort of beginning for fruitful inquiry which in science traditionally is at least supposed to be as significant as specific findings.

## REFERENCES

AULD, F., JR., & MYERS, J. K. Contributions to a theory for selecting psychotherapy patients. *Journal of Clinical Psychology,* 1954, 10, 50–60.

BALDWIN, J. A., GELFAND, S., KELLY, J. G., LANGE, H., NEWBROUGH, J. R. & SIMMONS, A. J. *Community mental health and social psychiatry: A reference guide.* Cambridge, Mass: Harvard University Press, 1962.

BATESON, G., JACKSON, D. D., HALEY, J., & WEAKLAND, J. H. Toward a theory of schizophrenia, *Behavioral Science,* 1956, 1, 251–264.

BATESON, G., JACKSON, D. D., HALEY, J., & WEAKLAND, J. H. A note on the double bind—1962. *Family Process,* 1963, 2, 154–161. (Includes extensive bibliography of the group's work.)

BATESON, G., & MEAD, M. *Balinese character: A photographic analysis.* New York: Special Publications of the New York Academy of Sciences, II, 1942.

BENEDICT, P. K. Sociocultural factors in schizophrenia. In L. Bellak (Ed.), *Schizophrenia, a review of the syndrome.* New York: Logos Press, 1958. Pp. 694–729.

BENEDICT, P. K., & JACKS, I. Mental illness in primitive societies. *Psychiatry,* 1954, 17, 377–389.

CAROTHERS, J. C. A study of mental derangement in Africans, and an attempt to explain its peculiarities, more especially in relation to the African attitude of life. *Journal of Mental Science,* 1947, 93, 549–597.

CAROTHERS, J. C. The African mind in health and disease. *World Health Organization Monograph 17.* Geneva: World Health Organization, 1953.

CLARK, R. E. Psychoses, income, and occupational prestige. *American Journal of Sociology,* 1949, 54, 433–440.

CLAUSEN, J. A. *Sociology and the field of mental health.* New York: Russell Sage Foundation, 1956.

CLAUSEN, J. A. The sociology of mental illness. In R. K. Merton, L. Broom, & L. S. Catrell (Eds.), *Sociology today.* New York: Basic Books, 1959. Pp. 485–508.

DRIVER, E. D. *The sociology and anthropology of mental illness: A reference guide.* Amherst, Mass.: University of Massachusetts Press, 1965.

DUNHAM, H. W. Current status of ecological research in mental disorder. In A. Rose (Ed.), *Mental health and mental disorder.* New York: W. W. Norton, 1955. Pp. 168–179.

DUNHAM, H. W. Social structures and mental disorders. In *Causes of mental disorders: A review of epidemiological knowledge, 1959.* New York: Milbank Memorial Fund, 1961. Pp. 227–265.

ELLIS, E. Social psychological correlates of upward social mobility among unmarried career women. *American Sociological Review,* 1952, 17, 558–563.

FARIS, R. E. L., & DUNHAM, H. W. *Mental disorders in urban areas.* Chicago; University of Chicago Press, 1939.

FELIX, R. H., & KRAMER, M. Extent of the problem of mental disorder. *Annals of the American Academy of Political and Social Science,* 1953, 286, 5–14.

FORTUNE, R. F. *The sorcerers of Dobu.* New York: Dutton, 1932.

FRANKLIN, R. M. Occupation and major mental disorders. In A. Rose (Ed.), *Mental health and mental disorder.* New York: W. W. Norton, 1955. Pp. 136–160.

FRUMKIN, R. M. Occupation and major mental disorders. In A. Rose (Ed.), *Mental health and mental disorder.* New York: W. W. Norton, 1955. Pp. 136–160.

GOFFMAN, E. The moral career of the mental patient. *Psychiatry,* 1959, 22, 123–142.

GOLDHAMER, H., & MARSHALL, A. *Psychosis and civilization.* Glencoe, Ill.: The Free Press, 1953.

HALEY, J. An interactional description of schizophrenia. *Psychiatry,* 1959, 22, 321–332. (a)

HALEY, J. The family of the schizophrenic: A model system. *Journal of Nervous and Mental Disease,* 1959, 129, 357–374. (b)

HOLLINGSHEAD, A. B., ELLIS, R., & KIRBY, E. Social mobility and mental illness. *American Sociological Review,* 1954, 19, 577–583.

HOLLINGSHEAD, A. B., & REDLICH, F. C. Social stratification and schizophrenia. *American Sociological Review,* 1954, 19, 302–306.(a)

HOLLINGSHEAD, A. B., & REDLICH, F. C. Schizophrenia and social structure. *American Journal of Psychiatry,* 1954, 110, 695–701. (b)

HOLLINGSHEAD, A. B., & REDLICH, F. C. *Social class and mental illness.* New York: John Wiley & Sons, 1958.

HUNT, R. G. Socio-cultural factors in mental disorder. *Behavioral Science,* 1959, 4, 96–107.

HUNT, R. G., GURSSLIN, O., & ROACH, J. Social status and psychiatric service in a child guidance clinic. *American Sociological Review,* 1958, 23, 81–83.

JACKSON, D. D. The question of family homeostasis. *Psychiatric Quarterly Supplement,* 1957, 31, 79–90. (a)

JACKSON, D. D. A note on the importance of trauma in the genesis of schizophrenia, *Psychiatry,* 1957, 20, 181–184. (b)

JACKSON, D. D., & WEAKLAND, J. H. Schizophrenic symptoms and family interaction, *Archives of General Psychiatry,* 1957, 1, 618–621.

JACKSON, D. D., & WEAKLAND, J. H. Conjoint family therapy; some considerations on theory, technique, and results. *Psychiatry,* 1961, 24 (Supplement to No. 2), 30–45.

JACO, E. G. The social isolation hypothesis and schizophrenia. *American Sociological Review,* 1954, 19, 567–577.

LABARRE, W. Some observations on character structure in the Orient: II. The Chinese, Parts One and Two. *Psychiatry,* 1946, 9, 215–237, 375–395.

LEACOCK, E. Three social variables and the occurrence of mental disorder. In A. H. Leighton, J. A. Clausen, & R. N. Wilson (Eds.), *Explorations in social psychiatry.* New York: Basic Books, 1957. Pp. 308–337.

LEMKAU, P. Y., & CROCETTI, G. M. Vital statistics of schizophrenia. In L. Bellak (Ed.), *Schizophrenia: A review of the syndrome.* New York: Logos Press, 1958. Pp. 64–81.

LIN, TSUNG-YI. A study of the incidence of mental disorder in Chinese and other cultures. *Psychiatry,* 1953, 16, 313–336.

LINTON, R. *Culture and mental disorders.* Springfield, Ill.: Charles C Thomas, 1956.

MINER, H. *The primitive city of Timbuctoo.* (Rev. ed.) Garden City, N.Y.: Doubleday Anchor Books, 1965.

MISHLER, E. G., & Scotch, N. A. Sociocultural factors in the epidemiology of schizophrenia. *International Journal of Psychiatry,* 1965, 1, 258–305.

MYERS, J. K., & SCHAFFER, L. Social stratification and psychiatric practice: A study of an outpatient clinic. *American Sociological Review,* 1954, 19, 307–310.

QUEEN, S. A. The ecological study of mental disorders. *American Sociological Review,* 1940, 5, 201–209.

ROBINSON, H. A., REDLICH, F. C., & MYERS, J. K. Social structure and psychiatric treatment. *American Journal of Orthopsychiatry,* 1954, 24, 307–316.

ROSE, A., & STUB, H. R. Summary of studies on the incidence of mental disorders. In A. Rose (Ed.), *Mental health and mental disorder.* New York: W. W. Norton, 1955. Pp. 87–116.

STAINBROOK, E. Some characteristics of the psychopathology of schizophrenic behavior in Bahian society. *American Journal of Psychiatry,* 1952, 109, 330–335.

TIETZE, C., LEMKAU, P., & COOPER, M. Schizophrenia, manic-depressive psychoses, and social-economic status. *American Journal of Sociology,* 1942, 47, 167–175. (a)

TIETZE, C., LEMKAU, P., & COOPER, M. Personality disorder and spatial mobility. *American Journal of Sociology,* 1942, 48, 29–39. (b)

WEAKLAND, J. H. The double-bind hypothesis of schizophrenia and three party interaction. In Jackson, D. D. (Ed.), *The etiology of schizophrenia.* New York: Basic Books, 1960. Pp. 373–388.

WEAKLAND, J. H. Family therapy as a research arena. *Family Process,* 1962, 1, 63–68.

WEAKLAND, J. H., & FRY, W. F. Letters of mothers of schizophrenics. *American Journal of Orthopsychiatry,* 32, 604–623 (1962).

WEAKLAND, J. H., & JACKSON, D. D. Patient and therapist observations on circumstances of a schizophrenic episode. *A.M.A., Archives of Neurology and Psychiatry,* 1958, 79, 554–574.

WEINBERG, S. K. *Society and personality disorders.* New York: Prentice-Hall, 1952.

WINDER, A. E., & HERSKO, M. The effect of social class on the length and type of psychotherapy in a Veterans Administeration mental hygiene clinic. *Journal of Clinical Psychology,* 1955, 11, 77–79.

*In March 1967 Jackson presented to the First Rochester International Conference on "The Origins of Schizophrenia" his views on this highly*

*problematic and debated entity, as they had evolved further since the pub-
lication of his book* The Etiology of Schizophrenia[1] *in 1960. This paper
is of particular interest, not only because it is the last comprehensive presentation made by this outstanding psychiatrist less than a year before his
untimely death, but also because it utilizes the concept of schizophrenia
first of all to explain again why individual personality theories (and, by
implication, individual treatment methods) cannot be applied to the pathologies of a human system like the family; secondly, to show the inter-
dependence between the behavior of the so-called identified patient and his
family; and thirdly to introduce the concept of restrictiveness as a major
factor of systems pathology. As Jackson demonstrates from his ample
clinical experience, restrictiveness appears to be based on a family rule
against the changing of rules, and this in itself creates a hopelessly paradoxical situation. This paper also corrects a general assumption, common
to many family studies (especially those of a sociological orientation),
according to which disturbed families are chaotic and "normal" families
are stable. Here, as elsewhere in scientific observation, it is the position of
the observer that determines his results: At the interface with society, disturbed families may indeed appear chaotic and unpredictable; seen as systems that manage to close themselves off against most contacts with
society, these families reveal a stifling degree of rigidity and inability to
change.*

# SCHIZOPHRENIA: THE NOSOLOGICAL NEXUS

Don D. Jackson

## Section I

*Introduction*

For many years there has been a general discontent with psychiatric
nosology. The hope we once had that individuals could be classified with
rigorous diagnoses has slowly dissipated. Not only is there dissatisfaction

Originally published in Excerpta Medica International Congress Series No.
151, *The Origins of Schizophrenia* (Proceedings of the First Rochester International Conference, March 29–31, 1967). Reprinted with permission.

[1] Don D. Jackson, ed. *The Etiology of Schizophrenia* (New York: Basic
Books, 1960).

with specific diagnostic labels, but the concepts on which these labels are based are continually being questioned. Evidence has accumulated that any attempt to classify an individual with static labels such as "depression" or "schizophrenia" ignores the facts of life which dictate such things as variations in individuals (normal or otherwise) from day to day, the fact that every year a patient spends in a mental hospital increases the likelihood that he will finally be labelled "schizophrenic," and Grinker, Rosenthal and others have demonstrated the crucial impact of the labeller on which label is chosen.

Furthermore, labels perpetuate the notion of "disease". Hopes for easy answers by developing biochemical or neurophysiological labels, for example, utilizing the EEG or finding Taraxen, have not worked out. Studies of identical twins have varied from the ineluctable 86 percent of Kallman to a recent study by Tienari which revealed no concordance in monozygotic twins one of whom was diagnosed as "schizophrenic."

As a result of these dissatisfactions, a number of people have been turning from the problem of classifying the individual to the problem of classifying *the context* in which the individual lives, e.g., his family. As family study has mushroomed, and as being family-oriented has become "In", many workers have cherished the hope that new or more useful diagnostic labels might spring forth from the forehead of Zeus or a new Freud. So far, a peculiar thing has been happening: people have been attempting to classify families with the terms and ideas of individual diagnosis—even though these have proven inadequate in the past. Instead of the development of categories of families, we find merely the claim that individuals of a particular nosological class come from a particular kind of family. Thus we now have terms such as "schizophrenic family", "schizophrenogenic parents", "delinquent families", and so on. This use of terms designed for individuals to characterize families is obviously inadequate, since a "schizophrenic family" contains a number of members who are not formally schizophrenic. This practice does *not* characterize a type of family interaction, nor does it distinguish the "schizophrenic family" from "non-schizophrenic families". Worse yet, all the errors and deficiencies of individual nosology are carried over and become firmly transplanted into family study. Continuing this trend will put us in the position of the neurotic who, by Freud's definition, makes worse what he seeks to cure.

The purpose of this paper is three-fold: (1) to dispel any lingering hopes that the study of the family can proceed by applying individual personality theories to families; (2) to present the level of general descriptions from which, in my opinion, we must proceed if we are to connect the individual and the family, especially in a complex disorder like schizophrenia; and (3) to consider what such a new framework might ultimately do for our view of the individual, especially for our nosological view of psychopathology including schizophrenia.

I.  Let me list a few of the reasons why the language of the individual's pathology cannot be usefully applied to the family:

A.  One of the reasons family study developed was because of the dissatisfaction with the monadic approach; hence describing families in terms of the characteristics of individuals will leave us with the same old dissatisfaction, plus some new ones.

B.  The past descriptions of individuals, by definition, ignored the context in which the individual functioned, whereas family studies must focus upon context—witness, e.g., the trend toward interviewing families in their own homes and including the extended family.

C.  The language of individual study is largely about processes assumed to be occurring within the individual. Families cannot reasonably be said to have "drives", "attitudes", "perceptions", "motivations", or the like. These can only be construed as the characteristics of individual family members, not of the family as a unit.

D.  The language of individual pathology provides a family description which is distorted by its very nature. One cannot say a family is "phobic" when only one member has a phobia. Not only the specific terms for the individual cannot be used, but the concepts on which these are based must be questioned as well. The medical model of "mental illness"—which considers pathology a property of a sick cell, a sick organ, or a sick person—is entirely unsuited to the study of transactional processes within a family.

In contrast to the description of individuals, family research emphasizes:

A.  Interpersonal and contextual factors which research on individuals so often neglects or even seeks to eliminate by holding such factors constant.

B.  The study of several people's typical, reciprocal responses *to* one another in all their variability; not the individual's response to a novel and standardized stimulus (e.g., Rorschach or TAT).

C.  An emphasis on the present; *not* how the person got to be the way he is, but *how* the system he inhabits maintains itself. Not *linearly* causal relations but *circular* ones. Retrospective data has been shown to be surprisingly unreliable.

D.  Behavior in the widest sense is the subject of family study, whereas individual study provided not so much a description of behavior as of the processes assumed to be occurring within people which led to behavior. In individual study, behavior was looked upon as simply an indication helpful for intrapsychic pigeon-holing. In family research, behavior is considered to be the continuing causal agent in the maintenance of a particular system. It is therefore essential to grapple with the problem of describing behavior.

E. Even if it were possible to translate individual theory into interpersonal terms, the goals of such an effort would be of questionable value. The product would be a sterile one, with no promise of new orders of knowledge. As the eminent scientific historian Kuhn has shown, important scientific discoveries have occurred from breakthroughs *not* orderly accretions.

It might appear, then, that the language and concepts for describing an individual are different in nature from the family description which is needed, and the twain shall never meet. Fortunately, this is not quite so. We feel that those who hope they can bridge from the individual to family study by using individual concepts are going to be disappointed. A bridge is possible but it would seem to be a one-way bridge. We must first develop a description of the family and then return with a new point of view about the individual.

II.   What is new and different in the family approach is not merely a numercial increase in the size of the unit of study. Let us examine the changes in thinking which have imposed themselves upon us in our study of families, and how these changes might be relevant to an ultimately more rigorous classification of individuals.

One immediate revision offered by family study has been the *order* of data studied. One shifts from description of the "nature of" someone to description of the "relations between" someone and someone else. This latter approach has required the use of observable behavior as a source of data, rather than the unseen "properties" inside the individual. The data become sequences of repetitive, observable "acts" between family members, and with this shift to a new type of data comes a possible new way of conceptualizing the problem.

III.   *Organization and limitation:* One way of classifying behavior in relation to other behavior is by the fundamental notion of redundancy, constraint, or limitation within a given range.

A. Definition:

1. Organization means limitation, since it can be behaviorally defined as a specific patterning of repetition and exclusion.

2. The family is organized; no family which stays together can behave "randomly" i.e., collide and bounce off each other like atoms in a cloud chamber.

3. Given a range of behavioral possibilities which are equally likely in theory, an organized entity will use some more than others. E.g., of possibilities "a" through "f" perhaps only "a" and "b" will be used; or perhaps "d" will not occur at all.

B. This is the underlying assumption in all family work: that the family-as-a-unit does and will behave with some form of consistency—not randomly. Family research can be seen as an attempt to tap that consistency and verify its existence. Our descriptions of family interactions are shorthand representations of the organization which we observe, in that they indicate the repetition or exclusion of behavioral possibilities.

C. It should be made clear here that this theory is *not* compatible with the older, sociologically-based notion that "disturbed" families (such as that of the schizophrenic) are disorganized and that this is of etiological significance. To the contrary, the evidence thus far indicates that the "disturbed" family is even more highly organized than the normal family, in that such a family utilizes relatively few of the behavioral possibilities available to it. (See section on "restricted" families.)

1. Certainly one has the impression that "disturbed" families (and their members) behave bizarrely, maladaptively, and often with a great deal of verbal or nonverbal distraction, and that they leave many transactions incomplete, thereby befuddling the observer and perhaps one another, too.

2. But if such behavior is observed only in terms of all possible behaviors, it can be readily established that the behavioral repertoire is extremely limited. To illustrate the level at which we intend "limitation" to be applicable, imagine the behavior of a family *with only one rule: that no other rules are to be followed.* One can easily imagine the apparent chaos in such a family organization, but it should also be obvious that the limitation imposed by their one rule would be extreme and that great organization is required to consistently *not* follow any rules. The price in terms of demands on individual members, as well as in terms of the family's adaptation to society, might be high, but the pathological family is highly organized unto itself. Some years ago I described how an apparent change for the better in one individual (such as helping a schizophrenic improve) can have disastrous consequences for other family members.[1] I am now saying that

this represents an attempt to introduce greater randomness in a rigid system.

IV.  Individual psychopathology can also be viewed as an extreme limitation in the kinds of behavior the individual can utilize. The richness, variety, and flexibility of his behavior responses are certainly limited, compared to the normal range of behavior.
A.  Examples:
  1. A phobic patient cannot enter an elevator, go up high buildings, or out into open spaces, whereas normal persons can.
  2. The delinquent has to steal, while normal persons steal or not, as they choose—especially around April 15th.
  3. The schizophrenic may talk with God, a dubious ability that most of us do not have; but he cannot *not* talk to God, and frequently he can *only* talk to God and not to mortals—a considerable social restriction for life on earth!
B.  A practical application of a nosological system based on behavioral limitation would be the redefinition of neurosis and psychosis along these lines: certain restrictions of behavior so limit the person that he is restricted in social development and such restrictions beget other restrictions. Further pathology, the observer reports, will depend on how the individual's restrictions relate to the *present* context.
  1. Darwin got along quite well with his heart phobia; a pole vaulter couldn't have.
  2. Restrictions of one's conversation to schizophrenic "nonsense" in itself will drastically limit the sort of life a person can lead.
C.  The ability of an individual to engage in a certain percent of the transactions available to him might be called his adaptability.
  1. If the number of these possibilities (compared to the theoretical possibilities open to him in the culture) is limited only by socioeconomic factors, we would say an individual is "normal" for his particular ecological niche. If his contingency possibilities are significantly further restricted, we would say he is "abnormal" or "restricted". That is, the absence of rape from a man's social repertoire is not an indication of pathology: limitation of culturally approved sexual activity is considered pathological.
  2. The promise of this approach to psychopathology is that it lends itself readily to interactional analysis. For instance complementarity

---

[1] Jackson, Don D. The Question of Family Homeostasis. *Psychiatric Quarterly Supplement* 31:79–90, part I (1957).

in marital couples often imposes complementary restrictions on each other on a mutually contingent basis. This leads to a vicious circle, e.g., the wife who nags and the husband who withdraws, each using the other as the stimulus for his own behavior.

3. Such a nosological basis may offer several advantages:
   a. observability;
   b. predictability;
   c. theoretical consistency;
   d. it is broad enough to encompass many specific theories of psychopathology;
   e. it spans both individual and family study.

V. Another possible meeting point of family and individual work is in the *class of behaviors* of which the symptom is an item:

A. We are often puzzled by the parents of middle-class delinquents who do not steal or vandalize; yet if one steps to a higher level of generality and views delinquency as essentially "breaking the rules and lying about it", then
   1. The labelled patient's behavior falls in this category;
   2. His parents' hypocrisy and other specific behaviors of theirs also fall in the class of "breaking rules and lying about it".
   3. The restrictions on the labelled patient's behaviors will *not* be observed in certain other families; and restriction also means in this context *not* being allowed to be honest (we have actual examples of this from the delinquency study at the Mental Research Institute by Dr. Jerome Rose).

B. The schizophrenic's symptomatic behavior has been described as essentially "confusion of logical levels".
   1. Unlabelled metaphor, disqualification, denial of communication coupled with denial of that denial.
   2. It has also been observed that the family of the schizophrenic, though non-psychotic in the present nosological sense, is notorious for confusion of logical levels: cf. double-bind, fragmentation, mystification, disqualification, as shown by the Palo Alto group, Lidz, Singer and Wynne, Laing and others.

C. The method of analysis fits another, still intuitive, aspect of family work: that the symptomatic behavior is somehow appropriate, not "sick", when the particular family system is considered. For example, when one observes the schizophrenic in his family, his behavior appears distressingly appropriate to the peculiar context in which he lives. In fact, one finds oneself admiring the skill with which a schizophrenic manages an extraordinarily complex situation in his family, and helps perpetuate it. Rather than see the schizophrenic as one who is "impaired" in his functioning, it begins to seem possible to see him as a person who must be more perceptive and acute than the normal person to deal with the conflicting rules of the system which he inhabits. His behavior may appear bizarre and inappropriate when he steps into a different system, but who among us is as capable as the schizophrenic of dealing with the extraordinarily complex family in which he matured—and the hospital system he later inhabits?

### Section II

*Introduction*

Man has his behavior prescribed and proscribed by the simple fact that, unlike animals, he cannot obtain necessary information from his instincts; instead he *must depend upon his fellow man*. If he is to remain a social animal he must hear and see inputs which have to be made into some kind of information.

This dependence on his fellows exposes man to obvious limitations on his behavior, and also to mind-bending. If he accepts required information, he also must accept messages about *himself* that may be *incompatible* or *antithetical* with the required information that he seeks. He also may receive paradoxical information that presents monumental difficulties in logic. For example, a young man may be reared by a mother who insists on the importance of marriage by protecting him from "ordinary" girls, so he ends up unmarried. One way of making such a situation "fit" is to believe that mother is protecting him from the "truth", which he may decide is "that he is incapable of marriage". The next step might be the thought "ergo I am a homosexual", yet this is paradoxical because he has not had isophilic sexual contact, and what does it imply about dad, about mother, etc.?

There exists considerable evidence that "mind-bending" occurs in the nuclear family's relationships with the offspring who bears the label of "schizophrenic". It has been postulated by myself and my colleagues in the "double bind theory" that a necessary mediating variable between schizophrenic behavior and mind-bending is an inability to escape the field.

The individual is trapped so he cannot escape the nature of the messages he is receiving from his family context. Another way to put this is to state hypothetically: "Individuals who live with their nuclear families and who later behave in such a fashion as to be labelled "schizophrenic" by an appropriate agent of their culture will give historical (genetic) and interactional evidence of having been restricted in some aspects of their behavior so that many contingency possibilities open to individuals from similar socio-economic-ethnic backgrounds have not been available to them".

The exact description of what constitutes "restrictiveness (i.e., the act of restricting another's behavior) depends on what categories of behavior one uses. They could be as obvious as noting that a child who is not allowed to speak has his verbal behavior restricted, to the hopelessly arcane observation that "the mother's unconscious hostility produces castration fear in her son".

In Part II of this paper I would like to offer categories of "restrictiveness" and "restricted behavior" which seem to me to have potential in the formulation of operational definitions of schizophrenia and some other serious disorders.

The definition of restricted behavior is the inability to engage in, or even to choose, contingency possibilities. This inability is judged in two ways, by the subject himself, usually a psychiatric patient (giving a history), or by an observer. The areas in which the individual is restricted need to be enumerated but can include all forms of human endeavor and activity. It is assumed that restricted individuals come from restricted families and some of these families practice "restrictiveness" on each other, i.e., they are not merely limited by illness, socio-economic position, etc., but actively restrict one another's behavior.

*I. The Individual*

A. Complains of restricting himself;
B. Complains of being restricted by others;
C. Complains of being restricted by a situation: for example, physical health, job, cultural or legal matters such as army, conformity, laws, etc.;
D. Complains that he is restricting someone else: e.g., occasionally a spouse will complain of his behavior in relation to the other spouse, but rarely recognizes it is difficult to say who is the kept and who the keeper.

*II. The Dyad or larger group (families, social groups, etc.)*

A. The identified patient, or some other chosen individual, is accused of restricting the group (for example: "My spouse is ruining our marriage", "My mother won't let me become a doctor", etc.).

B. An outside group (for example, an agency of the society) is restricting the group (seen as a complaint in *folie à deux*, complaints of injustice, unfair action by police, etc.).

C. The group relationship is complained of as restricting by the members of the group itself. For example, a couple in deciding on a divorce may state that they are bad for each other. Parents and children may sometimes decide that they are bad for each other and should live in separate domiciles.

D. The culture is restricting the group (e.g., families that complain of having to keep up with the Joneses. Families that complain of conformity, couples who want to engage in free love but feel society won't let them, etc.).

E. The group is being restricted by contingencies beyond their control (e.g., poverty, unemployment, police, physical illness, etc.).

There are certain concepts and observations that go along with the idea of restrictedness, and the kind of classification given above. For example, one might define the feeling of euphoria or well-being as a condition based on the myth or the reality or some combination of both, that new contingency possibilities exist and that new contingency possibilities can be utilized. For example, the obvious euphoria of Major White when he took his famous walk in space was apparent even to television observers. Yet, another view of the reality shows that he had little room to literally maneuver in, being at the end of a 25-foot tether. However, the aura of the vastness of space, combined with Major White's weightlessness, might account for his euphoria.

On the other hand, concepts like duty, patriotism, and so on, imply that the individual sacrifices, or has the will power to resist, seeking new contingency possibilities for a certain period of time. Thus, the loyal employee, who is honored by a gold watch after 30 years, is the one who regularly does the same job over and over again without fail and does not complain of being bored.

There is a possibility that only time-bound rebellion is healthy (i.e., is utilized for personal growth), since chronic rebellion implies that the aim is not towards utilizing new contingency possibilities but is directed at continuing the same relationship; for example, a couple who chronically fight, but stay together, indulge in the same pattern over and over again. The most restricted family possible would be the family which engaged in only one behavior, based on a single rule, namely, *that they would not obey any rule!*

The concept of novelty also fits in here because it appears to be a myth to think that people like sameness, for example, the tranquil, pastoral scene with the farmer and his sheep doing the same thing day after day, even if the individual appears to like sameness, for example, the hermit. Individuals grow older, and hence one day cannot be like another, if only because there is one fewer day left. It is probably that such concepts of sameness and peace, or peacefulness, are because we are not looking at large enough time periods. Most individuals look forward to weekends, to vacations, or at least to heaven, in the longer time periods.

It is apparent in our culture that too much emphasis has been placed on what parents should do for children, rather than in noting ways in which family patterns prescribe and proscribe behavior, including patterns of restrictiveness, in the child. This sort of thing is obvious in the spoiled child, or the crybaby, or the fearful child where parental attitudes, overt or covert, encourage reactions which limit the child's ability to participate in novel or new situations—or, in other words, to avail himself of possible contingencies. However, much more subtle familial forces may be at work and current family research indicates some of these may be observable and testable. In a structured interview developed at the Mental Research Institute, the parents may ask the child the meaning of the proverb "A rolling stone gathers no moss" instead of teaching it as they have been instructed. The way that they ask the child what it means may be larded with instructions not to leave the most literal level or make creative or novel responses; thus, a father may say, "You know what moss is, that green stuff that grows on trees, well it's really a lichen". A seven or eight-year-old child is naturally going to have to inquire what a lichen is and thus the answer that the parents overtly ask for is not the major part of the communication. The father is also saying, "Don't know more than I do".

If an individual, especially a child, does not react to contingency possibilities available to him, and there appear to be only personality reasons why he doesn't (rather than obvious physical or cultural reasons), then it is likely that he has learned prohibitions, and these should be available for observation *at least when transgressions invoke their reassertion*. This is a terribly important point which is overlooked when one sees the individual as a *whole* potential person who needs to have the infant inside of him (a dormant homunculus who somehow has been keeping in touch with the world but doesn't let the ego know it) grow up.

In such observations there are three likely considerations:

A.   The individual behaves in such a way that he invites sanctions from others and responds to the feedback as a command. For example:

Husband (hesitantly): "I was thinking of going to a show by myself tonight".

Wife: "Oh, don't go, you'll be too tired tomorrow".

Husband: "Okay" in a resigned tone.

Such individuals as the husband above might be called passive, masochistic, etc., in individual personality theory. But usually such labels implicitly—or in some personality theories, explicitly—ignore the evidence of present active sanctions from sources outside the individual such as spouses, relatives, the law, physicians, clergymen, etc.

B. The individual may utilize restricting techniques on significant others and in the process is also restricted himself, in one of two ways:

1. The relationship to the one that he is restricting in turn restricts himself, as may be the case for the husband of a phobic wife.

2. He influences others to join him in a restricted pattern, as in *folie à deux,* shared phobias, asocial two against the world, etc.

C. The observer may not be viewing a context in which "restrictiveness" is invoked. The design of a structured interview must take this into account

Restrictiveness is the behavior during which the process occurs of a person being restricted from engaging in contingency possibilities. Thus the restrictiveness of a family, such as is so strikingly obvious in the ulcerative colitis families, consists of those behaviors which can be labelled as limiting responsiveness, new behavior, unusual behavior such as humor, novelty, creative responses, etc. There are some possibilities for testing and further research in this. For example, children can be presented with the opportunity for novel situations and their ability to respond to them and the manner of the response can be rated, and then compared with the family interaction. Thus the simplest kind of response such as "I don't want to", or "I'm not interested" can be looked for in family interaction in terms of (*a*) the child being prohibited in his behavioral responses by the family, or (*b*) the family prohibiting itself as a group, such as is more frequent in the ulcerative colitis families.

### III. *Patterns of restrictiveness*

A. GENERAL AND MULTI-TOPICAL PATTERNS (for example, the overall kind of restrictiveness and restrictedness that one sees in ulcerative colitis families)

The rule is to avoid behavior that might be taken as a comment on the family or as a comment on inter-family relationships, event be-

tween siblings. If an individual engages in outside activities other than
those prescribed by law and custom, for example, school, church,
etc., it might be taken to be (*a*) avoidance of the family, (*b*) being
better than someone else in the family, or (*c*) a comment that the
family is not sufficient unto itself.

B.  GENERAL TOPICAL NON-RESTRICTEDNESS
These families engage in a wide range of activities as long as there
are not obvious physical harmful interferences such as danger, lack
of nutrition, sleep, etc., and not done at too great cost to other family
members. If it is done at a cost to family members it is assumed that
this will be made up in some way, such as through rotation, etc. This
kind of non-restrictedness can be noted in an interview by the range
of exchange of behaviors. These are usually of two kinds:
1. Stated and observed democratic rules: The family states its members are individuals and free to behave as such, and appears to mean
this as demonstrated in observed behavior in a variety of contingencies.
2. Spontaneous behavior, laughter, comments, criticism, sarcasm,
and so on, occur in a non-regularized way so that the observer feels
the family is interacting in a lively spontaneous fashion, enjoys each
other, and measures like Haley's "who speaks after whom?" reveal
on retest that there is non-regularity.

C.  SPECIFIC RESTRICTIVENESS
1. *Values;* for example, the Catholic family restricts eating of meat
on Fridays. Everyone in the family has a savings account, etc.
2. *Norms;* exchange of behaviors is proscribed in certain areas by
covert rules, while in most areas of functioning this *is not true.* For
example, there may be a rule in one family that no one is allowed to
be pessimistic. This restricts the individual's freedom since (*a*) he
cannot share or relate to certain other kinds of people and to some
circumstances, e.g., he cannot participate in a pessimistic discussion;
(*b*) he does not have the experience of feeling sad, hopeless, etc.,
even when this would be considered appropriate by others. Both (*a*)
and (*b*) leave this area of his personality undeveloped and, further,
such a rule dictates the selection of certain contingencies and avoidance of others. A child may not only be not allowed to be pessimistic,
but he will choose happy movies over sad ones by his own "free will"
and thus reinforce the non-experiencing that is also lacking at home.

(As an aside, people from this category of isolated restrictedness can do well in therapy and other types of influencing attempts since they basically have been taught to relate, and if the therapist says, "It's okay to feel sad, in fact you should" they can obey the therapist. Naturally, if the person still lives at home, he may experience resistance to his changing, but there may be a solution worked out that is pragmatic, namely, that he will be able to exercise his newfound talent on the outside, but still behave as the rest of the family does when he is at home.)

The concept of measuring a family's restrictedness allows for a certain kind of typology which is partially, briefly presented below.

A. SEVERE RESTRICTEDNESS

Severe restrictedness would include a rule against changing rules; hence, virtually any new contingency must be treated in the same new way. This is exemplified by the man who did not have fifteen years experience on his job, but one year's experience fifteen times. There would be two extremes of the severely restricted family on a continuum: the "chaotic family" and the "quiet family". The chaotic family has a rule that they will not obey rules and are restricted in that they, in effect, have to be against everything. The quiet family is the one who can only exchange very limited behaviors, rather than run the risk of any behavior being taken as a relationship message.

B. MODERATE RESTRICTEDNESS

In this category of families only certain areas of relationship rules and norms cannot be altered. For example, mother and father have to be perfect and always respected, but what constitutes acceptable behavior for acknowledging parental infallibility can fluctuate. For example:

Son: "I just went out and got a job".
Father: "I felt for a long time that you should be working".
Son: "You're right".

Thus the rule is bypassed and observed at the same time. When this kind of behavior is carried out to perfection, it is called diplomacy.

C. MILD RESTRICTEDNESS

This is a class of families in which it is assumed that rules which are to everyone's benefit in the family will be observed, but the individual is still left with a wide range of behavior in which he may engage. There are two types of families, at least, under this category: (*a*) the democratic family, and (*b*) the collaborative family. In the democratic family they may not relate in any particularly close way, but they do protect each other's individuality. The collaborative family interacts a great deal and enjoys exchanging behaviors because the exchanges add something. Almost invariably they will have humor, arguments, sarcasm and spontaneous expressions of enthusiasm.

## Summary

He who would define human behavior in such a way as to organize a diagnostic nosology must penetrate the enigmas swaddled in onion skins which fold and open in varying contexts. In other words, it is more apparent than in a group of patients we now loosely label schizophrenic.

It is suggested in this paper that monadic labels are old fashioned, indeed, damaging to therapeutic efforts and understanding, and that human interactional patterns offer a richer field of diagnostic exploration because they always take into account context.

One aspect of interaction is the process of restrictiveness and the resultant restricted behavior on the part of him who is responding to the restrictiveness. This is quite observable in certain families, particularly between the parents who have formed a coalition in order to invoke restrictiveness against certain behaviors of one of the children. Two such families in which this is most obvious are the schizophrenic and the families of the ulcerative colitis child. A beginning classification of these concepts is offered and loosely related to individual nosological terms currently en vogue.

It is suggested that the individual can be restricted in a variety of ways but especially through the use of relationship messages which are tied to content messages and through the use of disapproval, withdrawal or other nonaffiliative behavior. The schizophrenic family corresponds more to the former while the ulcerative colitis patient utilizes the latter technique.

*Throughout the preceding papers, the concept of the* double bind *was repeatedly mentioned. This specific pattern of interaction was first proposed by the Bateson group in 1956,[1] and ever since a large amount of*

[1] Gregory Bateson, Don D. Jackson, Jay Haley, and John Weakland, "Toward a Theory of Schizophrenia," *Behavioral Science* 1:251–64 (1956). In 1961 the Frieda Fromm-Reichmann Award of the Academy of Psychoanalysis was given for this significant contribution to the understanding of schizophrenia.

work has been done to operationalize it.[2] In a paper written jointly by members of MRI and the Psychopathology and Neurology Service of the G. Aráoz Alfaro Hospital in Lanús (Buenos Aires Province), the reader will find a first taxonomy of the elements of a double bind, based on clinical examples and showing that in spite its complexity some basic ingredients of this paradoxical pattern can be identified in families with a schizophrenic member.

# TRANSACTIONAL DISQUALIFICATION:
# RESEARCH ON THE DOUBLE BIND

Carlos E. Sluzki, M.D., Buenos Aires;
Janet Beavin, A.B., Palo Alto, Calif.; Alejandro Tarnopolsky, M.D.;
and Eliseo Verón, Ph.D., Buenos Aires

This is a report on some theoretical and technical contributions to the investigation of the double bind; they are the product of an ongoing research project on communication in the families of schizophrenic patients. The purposes of the present paper are to describe a researchable elaboration of the double bind theory, specifying the minimum level of complexity deemed necessary for such a communicational study and suggesting a method of breaking the data into units which are neither meaninglessly isolated nor too complex to be handled. Having proposed disqualification as an operational component of the overall double bind pattern, we will

Originally published in *Archives of General Psychiatry* 16:494–504 (1967). Copyright 1967, American Medical Association. Reprinted with permission.

This research was conducted at the Psychopathology and Neurology Service of Prof. G. Aráoz Hospital, Lanús, Buenos Aires Province, where it was supported by a grant from the Foundations Fund for Research in Psychiatry, administered by the Pan American Health Organization (World Health Organization).

[2] The literature on the double bind is by now extensive. One of the most recent and comprehensive publications is *Double Bind: The Foundation of the Communicational Approach to the Family,* ed. by Carlos E. Sluzki and Donald C. Ransom (New York: Grune & Stratton, 1976). Another important contribution was published recently by the Istituto per lo Studio della Famiglia in Milan (Mara Selvini Palazzoli, Luigi Boscolo, Gian Franco Cecchin, and Giuliana Prata), *Paradosso e Controparadosso* (Milan: Feltrinelli, 1975).

identify, define, and illustrate some varieties of what will be called transactional disqualification and emphasize another equally essential component, the response of the "victim."

## The Double Bind Hypothesis

In essence, we will describe disqualification as one, but definitely not the only, type of double bind. The double bind, then, is considered a class of phenomena and disqualification one of its observable forms.

To begin at the most general level, we concur with the growing number of investigators who are examining patterns of communication not only of the schizophrenic patient but of his family group as well, with the assumption that such detailed analysis will yield clues to the nature and context of schizophrenic behavior. One such pattern of communication was described by Bateson, Jackson, Haley, and Weakland as the *double bind*.[1] We consider the double bind, in its communicative aspects, as a generic form of *paradoxical injunction*[2] delivered in a vital ongoing relationship. That is, it describes the outline of a communication pattern which is composed of a series of requisite elements the specifics of which (content, unit, mode, participants, etc) may vary with different concrete types of double binds. For instance, the double bind may refer to a wide variety of content areas, and may also range from specific isolated incidents (the classic example being the mother who says coldly to her child, "Come here, dear") to macroscopic life situations (for example, Lu's description of dependency-achievement dilemma of some schizophrenic patients;[3] also, Weakland and Jackson's analysis of the situational antecedents of a schizophrenic episode[4]).

Before specifying the particular double bind on which this research has focused, some review and comments on the general pattern should be made. The distinctive characteristics of the double bind are described by the authors as the following: (1) two or more persons; (2) repeated experience; (3) a primary negative injunction; (4) a secondary injunction conflicting with the first at a more abstract level, and like the first enforced by punishments or signals which threaten survival; (5) a tertiary negative injunction prohibiting the victim from escaping from the field; (6) finally, the complete set of ingredients is no longer necessary when the victim has learned to perceive his universe in double bind patterns.[1 (pp253-254)]

For (1) we specify family members; further, assumptions about the intense nature of parent-child relations will influence our evaluation of other elements of the pattern.

Repeated experience (2) cannot be readily proven or directly demonstrated. High frequency may be observed in a given time sample, but this does not in itself prove that the experience is habitual. However, if *both* the incongruent messages (3) and (4) (see below) *and* a consistent type of response to these messages are observed in the time sample, it is more reasonable to conclude that the pattern has been learned through repeated experience. That is, if we observe $x$ and then $y$ (more than any other responses to $x$), we can assume more certainly that these two were linked in prior repeated experience. It is important to note here a point which will recur in this paper: the *response* of the receiver to a "binding" message is as important as such a message itself.

The issue of whether the "primary injunction" (3) need be specifically a negative one (having the form "do not . . .") appears to be only a matter of emphasis. The paradigm used in the original definition is ". . . either of two forms: (*a*) '*Do not* do so and so, or I will punish you,' (*b*) '*If you do not* do so and so, I will punish you' "[1](p253) (italics ours). Since any injunction has, implicitly or explicitly, one of these negative forms, this point can be phrased more simply as *any* injunction enforced by punishment or threats.

To avoid the sticky problem of a hierarchy of levels (4), "more abstract" can be understood here to mean simply "different" levels. At present, criteria for a fixed hierarchical classification of the levels of communication are arbitrary ones; this does not, however, deny the existence and relevance of the multiplicity of levels in human communication. At any rate, the "secondary injunction" must be at some specified *different level* from the first-mentioned (3).

The tertiary negative injunction prohibiting the victim from leaving the field (5) is, at the author's own suggestion, implicit in a relationship of survival value and need not be manifestly invoked each time a double bind occurs. Parenthetically, such a message may itself be a powerful double bind. As Weakland has pointed out:

> When dependency is inherent in the situation (as with childhood and illness), this point (5) is obvious. More complex, however, are the important situations where dependency (or effective belief in it) is fostered by other messages of total double-bind communication to a degree far beyond the psysical or emotional "realities" of the person's current life situation.[5](p376)

That is, for example, the parent may indicate to the child in a variety of ways that he (the child) is not adult, is incapable of independent decisions, needs the parent, cannot see things "right," etc. In certain settings (eg, where the parent also demands independent behavior, or where the "child" is an adult and there is no comment on such incongruency), these messages are not only themselves double binding, but set up a relationship within which other double binds can occur.

In such a relationship, or any relationship of survival value, the injunction in items (3) and (4) need not be overt either. That is, it is in the nature of familial relationships as viewed by contemporary genetic psychology that the child can ignore virtually nothing a parent communicates to him, in the sense that he must apprehend it as accurately as possible and respond to at least the minimal implicit injunction: This is how you should see so-and-so. In sum, we are suggesting that on the basis of (1), the vital relation of family members to each other, both punishment and survival are implicit for the child, and every message is an injunction of sorts. The final item (6) supports this argument indirectly. Then (3) and (4) become more simply *two mutually incongruent messages imposed at different levels.*

This complex set of ingredients was, in fact, reduced by the original authors to the following general characteristics of a situation (headings ours).

*Setting:* The individual is involved in an intense relationship; that is, a relationship in which he feels it is vitally important that he discriminate accurately what sort of message is being communicated so that he may respond appropriately.

*Messages Imposed:* The individual is caught in a situation in which the other person in the relationship is expressing two orders of message and one of these denies the other.

*Response:* The individual is unable to comment on the messages being expressed to correct his discrimination of what order of message to respond to, i.e. he cannot make a metacommunicative statement.[1, (p254)]

As already noted, the effect of the setting can quite reasonably be assumed in a family, though of course it can never be demonstrated. Given the family setting, then, our study of double bind patterns will focus on the two other characteristics: the occurrence of mutually incongruent messages of a specified type, and the study of responses to these messages. It is important to include here not only the incongruent message of the binder, but also *the response of the recipient of the bind.* Hereafter, agreeing with Weakland,[5] the original term "victim" will be avoided because its passive connotation implicitly places his response outside the total pattern. The double bind requires a transactional perspective for its understanding; if the incongruent messages are neutralized by the response, there is no bind.

The term *disqualification* has frequently been used to describe the first of these two characteristics (incongruent messages, or messages denying each other), and in this work, we have continued to refer to such incongruency as the relation of disqualification between messages or aspects of messages. However, the term has generally been used in regard to two different units of analysis: a single *message,* that is, each person's successive (usually alternating) communicative behaviors, the "package" of verbal utterances, tone, kinesics, etc, in an interactional situation; and a *transaction,* that is, the relation of one, usually contiguous, message, to another. The former would be self-disqualification, described by Haley[6] and Weakland and Fry[7]; the latter, disqualification of the other person, is mentioned by Haley[6] and also corresponds to the "mystification" described by Laing.[8] Our preferred focus for analysis of the interaction of families of schizophrenic patients is on the transaction, in which the interpersonal impact is clear.

## Transactional Disqualification

It is possible to disqualify virtually anything that occurs in communication;[6] further, the means by which this can be done seem similarly unlimited when one considers the multiple levels of expression constantly operating in an interpersonal situation. In order to be able to identify, definitively if not exhaustively, *what* is being disqualified *how,* we have limited our analysis to transcribed verbal interaction and focused on *incongruity in the response of one speaker in relation to the thesis (content) of the previous message of another.* The previous message, then, is seen as a frame for any response to it or, more accurately, as a part of a wider contextual frame which includes various other metacommunicative components.

In studying this relation, we assume that most messages have a potential for continuation—that is, they can be responded to—and that in many interpersonal situations, such as a group discussion of a common problem or question, there are strong contextual cues operating which ordain that, unless labeled otherwise, succeeding contiguous messages are responses to their predecessors. With a dyad this assumption is straightforward and virtually unquestionable; with a family group of more than two, things become more complex, because any individual statement can quite reasonably be seen as addressed to any or all other individuals, and it seems pedantic to insist on strict continuity. However, this can be handled in research by matching a message with the preceding message of *each* other person, not only the contiguous one, hoping thereby to do justice to the complexity which in fact faces the participants of such a discussion. That is, given message *a,* its content delimits a probabilistic repertory of types of succeeding messages. For instance, if *a* is a question, it is more probable that the next message will be an answer than another question, and much more than an unrelated statement. In each case the answer, the new question, or the unrelated statement is answer, question, or unrelated to message *a;* that is, it can be understood as occurring in a frame set by message *a,* the original question. (Of course, the same applies to any other sort of message *a.*) The relation between consecutive messages such as these can be inferred from the analysis of the content of both messages, and the existence of overt comments about such a relation (ie, metacommunicative clues). Without doubt, in colloquial interaction, overt metalinguistic clues are much less frequent than in formal interaction or communication in which the noise is greater or the channels more restricted. Many metacommunicative clues are implicit and are habitually inferred from the context in which the message is sent, which stresses again that the messages previous to the one under analysis must be considered an important part of such a context.

Thus the contextual aspect of message *b*—the fact that *a* preceded it— is unavoidable and, unless labeled otherwise, message *b* always implicitly contains it. For example, unless labeled otherwise, any message *b* which appears after question *a* is an answer to that question. *If metacommunicative indicators are absent and the content is incongruent with the context, or if these indicators are present but the content is incongruent with them, there is a disqualification of message* a *by message* b. *Message* b, then, has one meaning if analyzed out of context (by pure content aspects) and another meaning if studied within the interactional context, that is, the communicational sequence. It must be further stressed that each meaning is consistent within its own frame of reference; this is one of the main formal features of *paradox,* which in fact distinguishes it from simple contradiction: two propositions which are consistent within their own respective frameworks are incongruent with each other. From this comes the peculiarly irresolvable—but pragmatically present—yes-and-no, true-but-false quality of paradox.[9]

The immediate effect of a disqualification varies greatly with the context in which it occurs. It may provoke laughter or anger, or, most frequently, confusion, since the first speaker has no clear indication if the second agrees or disagrees with, scorns, resents, or already knew the content of *a;* he is left hanging in mid-air. Again, this is because either of both possible meanings—the contextual one and the one out of context— can be alleged by the sender to be the "real" one *without changing the text* of the disqualifying message.

Without further preface, several types of transactional (verbal) disqualification will illustrate the above, as well as the more complex permutations of each.

## Examples of Transactional Disqualification

The following examples are real ones, taken from transcripts of exploratory conjoint interviews of several families composed, in every case, of father, mother, adolescent schizophrenic son, and one sibling. The interviews were held at the Psychopathology Service of G. Aráoz Alfaro Hospital, Lanús, Province of Buenos Aires. The original analysis was made in Spanish, and the examples have been translated with considerable attention to both accuracy and clarity. As a marginal comment, it can be noted that at this (communicational) level of analysis the cultural differences between these and the schizophrenic American families described in the literature or observed by the authors seem to be remarkably small. The group could be globally characterized as schismatic.[10]

*Evasion—Change of Subject*

If $a$ is a statement which does not clearly end a topic of discussion, and $b$, the next statement, is in a new subject area but contains no labeling of this switch, then message $b$ disqualifies $a$, being incongruent in the fact that it is in content *not* a response to $a$, while in context it must be. It is not relevant whether or not $b$ makes sense in itself; it is the relation of $a$ to $b$ which determines the transactional disqualification.

Example I:

$a$ Son:   Well, then, I'll have to repeat again what I said. You, shall we say, started [in this interview]—of that I am sure—started to attack her first, that is, with nothing clarified, very hurried.

$b$ Mother: I love both of you, and I always try to make things at home work out better, but I can't manage it.

Example II:

$a$ Son:   When I talk to my sister, we get along, shall we say, as friends, but in the family, things are different, because something new always seems to appear, with these discussions and all these sort of. . . .

$b$ Mother: I don't want to speak all the time, doctor.

It is clear that the identification of evasion depends in large part on the definition of the subject area, with too broad or too narrow a definition resulting in no evasions or spurious ones, respectively. This definition, in turn, rests primarily on the situational context of the entire interaction. For the purpose of simplification, the examples given above are extreme— clearly evasive in their actual context and probably evasive in almost any context.

Besides the context/content incongruency, there may be other complexities in the evasion. For instance, it may be readily denied as a disqualification in several ways; if the observation is made that *b* ignored *a*, B (A and B refer, respectively, to the senders of the messages) may say "I didn't hear you," "I didn't know you wanted an answer," or may suggest that his change of subject is not really a change of subject because there is in fact an (unlabeled) relevance to *a*. The effect is to leave A without any clear indication of B's responses to *a*—no indication, in fact, that *a* existed at all.

*Sleight-of-Hand*

A change of subject is labeled as an answer. That is, as in evasion, *b* is in content a new subject, but additionally it is labeled as an answer to *a*. Such labels need not be literal ("I am answering you") but rather include, broadly, all overt *indicators of reception* of the first message.

Example III:

*a* Son:  Then, you say it is exactly the opposite of what I say.
*b* Father:  No, no, no, no, I say that you say . . . let . . . say whatever you you want, that's all.

Father's "No . . . I say . . ." indicates that he has heard and is answering (specifically, disagreeing with) the son's message; however, what he says cannot in fact be construed as an answer, because he has switched to what the son *can say* rather than what he (the father) *did say*.

Example IV:

*a* Daughter:  We have always gotten along well.
*b* Mother:  Yes, I've always loved you . . . in the same way.

Again, "Yes" indicates an answer, but the content is now on the new issue of love, which is treated as similar to the issue of getting along. Note that this transaction is quite similar to Example I, which is an evasion because *b* was not overtly labeled as an answer, nor did it contain any signs that the previous message had been received. In sleight-of-hand, then, the content is incongruent with not only the context, but the explicit metacommunicational label.

Example V:

Mother:     [to daughter] I've noticed lately that you don't want your girl friends to be in contact with Daniel; I've seen it lately.
*a* Daughter:    But—why, Mama?
*b* Mother:    Well, *I* don't know why.

The daughter's question obviously meant "What makes you say that?" Her mother answers as if the question had been "What are my motivations for doing that?—which assumes that the daughter had not only stipulated that "that" (not wanting her friends to see her brother) was true, but had moreover expected her mother to be more expert on her own motivations than she herself is.

Example VI:

*a* Mother:    The girl's [her daughter's] character is more like her father's.
*b* Father:    Well, there she's [his wife is] right. The characters of mother and daughter are different.

Mother simply said that their daughter resembles her father, asserting only by implication any comparatively lesser resemblance to her own character. Father, as if answering, agrees to a (qualitative) *difference* between mother and daughter. Within the general format described as sleight-of-hand, some specific subtypes involving changes of levels within subjects can be described:

*Literalization* This is a switch from the obvious content of *a* to the literal level in *b*, without any framing or labeling of the change; *b*, then, is not an appropriate response to *a*.

Example VII:

*a* Son:    You treat me like a child.
*b* Mother:    But you are my child.

The son clearly meant that he was now an adolescent and not a small child—in the sense of relative age; the mother refers to his literal, biological status as her child.

*Specifications.*—There is a specific response to a general theme.

Example VIII:

*a* Daughter:   We went swimming together all last summer.
*b* Mother:     Not the last week, you didn't.

If, however, the issue at hand is the universality of a phenomenon—all or none, always or never—then a specific counterexample, even unlabeled, is an appropriate form of disagreement, and *not* a disqualification.

Example IX:

*a* Father:     I never yell.
*b* Daughter:   You're yelling now.

Note that specification differs from literalization in that the levels involved are general→specific and metaphorical→literal, respectively.

*Status Disqualification*

The subject is changed from content to speaker (either A or B), with the added invocation of (relative) status; that is, *b* implies that *a* (the message) is not valid either because of A (the person) or because of B's superior knowledge, right, etc. Of course, if the subject of *a* involves such characteristics of either A or B (the persons), then there is no change of subject and no disqualification of this type.

Example X:

Mother:       The brother [her son], as he is alone and he was somehow con-
              fused, he wants to be with the sister, and the sister, to tell the
              truth, wanted to have her share of life . . . but. . . .
*a* Daughter:  No, it is not that I want to have "my share of life". . . .
*b* Mother:    [interrupting] She doesn't realize it because she's too little. She
              doesn't see it, but she loves her brother.

Example XI:

Mother:       I have seen, lately, that's my impression, I have observed, that
              she doesn't mix very well with Daniel.
*a* Daughter:  Why not, Mama?
*b* Mother:    Well, a mother knows. . . .

Status disqualifications, then, involve more than the basic change of subject. First, the subject is changed in a specifically personal direction with an implicit, rather ambiguous and unanswerable derogatory effect. Further, this effect is not only immediate but *prospective,* in that an undefinable number of A's future statements may be seen in the context of the same disqualification. The individual need not even have spoken yet for this prospective effect to have been established.

Example XII:

Interviewer: I've heard your [the parents'] opinions, but I would like to hear further the opinion of the youngsters . . .
Mother: [interrupting] They are kids, doctor.
Interviewer: [interrupting] . . . in regard to . . .
Mother: [interrupting] They are kids, doctor, they can't discern the past.

*Redundant Question*

Message *a* is a declarative statement; *b* is a question on the same level as *a* (not a metacomment, such as "how," "why," etc), repeating at least part of what has been previously said in *a*. This implies doubt or disagreement without openly stating it.

Example XIII:

*a* Son: I get along well with everybody.
*b* Father: Well with everybody, Peter?

The father could label his question, not as a disagreement, but as a desire for more information, though its ambiguity and echoing quality imply the former.

A good example of the possible double meaning of the disqualifying message can be given by transcribing the continuation of this interaction:

Son: Of course.
Daughter: Why not? We may have a quarrel or two, but. . . .
Son: But, generally no.
Father: Well, it seems clear that between the two of them there might be some occasional small thing, but that's all.

One of the two meanings of the disqualification ("Well with everybody?" meaning "I don't believe it") is tackled by the daughter's comment, which stresses this aspect ("Why not?"). The other meaning is followed by the father, whose last statement implies the other, "I was just asking," line.

*Summary of Disqualification Material*

The above do not cover all the ways in which, even within the limited area of transactional verbal material, disqualification can occur. Some possibilities can be imagined which were not yet observed; for instance, there might be a counterpart to specialization (disqualification by over-generalization) or to literalization (an inappropriate switch to metaphor). (Here we are referring to the communication of the "normal" family members; unlabeled metaphor is, of course, a common form of disqualification in schizophrenic speech.) Other observed patterns are clearly disqualifying, but cannot be conceptualized as formally as those described; therefore they remain idiosyncratic and impressionistic, however valid.

Our focus, as specified earlier, is the relation of the content of one message to that of the previous message of another speaker. In examining this relation, two parameters have been used: the *continuity* between contents of messages and the *indication of reception* of a message. Continuity refers to one meaning, subject, area, or level being pursued in successive messages. Indicators of reception are implicit or explicit cues (metacommunications) that the previous message was received; more operationally stated, they are elements of a message which refer to the existence of a previous message from another person. In family study, rather wide latitude should probably be given to the definition of such cues, especially in view of the informality of the interaction and the shared history of a family, whose communication would therefore not reasonably contain the same overt, careful labeling as that of strangers in a formal relationship. Within this broad area, then, are included not only overt metalinguistic comments ("I heard you . . ." or "That's a point . . ."), but also reconstructed indicators of reception such as "Yeah," "Well," or some clear incorporation of $a$'s content into $b$.

It is by crossing these two dichotomous parameters that the definition of transactional disqualification is obtained: *discontinuity of content without (accurate) indication of reception.* (The three other classes which result from combining both dichotomous variables would refer to different types of nondisqualifying transactions: continuity with or without indications of reception [which may be redundant in the case of continuity], and discontinuity with indication of reception [eg, labeled changes of subject, or the contextually appropriate specification mentioned in Example IX]). It is necessary to specify "accurate" reception indication because, as was seen in the examples above, message $a$ frequently did not seem to be received accurately, so the existent indicator of reception was inappropriate. Or, in a formulation less dependent on inference, $b$ did not appear a response to $a$ as sent. Reviewing the different types of disqualification in this light, the following emerges.

Evasion is the straightforward case of discontinuity of content with no indication of reception (so far as $b$ indicates, $a$ may not have occurred).

Sleight-of-hand involves discontinuity of content with inappropriate indication of reception—accurate reception is belied by the incongruency of contents. In the cases of literalization and specification, there is discontinuity in the *level* of the subject (metaphorical-literal, general-specific); with or without overt signals of reception, there is an indicated response to *a*, but not as sent.

Status disqualification is discontinuity (from content to speaker) with unclear or inaccurate indication of reception of *a;* that is, *b* may indicate that there was a message *a*, but not as sent. (As noted, there is the added element of relative status.)

Redundant questions are a peculiar case since there is, by definition, not only continuity but repetition of content—in question form; however, this question (*b*) is one which could best be answered by *a*, *which preceded it*, so it implies at once that *a* did and did not occur, and the continuity of content denies itself.

### Disqualification in Other Than the Verbal (Linguistic) Channel

As previously stated, we have analyzed primarily verbatim transcripts of family interviews, leaving aside the great amount of information conveyed by *other* channels than the verbal and by the *simultaneous presence,* in combination, of these different channels, verbal included. There are without doubt many types of transactional disqualifications that can only be detected and described through a complex multiple-channel analysis (Scheflen's observations on "modality splitting"[11]). Even if these types will not be discussed herein, it is worthwhile mentioning, as an example, *incongruency between channels;* that is, message *b* might answer *a* in content while another aspect of *b*, say, B's facial expression, incongruently indicates lack of interest, disdain, or exasperation—expressions the meaning of which can be denied if a comment is made about them. In fact, some of the examples given by the authors of the double bind theory can be identified as this type.

Another type of disqualification which is difficult to establish in a verbatim analysis is the one created by *silence* after a statement which requires an answer. Silence, in the middle of a sequence, can present several possible meanings, with a considerable margin of ambiguity; "I did not hear you" or "I was thinking of an answer" are responses which can neutralize any eventual derogatory meaning attributed to the mute statement. But the fact that nonverbal clues can often replace, or at least qualify, verbal messages stresses the necessity for an analysis covering channels other than the verbal in order to establish this type of disqualification.

### Some Comments on Pathogenicity: Setting and Response

The issue of the specific pathogenicity of double binds is neither a new nor a settled one, and the position of the present research should be made clear in this regard.

Disqualification is a fairly common and even convenient communicational maneuver which occurs not only in schizophrenic pathological groups, but in normal ones as well. It is, in fact, intimately related to play, fantasy,[12-13] psychotherapy,[13,14] and humor,[15] and hence has no pathological power per se. There is no such thing as a "more harmful" (ie, pathogenic) or "more benign" disqualification, since the pathogenicity does not rest in the disqualification itself as an isolated communicational event, but in the learned pattern of how to behave in such circumstances and the reinforcing effect of each repetition of the whole set. This brings us again to the distinction made at the outset between the entire double bind pattern—setting, messages imposed, and response—and the second of these elements, which we have here called disqualification. The incongruent messages are clearly empirically crucial; they cue the observer, drawing attention to a particular communicational sequence. But they are not isolated, linearly causal traumatic events; *the double bind is a pattern of interaction between two or more persons.*

This pattern of interaction has a certain general context or setting, here assumed to be the nuclear family; possibly certain areas of behavior within the family are more important than others, so that the concept of setting should be even more narrow than all of family interaction. The influence of the setting can be safely assumed in general, though it is difficult to assess exactly.

The other element, response to the incongruent messages, is, however, not only readily observable but directly related to the study of the nature and context of schizophrenic communication. The approach we take is to consider the possible responses to a disqualifying message and then construct a hypothetical repertory of alternative responses to such communicative events. This is done on the assumption that the selection of a particular response is not a random process, but the result of a deutero-learning process, in the sense that an individual will tend to respond in a way which has proven most successful for him in coping with the situation.

There are four classes of possible responses to a disqualifying message: explicit comment, withdrawal, acceptance, and counterdisqualification. According to the general model, the first two would avoid or offset the double bind.

*Comment*

This would be any form of request for clarification of or explicit comment on the incongruency in the messages imposed.

Example XIV (an extension of Example IV):

Daughter:  We have always gotten along well.
Mother:    Yes, I've always loved you . . . in the same way.
Daughter:  [overlapping] Well, that may be. I loved you and I always love you, so I don't see what that has to do with the whole matter.

The sleight-of-hand is countered by the comment of the daughter on both its valid *and* its irrelevance to the present sequence. When such meta-communicative statements are made, and made to stick, there is no bind.

*Withdrawal*

This need not be physical, that is, literally abandoning the field to some degree. Silence, refusal to interact further, or even cancelling the interaction and starting all over again might also evade the bind. An example of this type of response can be found in speech No. 12 of Example XV below, in which the son does not comment explicitly on the incongruency of the father's previous sleight-of-hand disqualification, but still seems to get around it by not accepting it and withdrawing doggedly to his original point.

In general, however, it might be well to question how effective withdrawal can ultimately be. The nature of the relationship which is the setting for the interaction proscribes withdrawal past a certain degree: the child cannot withdraw more than temporarily or partially. We suspect that if withdrawal is extreme or continued, it must be effected in such a way as to deny that it is occurring; the most obvious form would be a counter disqualification, or symptomatic behavior.

*Acceptance*

Another way of responding to the disqualification is to choose one level of the disqualifying message, that is, one of the two or more possible meanings, and to respond only to that as if it were the right one, leaving the other one(s) without explicit recognition. This ordinarily means to accept the disqualifier's terms in the redefinition of the situation, without acknowledging that this change has taken place.

This is well illustrated by the last speech (No. 15) in the following larger sequence, in which Examples I and III occurred.

Example XV:

| | |
|---|---|
| 1 Mother: | That's why we come here, to elucidate our situation without any bad intention at all, isn't that right? |
| 2 Son: | Mama, if—if she (the sister) defends herself, you are attacking; you must know that. You started to attack first. |
| 3 Mother: | Well, she—I don't know why she is defending herself because I am not saying anything that is reproachable. |
| 4 Son: | But, listen—I want to say, basically, that you started to attack first. |
| 5 Mother: | I don't attack anybody. We are here precisely to clarify a lot of things. |
| 6 Father: | Well, we are talking here, Daniel, that's all . . . |
| 7 Son: | (totally overlapping) Of course. |
| 8 Father: | . . . to clarify things, that's all, Danny. |
| 9 Mother: | (totally overlapping) It's for the good of everybody, and your own. |
| 10 Son: | Then you (the father) say it is exactly the opposite of what I say |
| 11 Father: | No, no, no, no. I say that you say . . . let . . . say whatever you want, that's all. |
| 12 Son: | Well, then, I'll have to repeat again what I said. You (the mother) shall we say, started—of that I am sure—started to attack her first, that is, with nothing clarified, very hurried. |
| 13 Mother: | I love both of you, and I always try to make things at home work out better, but I can't manage it. |
| 14 Interviewer: | (to son, who is mumbling something) Yes? |
| 15 Son: | No, nothing, I was commenting about Mama, yes, she's right. |

In this superficially benign, or at worst confused, conversation, an extraordinary amount of disqualification and double binding occurs. The mother has made some comments about the daughter which the son (the identified patient) insists are critical and attacking. The mother (1) emphasizes her benevolent intentions, and the son (2) restates his defense (though his formulation is at the beginning bizarre, because the causal chain is reversed). Mother (3) denies this, and the son (4) repeats it. Mother (5) denies again, and the father (6), in coalition with her, disqualifies the son by switching to the literal level. Son accepts the literalization of the father, thereby completing the bind. Another disqualifying aspect of the father's continuing statement (8) is his switch to the diminutive "Danny," a status disqualification which stresses that he is "just a kid." Mother (9) maintains the coalition with the father, framing the situation in terms of good or ill will and referring to the sickness of the son (and perhaps his responsibility for everyone else's sacrifice). Son (10) tries to clarify, if only just what people are saying, and his father (11) again disqualifies him by a totally tangential answer (a sleight-of-hand disqualification), without confirming or denying the statement of the son. The son (12) leaves that, retrenches, and restates his original thesis in a real effort to get it across. The mother (13) disqualifies with an evasion which has several other facets as well: "I do my best for you," "I do it for love," and "I am only human." (This type of response is what the original double bind paper described as a punishment more devastating than withdrawal of love or expression of hate or anger: "the kind of abandonment that results from the parent's expression of extreme helplessness"[1 (p253)].) Son (15) resigns his own position and completes the bind by accepting her definition of the situation. It should be noted that this choice, however, involves only the "illusion of alternatives":[4] both levels are valid per se, but when they are presented as alternatives which deny each other they form a paradox in which, in contrast to simple contradiction, either alternative is wrong.[9]

*Counterdisqualification*

A response of great significance for our study is that of another disqualification, especially in the form of symptomatic behavior. If one must respond and yet there is no correct response, then a communication which denies that it is a communication—a self-disqualification or disqualification of the other—is a possible, even an appropriate, response. This does not reinstate the original subject or level of discussion, but only increases the confusion about this subject in a bizarre succession of redefinitions. This possibility further stresses the necessity to avoid formulations such as binder and victim, since the disqualified and the disqualifier can change positions, and the latter is quite caught in his own trap.

Example XVI:

1 Son: (mumbles something unintelligible)
2 Interviewer: Louder, Daniel, louder.
3 Son: And I was saying that she (the mother) attacked me and that I won't take, that's all.

4 Interviewer:   Well, "that I won't take"—what does that mean?
5 Mother:        (overlapping) I am not attacking, we are, we are clarifying family matters, ah, the doctor invites us to speak. . . .
6 Father:        Don't think, not for a moment, Daniel, that they are attacks or counter-attacks, they are simply clarifications. Mama thinks that she couldn't get along well lately. She says it, but it is not an attack.
7 Mother:        With some . . .
8 Son:           (overlapping) *But the doctor, the doctor forced me speak loudly, Papa, what are you going to do?*
9 Father:        What?
10 Son:          *The doctor forced me to speak loudly, what are you going to do?*
11 Father:       (overlapping) And you do right. Everything you want to say, you have to say.
12 Son:          *Things spoken softly are not, not, not very detail* (sic).

In speeches 8, 10, and 12, the patient counterdisqualifies the father (and, implicitly, the mother) with frankly schizophrenic communication. The sequence which leads up to this is worthy of close attention. In an obfuscation of "attacking," "clarifying," and—in the most mechanical sense— "speaking," the son is disqualified with literalization by both Mother (5) and Father (6) in succession. The mother's literality ("the doctor invites us to speak") is also oddly impersonal and involuntary. Father makes a pacific though illogical distinction ("she says it, but . . ."). Further, the father begins the first of two remarkable prescriptions of schizophrenic thinking. In the first (6), he strongly states, "Do not think X," and compounds this with an "explanation" of what it is accurate to think, but which is, in fact, almost impossible to follow. (For instance, the mother had not said, even earlier, what she is paraphrased as having said.) The patient's self-justification (8 and 10) clearly incorporates the interviewer's previous instructions to speak louder (2)* and distorts them by literalization in the same way his father had confused speaking and attacking. The difference between his statement and the "only speaking" theme of both parents is not great. Furthermore, this statement of the son's echoes in exaggerated form the mother's implicit claim (5) that her statements are impersonal and involuntary: "the doctor invites us to speak" becomes "the doctor forced me to speak loudly." Thus the patient has counter-

---

* Although these instructions are in one sense purely mechanical, they convey the interviewer's opinion that the patient should speak up and be heard. Thus the patient does not have the option to withdraw temporarily into mumbling or silence, since the interviewer has, in effect, closed that possibility.

disqualified both parents in a direct, although condensed, imitation of the formal characteristics of their own disqualification. The father (11) apparently accepts the son's peculiar redefinition of the issue; however, the "you" in the son's question was not, as one might have expected, general (ie, meaning "what can one do?"), but rather the second-person familiar, referring to the father personally. So the father's answer is a sleight-of-hand in which the "you" is turned back to the son, as if he had asked "what can *I* do?" Further, having previously instructed the son not even to think certain things (6), he now adds, "Say whatever you want," or even, "You *must* say what you want to say." Not to think, "not for a moment," what one has already said one thinks, but to have to say whatever one wants to say—these instructions can only be followed by denying one's thoughts and the validity of what one says, and in his "disorganized" response (12), the patient conveys that he is not thinking and that he is not really saying anything, either.

Finally, if one would follow systematically the implications of such a theory, the test for the occurrence of the bind pattern must be the *response to the response.* That is, can clarification be made? Is it encouraged, supported, or even permitted? Is withdrawal blocked? If one level is accepted and followed, is this reinforced by the other? Or if counterdisqualification, especially that corresponding to schizophrenic behavior, occurs, is this tolerated? In examples such as that just given it seems almost prescribed or encouraged, and a pathological circle is formed. In studying these responses, one can reasonably reconstruct the general pattern of this type of interaction and infer therefrom the deutero-learning aspects[1] which have the greatest importance for pathogenic hypotheses.

### Final Comment

As indicated before, the stress in this paper, and in our research generally, is on the search for patterns of interaction. We are consistently finding, in families with a schizophrenic member, disqualifications followed by special types of sequences, such as the ones described, which tend to consolidate the bind and hence reinforce idiosyncratic modes of interaction. In this process, which implies a whole style of relation with the world and in which certain stimuli are systematically denied, certain meanings are systematically repressed, lack of recognition is reinforced and rewarded, and clarification is punished—in this, we concur in believing, might rest the pathogenesis of schizophrenia.

## REFERENCES

1. BATESON, G., et al: Toward a Theory of Schizophrenia, *Behav Sci* 1:251–264, 1956.
2. WATZLAWICK, P.: Paradoxical Predictions, *Psychiatry* 28:368–374, 1965.
3. LU, Y. C.: Contradictory Parental Expectations in Schizophrenia, *Arch Gen Psychiat* 6:219–234, 1962.
4. WEAKLAND, J., and JACKSON, D. D.: Patient and Therapist Observations on the Circumstances of a Schizophrenic Episode, *Arch Neurol Psychiat* 79:554–574, 1958.
5. WEAKLAND, J.: "The Double-Bind Hypothesis of Schizophrenia and Three-Party Interaction," in Jackson, D. D. (ed.): *The Etiology of Schizophrenia,* New York: Basic Books Inc., 1960.
6. HALEY, J.: The Family of the Schizophrenic: A Model System, *J Nerv Ment Dis* 129:357–374, 1959.
7. WEAKLAND, J., and FRY, W. F. JR.: Letters of Mothers of Schizophrenics, *Amer J Orthopsychiat* 32:604–623, 1962.
8. LAING, R. D.: "Mystification, Confusion and Conflict," in Boszormenyi-Nagy, I., and Framo, J. L., (eds.): *Intensive Family Therapy: Theoretical and Practical Aspects,* New York: Harper and Row, Publishers Inc., 1965, pp. 343–363.
9. WATZLAWICK, P.; BEAVIN, J.; and JACKSON, D. D.: *Pragmatics of Human Communications: A Study of Interactional Patterns, Pathologies and Paradoxes,* New York, W. W. Norton, 1967.
10. LIDZ, T., et al: "Schism and Skew in the Families of Schizophrenics," in Bell, N. W., and Vogel, E. F. (eds.): *A Modern Introduction to the Family,* Glencoe, Ill: Free Press of Glencoe, Inc., 1960, pp. 595–607.
11. SCHEFLEN, A. E.: "Stream and Structure of Communicational Behavior: Context Analysis of a Psychotherapy Session," *Behavioral Studies Monograph No. 1,* Philadelphia: Eastern Pennsylvania Psychiatric Institute, 1965.
12. BATESON, G.: A Theory of Play and Fantasy, *Psychiat Res Rep Amer Psychiat Assoc* 2:39–51, 1955.
13. HALEY, J.: Paradoxes in Play, Fantasy, and Psychotherapy, *Psychiat Res Rep Amer Psychiat Assoc* 2:52–58, 1955.
14. HALEY, J.: *Strategies of Psychotherapy,* New York: Grune & Stratton Inc., 1963.
15. FRY, W. F., JR.: *Sweet Madness: A Study of Humor,* Palo Alto, Calif: Pacific Books, 1963.

*Paradox has many faces. Not too long ago it was merely the delight or the despair of the logician. But ever since the advent of cybernetics, its impact and its disconcerting qualities have been felt in many areas of modern science, mostly because it casts doubts over the consistency and provability of classic scientific paradigms based on the idea of absolute or final truth. And, as we have seen in the foregoing, its occurrence in human communication may threaten the sanity of the communicants.*

*The simplest form of paradox is the famous statement, "I am lying." If it is true, then he who uttered it was lying, therefore it cannot be true. But if it is indeed a lie, then it is true precisely because it is a lie—and so forth ad infinitum. Although it is entirely possible to find self-definitions of this kind in human communication (and not just text books of logic), this is not the form of paradox most frequently encountered in clinical communications research. Rather, there the prototype is the demand "Be spontaneous!" in its many possible variations and guises.*

*The "Be spontaneous!"–paradox\* creates an untenable situation, since the demand contained in it makes impossible that which is demanded, i.e., spontaneous behavior. In 1970 Sluzki and Verón published a paper in which they undertook the important step of expanding the double-bind theory from its then almost exclusive concern with schizophrenic behavior to the study of the neuroses. What specific demands for spontaneous behavior, they asked themselves, may account for the development of hysteric, phobic and obsessive-compulsive symptoms? And they realized that, if this question can be answered, then the double bind theory has universal importance and double-binding in schizophrenia is only a special case.*

# THE DOUBLE BIND AS A UNIVERSAL
# PATHOGENIC SITUATION

*Carlos E. Sluzki, M.D., and Eliseo Verón, Ph.D.*

A few months ago the first author started the psychotherapeutic treatment of a university student who has a study problem: in spite of this man's positive motivation and his interest in studying, he is incapable

Originally published in *Family Process* 10:397–410 (1971), (translated by Paul Watzlawick). Reprinted with permission.

\* To the best of our knowledge, this term was first used by Ronald D. Laing.

of concentrated effort as soon as he sits down in front of a textbook. Otherwise he is a voracious reader, and his mental block interferes only with the reading of school books. He will sit before them for hours, his mind wandering, while making fruitless attempts to concentrate on the reading. Nobody forces him to study, although it should be mentioned that in his family high value is placed on academic achievement and both his parents are university graduates.

Here, then, is a person who wants to study but cannot. In one of the sessions he mentions, as an aside, that he also has a problem with brushing his teeth. He knows that he should but uses all sorts of subterfuges to avoid brushing them; he simply does not like the idea but does not know why. What he typically does is to delay brushing his teeth until it is time to leave the house, and then he would be late if he started brushing them. He realizes that his behavior amounts to a trick, and he himself calls it irrational. He mentions that as a child he had painfully irritated gums and therefore avoided brushing his teeth whenever possible, although both his parents stressed the necessity and importance of having clean teeth. He goes on to say that the way his parents tried to give special weight to their demands regarding tooth brushing, as well as many other of his activities, was to argue that to do all this *on his own initiative* would be clear proof of his being "grown up," i.e., independent. In his childhood the patient soon began to resort to little tricks, such as moistening the toothbrush and displacing the tooth paste on the shelf, to make believe that he had brushed his teeth, and this, to his great surprise and self-admiration, fooled the adults. He reports that hitting upon this deception was a fascinating experience for him. If we compare this recollection with the problem he now has brushing his teeth, we find that the two phenomena are structurally identical, although there is one difference: nowadays the injunction comes from within. Furthermore, it can be seen that the two phenomena are structurally identical with the complaint that brought him into therapy, i.e., his study problem. In both his present problems, that is, the trivial one with his toothbrushing and the very upsetting one related to his studying, the injunctions come from within the subject himself but are treated as if they originated from some outside authority that cannot be directly flouted, but can very well be fooled. This fooling is achieved by a sort of "I want to, but cannot" premise by means of which he, on the one hand, cannot be accused of not complying with the injunction but, on the other hand, need not comply with it. What, then, were the original messages given by his parents as they trained him to brush his teeth? First of all, "You must brush your teeth," and secondly, "To want to brush your teeth is an adult attitude," and, therefore, independent and commendable. These two messages, however amount to the paradox, "Do exactly as we say, but on your own initiative," and could be elaborated into, "If you do not obey, we shall be angry with you, but if you obey only because we are telling you, we shall also be angry, because you should be independent" (that is, to *want* to do whatever one *should* do of one's own will). This injunction creates an untenable situation, because it demands that an external source be confused with an internal one. But, on the other hand, it is also the almost ubiquitous model for the internalization of social rules. Its universal occurrence in no way alleviates its paradoxical nature. How can it be counteracted? Perhaps by dealing with its external aspect only? But with regard to this, the patient's childhood world contained yet another rule: any opposition to the parents was considered an act of badness, which produced annoyance and charges of disaffection, another not exactly infrequent complication. Thus, the explicit injunction, "You must mind us," was reinforced for this patient by assigning to any act of rebellion an intensely negative meaning. So there is no exit: to mind is a good thing, because it satisfies the demand for obedience, but it is bad because it does not comply with the demand for independence; while not minding, on the other hand, implies independence, which in itself is good, but violates the injunction to be obedient. And finally, the injunction, "You must do this of your own will," wedged in as it is between the other injunctions, eventually leads to the internalization of not only the source of these injunctions, but of the whole complex of binds inherent in the paradox. To want to brush one's teeth but "to have no time" and to want to study but "to be unable to" thus becomes the only legitimate way out of the impasse between minding and not minding, or of satisfying both the premises of obedience and independence.

There is every reason to assume that this pattern must have repeated itself throughout the patient's early learning experiences and that it has led him to see a whole range of situations as determined by the same contradictory injunctions and, therefore, as a member of the class of paradoxical situations produced by his family milieu.

What are the essential ingredients of this phenomenon? They are its occurrence within a framework of relationships with significant others; the need to discriminate correctly (given the importance of the dependence-independence conflict); the impossibility of leaving the field (given the dependency inherent in childhood); the impossibility of asking for clarifications (due to the vicious-circle nature of the paradox involved, and perhaps to the label of "rebellion" given to such a request for clarification); and, finally, a message that contains an injunction regarding a concrete fact and a second injunction regarding this class of facts, that contradicts the first. But what we have just presented is nothing but a list of the essential components of a *double bind,* the core element of the communicational theory of schizophrenia.

Expanding on this theoretical model we want to turn next to a brief presentation of a body of hypotheses we derived from a systematic, empirical study of the speech patterns of neurotic patients. This approach leads to an appreciation of the double bind model as a universal (and not only schizophrenia-specific) theory of pathogenesis.

We adopted the view that neurosis is "a technique (or a system of techniques) for the manipulation of meaning transmitted in interpersonal situations" (7). This means that the neurotic processes information according to a body of codification rules, that is, of "norms for the attribution of meaning to the objects in the 'real world' (including the subject himself as well as his behaviors), and at the same time of norms which define the relations between these meanings" (7). We further assumed that an understanding of the rules of interaction, which tell us something about the subject's "world view," will also permit us to make inferences about the learning contexts that produced these rules in the first place.

As we developed these genetic hypotheses, which may be considered an attempt to formulate a communicational theory of the neuroses, we based ourselves on Ronald Fairbairn's (4) postulates about the mental development of the child. According to this author, the child passes through the following three evolutional stages: (1) *infantile dependence,* marked by a relative lack of differentiation between the self and the non-self and a preponderance of the incorporation or the "taking" of objects; (2) *transition;* and (3) *mature dependency,* characterized by "relations between two independent beings who are completely differentiated" and by a predominance of "giving" in object relations.

The transitional stage ushers in the core dilemma of all mental development: *dependence versus independence.* This conflict between leaving the security of close object relations in favor of the inevitable uncertainty of independence is part and parcel of the process of socialization: parents tend to stimulate the impulse towards independence and to neutralize the needs for dependency. This process is a complex one, as the parents will have to redefine to their child almost daily, avoiding any overlap of boundaries, the respective areas of dependency (where action, except within a frame of compliance, is bad), of independence (where action based on compliance is bad), and a third, "experimental" one (which could be called one of "supervised experience in independence"). Obviously, to define these areas operationally will be all the more difficult for the parents if they themselves are having trouble in a specific area. Ultimately, however, these major or minor difficulties have their common denominator in the parents' own personality styles, which by themselves make certain modes of socialization more probable than others.

This is how the universal conflict between dependence and independence acquires specificity in each separate instance: whatever learning model predominates in a given family will determine the nature of the child's adaptation.

In the first stages of the learning process the search for "right" responses leads the child to a categorization of behaviors, that is, to a rudimentary codification system of what is good or bad, effective or ineffective. This codification will evolve and expand to the extent that the responses turn out to be well adapted to the learner's life situation and capabilities and will eventually become the basis for his understanding of the world as a whole.

It will be seen that our model takes into account an essential and well-documented feature of any learning process, namely the fact that, in any concrete situation in which learning occurs, there also takes place a transmission of the rules implicit to learning itself. We are referring here to the phenomena of acquiring a predisposition (a learning-set) or of what Bateson has called deutero-learning, i.e., learning to learn (2).[1] We want to stress that "learning to learn" is of a higher logical level than "learning" and that it, therefore, takes place on the level of meta-messages, which are about structures or *classes* of situations or messages of a given kind.

Applying this notion to what we said previously, it appears that learning typical of the transitional period may not only be beset by conflict on the content level (i.e., the basic problem inherent in the dependence-independence dilemma), but also by conflicts on the next higher (the

---

[1] *Predisposition,* a term originally used in experimental learning psychology, refers to the result of a subject's repeated exposure to a given learning situation, so that his trial and error behavior on any subsequent exposure to situations of the same type is drastically reduced. This is what Bateson (2, 1) calls *deutero-learning.* There are, then, two separate levels of information-processing involved: one that has to do with information about the contents of the *particular situation* and the other, on a higher logical level, with information about the type of task or situation.

It should be remembered what happens when, once a predisposition is established, the experimenter changes the nature of the learning situation so that it now contradicts the predisposition. In Bateson's terms this is the "experimental neurosis" produced by Pavlovian experiments. If these two separate levels of learning—the one related to the content, and the other to the pattern or structure responsible for the predisposition—did not exist, the particular contradiction that gives rise to the experimental neurosis could not exist either.

deutero-learning) level. This means that contradictions and incongruencies may arise from the way the parents define the learning situation. They derive in all likelihood from the parents' own conflicts and manifest themselves in their relationship to the child. The co-presence of these two sources of conflict—one universal, stemming from the dependence-independence dilemma (in all its multiple variations), and one potential and specific to each case, that of the parental conflicts—organizes the interaction in each person's learning process. The way these conflicts eventually turn into specific patterns of interaction—i.e., the stability and pervasiveness of the contradictory messages-structures and of the type of responses favored, its timing within the developmental process, et cetera—will, in the long run, give rise to specific forms of neurosis (conceived in terms of behavioral stereotypy). In other words, the contradiction contained in the original learning situations will make the child respond in a way that to him will seem the most successful and will eventually lead to a set of rules for dealing with the outside world. Once these rules are established he will "recognize" over and over again in new situations the familiar structure of the contradiction contained in his early learning experiences and, finally, he will provoke in others those behaviors that will reinforce and "justify" his own interpersonal conduct.

These rather abstract considerations now need to be made more specific. To do this we shall summarize here the way we have tried to define those contradictions inherent in the specific learning experiences that eventually generate hysteric, phobic, and obsessive-compulsive behaviors respectively.

### Hysteria

*Hysterics* show a positive orientation to external objects, but their evaluation of themselves is negative.[2] Their exhibitionistic and seductive behavior is in keeping with both these views for, on the one hand, it serves to attract the outside object, but on the other hand, it presupposes within the hysteric a lack of conscience and a kind of selective blindness for his own seductiveness. If, as a result of this, the external object is attracted to him, it must be rejected because it touches upon those aspects he values negatively. But this rejection will of necessity be temporary, for to stop attracting the other person is tantamount to renouncing the loved object. This contradiction is bound to create a "yes, but no" behavior that will tend to repeat itself indefinitely. The hysteric conceives of his role as

[2] According to Fairbairn, for the hysteric the accepted or "good" object is outside and the rejected or "bad" inside.

passive—i.e., he suffers the consequences of the others' actions. The others engage in activities, and he adopts inner states. In terms of who controls whom, one could say the hysteric engineers his inner states so as to produce specific actions on the part of others.

What kind of early learning experiences could lead to this behavior? One may assume it would be in the nature of this learning context to punish the subject whenever his behavior is actively geared towards achieving results but to reward him when he assumes the right inner states in response to parental action. Activity thus becomes associated with punishment and passivity with reward.[3] Now it is well known that any socializing medium will at times demand certain forms of active behavior. In the interpersonal situation we are here examining, the parents will metacommunicate to their child what kind of behavior they expect of him, but these implicit expectations will be in conflict with the explicit "rules of the game." The only viable way of not violating the explicit rules, while at the same time responding adequately to the implicit demands—whose violation also carries the threat of frustration and punishment—is through *indirect compliance* with these demands within the frame of the explicit rules. This amounts to a progressive ability to manipulate his inner states so as to adapt himself to the situation on hand. One example of this would be a child who, when actively demanding his parents' attention, is told "don't bother us," but when throwing a tantrum quickly gets it. Thus the parents pay attention only to those behaviors that do not explicitly demand it, and vice versa.

In view of the foregoing, the contradictory and paradoxical messages responsible for the emergence of hysteria can perhaps best be summarized in the formula: *"Take initiative, but remember that it is forbidden to take initiative."*

### Phobics

Passing now to the phobic patient, it appears that his basic problem lies in the distinction between dangerous and harmless situations, since for him the world never ceases to be potentially dangerous.[4]

[3] This would be a "classical Pavlovian context," as defined by Bateson (2), in which any information as to what the subject is supposed to *do* is excluded from the sequence of events that make up the learning situation. But at the same time the subject is included in the sequence to the extent that he is not expected to react to it actively and with a view towards modifying the situation, but through a self-modification.

[4] According to Fairbairn, in the case of the phobias both the accepted and the rejected objects are outside the subject.

What learning model may eventually account for phobic behavior? Explicitly, the learning situation will be such as to encourage the subject towards independence. But since the parents conceive of the world as full of dangers, they will meta-communicate to their child "the world is very dangerous." Thus taking risks of any kind will be punished and avoiding-behavior rewarded.[5] The simultaneous presence of both injunctions creates an incongruency: the explicit encouragement of independence contradicts the implicit rule to avoid exaggerated dangers, since, by parental definition, the world of independence is dangerous. There is, then, no other way out of this impasse than to act independently only in those areas that have been declared safe by the parents, or in other words, to act with fictitious independence.

All of the phobic's interactions can be seen as the outcome of this learning process. When he interacts with others, the immediate activation of his avoidance behavior is a mechanism for both judging the safety of his environment and defining the relationship with his partner through the meta-message, "I am not a grownup, I need protection." This attitude is as contradictory as the paradoxical injunction that produces it, which can be summarized by the formula, *"Be independent by depending on me."*

### Obsessive Compulsives

Yet another picture emerges with the *obsessive-compulsive* patients. They assign a positive value to certain of their actions and a negative one to others.[6] Both the danger of acting as well as the means of controlling this danger are internalized. One of the essential features of the obsessive-compulsive coping technique consists in utilizing one's own "acceptable" behaviors to control or neutralize "objectionable" or "bad" ones. As a result of this, however, the acceptable behaviors lose their meaning, since they now have no purpose of their own except to stand *in lieu of* the unacceptable actions: to be busy repeating an acceptable action prevents the emergence of the unacceptable ones, and this becomes the basis of

[5] The explicit learning context of the phobic seems to be identical with Bateson's (2) concept of "instrumental reward": it defines behaviors the learner must engage in *actively* in order to be rewarded. The learning situation acknowledges and encourages independence on the part of the subject. Implicitly, however, it meta-communicates that the situation is an "instrumental avoidance" context (for a definition of this term cf. footnote on page 236).

[6] This is in keeping with Fairbairn's postulate that with these patients both the accepted and the rejected object is internal.

obsessive-compulsive rituals.[7] The overwhelming need to avoid doing the wrong thing is compounded by the conviction that to think of doing something amounts to having done it. The occurrence of ideas or behaviors requiring rejection triggers off the ritual of undoing to re-establish the equilibrium. This process is complicated by the fact that "the bad" is conceived of as contaminating certain actions that until then were considered neutral or even good, and this eventually requires a re-structuring of the rituals.

Let us try to identify the learning context that may be conducive to the genesis of the obsessive-compulsive neuroses. The child is expected to attain independence following the rule that if he wants to avoid punishment he must learn "to do the right things." To comply with this rule is considered the right behavior, but there is no instrumental reward connected with it. If the child does something "bad" or does not do the "right thing," he is punished. If, on the other hand, he behaves properly, he is not rewarded but is simply considered to have done his duty.[8]

But while on one level the parents encourage the child to assume duties as a form of "independence," on another level they meta-communicate to him that he is *instrinsically bad* (e.g., "Of course, what else could one expect from you?"). Independent behavior is thus defined as good and the child encouraged to behave accordingly, while at the same time he is labeled bad and capable only of doing bad things. This creates an untenable situation.

This impasse probably originates from the premature imposition of certain demands. If the parents make demands that exceed the child's present capabilities, he is bound to fail. If they then attribute these failures to the child's ineptitude rather than to his immaturity, he himself will eventually conceive of his failures as "badness," deserving punishment.[9]

[7] "The obligation to do the right thing—or not to do the wrong one—camouflages the prohibition against doing the wrong thing. This prohibition is not recognized because it would otherwise generate anxiety and because any prohibition implies, by definition, the possibility of doing what is prohibited" (7).

[8] This situation is one of "instrumental avoidance," in which the conditioned stimulus is followed by a disagreeable experience—e.g., an electric shock—*unless* the subject responds with a certain action. The subject thus learns how to insert his own action into the sequence of events in order to avoid punishment. Therefore the reward lies in the avoidance of punishment.

[9] "Another important fact is that the parents couch their injunctions and punishments in abstract terms, such as referring to "what *one* must do," and thereby define themselves as the mere intermediaries between the child and the rules. This leads the child to attribute an impersonal nature to these injunctions" (7).

2. BATESON, G., "Social Planning and the Concept of 'Deutero-Learning,'"
his own initiative and since all spontaneous action has been defined as
necessarily bad, the emergence of badness becomes a constant danger.
This conflict can be summarized by the paradoxical formula, *"Be independent, although, of course, you are incapable of it."*

It should be noted that our *formulae* of paradoxical injunctions are
theoretical constructs. In real-life situations the contradictory rules are, of
course, transmitted in many different ways, through different channels of
communication, by different persons, and in different situations that all
together make up the vast repertory of learning contexts.

These mutually incompatible messages, pertaining to different logical
levels, can be transmitted (a) both through the same channel (verbal,
paralinguistic, nonverbal, or contextual) or through different channels; (b)
both by the same person or separately by more than one (10); (c) within
the frame of one given learning context or as an interference phenomenon
*between* learning contexts; and d) simultaneously or successively.

The paradoxes themselves can be similarly classified, depending on what
element of the entire learning context is primarily involved; e.g. (a) both
messages refer to the learner (as is the case with the paradoxes inherent
in the three forms of neurosis mentioned in the foregoing); (b) both messages refer to their sender (for instance, any statement amounting to: "Only
when I am suffering am I really happy"); (c) the frame of reference and
the source of the message are both linked, yet incompatible (as is the
case with, for instance, the Liar Paradox, i.e., the statement by Epimenides
the Cretan, "All Cretans are liars"). For an introduction to the problem of
paradoxes in human communication cf. Watzlawick *et al.* (9).

Anybody's typical behavior is the outcome of the different learning
contexts he has internalized. It thus makes sense to think in terms of
principal and secondary contexts (or of paradoxes produced by them),
just as it makes sense to talk about predominant and accessory behavior
traits.

Now, if the codification rules imposed by the socialization process do
condition the subject towards a certain "world view," this also implies that
the neurotic encounters over and over again the conflicts created by the
paradoxical nature of the original situation. For him this situation recurs
whenever the dependence-independence dilemma is reactivated in any one
of its many variations and, when this occurs, the paradoxical rules for
the resolution of the conflict, i.e., neurotic behavior, will be resorted to
again. The recurrent nature of this pattern suggests a sort of circular reinforcement, i.e., a positive feedback. The paradox has, therefore, both an

"historical" and a "present" aspect, and this is why the neurotic disturbance tends to be self-perpetuating.

Numerous variables impinge on the process of socialization, such as basic personality traits of the subject or the intensity of instinctual drives, etc., but there are also factors having specific bearing on the learning context that can determine the intensity, persistence, and virulence of a given clinical picture, or the question as to which clinical picture will emerge. These latter are: (1) the simultaneous or successive occurrence of the main learning contexts; (2) the very early occurrence of paradoxical injunctions; and (3) the intensity and nature of the many possible corrective experiences originating within the family or coming from the extrafamilial environment.

To summarize, the following are the characteristics common to all the learning models mentioned above. First of all, contradictory messages given simultaneously and belonging to different logical levels (one message contains an instruction and the other an instruction or an information that contradicts the first one but refers to the class of instructions of which the first one is a member). This takes place in a context—the family—that cannot be evaded and in which it is of fundamental importance for the subject to discriminate meanings correctly. Finally, the pattern repeats itself over time, since it is the context for a number of different learning experiences and thereby predisposes the subject to expect this kind of experience even in cases where the essential ingredients of the original situation are absent.

These characteristics are identical with what several authors consider the essential ingredients of a double-bind situation, e.g. (3) (6).

On the basis of the general considerations contained above, it may now be proposed that the double-bind theory is not specific to the etiology of schizophrenia but, rather, defines a *universal pathogenic situation:* any pathology of a psychological—and therefore interactional—nature would have to have as its antecedents a learning context in keeping with the premises postulated by the Palo Alto group fourteen years ago.

The hypothesis that double-bind situations may be involved not only in the pathogenesis of schizophrenia but also in other forms of psychopathology was advanced by Ferreira (5) who described double binds in delinquency, and Watzlawick (8) who suggested specific connections between certain clinical pictures and the particular areas of human functioning in which double-binding occurs.

It will be remembered that the double-bind theory was originally proposed in 1956 by Bateson, Jackson, Haley, and Weakland as an explanation of the etiology of schizophrenia. The early enthusiasm with which the psychiatric world accepted it has since been replaced by a continuous polemic that either takes issue with the undeniable gap between the theory and the evidence supporting it or merely the fact that very little work has been produced so far to support and go beyond the original formulation. This stagnation, we believe, is due largely to the lack of a suitable methodology for the analysis of patients' utterances, as well as for the conceptual reconstruction of the learning contexts involved and the validation of any hypotheses advanced so far.

What we propose is that the double-bind theory has a much wider applicability than originally postulated. We further propose that the first step towards validating his expanded conceptual model would consist in a reconstruction of the specific learning context underlying each of the clinical pictures by establishing a rigorous connection between the original paradox and the ensuing pathology. To this end, the approach described in this paper in respect to certain forms of neuroses could be applied in the sense that intermediate steps must be found between the double-bind theory (which in Bateson's own words is more an epistemology) and each clinical picture. The second step would then be to operationalize the concepts thus developed by applying them to the verbal productions of patients, and finally, by verifying them through longitudinal studies. It seems to us that the lack of longitudinal verification is due not so much to the practical difficulty of such studies, but to the lack of intermediate links between the theory and its practical application.

For the time being, the task of formulating specific hypotheses for the genesis of schizophrenia is beyond our capabilities. Very probably our research efforts will have to be directed towards a reconstruction of the meta-rules, i.e., of the rules governing the relation between learning models, that are perhaps the result of the consistently inconsistent imposition of learning contexts by the parents. It may well be that such inconsistencies as are contained in the erratic meta-communication of parental expectations will lead the child to internalize the rule that there are no rules for a clear interpretation of reality, with the result that he will tend to attribute to a situation meanings in conflict with the context in which it occurs. "Crazy" behavior may thus become the only "acceptable" way out of any injunction demanding, in one way or another, "Learn to live up to our expectations, but independently from what we may tell you," or, in other words, "Distrust your senses and learn to see the world as it really is."

## REFERENCES

1. BATESON, G., "Conventions of Communication: Where Validity Depends on Belief," in Ruesch, J. and Bateson, G., *Communication, the Social Matrix of Psychiatry*, New York, W. W. Norton, 1951 (Chapter 8).
2. BATESON, G., "Social Planning and the Concept of 'Deutero-Learning,'" in Bryson, L. (Ed.), *Science, Philosophy and Religion*, 2nd Symposium, New York, Harper & Row, 1942.
3. BATESON, G., JACKSON, D. D., HALEY, J., and WEAKLAND, J. H., "Toward A Theory of Schizophrenia," *Behav. Sci.*, 1: 251–264, 1956.
4. FAIRBAIRN, W. R. D., *An Object-Relations Theory of the Personality*, New York, Basic Books, 1952.
5. FERREIRA, A., "The Double Bind and Delinquent Behavior," *Arch. Gen. Psychiat.*, 3: 359–367, 1960.
6. SLUZKI, C. E., BEAVIN, J., TARNOPOLSKY, A., and VERÓN, E., "Transactional Disqualification," reprinted on pp. 208–227 of this volume.
7. VERÓN, E. and SLUZKI, C. E., *Communicación y neurosis*, Buenos Aires, Editorial del Instituto, 1970.
8. WATZLAWICK, P., "Patterns of Psychotic Communication," in Doucet, P. and Laurin, C. (Eds.), *Problems of Psychosis*, Amsterdam, Excerpta Medica Foundation, 1969.
9. WATZLAWICK, P., BEAVIN, J. H., and JACKSON, D. D., *Pragmatics of Human Communication*, New York, W. W. Norton, 1967.
10. WEAKLAND, J. H., "The Double-Bind Hypothesis of Schizophrenia and Three-Party Interaction," in Jackson, D. D. (Ed.), *The Etiology of Schizophrenia*, New York, Basic Books, 1960.

*The final paper of this chapter is a reconsideration of "Toward a Theory of Schizophrenia," twenty years after its publication, by one of its authors, John H. Weakland. The major theme is simple: What was most important about this paper was its general communicational viewpoint on behavior— a first departure from the established paradigm that madness is the result of deeply hidden intrapsychic conflicts. It may be observed that this theme has already been stressed more than once in the present work. But since we all tend to do—and to think—more of the same, it is no easy task to promote the adoption of a new paradigm, and another restatement of this basic message seems justified.*

# "THE DOUBLE-BIND THEORY"
# BY SELF-REFLEXIVE HINDSIGHT

*John H. Weakland*

Since the double-bind theory was first propounded—or, sticking more to simple description, since the original publication by Bateson, Jackson, Haley and me of "Toward a Theory of Schizophrenia" (2)—there has been, if not a scientific earthquake, at least a fair amount of commotion largely traceable to this work.

For example: There is a series of publications relating to the original article. (Many, though not all, of these writings are listed in Olsen's (4) review.) Such published works are the most substantial evidence of the paper's impact, or at least the sort of evidence taken most seriously according to scientific and professional conventions of significance. There is also, however, continuing oral discussion of the double bind in the family and psychiatric fields and various utilizations of the idea in treatment of patients. There is even some noticeable entrance of the term "double bind" into everyday language. Such an impact appears rather striking, especially in a time when there is so much scientific research and publication, in addition to an enormous amount of published writings of more general interest. Amid this mass of words, few new ideas create any lasting stir—though many, for related reasons of widespread communication, blaze up and burn out quickly or are preserved only within some devoted but limited cult.

Moreover, this impact has not been simple and straightforward, but complex and confusing. Some of the publications provoked by the original article support or extend it, but many oppose it—ranging from those that purport to disprove "the double-bind theory" to those that reinterpret its relevance rather sweepingly.

All this is especially interesting to me, as one of the original double-bind authors, and the more so because I note a related curiosity in my own professional life. For ten years I have written nothing further on the double bind, or even anything labeled as directly related to it. I have not even talked about it appreciably, except in discussions of a rather historical slant, usually with students; e.g., "How the double-bind concept arose

Originally published in *Family Process* 13:269–77 (1974). Reprinted with permission.

and developed in the context of the Bateson group's research." Yet I see much of my ongoing work—in several rather different areas—as importantly related to the double-bind idea, even if not explicitly referring to it, and I have remained quite interested in what others were writing about the double bind, with recurring thoughts of adding my own latter day two cents' worth. It seems the time for this has finally come.

My aim here, then, is to sketch my own reconsideration of "Toward a Theory of Schizophrenia" and, hopefully, to clarify this murky situation somewhat. The "hindsight" of my title refers, obviously, to this reconsideration. "Self-reflexive" is less obvious; it refers to the fact that the viewpoint from which I will be considering "Toward a Theory" largely derives from the article itself—or at least is consonant with some main principles therein, which over time have become progressively more pervasive and important in my own thinking and acting. Therefore, describing my present view of "Toward a Theory" will, I hope, concurrently make plain my viewpoint for observation, without going over similar ground twice. Such an approach may appear to some as tautological and subjective. My own position on this, however, is very different. It is based on the belief that *views*—conceptualizations, in fancier language—are all we really have to work with in ordering life experience, even in that part of it called science. If so, the best we can do is to make those views that are used clear and explicit. This has not always been the case in writings on the double bind. Instead, "the double-bind theory" has often been examined and discussed *within* some context of broad assumptions and premises, including conventions of scientific outlook and beliefs about "theories" and "facts" that were simply taken for granted, or at most implicit. While it may be impossible ultimately to define one's viewpoint and assumptions completely explicitly—and in many situations there may be no great need to attempt this—steps toward this ideal goal can be especially useful in instances, like the present one, that are marked by confusion and contradictions.

This account will, by necessity, overlap some prior writings on the double bind, since existing discussion of this subject is already extensive and varied. Yet this account will also, by a combination of necessity and choice, be partial. Not every aspect of "Toward a Theory of Schizophrenia" will be considered here. In the first place, that article involved many ideas and observations, varying both in particular focus and in level of abstractness and generality. Some of these were more fully developed than others; in addition, what was most explicitly stressed in the article and what has proven most significant—in my view—are not necessarily identical. Second, as the joint work of four authors who, despite shared interests and close working relationships, were four quite different individuals, this article does not really present one fully integrated point of view. Rather, it involves a common core plus diverse fringes of emphasis and direction—and perhaps even some fringes of disagreement. In these circumstances, I believe it is more useful to concentrate on what I see as the most important features of the original work than to attempt to trace and consider all of its various threads. For related reasons this account will, by choice, be brief, in an attempt to make the main features of "Toward a Theory"— according to this admittedly partial view—stand out with maximum clarity, unobscured by secondary detail.

So much for framing and disclaiming; now for the matter itself. My point of departure is the question, "What is 'Toward a Theory of Schizophrenia' about?". This may seem a silly question. The answer appears obvious: the title, the main content, and much of the subsequent discussion of this article combine to indicate that it is about schizophrenia, something called the double bind, and a theory relating the two. Nevertheless, I think this obvious answer is too simple, narrow, and specific. Schizophrenia was indeed the concrete object of inquiry, but here, as elsewhere, a labeled "entity" may be considered in itself, in terms of its more general relevance, or both. And I consider that, while schizophrenia was the specific subject matter, most fundamentally and generally our article was concerned with relationships between behavior and communication, and especially with an approach to investigating these areas of interest.

It is understandable that considerable confusion and misunderstanding might exist on this point. Certainly the article itself made the specific focus explicit and failed to state the more general one as plainly; perhaps it was not even plain in our minds. In addition, the fact that schizophrenia was the particular subject of our work may itself have promoted an overly narrow view of "Toward a Theory." Schizophrenia then was, and largely still is, seen as a great and pressing practical problem. And pressing problems—whether schizophrenia, cancer, or war—tend to be focused on as such, narrowly. An answer to the particular problem is sought, not its implications elsewhere and more broadly.

Yet in other important respects, the focus on schizophrenia was both appropriate and fortunate. Whatever schizophrenia may be—and even if it is not a specific thing at all—it plainly involved behavior that is varied, extraordinary, and "irrational." Such a subject is difficult to investigate and clarify, but any understanding gained is likely to have correspondingly sweeping scope; study of the "abnormal" has repeatedly proved illuminating for the "normal" as well.

"Toward a Theory," in the first place, treated schizophrenia as behavior, both conceptually and empirically. Today this sounds rather simple, perhaps even obvious, at least among those with an interactional orientation. But this view is not accepted everywhere even now, and it certainly was not common then. At that time, by being labeled as definitely a "pathology" and "irrational," schizophrenia was essentially set off and separated from behavior in general and was defined negatively—in terms of how it was not "normal." In consequence, rather little attention was paid to observing and defining schizophrenia in terms of its own positive characteristics. What it was like was taken as almost obvious, and attempts to explain its existence and nature commonly moved quickly, and largely by inference, into non-behavioral realms—whether these were mentalistic or physiologic. In contrast, to consider schizophrenia seriously—even if tentatively—as behavior, made for many significant differences in its study and understanding. The first step then became the more careful recording and examination of schizophrenic behavior as such—actions and especially speech—with the aim of characterizing this behavior more clearly and systematically in positive terms, and terms relatable to more familiar behavior or behavior generally. Such a concern also implied that one should focus attention not on what is most striking and dramatic, nor what is presupposed necessarily important, but what is observably basic—that is, regular and general features and interrelationships. This shift of approach was exemplified in the article's discussion of how much schizophrenic speech resembles ordinary metaphor, except that it is not labeled as metaphor in conventional ways.

This line of inquiry and explanation also implied that "normal behavior" itself may also require fresh observation and better characterization than, for instance, simple ideas of "rationality" provide. Indeed, the consideration of metaphor already began this move and was pursued further, though not altogether explicitly, elsewhere in "Toward a Theory" —for example, in discussion of humor, poetry, fiction, and hypnosis.

Beyond the question of "What sort of behavior is schizophrenia?," though closely related to it, lies the question of explaining its nature and occurrence: "How does this sort of behavior come about?" Here, rather than hastening to infer the underlying basis of "schizophrenic thought" from a few scraps of patients' speech isolated from their circumstances, a behavioral view led us to at least examine the occurrence of schizophrenia as one might other behavior—that is, by study of its behavioral contexts. The efforts of "Toward a Theory" in this direction were somewhat divided between consideration of possible learning contexts in the schizophrenic's developmental history and examination of the immediate interactional context of communication. While these two lines of inquiry and explanation are fundamentally similar in their focus on attempting to relate behavior to actual communication that is at least potentially observable, this dual emphasis in the original article certainly has been one source of confusion and uncertainty. The relative importance of the two was never settled—or even clearly postulated—in "Toward a Theory," and in fact this remains a matter of dispute both among the authors and more widely. Perhaps the most that can be said even now is to suggest that, before turning toward what is less directly observable, thorough study of the importance of the present, directly observable context, is most in line with the principles of behavioral study generally.

To study the relationship of behavior and communication, however, means that not only the behavior but the communication involved must be handled adequately—again both conceptually and empirically. Indeed, in my estimation, "Toward a Theory" made headway in understanding schizophrenia largely because it developed and utilized a new general view of communication. This view involved a number of different but closely interrelated elements. First, there was the beginning of a close identification of communication and behavior as two sides of one coin, so to speak—a recognition that the most important aspect of social behavior is its communicative effect and that communication is the major factor in the ordering of behavior socially. In pursuing these connections, "Toward a Theory" certainly took a one-sided or unidirectional view at important points—for example, in seeing a "binder" as imposing a double bind on a "victim." Nevertheless, even if less clearly and explicitly, the article also promoted a view of communication as pervasively and basically interactional—as a system, in which uni-directional *attributions* and various punctuations occur but in which these (even our own) should be seen only as aspects of the larger system. Again, as with schizophrenic behavior itself, what is important for understanding is to see the general pattern of communication, not specific events or messages, however dramatic or striking, in isolation. In fact, this whole approach proposed that there is no such isolated event or message. Not only should messages by various parties be seen in relation to one another, there is also no simple message even by one party. "Toward a Theory" pointed out that every message involves multiple channels of communication, modifying one another. Their relationships form a vital part of the pattern; whether they are congruent or contradictory, they must be taken into account jointly. This complexity of messages was considered and examined in various ways—in terms of framing, qualification and disqualification, the Theory of Logical Types, stylized types of communication, and others. Perhaps there are better ways yet to be conceived; the important point made was that *somehow* this complexity must be recognized and grappled with as a major feature of communication in itself, that it can only be misleading to fix on one aspect of a communication—or a series of aspects separately —as the real or important matter and scant the rest or their interaction. Within this general framework, what is significant in particular, and how, can only be found out by empirical study. Like the pattern called a double bind, what is significant may not be—probably will not be, or it would have been noted before—evident in advance. Rather, it is likely to be subtle and unnoticed, or visible but apparently trivial.

Finally, our viewpoint emphasized the influential aspect of communication as most important and inclusive. The germ of this already existed in Bateson's idea that every message is both a report and a command. That is, there is more than "information," in the common but limited sense of "facts," on the basis of which the receiver may decide action—a view related to the old rationalistic conception of behavior. Communication, with its multiplicity of messages, involves other forms of influence as well, and the whole must be examined. How? Essentially, again, by the only way it is possible to go from the general orientation to specifics— by empirical study focused on effects. What behavior appears to follow a given sort of communication, or, more precisely, what patterns of association of communication and behavior are actually observable? "Toward a Theory" certainly did not settle this question for communication and behavior generally, perhaps not even for schizophrenia and double binds. But it *raised* the question in such a way that it could usefully be pursued, and took some first steps.

This leads in conclusion, to what I see as central in evaluating "Toward a Theory." This article is a statement of certain observations and ideas, mainly about communication. It is, therefore, a communication about communication. It could, of course, still be judged from some external viewpoint—hopefully, one made explicit—but I have chosen to consider this particular communication here in terms of its own general view of communication. In these terms, this article, like any other communication, involved both reports—observations—and commands—proposals for a viewpoint. To judge it on the basis of its reports alone—inquiry as to "the truth of the theory" being a specific instance of this—is to take a limited standpoint and one which is at odds with the main thrust of the article itself. Man does not live by truth alone, but by ideas and influences. Man does not treat problems by truth alone. An interpretation of behavior —"His criticism is an expression of his loving concern for you"—may be helpful in easing a difficult situation even if its truth can never be determined. Man does not even pursue science by truth alone. The best hypotheses are "true"—that is, survive tests aimed at disconfirmation—only within certain limits, and this limited truth ordinarily is achieved only late in the development and the consensual *definition,* of a field. "Toward a Theory" is more an opening wedge, proposing a new way of conceptualizing and observing old problems (cf. Kuhn, 3). Although I believe that the observations reported in "Toward a Theory" are reasonably reliable, in such a situation especially (though not exclusively) the accuracy of specific statements may easily be less important than the general direction and viewpoint delineated—just as the general concern of the article with behavior and communication may be more important than its specific concern with schizophrenia. This, perhaps, is not far from Bateson's meaning in saying that "the double-bind theory" is not so much a specific theory as a *language* (1)—which like any language serves to orient both thinking and observation.

From this standpoint, most of the writings that have aimed primarily at getting more simple and specific than the original article, especially those attempting to prove or disprove "the double-bind theory," miss the main point. This point is to consider and evaluate this communication more comprehensively—that is, like any communication, primarily by its effects. This is not to claim that care and precision in observation and statement—at a level appropriate to the situation—are not important, but that they are important functionally, not absolutely. It is certainly not to claim that evaluation of the article's significance on the basis of its effects is any simple matter. Such an evaluation requires many difficult judgments—of the state of affairs before the communication, as its background; of its observable effects so far; even of estimated effects yet to come; and of the importance of any such changes and developments. I will not, in fact, venture to make any precise judgment in terms of this general standard. Broadly, however, against the background described earlier, I think it is plain that, despite any unclarities and confusions it included or led to, "Toward a Theory of Schizophrenia" did present a new general viewpoint on communication and behavior and the statement of this viewpoint has led to much other useful work, both practical and theoretical. In this connection, the various writings that have taken off from, and gone beyond, the original article (whether by expanding on matters merely touched on there or by seeking quite new connections) to consider other "pathologies," therapy, creativity, and even evolution do not appear as disqualifications. Rather, they represent developments consonant with the basic aims and framework of "Toward a Theory of Schizophrenia" and testify further to its usefulness and influence. And the end is not yet. To me, this seems the main thing, and enough.

CHAPTER 5

# Change

*Family (or interactional) psychotherapy, it will be remembered, was defined in the Introduction in two ways: as a new view of human problems and as a treatment method based on this view. It is not too difficult to appreciate that by focusing on the systemic qualities of a problem situation in the Here and Now, rather than on its genesis over time, the therapist can become effective at a relatively early stage of the treatment. Fairly rapid changes of this kind are, of course, only possible if he is willing to take an active stance through deliberate interventions rather than by passively waiting for change to well up spontaneously from the depths. Thinking in terms of systemic interaction makes possible interventions that have no place in other paradigms of therapy, and they may constitute turning points of difficult treatments.*

*A report by Jackson and Yalom provides an interesting case in point. With the enormous power of absorption that the families of schizophrenics can marshal against any threat to their rigid homeostasis, the treatment of this family had begun to show the typical characteristics of a systemic stalemate. For impasses of this kind we use the term Game without End\* and mean by it any situation in which a system cannot generate from within itself the rules for the change of its own rules. Consequently, such a system will endlessly run through the finite number of internal changes available to it, thereby achieving only "more of the same"†, without ever arriving at a resolution of the impasse. The metarule for systemic change can, therefore, be introduced only from the outside, and this is what interventions in interactional psychotherapy are all about.*

*It is perhaps worthwhile to stress here a particular point even though it is already emphasized in the paper: After making his intervention and*

---

\* Paul Watzlawick, Janet H. Beavin and Don D. Jackson, *Pragmatics of Human Communication,* New York, W. W. Norton, 1967, pp. 232–236.

† Paul Watzlawick, John H. Weakland and Richard Fisch, *Change.* New York, W. W. Norton, 1974, pp. 31–39.

*putting the family in a therapeutic double bind, Jackson achieves his most noticeable tactical gain not by a clever interpretation, but by the non-verbal expedient of bursting out laughing.*

# CONJOINT FAMILY THERAPY AS AN AID
# TO INTENSIVE PSYCHOTHERAPY

*Don D. Jackson and Irvin Yalom*

### Introduction

In the past two decades the basic focus and format of psychiatric therapy has undergone significant change. The classical intrapsychic focus has been infinitely enriched by the cultural and interpersonal contributions of such innovators as Adler, Horney, and Sullivan. The classical one-to-one doctor-patient format also has been enriched by the rise of such new formats as milieu therapy, group therapy, and more recently, conjoint family therapy. At this stage of our knowledge, it is sagacious to consider classical techniques as being enriched by newer approaches rather than being challenged by them. Not only may different approaches be the therapy of choice for different individuals but several different approaches may be indicated in the treatment of one individual. These different approaches may be utilized concurrently or sequentially. This paper will present an example of the latter instance in which conjoint family therapy was utilized as one of a sequence of therapies. In this instance family therapy was particularly efficacious in abruptly motivating an apparently chronically hospitalized schizophrenic to leave the hospital, to find a means of supporting himself, and to involve himself meaningfully in further individual therapy.

The drama of sudden improvement can obscure the heuristic aspects of such cases and leave us with anecdotes rather than therapeutic insight. We present the case, however, not as a claim for the efficiency of conjoint family therapy but as an illustration of the basic theory behind family therapy.

Reprinted by permission of the authors, the editor and the publisher from D. D. Jackson and I. Yalom, "Conjoint Family Therapy as an Aid to Intensive Psychotherapy". In A. Burton, ed., *Modern Psychotherapeutic Practice: Innovations in Technique.* Palo Alto, Science and Behavior Books, 1965, pp. 81–97.

Our basic theory stems, in part, from two observations made many years ago by innumerable therapists who came into contact with the families of hospitalized schizophrenic patients. One observation was that the families almost deliberately seemed to sabotage the treatment of the ill member. A harsh, even cruel charge, to be sure, and yet the behavior seemed so gross that no other conclusion could be reached. The other observation was that there occurred not infrequently an alternation or substitution of illness in the family. The patient's improvement was accompanied by the appearance of severe mental illness in some other family member—often the mother, less frequently a sibling or the father. What conclusion could be drawn from these two observations? It would seem that, despite the family's natural concern for the ill member, there are strong forces operating in the family to keep the patient sick.

Our major assumption, therefore, is that the family is a homeostatic system inextricably involving and influencing the patient.[1,2] Specifically, the family context of the schizophrenic is one in which the patient and only the patient has difficulties; and conversely, his position in the family is to be the problem. In addition to this we see the peculiar absence of personal problems in the cases of other family members. This assumption, of course, has many implications for therapy. The attempt to effect therapeutic change in a patient closely involved with his family without recognizing and dealing with opposing family forces is often foolhardy as well as futile. In fact, an important method of instigating some change in the patient is to tamper with the family system. Admittedly the schizophrenic family system is often ossified, and even when change occurs, it may be evanescent—the complex family forces quickly reinstating the *status quo*.[3]

The present case illustrates both the long-range use of family therapy and a specific technique for tampering with the family system in a crucial interview which appeared to be a turning point in therapy. We wish to call attention not only to the changes in the patient but to the changes in the family as well.

### The Patient

The patient, David Brown, is twenty-five years old, unmarried, and when therapy was first begun by one of the authors (I. Y.), had been

[1] Haley, J. The family of the schizophrenic: A model system. *J. Nerv. Ment. Dis.*, 1959, *129*, 357–374.

[2] Jackson, Don D. The question of family homeostasis. *Psychiat. Quart. Suppl.*, 1957, *31*, 79–90.

[3] Jackson, Don D. and J. Weakland. Conjoint family therapy. Some considerations on theory, technique, and results. *Psychiatry*, 1961, *24*, 30–45.

continuously hospitalized for one and a half years. Although in retrospect there were many ominous signs adumbrating his illness for a period of six years, he was first officially labeled a patient while in the service at age twenty. At that time, shortly after induction and assignment to Alaska, he was noted to appear confused, preoccupied, and withdrawn. He was unable to perform his work, had repeated episodes of extremely anxiety, and several inexplicable outbursts of anger and melancholy. The main thought-content involved the recent termination of a (largely autistic) relationship with a woman and marked indecision about future occupational plans. The confusion and withdrawal progressed to catatonia, and the patient was hospitalized and four months later medically discharged.

He returned home to live with his parents and his only sibling, a brother seven years his junior. His life pattern here consisted of numerous social and occupational failures. He dated often but characteristically misjudged the nature of the relationship and on several occasions made a premature and inappropriate proposal of marriage. Despite a high level of intelligence and a two-year college education, he was unable to negotiate even the least demanding jobs (janitorial work, messenger, etc.) and was invariably discharged because of his confused ineptness. He was seen by a psychiatrist in therapy during this time, but treatment was ineffective and hospitalization was advised.

The patient presented himself as an attractive, well-groomed young man, who, on casual examination, appeared to be in no distress. On thorough psychiatric examination, however, major impairment was obvious. His affect was peculiar—often indifferent, occasionally saddened, with periodic outbursts of inappropriate laughter or loud singing. He had had auditory hallucinations since the onset of his illness, chiefly derogatory, and resembling the voices of his family members. Present also were ideas of reference as well as bizarre somatic delusions that various parts of his body were decaying or vanishing and that maggots were infesting his blood stream. The chief impression one obtained from talking with him was one of vagueness, indecision, confusion, and a tendency to agree with everything the interviewer advanced. Because of his intelligence, attractiveness, good grooming, and presumably good potential, he elicited much interest and compassion from the ward personnel and on several occasions was involved in individual therapy. President of the ward community, editor of the hospital newspaper, he functioned well in the hospital setting, and the staff, like his family, tended to underestimate his inner turmoil. Student nurses and medical students identified with him, often vociferously taking issue with the diagnosis and ominous prognosis.

## Summary of the First 18 Family Interviews

Since individual and group approaches had failed to help, it was decided to involve Dave and his family in conjoint family therapy. His father
and mother together with Dave were seen once a week in ninety-minute
sessions. Because of school pressures, the younger brother, Charles, could
attend only a couple of the sessions. (The meetings, incidentally, entailed
some sacrifice on the part of the parents, since they lived over two hours
away from the hospital.)

In the initial sessions the therapist attempted to orient the family to the
rationale of family therapy. He expressed the opinion that the other family
members are invariably troubled, although the obvious distress of the identified patient tends to overshadow their pain. The family expressed a great
desire to help and accepted this orientation albeit tenuously and quizzi-
cally. During the early sessions much historical data was discussed, developing the history of the family from its origins (the first meeting of the
parents) as well as the early histories of each parent. These accounts,
though seemingly complete, were strangely impersonal. Conspicuously
missing were mentions of the typically human as well as the idiosyncratic
problems of living. Aside from the appropriate concern for Dave's illness
there was only happiness, cooperation, love, and inexorable social and
financial success. Dave's response to this was, at one point, to pound on
the table and shout, "My God, I come from a perfect family!" Mother
answered, "Dear, have we said anything that wasn't true?" Dave replied,
"No, but now I see what a goof ball I really must be."

Also absent was the occurrence of any "give and take" between the
parents. They seemed to function as a single person or system. It was not
until the sixth interview that the first semblance of individual differences
occurred. Father, during the session, informed Dave that on his last job,
he (father) had actually been paying Dave's salary and Dave's employer
retained him only as a personal favor to father. Mother wept at this, saying that father shouldn't have told Dave. The first overt disagreement occurred much later when father accused Dave of not working because of
laziness. Mother disagreed, gently serving as a peacemaker between father
and son. It was especially difficult to obtain a multidimensional view of
mother. A shadow figure, she smiled bravely and endlessly coined Norman
Vincent Peale-type cliches. When the therapist commented thereupon, the
family responded with disbelief or utter incomprehension, leaving the therapist with the maddened feeling that he had been the fall guy for father
and sons, all of whom withheld their true feelings. (The bewildering ex-

perience of the therapist who treats this type of family is graphically described by Schaffer, et al.)[4]

Despite statement of the therapist's theoretical position, it seemed impossible for the family to grasp that they were coming to help themselves as well as the patient. The feeling prevailed that they were there for Dave's sake, and the burden of keeping the discussions going fell on his shoulders. The parents after approximately eighteen sessions felt all "dried up"; there was nothing more to say. The sessions became increasingly unproductive, with all participants including the therapist growing discouraged.

## Consultant's Interview

Because the family was losing interest and the therapist felt conjoint family therapy was still the patient's best hope, he asked a consultant (D.J.) to interview the family, primarily to get a feel for them, but in addition to behave therapeutically if the opportunity offered itself. The consultant felt that like many of the families of chronic schizophrenics, the Browns were well defended and most of their energies were focused on maintaining the patient in the sick role, as well as maintaining the *status quo* of the family interrelationships. He decided beforehand to see if the family could be moved by placing them in a particular therapeutic bind; namely, they would be asked: *What problems might arise for the family if Dave improves?* Apart from that question, the interview was not structured.

The usual framework for psychotherapy is a restorative one; that is, we presume to remove the presenting complaint so that the patient and those close to him can go about their lives without this handicap. Clinical experience, however, often argues against this view. The evidence concerning relapse and/or psychopathological repercussions among other family members has led us to suspect that we have tampered with part of an ongoing system and altered its "normal" state in removing the labeled symptom of one member. Thus, the usual assumption that things will somehow get "back to normal" if the identified patient improves can obscure the possibility that the symptomatic behavior of the patient has a vital *present function* in maintaining the balance of family relationships.

In this case of a rigid family system, the physical presence of the other family members in a psychotherapeutic setting had not aided their understanding of their interlocking roles in Dave's schizophrenic symptoms.

[4] Schaffer, L. et al. On the nature and sources of the psychiatrists' experience with the family of the schizophrenic. *Psychiatry*, 1962, *25*, 32–45.

Indeed, these occasions only seemed to verify their myth that the family would be ideally happy but for Dave's misfortune, to which other problems could be traced with a truly remarkable consistency. The authors were in agreement that such a context was not likely to help the patient, and that family therapy was not going to succeed until each family member sought some help in it for himself. And no one at this point was even admitting to a problem.

The consultant felt that the situation warranted a sharp reversal from the prevailing view of Dave's psychopathology as aberrant behavior, and decided to use his authority as the consulting expert to focus the family's attention on their investment in Dave's illness. This was done by placing them in a particular therapeutic double bind. The question "What problems might arise for the family if Dave should improve?" is particularly forceful because it is a paradox in which the family as presently organized "can't win." The question encourages problems in a framework of help. Rather than arousing their guard by indirect probing, the consultant takes advantage of the family members' view of themselves as helpful individuals and implies they would be uncooperative if they did not produce some difficulties to discuss with him. Backed as it is by an expert, the question is heavily weighted to evoke at least token answers. Yet any indication of family difficulties which might be caused by Dave's remission can be amplified as barriers to his recovery and, hopefully, force the family to consider, at some level, that they must change before recovery is possible. If such a small dent can be made in the family's present rigidity, then further steps can be taken to get family members to assume some problems of their own.

This session was opened after polite formalities by the consultant's asking the above question. The family was incredulous at first, but the patient seemed intrigued by the question. The first break-through occurred when father admitted that if the patient improved and came home, he (the father) would be embarrassed socially. The mother was terribly hurt by this admission on his part, and the parents' usual coalition began to come apart at the seams.

Dave was helpful in suggesting several difficulties which might follow his improvement. He suggested that if he should fall in love and want to marry, it would be a problem for him to present his intended to his parents. Mrs. Brown said, on the contrary, she would be delighted, but qualified her statement by adding: " 'Course, I would always hope it would be the right one." The consultant agreed that this was a chancy thing, that every mother who loves her son is troubled by such questions as whether the girl is good enough for him or whether she might be too good for him. But while the mother agreed it was a "gamble," the rest of the family joined in to table this discussion on the grounds that it was a "natural" problem and, at any rate, "not that big of a problem."

The parents maintained that it was the opinion of many doctors that Dave should become "independent" of them if he were released, so therefore no problems for the family would arise. In the following example the consultant pressed them to admit that their plan for complete separation was neither practical nor desirable, and the patient attempted a rescue. Note that nonverbal intervention such as laughter is effective as interpretation while avoiding the sort of discussion in which the therapist must digress and risk becoming quite legalistic to make his point.

| | |
|---|---|
| Dave: | Wh-What if it goes completely the opposite, what if I don't even wanna see them? (pause) |
| Consultant: | (laughs) |
| Dave: | (laughs) |
| Mother: | (joining laughter) What's happened. . . ? |
| Consultant: | Mhm! |
| Dave: | (still laughing) |
| Consultant: | How far away would you have to get— |
| Dave: | (interrupting, laughs) |
| Charles: | Tahiti or some other— |
| Consultant: | (interrupting) Yeah, I—I was wondering—I was thinking of Timbuktu . . . (Dave, still laughing) Ah, you don't think that wouldn't cause a problem. |
| Dave: | Sure it would. But uh, I would . . . (sigh) I don't know what —there's a—there's a problem in family relations that goes something like this: Unless you're actually in a psychiatrist's office you never want to hear—if you're on your own—I don't —I feel you never want your family to know just exactly how y—how bad things are or maybe . . . how . . . uh . . . realistically what things are really like. At least—I think you put up a front in both lines—especially if y—the more you get independent and away from your family, the more you're likely to be like this. At least this is the way I see myself . . . So I see . . uh . . as I get well I see associations with my family more or less going down the drain. |
| Consultant: | Mhm. |
| Mother: | Well, other people's [relationships] don't. |

Mrs. Brown's comment illustrates a typical double bind which pervades the schizophrenic family: While he is instructed, on great authority, to be independent of his family and thus avoid causing them trouble, he is told at another level that if he improves and breaks some family ties, he is behaving unnaturally and unlovingly.

In addition to this "stay away closer" position, the parents maintained that if difficulties ensued from Dave's improvement, they would be problems for Dave alone and not for the family:

Dave:        What if—what if by some—some chance I should become more successful than my father, then how would my father feel about it?

Consultant:  Well, predictably, he would say 'Great going!'

Dave:        Mhm.

Consultant:  But how would he *feel* about it?

Dave:        Yeah.

Father:      If you want an answer . . . from me; I'd be thrilled.

Dave, Charles and Consultant laugh.

Such a patently superficial answer illustrates that not only Dave is trapped by his role as receptacle of the family problems. The others are as obligated to feel and speak only the positive aspects as Dave is to accept the negative aspects of a given situation. Once this system is set into motion, the others *cannot* admit to "bad" feelings in the many situations where this is appropriate or even necessary. Here, by laughing, however good-naturedly, as the consultant did earlier, the sons indicate some preverbal understanding of the untenability of their father's position. Lest we be accused of advocating filial impiety, let us hasten to add that laughter often serves as a synthesis and release of paradox, as in formally labeled humor, and here, when family members have been forced to realize that something is vaguely amiss in their usual patterns of interaction. Further, *laughing together* is a vital form of interpersonal confirmation, which the consultant used frequently to ally the patient while forestalling distracting sympotomatic behavior.

During the discussion of the drawbacks to Dave's improving, the younger brother had been silent but interested. When asked about Dave's weekends with the family (from which the patient usually returned quite agitated), Charles withdrew and relabeled Dave: "Before he comes home I'm a little nervous because I never know in what mood or how he'll be." The consultant pointed out that it seemed as if Dave were being asked to bear the intolerable burden of the whole family's solicitation. He was the total barometer of how well or how poorly things went on the weekend. Surprisingly, the patient burst in on this with:

Dave:          Well, I feel that sometimes my parents and Charles also are very sensitive to how I might feel, maybe overly sensitive about how I feel, 'cause I don't—I don't feel I raise the roof when I go home, or . . .

Mother:      Mhm. Dave, you haven't been like that either since you had your car, it's just—but *before* you did.

Dave:          Well, I know I did . . .

Mother:      (overlapping) Yeah, but even—yeah, lately, twice since you had your car.

Dave:          Yeah, OK, anyhow, ah, (sigh) that's-ah, I wish I didn't have to be that way, I guess, it'd be nice if I could enjoy myself or somethin' . . . (sighs, pause)

Consultant:  You change your story in mid-stream when your mother is nice to you, you know. Which . . . is understandable but in your position you just can't afford to do it. (Dave: Mhm.) It makes you kookier. Then you don't even know what you're thinking.

Mother:      What did he change?

Consultant:  That—ah, I can't read his mind so I'm just going by—I don't know what he was going to say precisely, I have a general idea, I think, just from experience—

Dave:          Well, it's just, just the story that I'm the sick one in the family and so this gives everybody else a . . . a chance to be a good Joe and pick up Dave's spirits whether Dave's spirits are necessarily down or not. That's what it amounts to sometimes, I feel. In other words, I can't be anything but myself, and *if people don't like me the way they am—ah, the way I am*—then I appreciate when they, if they'd tell me or something is what it amounts to.

The patient's slip of the tongue captures the puppetry in which he is entangled; although he says "I can't be anything but myself," the question remains: is myself *I* or *they?*

At this point the consultant decided on a second major tactic to tamper with the family system: to use as a foil Charles, the younger brother, who was insipidly polite, smiling, and much too controlled for a boy not quite eighteen. It was felt that his loosening up might be beneficial to him and also would not make the patient's behavior appear so out of line with the rest of the family. Further, the goal of this single interview was not insight, but to set in motion family forces which would alter the previously stable but unhealthy patterns of interaction. If Charles could be labeled as a problem, even if only to cooperate with the consultant, then Dave is not only somewhat relieved of his role but other family members must try new ways of coping with Charles, and those changes must have repercussions in other family relationships.

He was asked if he ever had any moods, which question elicited explosive laughter from the patient and his father. Charles carefully explained that sure, occasionally he had little problems, but in continuing in this vein he strained his father's patience to the breaking point. The father mentioned "slamming doors," schoolwork, and alluded to a rocky love affair mentioned earlier in the interview. This, it turned out, was a romance with a girl one year older than Charles, and though he had protested there was not much to it, the father had stated that he hoped Charles would not marry until he finished college. When the patient, in a brotherly manner, had asked Charles if he were thinking of marriage, father and mother had invoked the family rule that there were no problems and brushed the question aside.

In discussing Charles, Mr. Brown unexpectedly confessed his feelings of inadequacy as adviser to his sons. But before this could be explored, Charles sought to restore the family facade:

Charles: And I think, I think it's better that way, too, because you get y-you—in other words, of course a big problem I'll take to my parents but smaller problems 'n things I try to solve myself 'cause that way, even if I do make a mistake I learn that way.

Consultant: I didn't know there were any big problems . . .

Charles: Well, I say "if."

Consultant: (laughing, with Charles) If there are none then you haven't had the . . .

Charles: (overlapping) Well, I—I . . .

Consultant: . . . experience of taking it to them.

Such examples illustrate the tenacity of the family rules even in the face of logical contradiction. Seeking to construct a situation in which it would be impossible to deny there were other family difficulties beside Dave, the consultant made a specific suggestion:

. . . there's something, Charles, that you could do that would be, I think, of immeasurable help to your brother. And I think of help to you, but I can't prove that to you. And that is that you would agree that you would become more of a problem, during the time that Dave wasn't coming home. (pause) . . .

Charles: You mean rebel against my parents, or . . .

Consultant:    No . . . there are all sorts of ways of being a problem, what I mean is being a problem with a purpose, not just to—not a troublemaker—that's nothing—but I mean you would be more of a problem in the sense that you would get a little more honest about some of the things that trouble you, or some of the uncertainties you may have, or whatever you don't share with your parents now because you don't want to bug them.

His father protested that Charles was already a problem.

Father:    Well, ah, I'm thinking of Charles at home, though, it, ah, maybe you have a different idea of Charles than the way he is at home, ah, Charles, as, yells and hollers around the house and there's no question about what it—that something displeases him, you know it quick, and ah, he's very demonstrative, and ah, ah, ah, you sure do know what, what he likes and what he doesn't. He—he's not around trying to placate us.

Consultant:    Do you—are you aware of yelling, hollering around the house?

Charles:    Well, sure, I mean, but this is my temper, I mean, just the way I am, you know, I—I have a temper where—it'll—you know, fizzle out pretty fast and I'm all right again, you know it—it does—it's not a lasting, you know, dislike . . .

Consultant:    It—there's no reason why it happens. It's just some kind of chemistry inside of you that . . .

Charles:    No, no. There's something that certainly has to tee me off, but I mean, you know . . .

Consultant:    Mhm. But—you see—

Charles:    Just a little thing—

Consultant:    —it's obvious, I would think, that what tees you off is something that the three of you don't have consensual validation about. You don't—that, you know, there's no agreement; "Yes, this did happen, and this tees you off and it's going to continue to happen whether you like it or not, or we'll make some reparation . . ." It's treated as if you have a temper, not as if—this is part of working out a relationship. If you're going to become more of a problem, in order to help your brother, then instead of just blowing up, you'll have to state, you know, what the problem is: "I feel unfairly treated," or "I'm not getting enough allowance," or whatever the thing, and have a discussion about it.

Mother:    Well, it isn't those kind of things that—

Consultant:    Whatever it is.

The only example the three could agree on was Charles' agitation at misplacing his glasses or keys. Charles agreed to become more of a problem, and the consultant ended the interview with the suggestion that unless they found some personal reason for family therapy, they should not burden Dave with their continued benevolence by attending sessions.

## Subsequent Family Interviews

The changes in the family following the consultation were dramatic; temporarily, at least, the therapist was able to break into the family system. Father began the very next session by stating that he had been thinking that he was tired of carrying all the family burdens and he would like to be a problem for a change. When he was asked how he might go about being a problem, he replied that he might come home late from the office one day without previously informing his wife. This opened up the crucial but previously unmentioned issue of mother's possessiveness, and immediately there was a deluge of pertinent and important material. The younger brother, Charles, commented that the family slogan or joke is "Mother has to know!" Everyone knew that mother became upset and worried if some family member went almost anywhere without "signing in" with her first. The issue was treated as gently as possible by the family, mother's contribution being to point out all the ways in which she had improved over the past few years. Following this meeting mother became quite depressed, and in the following sessions for the first time really began to talk about herself. She brought up the fact that her first marriage would have failed anyway even if her husband hadn't been killed in an automobile accident, since he had been flagrantly unfaithful to her. Mother suggested that this may have destroyed her trust in men and might explain her intrusiveness into the lives of her husband and sons.

She also related that her mother, who died when Mrs. Brown was six, was a severe asthmatic and had become addicted to narcotics. After her mother's death she lived in terror lest her father remarry, bringing an evil stepmother into the house. Some of these facts and others were heard for the first time by the family, and the two sons were quite astonished to hear of the previously unsuspected unhappiness in mother's life.

Father continued to bring up things that had been worrying him. He mentioned, for example, that during the family sessions he had often been a "nervous wreck" because he felt it necessary to walk a tightrope to avoid on the one hand upsetting Dave and on the other hand wounding mother if phrases were not carefully chosen. Father again expressed his utter lack of confidence in himself as a parent and his reluctance to counsel Charles about almost any matters because of his total failure with Dave.

On several occasions when father was trying to proceed, Dave attempted to focus the meeting on himself by direct request or by acting crazy in a fashion that demanded therapist's and family's attention. The therapist commented on these moves and in addition kept the family from focusing on them. Father told Dave that the fact he (father) liked peace and quiet and therefore kept things to himself was misleading. "If you think I'm superhuman, that I don't have feelings or hurts or problems, that nothing inside bothers me, then I've got news for you!"

And this was news for Dave as he began to see his parents with their frailties and disappointments in a way he had not previously perceived them. The parents became so involved themselves in the sessions that there was a marked de-emphasis of Dave's problems. He reacted to this at first with diversionary tactics as mentioned above and then with sadness and fear at being extruded from the family. He saw more clearly than before the dilemma which had perpetuated his illness: that getting well and relinquishing his function as the problem meant losing mother and father and facing the loneliness of life without them.

Charles was made an important part of the therapy by the prescription given him to be more of a problem so that Dave would be able to be less of one. Whereas previously he had attended only a couple of sessions and remained on the periphery, now he attended every one and was cast in a central role. His attempts to be more of a problem were at first feeble, and he was dealt with severely by the therapist and, surprisingly enough, by his parents, who objected he was not trying hard enough to be a problem. If, for example, he was able to tell his parents that he was worried about breaking up with his girl friend he was criticized for not bringing it up earlier. He was told that by waiting a couple of days and working it through, he was depriving his parents of a chance of worrying with him and helping him find a solution. Any protests by Charles were countered with, "It looks like you just won't let Dave stop being the problem in the family." Charles ultimately was helped to grow more spontaneous and honest with himself.

The third session after the consultation was an important one—containing among other things, father's aforementioned "news" for Dave about his own problems, and including a detailed description of some of his early unhappy times. Immediately afterward Dave answered a want ad and obtained a job on his own for the first time in years. He worked at this for a month before being discharged because his employer obtained a skilled worker and possibly because of the patient's lack of manual dexterity (the job was making and installing awnings). When he lost this job the family response was appropriate and encouraging. When he expressed shame at failing them after all their effort in therapy, they all reminded him that they were also coming for themselves and pointed out to him the ways in which they had all benefited. It is of interest to note that once when Dave was working and could not attend a session, the family elected to meet anyway, an inconceivable proposition to them earlier in therapy. There was competition for the therapist's attention. After the brother's last session (before leaving for college) he privately expressed to the patient his annoyance at the parents and the therapist for not having devoted enough of the last session to him. Later the patient passed this confidence along to the therapist with obvious relish.

### Subsequent Individual Therapy

At the time of this writing the patient has been out of the hospital for a year, living alone and supporting himself. He held one job for nine months, and then graduated to a more responsible, higher paying position.

With Dave's gradual maturation and disengagement from his family, a new stage in therapy began and conjoint family sessions have gradually been replaced by individual sessions.

The family therapy context was directly pertinent to subsequent treatment and greatly enriched the scope of individual therapy. For example, Dave repeatedly created for himself a particular interpersonal dilemma. Early in a relationship he revealed everything about himself and later resented his friends for their premature intimacy and intrusiveness. The concept of roles was an utterly alien one to him. The idea that one has different roles (student, patient, employee, boy friend, etc.) and that one reveals different parts of himself in different roles seemed grossly dishonest and evil. However, when this dilemma was considered from the vantage point of the family and "Mother has to know," it became more comprehensible both to the therapist and to Dave. "Tell all to Mother" and "be strong and self-sufficient" were conflicting messages delivered to Dave all his life.

The examination of Dave's indirect methods of communicating with others was another crucial part of therapy. For example, one day he came to his therapy hour angry and discouraged. He had proposed marriage to a girl he had been dating and was rejected. It turned out, however, that the proposal had been far from a spirited one, and when he was asked what he would have done had she said "yes," he replied, "I guess I would've gotten the hell out of the state." Therapy then focused on the task of finding more adaptive techniques of learning whether one is liked.

Another example occurred shortly after the patient was officially discharged from the Veterans Administration and began paying a fee for outpatient visits. The therapist was late for a session and, although he denied concern about this, during the hour he reported hearing a voice within him say, "You are robbing me." The therapist helped Dave to understand both that he was angry at the therapist and that he could, with safety, openly say so without resorting to indirect, crazy devices—in this instance, a fledgling hallucination. On several occasions the patient found himself in an inextricable bind. His boss disapproved of psychiatry and refused to allow him time off for therapy hours. The therapist, of course, strongly urged him to remain in treatment, but only rarely could he offer him evening hours. This bind, which was constructed by two important survival figures, was experienced by him as one which he could neither attack, avoid, nor comment upon. It is interesting that this "independent-dependent" bind was similar to the previous one mentioned in relation to his mother. Dave's repertoire of responses to this type of life situation was limited—almost stereotyped—and he resorted to periods of confused, bizarre behavior or inappropriate laughter. In therapy Dave was helped to understand the nature of the bind and that more adaptive responses were possible. A discussion of this incident led to the development of tactics to handle Mother (especially humorous overstatement), and the patient seemed to benefit from these discussions, although he is still far from adroit in handling his parents.

The paramount significance of all these incidents, however, is that the patient repeatedly gets into difficulty because of his inability to label situations and to comment directly on his affective responses—especially when his feelings involve anger or love. This defect is, of course, glaringly present in his family, and comparisons were frequently made between Dave's communication problems and the pathological communication in the entire family. It was at this point that Dave stated he finally clearly understood the role of his family in his illness and the rationale behind the family sessions.

Another important double bind that Dave's mother, like so many mothers of schizophrenics, created was in the area of achievement. Fundamentally, the contradictory messages that Dave received were: "You shall be a very great man—the man among men" and "You cannot attend to even the basic necessities in life and without me would not survive." Dave's mother, who was somewhat of a mystic and belonged to a group of glossolaliacs, cherished a prophecy made by her sect when Dave was an infant that he "would one day be in India with an eagle on his shoulder." This prophecy was known by all and formed part of the family folklore. While Dave was in the hospital he ruminated endlessly about what he should be in life and subscribed to many correspondence courses. This rumination disconcerted the family who beseeched him to stop. Mother reinforced the double bind by frequently telling Dave, "Stop worrying about jobs because when you get well *you can be anything you want to be.*" When Dave obtained his new job (which happened to necessitate a move to another apartment), he called home to give his parents the good news. Mother's response, however, was "What did you do with the clothes you had in storage at the old place?" Dave's response to this was predictable—a feeling of confusion and a diffuse anger, culminating in his shrieking, "That's personal."

## Discussion

The utilization of conjoint family therapy as part of intensive individual psychotherapy is in need of further exploration. We have used conjoint family visits in connection with the psychotherapy of college students living away from home where the therapist would ordinarily not have the opportunity to meet the patient's parents. Many other situations arise that seem tailor-made for family sessions as a part of ongoing psychotherapy. Occasions such as contemplated matrimony, discharge from a hospital, moving of a relative into the home, divorced parents who share child visitation, and many others need study and documentation. If the psychotherapist is flexible in his approach, we feel that he will discover many indications for implementing psychotherapy with family sessions.

## Summary

An increased flexibility of therapeutic approaches has been one of the concomitants of the developing maturity of the psychotherapeutic fields. Not only may different techniques be applied to different individuals, but different techniques may be employed concurrently or sequentially with the same individual as he passes through various stages of therapy. A course of therapy is described in which family therapy was used to liberate a chronic schizophrenic patient from a restraining family system which operated to impede his efforts at individualization. A therapeutic tactic, designed to rupture the premise system of the family, was employed. Some family disorganization ensued at first, but eventually the patient was able (at least temporarily) to relinquish his obligatory role as the problem in the family. The patient subsequently engaged himself gainfully in individual therapy which explored in depth many issues which had been raised in the conjoint family therapy sessions.

*One of the sobering experiences of young psychotherapists is that change, although usually clamored for, is rarely welcomed when it is imminent. But the psychiatric community itself is not immune to this apparent perversity of human nature. Philosophies of therapy are a little like religious convictions, and history provides a plethora of examples for the stubbornness of the latter. In the following paper, Richard Fisch highlights the paradox of the resistance to change in a profession devoted to effecting change.*

# RESISTANCE TO CHANGE IN THE PSYCHIATRIC COMMUNITY

*Richard Fisch, M.D.*

As psychotherapists, we are constantly involved in encouraging change in our patients. In one way or another we devote a major portion of our working lives hoping that we may be of some assistance in the broadening of their experiences in the world. Yet less attention is paid to the broadening of our own professional lives or the tools we use to help patients achieve changes in themselves. I am sure that most therapists, at some points in their career, have paused to take a backward look over the growth of their work. However, the press of work keeps up and it is difficult to keep questions about one's own development in mind for long. We continue trying to help, using the tools we know best and perhaps not varying them very much until more years go by and again we may pause to look back on our own change, or lack of it.

Some time ago the pressure of working in a clinic overloaded with patients, most of whom lacked sophistication but who were badly in need of help, forced me to reevaluate the techniques I had been trained in,

Originally published in *Archives of General Psychiatry* 13:359–66, 1965. Copyright 1956 by American Medical Association. Reprinted (in abbreviated form) by permission.

primarily psychoanalytic psychotherapy. I decided to use more symptom-oriented methods which departed widely from my own technical background. It was the reaction of colleagues to these innovations that brought into sharper focus the questions I raised above: how ready are psychotherapists to change and explore? I decided to condense the experiences with colleagues into some organized form so that other psychiatrists who are starting to settle into their careers might take a backward look a little sooner and to gain some understanding of the difficulty that might be faced in attempting to make alterations in that career.

In order to develop new approaches, psychiatrists at all levels of involvement—training, private practice, hospitals, and research organizations—must be maximally free to entertain, plan, and test new techniques.

In this paper I am concerned with obstacles to the opening up of new pathways; obstacles manifested by orthodoxy, sectarianism, overspecialization, and a shying away from dissension.[1-3,6] The second portion of this paper is devoted to suggestions that can be undertaken at various levels of psychiatric organization in overcoming trends toward stagnation.

## I. Sources

New approaches for dealing with deviant behavior and altering it have run into resistances that stem from multiple sources: the presumption that psychoanalytic concepts are to be the yardstick used to measure new techniques, the evaluation of new ideas by examining the innovator's motivation rather than his ideas, and overt and covert pressures on innovators deriving from the nature of formal and informal psychiatric organizations.

### A. "The Psychoanalytic Yardstick"

When one considers the overall direction of psychiatric training in the United States, there can be little doubt that its principal vector is psychoanalytic, either in its pure form or in some attenuated state.[10]* The large mass of private practitioners reflect this trend also. The vocabulary of psychiatry today—unconscious, transference, resistance, orality, anality, etc—indicates the widespread use of psychoanalytic concepts and methodologies. Other approaches to treatment—somatic therapies, hypnosis,[8]

---

* For example, many of the renowned training centers are in some fashion associated with formal psychoanalytic institutes, such as the Menninger Clinic, the Yale Department of Psychiatry, or the New York Psychiatric Institute.

behavior therapy, social case work, family therapy, milieu therapy, psycho-drama—are usually considered tangents of the main core of treatment, psychoanalytic psychotherapy. Yet no study of results has ever adequately documented the superiority of this method over any of the preceding techniques.[10] Thus the choice of therapeutic method may be unrelated to effectiveness and this has ramifications when clinicians evaluate new techniques. Because of the priority given to psychoanalytic concepts in training and practice, a major source of resistance to change in psychiatric approaches is the use of a "psychoanalytic yardstick" and the following illustrates how it is used.

### B. *The Dependence on Insight*

While it is not the sole property of psychoanalytic forms of therapy, insight as the conditio sine qua non of behavior change has received its greatest impetus from psychoanalytic theory and practice. The greatest bulk of time spent in treatment revolves more around this one basic assumption than any other approach (such as suggestion, alterations in milieu, directions, etc). Often, insight itself is regarded as the goal of treatment and therapists will report "progress" in patients solely on the acquisition of insight. New methods that do not include insight will therefore be criticized simply on the basis that it does not include this "essential." One experimental therapist, after describing the rapid and apparently durable results achieved in relieving a patient of symptoms through a variant of behavior therapy, was criticized by a more conventional colleague because her symptoms were relieved before she could "get insight into her problems."

### C. *"Transference Cure"*

Another phenomenon, stemming from psychoanalytic thought, is that new forms of therapy are often discounted on the basis that results achieved through any wide departure from psychoanalytic therapy are "only transference cures" or "flights into health." Thus, what in all other scientific fields is the essential criterion—results—in psychoanalytic psychiatry is relegated to a secondary position in favor of consistency with a prevailing theory. I have heard therapists claim that, even should symptom relief achieved without insight prove to last the lifetime of the patient, they would still regard it as a transference cure and something less than desirable. The concept of flight into health is also an unfortunate and devastating one. One wonders how often patients who have achieved marked relief and ego enhancement in early stages of treatment are subsequently convinced of the "illusory" nature of their improvement and seduced into lengthy if not interminable treatment with attendant loss of confidence in their ability to gauge improvement because symptom change was labeled as flight into health. Telling patients that we are not interested in results may be a useful stratagem of treatment, but to disregard results in evaluating any form of therapy is dangerous.

Therefore, even if innovators can cite impressive results with new techniques they run the risk of criticism that their methods, in departing from psychoanalytic practice, have achieved results less than desirable, i.e., only transference cures.

### D. *Covert Manipulation by Therapists*

Psychoanalytically oriented therapists often fail to see their manipulation of patients which is inherent in any interaction, especially in a psychotherapeutic one. Conversations are continually being steered by the therapist not only in obvious ways, such as questions, but often by such subtle clues as variations in attention, manifestations of tension such as changes in breathing, tonal emphases, and even the display of books which indicate the therapist's areas of interest.[4] Thus, while therapists exert covert manipulation of patients, they can continue the myth of "nondirectiveness." Being nondirective or noncommittal has come to be a hallmark of modern psychotherapy, so much so that patients will often state that they realize they should not ask their therapists advice of everyday matters nor expect answers to questions.

As a result of the high value placed on nondirection, and because of the blind spots to covert direction, there is resistance to forms of treatment that involve open directiveness, such as hypnosis, behavior therapy, milieu therapy, etc.

### E. *Questioning Motivation of Clinicians*

Clinicians would be freer to evaluate the pros and cons of new ideas if they simply focussed on the content of those ideas. What does the innovator propose? How does he organize his ideas? How has he applied them? What kind of results has he achieved? These are the questions that should be raised. They are often not raised, and instead there is a preoccupation with what the innovator's motivation was in bringing forth divergent ideas. Again, while not the sole property of the psychoanalytic movement, the impetus for this has come from the priority given to psychoanalytic therapy, especially that of "countertransference." Clinicians who depart from the psychoanalytic yardstick find that colleagues may be more interested in their "countertransference distortions" than in the method and results of any new ideas brought forward. Probably the clearest example of this is found in an editorial letter in the *International Journal of Psychoanalysis* on the very subject of deviance from classic analytic practice:

> If we ask ourselves what may be at the root of such dissidence as presents itself in the phenomenon of the neoanalytic movement, we must come up with answers bearing on the problem of our selection of candidates, and on those qualities of the training analysis and of the supervisory system which eventuate in failure of resolution of *pathological narcissism,* in survival of *narcissistic identification* in the transference and counter-transference, and in the persistence of the *transference neurosis* itself. Our failure to be uncompromising in the application of our psychoanalytic insight into our authoritarian roles as teachers and educators may have something to do with the fact that at least some of our colleagues and students find solace for *narcissistic injury* in alliance as dissident coteries (italics mine).[7]

Psychoanalysis is burdened with a theory that permits the invalidation of attempts to alter it, as well as disqualify techniques operating outside the analytic framework.

F. *Organizational Pressures on Innovators*

Clinicians who experiment within a formal organization such as a hospital or clinic, are subject to pressures, both open and covert, which may discourage innovation. For example, one of the ward psychiatrists at a local state hospital attempted to reorder his ward using concepts of a "therapeutic community." He was never told to desist, but instead was transferred to one of the chronic services, an oft-used form of censure. In such cases, the resistance to innovation is based not so much on resistance to any particular concept of treatment so much as a perceived threat to the status quo of the hospital.

In more subtle forms, supervisors in residency training programs may discourage innovation by asking that supervisees explore their own motivation for deviation from conventional treatment. Residents who hope to practice in the area in which they are taking their training are particularly vulnerable to this kind of discouragement since they will have to depend on senior clinicians and their hospital for recognition and sources of referral. The same applies to young psychiatrists in the community who also depend on the senior members of the profession to introduce them into the professional community and provide referrals. A reputation for being "far out" may seriously jeapardize the newcomer's practice.

More experienced therapists, at the same time, subject themselves to similar restraints by failing to encourage or allow for discussion of divergent ideas and practices among members of professional societies and hospital staffs. Time that might be devoted to such discussion is frequently taken up with plodding administrative details, or "sociability hours." Often clinical material is relegated to "safe" outside speakers who are freer to present controversial ideas since they are more independent economically and professionally from the hosting group. Since there is probably more innovation by conventional therapists than is apparent, such "off-beat" speakers may encourage innovators simply by demonstrating that respected others are pursuing similar lines. That conventional clinicians depart from "proper" technique is most usually revealed in small "trusted" groups, and as asides, rarely in an open formal meeting. Even so, such asides still allow for the realization that orthodoxy is not all that popular or slavishly followed and younger therapists in particular may soon realize the illusory nature of "standard practice." I am not suggesting that formal professional groups, such as local psychiatric societies, are composed of members all burning for the opportunity to present new and revolutionary ideas, nor, if this were so, that this would be the best use of such societies; but where pertinent issues are strongly felt by many therapists, the airing of these issues is discouraged. For example, in one psychiatric society, several therapists were concerned over the loose and confusing interpretation of psychiatric indications for therapeutic abortion and asked that a panel discussion be held to try to shed some light on the matter. Despite repeated requests, even in the face of programless meetings, no such discussion has been held even though the initial suggestion was raised some two or more years ago.

It also seems difficult for therapists to describe what they do with patients during therapy sessions. At one hospital the psychiatric department was asked to present clinical material at their department meetings much as it is done in other medical and surgical sections. Psychiatrists then rotated in describing their own clinical experiences. However, the descriptions were inclusive of everything except what the therapist himself did. The history of the patient's illness occupied the major bulk of the time; this was followed by the various insights or resistive maneuvers the patient availed himself of, and finally some material related to improvement. Members, both those presenting as well as the audience, seemed uninterested in this form of participation and finally it was done away

272   THE INTERACTIONAL VIEW

with altogether. (As a recognition by members of the resistance to revealing one's work, the first presenter was roundly congratulated, not on his presentation, but for the fact that he had the courage to go first and "break the ice.") In no other branch of medicine is there such secrecy as to what the practitioner does with his patient. In hospital practice, the psychiatrist is free from observation of his work which his medical and surgical colleagues accept as a daily part of their routine, and since a consensus of what constitutes successful psychiatric treatment is lacking, even this area is unmonitored.

Finally, there is a tacit acceptance among psychiatrists that while various approaches to treatment are useful, most of these should be left to "specialists" to handle while the average therapist should continue to devote himself to individual psychoanalytic psychotherapy. For example, while most psychiatrists in the local area regard themselves as flexible in approaches to each patient, this usually means utilizing some variant of psychotherapy with occasional prescribing of psychotropic drugs. For other techniques, patients are referred to the "specialists" in group therapy, family therapy, hypnosis, shock treatment, or brief therapy. In this way, therapists avoid testing out, exploring, or understanding newer, divergent methods of treatment and "encapsulate" these to a relatively small number of their colleagues.

**REFERENCES**

1. THOMPSON, C.: A Study of the Emotional Climate of Psychoanalytic Institutes, *Psychiatry* 21: 45–52 (Feb) 1958.
2. RADO, S.; GRINKER, R. R.; and ALEXANDER, F.: Editorial, *Arch Gen Psychiat* 8:527 (June) 1963.
3. ROSE, M., and ESSER, M. A.: The Impact of Recent Research Developments on Private Practice, *Amer J Psychiat* 117:429–433 (Nov) 1960.
4. ROGERS, J. M.: Operant Conditioning in a Quasi-Therapy Setting, *J Abnorm Soc Psychol* 60:247, 1960.
5. SZASZ, T.: *The Myth of Mental Illness,* New York: Paul B. Hoeber, Inc., a division of Harper & Brothers, 1961.
6. HOLLINGSHEAD, A., and REDLICH, F. C.: *Social Class and Mental Illness,* New York: John Wiley & Sons, 1958.
7. GITEL, M.: Letter, *J Int Psychoanal Assoc* 43:375, 1962.
8. WOLFBERG, L. R.: *Medical Hypnosis,* New York: Grune & Stratton, Inc., 1948, p 12.

9. GOFFMAN, E.: *Asylums,* Garden City, N.Y.: Anchor Books, Doubleday & Co., 1961.
10. GRINKER, R. R.: "A Philosophical Appraisal of Psychoanalysis," in Masserman, J. (ed.): *Science and Psychoanalysis,* New York: Grune & Stratton, Inc., 1958, vol 1.

*It stands to reason that a new technique does not spring into being in a final, definitive form. Rather, its elaboration is a slow, uncertain and often circuitous process, always open to improvements and simplifications. A new treatment approach like family therapy is no exception. As we survey the field in the mid-Seventies, we not only find different and even contradictory theories and practices co-existing under this rubric, but even within a given school of thought changes are bound to occur over time.*

*In the early Sixties, for instance, we firmly believed that family therapy was only possible when the entire family was together in the treatment room and we would send them home when one of them failed to show up. But the obvious question soon arose: How entire is the "entire" family? Is the uncle who lives five miles away and in his bitter old age refuses any dealings with the family, part of the family or not? Or the student who is renting a room—is he part of the family? To cut a long story short, we now are convinced that once a therapist thinks primarily in terms of interaction, he can do family therapy even with a single individual.*

*However, probably the most important improvement and simplification regards the brevity, effectiveness and goal-directedness of treatment which interactional therapy has made possible. While these three terms are interdependent, the first—brevity of treatment—carries special social importance at a time when the demand for help far exceeds the services available to other than those who can afford long-term therapy.*

*In 1968 a new project was undertaken at MRI to investigate the phenomenon of therapeutically induced as well as of spontaneous change and to see what conclusions could be drawn for the design of novel, brief and effective interventions. Out of this study there grew a body of general principles of problem formation and problem resolution whose special applications to psychotherapy and human conflicts in the wider sense are the subject matters of a recently published book.\* The following*

* Paul Watzlawick, John H. Weakland and Richard Fisch, *Change. Principles of Problem Formation and Problem Resolution.* New York, W. W. Norton, 1974.

*article is a summary description of the work of the Brief Therapy Center* (*as this project is called for lack of a better name*) *and its underlying assumptions.*

# BRIEF THERAPY: FOCUSED
# PROBLEM RESOLUTION

*John H. Weakland, Richard Fisch, M.D.,*
*Paul Watzlawick, Ph.D., and Arthur M. Bodin, Ph.D.*

In the last few years, brief treatment has been proliferating—both growing and dividing. As Barten's (2) recent collection of papers illustrates, "brief therapy" means many different things to many different therapists. The brief therapy we wish to present here is an outgrowth of our earlier work in that it is based on two ideas central to family therapy: (a) focusing on observable behavioral interaction in the present and (b) deliberate intervention to alter the going system. In pursuing these themes further, however, we have arrived at a particular conceptualization of the nature of human problems and their effective resolution, and of related procedures, that is different from much current family therapy.

We have been developing and testing this approach at the Brief Therapy Center over the past six years. During this period the Center, operating one day a week, has treated 97 cases, in which 236 individuals were seen.

The Brief Therapy Center was initiated by a grant from the Luke B. Hancock Foundation and matching funds from the T. B. Walker Foundation and the Robert C. Wheeler Foundation, whose support is gratefully acknowledged. In addition to the authors, the work of the Center has depended heavily on the services, largely volunteered, of Mrs. Barbara McLachlan as project secretary and of Mrs. Elaine Sorensen, Paul Druckman, M.D., Frank D. Gerbode, M.D., Jack Simon, M.D., Thomas M. Ferguson, Lynn Segal, George S. Greenberg, and Joel Latner as research assistants, at various periods.

We would also like to acknowledge the help of a number of guest therapists, whose work allowed us to observe and compare various treatment styles; these included Don D. Jackson, M.D., Arthur B. Hardy, M.D., Ralph I. Jacobs, M.D., Roland C. Lowe, Ph.D., Patricia Hewitt, Ph.D., Constance Collinge Hansen, M.S.W., and Jay Haley, M.A.

Originally published in *Family Process* 13:141–68 (1974). Reprinted by permission.

(We have also had extensive experience using the same approach with private patients, but these cases have not been systematically followed up and evaluated.) These 97 cases reached us through a considerable variety of referral sources, and no deliberate selection was exercised. As a result, although probably a majority of our cases involve rather common marital and family problems, the sample covers a wide range overall. We have dealt with white, black, and oriental patients from 5 to over 60 years old, from welfare recipients to the very wealthy, and with a variety of both acute and chronic problems. These included school and work difficulties; identity crises; marital, family, and sexual problems; delinquency, alcohol, and eating problems; anxiety, depression, and schizophrenia. Regardless of the nature or severity of the problem, each case has been limited to a maximum of ten one-hour sessions, usually at weekly intervals. Under these circumstances, our treatment has been successful—in terms of achieving limited but significant goals related to the patients' main complaints—in about three-fourths of these cases. We have also demonstrated and taught our approach to a number of other therapists in our area.

We present our approach here for wider consideration. Any form of treatment, however, is difficult to convey adequately by a purely verbal account, without demonstration and direct observation. We will, therefore, begin by discussing the significance and nature of our basic premises in comparison with other forms of treatment. Hopefully, this will provide an orienting context for the subsequent description—supplemented with illustrative case material—of our interrelated concepts, plan of treatment, specific techniques, and results.

### Psychotherapy—Premises and Practices

In characterizing treatment approaches, although some over-simplification may result, outlining basic premises may make their nature—and especially, their implications—more plain. Often, attention is concentrated on what is explicit and detailed, while what is common and general is neglected. Yet, the more general an idea, the more determinative of behavior it is—especially if its existence is not explicitly recognized. This holds for interpersonal influence as well as individual thinking and behavior; Robert Rosenthal's (21) experiments demonstrate how the beliefs, assumptions, expectations, and biases of an experimenter or interviewer have a profound effect on his subjects. Similarly, the beliefs and theories held by a therapist may strongly influence not only his technique but also the length and outcome of his treatments—by affecting his patient's behavior, his evaluation of that behavior, or both.

For instance, if schizophrenia is conceptualized as a gradual, irreversible mental deterioration involving loss of contact with reality, then attempts at psychotherapeutic contact make little sense, and the only reasonable course of action is long-term hospitalization. The hospitalized patient is then likely to react in a way that clearly justifies this initial "preventive" action. Alternatively, if schizophrenia is seen as a manifestation of a dysfunctional structure of family relationships, the outlook is different and more hopeful, although basic restructuring of the family system is now likely to be seen as necessary. Again, in terms of the postulates of classical psychoanalytic theory, symptom removal must perforce lead to symptom displacement and exacerbation of the patient's condition, since it deals only with manifestations of deeper problems. The premises of the theory permit no other conclusion, except the alternative of claiming that the problem must not have been a "real" one (22). On the other hand, in therapies based on learning or deconditioning theories, symptom manipulation is consistent with the theoretical premises. This enables the therapist to try very different interventions—and, to some extent, constrains him to do so.

That is, all theories of psychotherapy (including our own) have limitations, of practice as well as conception, that are logically inherent in their own nature. Equally important, these limitations are often attributed to *human* nature, rather than to the nature of the theory. It is all too easy to overlook this and become enmeshed in unrecognized, circular explanations. Stating the basic premises of any psychotherapeutic theory as clearly and explicitly as possible at least helps toward perceiving also its implications, limitations, and possible alternatives.

### Our Brief Therapy—Bases and Comparisons

Much of the shorter-term treatment that has recently developed in response to the pressure of patient needs and situational limitations consists essentially of briefer versions of conventional forms of individual or family therapy. The same basic assumptions are involved, and, correspondingly, the methods used are similar, except for limited adaptations to the realities of fewer sessions (3, 5, 20). This is expectable, as the usual frameworks naturally offer more restraints to innovation than encouragement and guidance. Within their terms, new methods are apt to appear strange and unreliable (15). Consequently, "brief therapy" ordinarily connotes an expedient that may be necessary when a preferred treatment is not available or is considered not feasible—since the "best" therapies often require patients equipped with rather exceptional resources of time, money, intelligence, persistence, and verbal sophistication. The goals of such brief therapy correspondingly are conceived as limited "first aid"—such as relief of some pressing but not fundamental aspect of the patient's problem, or a supportive holding action until really thorough treatment becomes possible.

We recognize and value the practical and economic advantages for patients and society of shortening treatment. We do not, however, see our own kind of brief treatment as an expedient, nor is brevity in itself a goal to us, except that we believe setting time limits on treatment has some positive influence on both therapists and patients. Rather the nature of our therapy, including its brevity, is primarily a consequence of our premises about the nature and handling of psychiatric problems.

Our fundamental premise is that regardless of their basic origins and etiology—if, indeed, these can ever be reliably determined—the kinds of problems people bring to psychotherapists *persist* only if they are maintained by ongoing current behavior of the patient and others with whom he interacts. Correspondingly, if such problem-maintaining behavior is appropriately changed or eliminated, the problem will be resolved or vanish, regardless of its nature, origin, or duration (24, 26). Our general principles and specific practices of treatment all relate closely to these two assumptions.

This view, like any other, must be judged by its fruits rather than by its seeds. Yet, a brief consideration of two areas of shared prior experience and interest that appear to have had major implications for our present joint position may clarify it and give some due acknowledgement.

Our present brief therapy is visible first as pursuing further two main aspects of family therapy, in which we have all been extensively involved. A decade-and-a-half ago family therapy began to focus attention on observable behavioral interaction and its influence, both among family members and between them and the therapist, rather than on long-past events or inferred mental processes of individuals (10). In line with this, we now see disturbed, deviant, or difficult behavior in an individual (like behavior generally) as essentially a social phenomenon, occurring as one aspect of a system, reflecting some dysfunction in that system, and best treated by some appropriate modification of that system. We differ, however, with those family therapists who consider the dysfunction involved to be necessarily a fundamental aspect of the system's organization and requiring correspondingly fundamental changes in the system. Instead, we now believe that apparently minor changes in overt behavior or its verbal labeling often are sufficient to initiate progressive developments. Further, while we recognize that along with its obvious disadvantages symptomatic behavior usually has some recognizable advantages or "pay-offs"—such as providing leverage in controlling relationships—we no longer consider these especially significant as causes of problems or obstacles to change.

Family therapy also has prompted greater activity by therapists. Once family interaction was seen as significant for problems, it followed that the therapist should aim to change the going system. Extending this, we now see the therapist's primary task as one of taking deliberate action to alter poorly functioning patterns of interaction as powerfully, effectively, and efficiently as possible.

On the matter of *how* the therapist can actively influence behavior effectively—the strategy and techniques of change—we are especially indebted to the hypnotic work of Milton Erickson and his closely related psychotherapy.[1] Two points have been particularly influential. First, although Erickson is much concerned with how overt behavior affects feelings or states of mind, his moves to change existing behavior usually depend upon implicit or indirect means of influence. Even when behavior is explicitly discussed, his aim often is not to clarify the "reality" of a situation but to alter and ameliorate it by some redefinition. Second, both as hypnotist and therapist, Erickson has emphasized the importance of "accepting what the client offers," and turning this to positive use—in ways we will illustrate later—even if what is "offered" might ordinarily appear as resistance or pathology.

While our present approach thus derives directly from basic family therapy, in part, and from Erickson's work, in part, it also differs from both. For example, many family therapists attempt to bring about change largely by explicit clarification of the nature of family behavior and interaction. Such an attempt now seems to us like a family version of promoting "insight," in which one tries to make clear to families the covert rules that have guided them; we ordinarily avoid this. Meanwhile, our conceptualization of problems and treatment appears at least more general and explicit than Erikson's and probably different in various specific respects.

On the other hand, similarities as well as differences are observable between our treatment approach and other approaches with which we have had little interaction. For example, within the general field of family

---

[1] The work of Jay Haley (11, 12, 13) has been valuable in making Erickson's principles and practices more explicit, as well as in providing additional ideas from Haley's own work in family therapy and brief treatment.

therapy, we share with the crisis-intervention therapy of Pittman, Langsley, and their co-workers (18) beliefs in the importance of situational change for the onset of problems and of both directive measures and negotiation of conflicts in promoting better functioning in family systems. Minuchin and Montalvo (16), together with a number of their colleagues at the Philadelphia Child Guidance Clinic, have increasingly emphasized active intervention aimed at particular reorderings of family relationship structure to achieve rapid problem resolution; we often pursue similar aims. Other family therapists than ourselves, notably Bowen, assign patients homework as part of treatment. Work with families similar to our own is also being developed abroad, for instance, at the Athenian Institute of Anthropos under Dr. George Vassiliou and at the Istituto per lo Studio della Famiglia in Milan, under Prof. Dr. Mara Selvini Palazzoli. In addition, the behavior modification school of therapy involves a number of ideas and interventions rather parallel to ours, although that field still appears to give little attention to systems of interaction. Furthermore, as noted later, a number of the techniques of intervention we utilize have also been used and described, though usually in a different conceptual context, by other therapists.

In sum, many particular conceptual and technical elements of our approach are not uniquely ours. We do, however, see as distinctive the overall system of explicitly stated and integrated ideas and practices that constitute our approach.

### Main Principles of Our Work

1. We are frankly symptom-oriented, in a broad sense. Patients or their family members come with certain complaints and accepting them for treatment involves a responsibility for relieving these complaints. Also, since deviant symptomatic behavior and its accompanying vicious circles of reaction and counter-reaction can themselves be so disruptive of system functioning, we believe that one should not hasten to seek other and deeper roots of pathology. The presenting problem offers, in one package, what the patient is ready to work on, a concentrated manifestation of whatever is wrong, and a concrete index of any progress made.

2. We view the problems that people bring to psychotherapists (except, of course, clearly organic psychiatric syndromes) as situational difficulties between people—problems of interaction. Most often this involves the identified patient and his family; however, other systems such as a patient's involvement with others in a work situation may be important at times.

3. We regard such problems as primarily an outcome of everyday difficulties, usually involving adaptation to some life change, that have been mishandled by the parties involved. When ordinary life difficulties are handled badly, unresolved problems tend increasingly to involve other life activities and relationships in impasses or crises, and symptom formation results.

4. While fortuitous life difficulties, such as illness, accidents, or loss of a job sometimes appear to initiate the development of a problem, we see normal transitional steps in family living as the most common and important "everyday difficulties" that may lead to problems. These transitions include: the change from the voluntary relationship of courtship to the commitment of marriage, and from this to the less reversible commitment when the first child is born; the sharing of influence with other authorities required when a child enters school, and with the child himself and his peers in the adolescent period; the shift from a child-oriented marital relationship back to a two-party system when the children leave the home, and its intensification at retirement; and return to single life at the death of one spouse. Although most people manage to handle these transitions at least passably well, they all require major changes in personal relationships that may readily be mishandled. This view is similar to that of Erickson and Haley (12).

5. We see two main ways by which "problems" are likely to develop: if people treat an ordinary difficulty as a "problem" or if they treat an ordinary (or worse) difficulty as no problem at all—that is, by either overemphasis or underemphasis of difficulties in living.

The first appears related to utopian expectations of life. There are countless difficulties which are part and parcel of the everyday business of living for which no known ideal or ultimate solutions exist. Even when relatively severe, these are manageable in themselves but can readily become "problems" as a result of a belief that there should or must be an ideal, ultimate solution for them. For instance, there apparently has been a "generation gap" for the past 5000 years that we know of, but its difficulties only became greatly exacerbated into a "problem" when many people became convinced that it should be closed.

Inversely, but equally, "problems" can arise out of the denial of manifest difficulties—which could be seen as utopian assertions. For instance, the husband and wife who insist their marriage was made in heaven, or the parents who deny the existence of any conflicts with their children—and who may contend that any one seeing any difficulty must be either bad or mad—are likely to be laying the foundation for some outbreak of symptomatic behavior.

Two other aspects of this matter need mention. First, over- or under-emphasis of life difficulties is not entirely a matter of personal or family characteristics; this depends also on more general cultural attitudes and conceptions. While these often may be helpful in defining and dealing with the common vicissitudes of social life, they can also be unrealistic and provoke problems. For example, except for the death of a spouse, our own culture characterizes most of the transitions listed earlier as wonderful steps forward along life's path. Since all of these steps ordinarily involve significant and inescapable difficulties, such over-optimistic characterization increases the likelihood of problems developing—especially for people who take what they are told seriously. Second, inappropriate evaluation and handling of difficult situations is often multiplied by interaction between various parties involved. If two persons have similar inappropriate views, they may reciprocally reinforce their common error, while if one over-emphasizes a difficulty and another under-emphasizes it, interaction may lead to increasing polarization and an even more inappropriate stance by each.

6. We assume that once a difficulty begins to be seen as a "problem," the continuation, and often the exacerbation, of this problem results from the creation of a positive feedback loop, most often centering around those very behaviors of the individuals in the system that are intended to resolve the difficulty: The original difficulty is met with an attempted "solution" that intensifies the original difficulty, and so on and on (26).

Consider, for instance, a common pattern between a depressed patient and his family. The more they try to cheer him up and make him see the positive sides of life, the more depressed the patient is likely to get: "They don't even understand me." The action meant to *alleviate* the behavior of the other party *aggravates* it; the "cure" becomes worse than the original "disease." Unfortunately, this usually remains unnoted by those involved and even is disbelieved if any one else tries to point it out.

7. We view long-standing problems or symptoms not as "chronicity" in the usual implication of some basic defect in the individual or family, nor even that a problem has become "set" over time, but as the persistence of a *repetitively* poorly handled difficulty. People with chronic problems have just been struggling inappropriately for longer periods of time. We, therefore, assume that chronic problems offer as great an opportunity for change as acute problems and that the principal difference lies in the usually pessimistic expectations of therapists facing a chronic situation.

8. We see the resolution of problems as primarily requiring a substitution of behavior patterns so as to interrupt the vicious, positive feedback circles. Other less destructive and less distressing behaviors are potentially

open to the patient and involved family members at all times. It is usually impossible, however, for them to change from their rigidly patterned, traditional, unsuccessful problem-solving behavior to more appropriate behavior on their own initiative. This is especially likely when such usual behavior is culturally supported, as is often the case: Everyone *knows* that people should do their best to encourage and cheer up a loved one who is sad and depressed. Such behavior is both "right" and "logical"—but often it just doesn't work.

9. In contrast, we seek means of promoting beneficial change that work, even if our remedies appear illogical. For instance, we would be likely to comment on how sad a depressed patient looks and to suggest that there must be some real and important reason for this. Once given some information on the situation, we might say it is rather strange that he is not even *more* depressed. The usual result, paradoxical as it may seem, is that the patient begins to look and sound better.

10. In addition to accepting what the patient offers, and reversing the usual "treatment" that has served to make matters worse, this simple example also illustrates our concept of "thinking small" by focusing on the symptom presented and working in a limited way towards its relief.

We contend generally that change can be effected most easily if the goal of change is reasonably small and clearly stated. Once the patient has experienced a small but definite change in the seemingly monolithic nature of the problem most real to him, the experience leads to further, self-induced changes in this, and also, in other areas of his life. That is, beneficent circles are initiated.

This view may seem insensitive to the "real," "big," or "basic" problems that many therapists and patients expect to be changed by therapy. Such goals are often vague or unrealistic, however, so that therapy which is very optimistic in concept easily becomes lengthy and disappointing in actual practice. Views of human problems that are either pessimistic about change or grandiose about the degree of change needed undermine the therapist's potentially powerful influence for limited but significant change.

11. Our approach is fundamentally pragmatic. We try to base our conceptions and our interventions on direct observation in the treatment situation of *what* is going on in systems of human interaction, *how* they continue to function in such ways, and *how* they may be altered most effectively.

Correspondingly, we avoid the question *"Why?"* From our standpoint, this question is not relevant, and involvement with it commonly leads toward concerns about "deeper" underlying causes—historical, mental, familial—of problem behavior and about "insight" into these.

That is, the question "Why?" tends to promote an individualistic, voluntaristic, and rationalistic conception of human behavior, rather than one focused on systems of interaction and influence. Moreover, since underlying causes inherently are inferential rather than observable, concern about them distracts a therapist from close observation of the present problem and what behavior may be perpetuating it.

On the basis of this general conception of problems and their resolution, which is discussed more fully in Watzlawick, Weakland, and Fisch (25), we can now describe the overall practical approach and specific techniques that we utilize.

### Operation of the Brief Therapy Center

The Brief Therapy Center was established as one of the projects at the Mental Research Institute in January, 1967. Since the termination of our founding grants, we have continued our work on a somewhat reduced scale on volunteered time. Some direct operating expenses have been met by donations from patients, although we provide free treatment where appropriate.

Our working quarters consist of a treatment room and observation room, separated by a one-way viewing screen, with provision for simultaneously listening to and tape-recording sessions. There is also an intercom phone between the two rooms. At the outset of our work, a therapist and an official observer were assigned, in rotation, to each case. More recently, we have been working as an overall team, with several observers of equal status usually present.

Our handling of all cases follows a six-stage schema, although in practice there may be some overlap among these:

1. Introduction to our treatment set-up.
2. Inquiry and definition of the problem.
3. Estimation of behavior maintaining the problem.
4. Setting goals of treatment.
5. Selecting and making behavioral interventions.
6. Termination.

Each of these will now be considered in order.

#### Introduction to Our Treatment Set-Up

Patients intentionally are accepted with no screening. A first appointment is set by the project secretary whenever an applicant calls and there is a vacancy in our schedule. No waiting lists are kept; when we have no vacancy, people are referred elsewhere.

At the first meeting, our secretary has the patient or family fill out a form covering basic demographic data and brings him or them to the treatment room. The therapist begins by explaining the physical and organizational arrangements, mentioning the potential advantages for treatment of the recording and observation, and requests written consent to this. Only two patients have ever declined to proceed on this basis. The therapist also tells the patient at once that we work on a maximum of ten sessions per case; this helps to set a positive expectation of rapid change.

*Definition of the Problem*

Since our treatment focus is symptomatic, we want first to get a clear and explicit statement of the presenting complaint. Therefore, as soon as the therapist has taken a brief record of the referral source and any previous treatment, he asks what problem has brought the patient to see us. If a patient states a number of complaints, we will ask which is the most important. In marital or family cases, since viewpoints may differ, although they often are plainly interrelated, we ask each of the parties involved to state his own main complaint. From the beginning, then, we are following a form of the general principle, "Start where the patient is at."

Fairly often, the patient will give an adequate answer—by which we mean a clear statement referring to concrete behavior. In many cases, however, the response will leave the presenting problem still in doubt. Further inquiry is then needed to define more clearly this point of departure for the entire treatment. For example, patients with previous treatment experience or psychological sophistication are likely, after only the briefest mention of any present behavioral difficulty, to launch into discussion of presumed underlying matters, especially intrapsychic factors and family history, presenting these as the "real problem." We then press the question of what particular difficulties in living have brought them to see us *now*. To make things more specific, we often ask such questions as "What do you now do because of your problem that you want to stop doing, or do differently?" and "What would you like to do that your problem interferes with doing now?" Such inquiries also begin to raise the related question of treatment goals.

Other patients, especially younger ones, may state their complaints in vague terms that lack reference to any concrete behavior or life situation: "I don't know who I really am"; "We just can't communicate." Such patients can be particularly difficult initially. We find it important not to accept such statements as appropriate and informative but to continue inquiry until at least the therapist, if not the patient, can formulate a concrete, behavioral picture of the problem—of which such attachment to vague and often grandiose thinking and talking may itself be a major aspect.

*Estimation of Behavior Maintaining the Problem*

Our view, as mentioned earlier, is that problem behavior persists only when it is repeatedly reinforced in the course of social interaction between the patient and other significant people. Usually, moreover, it is just what the patient and these others are doing in their efforts to deal with the problem—often those attempts at help that appear most "logical" or unquestionably right—that is most important in maintaining or exacerbating it.

Once behavior is observed and considered in this light, the way this occurs is often rather obvious: The wife who nags her husband and hides his bottle in her efforts to have him from his alcohol problem and succeeds only in continually keeping drinking uppermost in his mind; the forgiving husband who never criticizes his wife until she feels he doesn't care anything about her, whatever she does, and becomes depressed—and he is forgiving of that too; the parents of a child dissatisfied with school who "encourage" him by taking all the more about how important and great education is—instead of it being a necessary drag. In other instances, of course, the reinforcements may be more difficult to perceive, either because they are subtle or complex—nonverbal behaviors, contradictions between statements and actions, different behaviors by several persons— or because even therapists are conditioned to accept cultural standards of logic and rightness without examining whether things really work that way.

In practice, the therapist first simply asks the patient and any family members present how they have been trying to deal with the problem. This alone may lead rapidly to a view of what keeps things going badly. If not, the inquiry, aiming always at concrete behavior, can be pursued at more length and in more detail, but sympathetically—the therapist's aim is to get enough information to understand what is happening, for which he needs cooperation, not to confront people with their mistakes. In addition to what the patient or others state explicitly, it is important to note *how* they discuss the problem and its handling, including their interaction. Such inquiry is likely to disclose a number of things that play some part in maintaining the problem, but working briefly demands choosing priorities. On the basis of observation and experience, one must judge which behavior seems most crucial.

*Setting Goals of Treatment*

Setting a goal both acts as a positive suggestion that change is feasible in the time allotted and provides a criterion of therapeutic accomplishment for therapist and patient. We, therefore, want goals stated clearly in terms of observable, concrete behavior to minimize any possibility of uncertainty or denial later. If parents bring us a child because he is failing in school, we ask for an explicit criterion of satisfactory progress—because we want to avoid subsequent equivocations such as "He is getting B's now instead of F's, but he isn't really learning enough." Also, we steer toward "thinking small" for reasons already discussed. Therefore, our usual inquiry is something like "At a minimum, what (change in) behavior would indicate to you that a definite step forward has been made on your problem?"

Concerning goals especially, however, patients often talk in vague or sweeping terms, despite our efforts to frame the question in terms of specific behavior. We then try to get more concrete answers by further discussion, clarification, and presentation of examples of possible goals for consideration. With vague, grandiose, or utopian patients, we have found it helpful to reverse our field, bringing them down to earth by suggesting goals that are too far out even for them. This again involves accepting what the patient offers, and even enlarging on this, in order to change it. For example, a student who was already in his mid-20's and was still being supported by a working mother told us he was studying "philosophical anthropology" in order to bring the light of India and China to bear on the West. He also, however, mentioned some interest in attending a well-known school of Indian music. It was then pointed out to him that this represented a rather limited aim compared to his concern to unite the spirituality of India with the practical communism of China and use both to reconstruct Western society. He then said that, since he was not doing well in his studies and was short of money, if he could secure a scholarship and really learn Indian music, this would be quite enough accomplishment for the present.

We usually are able, directly or indirectly, to obtain a stated goal that appears sufficiently explicit and appropriate to the problem. In some cases, however, we have not been able to do so. Either the patient persisted in stating only vague, untestable goals, or, rarely, the patient stated and stuck to an explicit goal which we judged inappropriate to his problem. Then we do not dispute what the patient insists on but privately set our own goal for the case by joint staff discussion of what sort of behavior would best exemplify positive change for the particular patient and problem. In fact, some such discussion occurs for all cases; at the least, the staff must always judge whether the patient's statement of his goal is adequate. Also, there is always staff discussion of intermediate behavioral goals; how does the patient—or his family members—need to behave so that the specific goal of treatment will follow?[2]

Our aim is to have a definite goal established by the second session, but gathering and digesting the information needed for this sometimes takes longer. Occasionally, we may revise the original goal in the course of treatment or add a secondary goal.

*Selecting and Making Interventions*

Once we have formed a picture of current behavior central to the problem and estimated what different behavior would lead to the specific goal selected, the task is one of intervening to promote such change. This stage must be discussed at some length, since it ordinarily constitutes the largest, most varied, and probably most unusual part of our treatment.

*Change and "insight."* We have already stated that our aim is to produce behavior change and that we do not see working toward insight, at either an individual or a family level, as of much use in this. In fact, working toward insight can even be counter-productive. Simple, practical-minded patients are often put off by this, since they want action and results, while more intellectually minded patients are likely to welcome such an approach but use it to delay or defeat any change in actual behavior. However, in addition to suggesting or prescribing changes in overt behavior, we do utilize interpretations. Our aim, though, is simply the useful relabeling of behavior. Patients often interpret their own behavior, or that of others, in ways that make for continuing difficulties. If we can only redefine the meaning or implications attributed to the behavior, this itself may have a powerful effect on attitudes, responses and relationships. Such interpretation might look like an attempt to impart insight, but it is not. Using interpretation to promote insight implies that truth can helpfully be disclosed and recognized. This is not our aim or our belief. Rather, our view is that redefining behavior labeled "hostile" as "concerned interest," for example, may be therapeutically useful whether or not *either* label is "true," and that such truth can never be firmly established. All that is observable is that some labels provoke

---

[2] Our schedule is arranged to allow for one half-hour after each session for staff discussion and planning of goals, specific interventions to use, and so on. In addition, new cases and general issues are considered at more length in separate, weekly staff meetings.

difficulties, while others, achievable by redefinition, promote adjustment and harmony—but this is enough.

Such relabeling may be especially important with rigid patients. It does not require overt behavior change, and it may even be accomplished without the need for *any* active cooperation by the patient or any family member. If the therapist's redefinition of an action or situation is not openly challenged—which can usually be arranged—then the meaning and effects of that behavior have already been altered.

*Use of idiosyncratic characteristics and motivation.* We attempt early in treatment to determine what approach would appeal most to the particular patient—to observe "where he lives" and meet this need, whether it is to believe in the magical, to defeat the expert, to be a caretaker of someone, to face a challenge, or whatever. Since the consquences of any such characteristic depend greatly on the situation in which it operates and how this is defined, we see these characteristics of different individuals not as obstacles or deficiencies, but as potential levers for useful interventions by the therapist.

For example, certain patients appear inclined toward defeating therapists, despite their request for help. This may be indicated by a history of unsuccessful treatment, repeated failure to understand explanations or carry out instructions, and so on. In such cases, the easiest and most effective course may be for the therapist to insist that the patient cannot possibly resolve his problem and that treatment can at most help him to endure it better. The patient is then likely to defeat *this* stance by improving.

A middle-aged widow first came to us with a complaint about the behavior of her 18-year-old son: delinquency, school failures, anger, and threatened violence toward her. She stated this was her only problem, although she also mentioned that she was an epileptic and was unable to use her right arm as a result of a work injury. Both mother and son had had about two years of previous therapy. We first suggested directly that her son was acting like a difficult, provoking, overgrown kid and, accordingly, she might gain by handling him more firmly in a few simple ways. She quickly thwarted such suggestions by increasing claims of helplessness: Now the epilepsy was emphasized; there was trouble with the other arm, too; a hysterectomy and appendectomy were also reported, along with childhood rheumatic fever, bleeding gums, troubles with her former husband and with her mother-in-law, constant worsening financial crises, and much more. In short, she was already a woman carrying on bravely amidst a sea of troubles that would have totally swamped anyone else; how could we ask her to do more yet? We then changed our approach to utilize this characteristic opposition. We began to insist to her that she was being unduly optimistic, was minimizing her troubles in an unrealistic way, and was not recognizing that the future very probably held even greater disasters for her, both individually and in terms of her son's behavior. It took some doing to surpass her own pessimistic line, but once we were able to do so, she began to improve. She started to oppose our pessimism—which she could only do by claiming and proving that she was not *that* sick and helpless—and to take a much more assertive attitude with her son, to which he responded well.

*Directed behavior change.* One of our main stated aims is to change overt behavior—to get people to stop doing things that maintain the problem and to do others that will lead toward the goal of treatment. While we are willing to issue authoritative directions, we find compliant patients rather rare. After all, most patients have already been exposed to lots of advice. If it was good, they must have some difficulty about profiting from advice; if it was bad, some preparation is needed for them to respond to quite different advice. Moreover, again, it is often just that behavior that seems most logical to people that is perpetuating their problems. They then need special help to do what will seem illogical and mistaken. When sitting on a nervous horse, it is not easy to follow the instructor's orders to let go of the reins. One *knows* the horse will run away, even though it is really the pull on the reins that is making him jump.

Behavioral instructions therefore are more effective when carefully framed and made indirect, implicit, or apparently insignificant. When requesting changes, it is helpful to minimize either the matter or the manner of the request. We will suggest a change rather than order it. If the patient still appears reluctant, we will back off further. We may then suggest it is too early to do that thing; the patient might think about it but be sure not to take any action yet. When we do request particular actions, we may ask that they be done once or twice at most before we meet again. We may request only actions that will appear minor to the patient, although in our view they represent the first in a series of steps, or involve a microcosm of the central difficulty. For example, a patient who avoids making any demands of others in his personal relationships may be assigned the task of asking for one gallon of gasoline at a service station, specifically requesting each of the usual free services, and offering a twenty-dollar bill in payment.

This example also illustrates our use of "homework" assignments to be carried out between sessions. Homework of various kinds is regularly employed, both to utilize time more fully and to promote positive change where it counts most, in real life outside the treatment room.

*Paradoxical instructions.* Most generally, paradoxical instruction involves prescribing behavior that appears in opposition to the goals being sought, in order actually to move toward them. This may be seen as an inverse to pursuing "logical" courses that lead only to more trouble. Such instructions probably constitute the most important single class of interventions in our treatment. This technique is not new; aspects and examples of it have been described by Frankl (8, 9), Haley (11), Newton (17) and Watzlawick, *et al.* (24). We have simply related this technique to our overall approach and elaborated on its use.

Paradoxical instruction is used most frequently in the form of case-specific "symtom prescription," the apparent encouragement of symptomatic or under undesirable behavior in order to lessen such behavior or bring it under control. For example, a patient who complains of a circumscribed, physical symptom—headache, insomnia, nervous mannerisms, or whatever—may be told that during the coming week, usually for specified periods, he should make every effort to increase the symptom. A motivating explanation usually is given, e.g., that if he can succeed in making it worse, he will at least suffer less from a feeling of helpless lack of control. Acting on such a prescription usually results in a *decrease* of the symptom—which is desirable. But even if the patient makes the symptom increase, this too is good. He has followed the therapist's instruction, and the result has shown that the apparently unchangeable problem can change. Patients often present therapists with impossible-looking problems, to which every possible response seems a poor one. It is comforting, in turn, to be able to offer the patient a "therapeutic double bind" (4), which promotes progress no matter which alternative response he makes.

The same approach applies equally to problems of interaction. When a schizophrenic son used bizarre, verbal behavior to paralyze appropriate action by his parents, we suggested that when he needed to defend himself against the parents' demands, he could intimidate them by acting crazy. Since this instruction was given in the parents' presence, there were two paradoxical positive effects: the son decreased his bizarreness and the parents became less anxious and paralyzed by any such behavior.

Not infrequently, colleagues find it hard to believe that patients will really accept such outlandish prescriptions, but they usually do so readily. In the first place, the therapist occupies a position of advice-giving expert. Second, he takes care to frame his prescriptions in a way most likely to be accepted, from giving a rationale appropriate to the particular patient to refusing any rationale on the grounds that the patient needs to discover something quite unanticipated. Third, we often are really just asking the patient to do things they already are doing, only on a different basis.

We may also encourage patients to use similar paradoxes themselves, particularly with spouses or children. Thus, a parent concerned about her child's poor school homework (but who prabably was covertly discouraging him) was asked to teach the child more self-reliance by offering incorrect answers to the problems he was asking help in solving.

Paradoxical instructions at a more general level are often used also. For example, in direct contrast to our name and ten-session limit, we almost routinely stress "going slow" to our patients at the outset of treatment and, later, by greeting a patient's report of improvement with a worried look and the statement, "I think things are moving a bit too fast." We also do the same thing more implicitly, by our emphasis on minimal goals, or by pointing out possible disadvantages of improvement to patients, "You would like to do much better at work, but are you prepared to handle the problem of envy by your colleagues?" Such warnings paradoxically promote rapid improvement, apparently by reducing any anxiety about change and increasing the patient's desire to get on with things to counteract the therapist's apparent overcautiousness.

On the same principle, when a patient shows unusually rapid or dramatic improvement, after acknowledging this change we may prescribe a relapse, on the rationale that it further increases control: "Now you have managed to turn the symptom off. If you can manage to turn it back on during this next week, you will have achieved even more control over it." This intervention, similar to Rosen's "re-enacting the psychosis" (18) and related techniques of Erickson, anticipates that in some patients improvement may increase apprehension about change and meets this danger by paradoxically redefining any relapse that might occur as a step forward rather than backward.

Since we as therapists are by definition experts, giving authoritative instructions on both thinking and acting, another pervasive element of paradox is created by the fact that ordinarily we do so only tentatively, by suggestions or questions rather than direct orders, and often adopt a "one-down" position of apparent ignorance or confusion. We find that patients, like other people, accept and follow advice more readily when we avoid "coming on strong."

*Utilization of interpersonal influence.* Although many of our treatment sessions include directly only one therapist, and one patient, we consider and utilize more extended interpersonal relationships constantly in our work. First, even when we see only the "identified patient," we conceive the problem in terms of some system of relationships and problem-maintaining behavior involving his family, his friends, or his work situation. Therefore, we believe that any interventions made with the patient must also take their probable consequences for others into account.

Equally, however, useful interventions may be made at any point in the system, and frequently it appears more effective to focus our efforts on someone other than the identified patient. Where a child is the locus of the presenting problem, we very commonly see the whole family only once or twice. After this we see the parents only and work with them on modifying their handling of the child or their own interaction. With couples also, we may see the spouses separately for the most part, often spending more time with the one seen by them as "normal." Our point is that effective intervention anywhere in a system produces changes throughout, but according to what the situation offers, one person or another may be more accessible to us, more open to influence, or a better lever for change in the system.

Second, the therapist and the observers also constitute a system of relationships that is frequently used to facilitate treatment. With patients who find it difficult to accept advice directly from a real live person, an observer may make comments to the therapist over the intercom phone to be relayed to the patient from this unseen and presumably objective authority. When a patient tends to disagree constantly, an observer may enter and criticize the therapist for his "poor understanding" of the case, forming an apparent alliance with the patient. The observer can then often successfully convey re-phrased versions of what the therapist was offering originally. With patients who alternate between two different stances, two members of the treatment team may agree, separately, with the two positions. Then, whatever course the patient takes next he is going along with a therapist's interpretation, and further suggestions can be given and accepted more successfully. Such therapist-observer interaction strategies can bring about change rapidly even with supposedly "difficult" patients.[3]

As may be evident, all of these techniques of intervention are means toward maximizing the range and power of the therapist's influence. Some will certainly see, and perhaps reject, such interventions as manipulative. Rather than arguing over this, we will simply state our basic view. First, influence is an inherent element in all human contact. Second, the therapist's functioning necessarily includes this fact of life, but goes much further; professionally he is a specialist at influence. People come to a therapist because they are not satisfied with some aspect of their living, have been unable to change it, and are seeking help in this. In taking any

[3] Team work facilitates such interventions but actually is seldom essential. A single therapist who is flexible and not unduly concerned about being correct and consistent can also utilize similar techniques—for example, by stating two different positions himself.

case, therefore, the therapist accepts the assignment of influencing people's behavior, feelings, or ideas toward desirable ends. Accordingly, third, the primary responsibility of the therapist is to seek out and apply appropriate and effective means of influence. Of course, this includes taking full account of the patient's stated and observed situation and aims. Given these, though, the therapist still must make choices of what to say and do, and equally what not to say and do. This inherent responsibility cannot be escaped by following some standard method of treatment regardless of its results, by simply following the patient's lead, or even by following a moral ideal of always being straightforward and open with the patient. Such courses, even if possible, themselves represent strategic choices. To us, the most fundamental point is whether the therapist attempts to deny the necessity of such choices to himself, not what he tells the patient about them. We believe the better course is to recognize this necessity, to try whatever means of influence are judged most promising in the circumstances, and to accept responsibility for the consequences.

*Termination.* Whether cases run the limit of ten sessions or goals are achieved sooner, we usually briefly review the course of treatment with the patient, pointing out any apparent gains—giving the patient maximum credit for this achievement—and noting any matters unresolved. We also remark on the probable future beyond termination, ordinarily in connection with reminding patients that we will be contacting them for a follow-up interview in about three months. This discussion usually embodies positive suggestions about further improvement. We may remind patients that our treatment was not intended to achieve final solutions, but an initial breakthrough on which they themselves can build further. In a minority of cases, however—particularly with negativistic patients, ones who have difficulty acknowledging help from anyone, or those fond of challenges—we may take an opposite tack, minimizing any positive results of treatment and expressing skepticism about any progress in the future. In both instances, our aim is the same, to extend our therapeutic influence beyond the period of actual contact.

In some cases, we encounter patients who make progress but seem unsure of this and concerned about termination. We often meet this problem by means of terminating without termination. That is, we say we think enough has been accomplished to terminate, but this is not certain; it can really be judged only by how actual life experience goes over a period of time. Therefore, we propose to halt treatment, but to keep any remainder of the ten sessions "in the bank," available to draw on if the patient should encounter some special difficulty later. Usually, the patient then departs more at ease and does not call upon us further.

## Evaluation and Results

If psychotherapy is to be taken seriously as treatment, not just an interesting exploratory or expressive experience, its effectiveness must be reliably evaluated. But this is far from easy, and rather commonly therapists offer only general clinical impressions of their results, with no follow-up of cases after termination, while researchers present ideal study designs that seldom get implemented.

We certainly cannot claim to have resolved this problem fully, even though we have been concerned with systematic evaluation of results from the outset of our work. Our method of evaluation still involves some clinical judgments and occasional ambiguities, despite efforts to minimize these. Until very recently, we have not had the resources needed to repeat our short-term follow-ups systematically after longer periods. And our evaluation plan is apt to seem overly simple in comparison with such comprehensive schemes as that of Fiske, *et al.* (6). At most, we can claim only that our method of evaluation is simple, avoiding dependence upon either elaborate manipulation and interpretation of masses of detailed data or elaborate theoretical inference; that it is reasonably systematic and practicable; and most important, that it is consonant with our overall approach to problems and treatment.

We see the essential task of evaluation as systematic comparison of what treatment *proposes* to do and its observable *results*. Our treatment aim is to change patients' behavior in specific respects, in order to resolve the main presenting complaint. Give the brevity of our work, the past refractoriness of most of the problems presented, and our frequent observation of behavior change immediately following particular interventions, we feel fairly safe in crediting observed changes to our treatment. Our evaluation then depends on answers to the two questions: Has behavior changed as planned? Has the complaint been relieved?

In our follow-up, the interviewer, who has not participated in the treatment, first inquires whether the specified treatment goal has been met. For instance, "Are you still living with your mother, or are you living in your own quarters now?" Next, the patient is asked the current status of the main complaint. This is supplemented by inquiring whether any further therapy has been sought since terminating with us. The patient is also asked whether any improvements have occurred in areas not specifically dealt with in treatment. Finally, to check on the supposed danger of symptom substitution, the patient is routinely asked if any new problems have appeared.

Ideally, such evaluation would divide our cases into two neat piles: successes in which our goal of behavior change was met and the patient's problem completely resolved, and failures in both respects. In reality, our treatment is not perfect; while results in these terms are clear for a majority of cases, several sources of less clear-cut outcomes remain: (a) Fairly often we have had cases in which our goal was reached or approached and considerable improvement was evident, but complete resolution of the presenting problem or problems was not attained. (b) Occasionally we have failed to formulate a goal explicit and concrete enough to check on its achievement with certainty. (c) In a very few cases, achievement of the planned goal and reported relief of the problem have been inversely related—hitting our target of change did not lead to relief, or we somehow got results in spite of missing our specific target.

In terms of our basic principles, all such mixed cases must be considered as failures of either conception or execution that demand further study. In the patients' terms, on the other hand, some of these cases have been completely successful, and many others represent quite significant progress. For the more limited and immediate purpose of evaluating the general utility of our approach, therefore, we have classified our cases into three groups according to practical results, recognizing that these correlate generally but not completely with achievement of our specific goals of behavior change. These groups represent: (a) complete relief of the presenting complaint; (b) clear and considerable, but not complete, relief of the complaint; and (c) little or no such change. For simplicity, the one case in which things were worse after treatment is included in the third group. We have not broken down our sample into sub-groups based on common diagnosis, since the conventional system of diagnostic categories and our conception of problems and their treatment are based on different assumptions and the nature of the presenting problem has appeared to make little difference for our rate of success or failure. It should also be noted that this evaluation refers directly only to the major presenting complaint. However, in none of our cases in which this complaint was resolved was there any report of new problems arising, and in many of these, improvements in additional areas were reported. On this basis, then, our overall results for 97 cases, involving an average of 7.0 sessions, are:

| | | |
|---|---|---|
| Success | 39 cases | 40 per cent |
| Significant improvement | 31 cases | 32 per cent |
| Failure | 27 cases | 28 per cent |

These results appear generally comparable to those reported for various forms of longer-term treatment.

## Conclusion: Implications

In this paper we have set forth a particular conception of the nature of psychiatric problems, described a corresponding brief treatment approach and techniques, and presented some results of their application. Clearly, further clinical research should be done, as important problems obviously remain; goals are still difficult to set in certain types of cases, the choice of interventions has not been systematized, evaluation is not perfected. Concurrently, though, there should also be more thinking about the broader significance of these ideas and methods. Our results already give considerable evidence for the usefulness of our general conception of human problems and their practical handling. Since this is both quite different from more common views and potentially widely relevant, we will conclude with a tentative consideration of some broad implications of our work.

The most immediate and evident potential of our work is for more effective use of existing psychiatric facilities and personnel. This could include reduction in the usual length of treatment and a corresponding increase in the number of patients treated, with no sacrifice of effectiveness. In fact, our approach gives promise of more than ordinary effectiveness with a variety of common but refractory problems, such as character disorders, marital difficulties, psychoses, and chronic problems generally. Further, it is not restricted to highly educated and articulate middle-class patients but is applicable to patients of whatever class and educational background.

In addition, our approach is relatively clear and simple. It might therefore be feasible to teach its effective use to considerable numbers of lay therapists. Even if some continuing supervision from professionals should be necessary, the combination of brief treatment and many therapists thus made possible could help greatly in meeting present needs for psychological help. Although this kind of development would have little to offer private practice, it could be significant for the work of overburdened social agencies.

Taking a wider view, it is also important that our model sees behavioral difficulties "all under one roof" in two respects. First, our model interrelates individual behavior and its social context instead of dividing them—not only within the family, but potentially at all levels of social organization. Second, this framework helps to identify continuities, similarities, and interrelations between normal everyday problems, psychiatric problems of deviant individual behavior, and many sorts of socially problematic behavior, such as crime, social isolation and anomie, and certain aspects of failure and poverty. At present, social agencies attempting to deal with such problems at the individual or family level are characterized by marked conceptual and organizational divisions—between psychological vs. sociological, supportive vs. disciplinary orientations, and more specifically, in the division of problems into many categories that are presumed to be distinct and discrete—reminiscent of the "syndromes" of conventional psychiatry. At best, this results in discontinuity; ineffective, partial approaches; or reduplication of efforts. At worst, it appears increasingly likely that such divisions themselves may function to reinforce inappropriate attempts at solution of many kinds of problems, as suggested by Auerswald (1) and Hoffman and Long (14). Our work thus suggests a need and a potential basis for a more unified and effective organization of social services.

Finally, our work has still broader implications that deserve explicit recognition, even though any implementation necessarily would be a very long-range and difficult problem. Our theoretical viewpoint is focused on the ways in which problems of behavior and their resolution are related to social interaction. Such problems occur not only with individuals and families, but also at every wider level of social organization and functioning. We can already discern two kinds of parallels between problems met in our clinical work and larger social problems. Problems may be reduplicated widely, as when concern about differences between parents and children becomes, in the large, "the generation gap problem." And conflicts between groups—whether these groups are economic, racial, or political—may parallel those seen between individuals. Our work, like much recent social history, suggests very strongly that ordinary, "common-sense" ways of dealing with such problems often fail, and, indeed, often exacerbate the difficulty. Correspondingly, some of our uncommon ideas and techniques for problem-resolution might eventually be adapted for application to such wider spheres of human behavior.

## REFERENCES

1. AUERSWALD, E., "Interdisciplinary vs. Ecological Approach," *Fam. Proc.,* 7:202–215, 1968.
2. BARTEN, H. (Ed.), *Brief Therapies,* New York, Behavioral Publications, 1971.
3. BARTEN, H., and BARTEN, S., (Eds.), *Children and Their Parents in Brief Therapy,* New York, Behavioral Publications, 1972.
4. BATESON, G., JACKSON, D., HALEY, J., and WEAKLAND, J., "Toward a Theory of Schizophrenia," *Behav. Sci.,* 1:251–264, 1956.

5. BELLAK, L., and SMALL, L., *Emergency Psychotherapy and Brief Psychotherapy,* New York, Grune and Stratton, 1965.
6. FISKE, D., HUNT, H., LUBORSKY, L., ORNE, M., PARLOFF, M., REISER, M., and TUMA, A., "Planning of Research on Effectiveness of Psychotherapy," *Arch. Gen. Psychiat.,* 22:22–32, 1970.
7. FRANK, J., *Persuasion and Healing,* Baltimore, Johns Hopkins Press, 1961.
8. FRANKL, V., *The Doctor and the Soul,* New York, Alfred A. Knopf, 1957.
9. FRANKL, V., "Paradoxical Interventions," *Amer. J. Psychother.,* 14:520–535, 1960.
10. JACKSON, D., and WEAKLAND, J., "Conjoint Family Therapy: Some Considerations on Theory, Technique, and Results," *Psychiatry,* Supplement to 24:2:30–45, 1961.
11. HALEY, J., *Strategies of Psychotherapy,* New York, Grune and Stratton, 1963.
12. HALEY, J., *Uncommon Therapy: The Psychiatric Techniques of Milton H. Erickson, M.D.,* New York, W. W. Norton, 1973.
13. HALEY, J. (Ed.), *Advanced Techniques of Hypnosis and Therapy: Selected Papers of Milton H. Erickson, M.D.,* New York, Grune and Stratton, 1969.
14. HOFFMAN, L., AND LONG, L., "A Systems Dilemma," *Fam. Proc.,* 8:211–234, 1969.
15. KROHN, A., "Beyond Interpretation," (A review of M. D. Nelson, *et al., Roles and Paradigms in Psychotherapy). Contemporary Psychology,* 16:380–382, 1971.
16. MINUCHIN, S., and MONTALVO, B., "Techniques for Working with Disorganized Low Socioeconomic Families," *Amer. J. Orthopsychiat.,* 37:880–887, 1967.
17. NEWTON, J., "Considerations for the Psychotherapeutic Technique of Symptom Scheduling," *Psychotherapy: Theory, Research and Practice,* 5:95–103, 1968.
18. PITTMAN, F. S., LANGSLEY, D. G., FLOMENHAFT, K., DE YOUNG, C. D., MACHOTKA, P., and KAPLAN, D. M., "Therapy Techniques of the Family Treatment Unit," pp. 259–271 in Haley, J. (Ed.), *Changing Families: A Family Therapy Reader,* New York, Grune and Stratton, 1971.
19. ROSEN, J., *Direct Analysis,* New York, Grune and Stratton, 1953.
20. ROSENTHAL, A., Report on brief therapy research to the Clinical Symposium, Department of Psychiatry, Stanford University Medical Center, November 25, 1970.
21. ROSENTHAL, R., *Experimenter Effects in Behavioral Research,* New York, Appleton-Century-Crofts, 1966.
22. SALZMAN, L., "Reply to the Critic," *Int. J. Psychiat.,* 6:473–478, 1968.
23. SPIEGEL, H., "Is Symptom Removal Dangerous?" *Amer. J. Psychiat.,* 123:1279–1283, 1967.
24. WATZLAWICK, P., BEAVIN, J., and JACKSON, D., *Pragmatics of Human Communication,* New York, W. W. Norton, 1967.

25. WATZLAWICK, P., WEAKLAND, J., FISCH, R., *Change: Principles of Problem Formation and Problem Resolution,* New York, W. W. Norton, 1974.
26. WENDER, H., "The Role of Deviation-Amplifying Feedback in the Origin and Perpetuation of Behavior," *Psychiatry,* 31:317–324, 1968.

*Resistance to change is not the only complication that may thwart the process of change. Another way of precluding it and of turning the attempted solution into its own problem—postulating a utopian goal—was already described briefly on page 280 of the preceding paper. Especially in our days this form of wrong problem solution is far more frequent than may appear at first sight. In the following essay, later incorporated into the book* Change\*, *Paul Watzlawick examines the practical consequences of attempted utopian changes, which invariably lead a system into more of what was to be changed.*

# THE UTOPIA SYNDROME

## Paul Watzlawick

> Truth is not what we discover, but what we create.
>
> —SAINT-EXUPÉRY

The preamble to the constitution of a Free University states: "The natural state of man is ecstatic wonder; we should not settle for less." The program of one of the rapidly proliferating esoteric institutes introduces its course for married couples with the words: "Marriage which means the compromise of love isn't worth the trip." Another course teaches physical scientists *cosmic thinking* "as a way of becoming more aware of ways for developing more harmony." And the description of a course offered by a highly respectable institution of higher learning confidently promises: "If your perception of yourself is vague and ephemeral, if you feel your relations with others are awkward and mixed-up, this series

Originally published in *Swiss Review of World Affairs,* Vol. 22, No. 12, March 1973, pp. 19–22. Reprinted by permission.

\* For reference see footnote on page 273.

of lecture-work-seminars may well turn you on to life and its deep richness and meaning for you."

But what if somebody fails to reach his natural state of ecstatic wonder, and if life's deep richness does not unfold itself?

Since 1516, when Thomas More described that distant island which he gave the name of Utopia ("Nowhere"), volumes have been written on the subject of an ideal society. Much less has been said, however, about the concrete, individual as well as societal results of utopian expectations. In our own Age of Utopia these results and their peculiar pathologies are beginning to become evident. Virulent, and no longer limited to particular societal or political systems, they prove once again that specific premises lead to specific consequences, and that these consequences may tend to perpetuate what the premises were meant to overcome. Heaven knows that this outcome is not surprising, but every generation apparently has to rediscover it through its own painful convulsions.

A passage from Dostoevsky's "Demons" is illustrative and could have been written today, not 100 years ago. Addressing a group of conspirators is Shigalyov, the author of an enormously complex "study of the social organization of the society of the future which is to replace our present one." He is willing to present his thoughts in abbreviated form in ten evening sessions, but warns that

my system is not yet complete. I'm afraid I got rather muddled in my own data, and my conclusion is in direct contradiction to the original idea with which I start. Starting from unlimited freedom, I arrived at unlimited despotism. I will add, however, that there can be no other solution of the social formula than mine.

The modern utopias are not that complex. Unlike Dostoevsky's character, the modern Shigalyovs are *terribles simplificateurs,* flat-thinkers all too often caught in the most banal dichotomies of yes and no. But like their literary predecessor, they are bound to run into what C. G. Jung has called *enantiodromia,* that is, the tendency of extreme attempts at change to somersault into their very opposite and to reinforce what they were intended to change. The superhuman and the inhumane are all too often the two sides of the same coin, and the decisive flip of the coin is usually beyond human control: the French Revolution with its lofty ideal of universal *liberté, égalité, fraternité* turned into a holocaust; and it is perhaps not generally known that during the last months of his life, Kant, the advocate of Pure Reason, was tormented by unbearable anxiety attacks.

Extremism in the solving of human problems seems to occur most frequently as a result of the belief that one has found the ultimate, all-embracing answer. Once somebody is caught in this belief, it is then logical for him to try to actualize this solution—in fact, he would not be true to his own self if he did not. The resulting behavior, which we shall call the "utopia syndrome," can take one of three possible forms, and these will now be presented in some detail.

The first form could be called introjective. Its consequences are more strictly psychiatric than social, since they are the outcome of a deep, painful feeling of personal inadequacy for being unable to reach one's goal. If that goal is utopian then the very act of setting it creates a situation in which the unattainability of the goal is less likely to be blamed on its utopian nature, but rather on one's ineptitude: my life should be rich and rewarding, but I am living in banality and boredom; I should have intense feelings, but cannot awaken them in myself. The psychiatrist Yalom has shown in a recent study that a severe and unattainable self-image, like Hemingway's, can lead to tragic consequences: "The individual cannot in real life approximate the superhuman scope of the idealized image, reality eventually intrudes, and he realizes the discrepancy between what he wants to be and what he is in actuality. At this point, he is flooded with self-hatred, which is expressed through a myriad of self-destructive mechanisms." Who is to cure his sickness? Certainly not those who claim that for them the utopian idea works, because their claim can only deepen and confirm his feelings of failure and sickness. And, on the other hand, certainly not those who do not share his utopia, but are likely to suggest solutions which to him are nothing but invitations to resign himself to a mediocre, cold and threatening world. The description of a panel discussion on "RAP-centers" at the 1971 meeting of the American Ortho-Psychiatric Association summarizes the problem only too well:

. . . These centers' populations differ from those of classic clinic populations in certain ways, e.g., "loneliness" is experienced as "unbearable" and is chronic; fear of "establishment institutions" or of being considered a "patient" precludes treatment elsewhere; expectation of constant instant happiness is not met and its absence is seen by rap-clients as "sickness"; inherent, indoctrinated concern with police (even when not warranted) is endemic; training in order to "help" is considered unnecessary and even harmful. Yet more people go to RAP-Centers than to Community Mental Health Clinics.

Other possible consequences of this form of the utopia syndrome are alienation, divorces, nihilistic world views; frequently alcohol or drugs are involved, but these brief euphorias are inevitably followed by a return to an even colder, grayer reality, a return which makes existential "dropping out" even more appealing. This attitude, too, has a predecessor in Russian literature: Oblómov, the hero of Goncharóv's novel of the same title (which in nineteenth century Russia made the expression *Oblomovism* into a fashionable, diagnostic term for this affliction). Of course, dropping out as well as Oblomovism are possible only where subsistence is guaranteed by society.* Oblómov's estates, even though he let them deteriorate, still produced enough to keep him going, while today's drop-outs can count on the parental allowance or on government welfare. But since we all tend to hate and fear those on whom we helplessly depend, parents or State may become almost paranoid symbols of persecution. Not surprisingly, in this view of the world, the fantasy of general destruction (produced actively or suffered helplessly) can become wisdom's ultimate resolve.

The second variation of the utopia syndrome is much less dramatic and even holds a certain charm. Its motto is Robert Louis Stevenson's well-known aphorism, "It is better to travel hopefully than to arrive," which he probably borrowed from a Japanese proverb. While Oblomov and his modern followers despair of their ability to reach the too distant goal, here the method of choice is a harmless and almost playful form of procrastination. Since the goal is distant, the journey will be long, and a long journey requires lengthy preparations. The uneasy question as to whether the goal can be reached at all or, if reached, will be worth the long trip, need not therefore be asked for the time being. In his poem *Ithaka,* the Greek poet Constantinos Cavafy depicts this very attitude. Pray that the way be long, he counsels the seafarer, that your journey be full of adventures and experiences. You must always have Ithaka in mind, arrival there is your predestination—but do not hurry the journey, better that it last many years. Be quite old when you anchor at the island. And Cavafy knows of a non-utopian solution: You enter harbours never seen before, and rich with all you have gained on the way, do not expect Ithaka to give you riches. Ithaka has given you your lovely journey, without Ithaka you would not set out.

But Cavafy's wise, conciliatory solution is open only to a few, for the

* In one of his essays, George Orwell has this to say about our own century: "The leading writers of the Twenties were predominantly pessimistic. Was it not after all because these people were writing in an exceptionally comfortable epoch? It is just in such times that 'cosmic despair' can flourish. People with empty bellies never despair of the universe, nor even think about it, for that matter."

dream of arriving in Utopia can be alarming: either in Cavafy's sense as fear of disenchantment, or in Hamlet's sense, that we shall "rather bear those ills we have than fly to others that we know not of." In either case, it is the journey, not the arrival, that matters; the eternal student, the perfectionist, the neurotic who invariably, predictably manages to fail on the eve of success, are examples of travellers who eternally wander and never arrive. The psychology of the unattainable necessitates that every fulfillment is experienced as a loss, as a profanation: for the devout Jew the political reality of the State of Israel is little more than the banal parody of an age-old, messianic longing; for the romantic lover who at long last conquers the beautiful woman, the reality of his victory is a far cry from what it was in his dreams.

The third variation of the utopia syndrome is essentially projective, and its basic ingredient is a moral, righteous stance, based on the conviction of having found the truth and sustained by the resulting missionary responsibility of improving the world. This is first attempted by various forms of persuasion and in the hope that the truth, if only made plain enough, will of necessity be seen and accepted by all men of good will. Consequently, those who will not embrace it are—by definition of this simplistic premise—acting in bad faith and their eventual destruction for the benefit of mankind is fully justified.

Thus, if my life is not a permanent state of ecstatic wonder, if universal love of everybody for everybody has not yet been actualized, if in spite of my exercises I have not yet attained *sátori*, if I am still unable to communicate deeply and meaningfully with my partner, if sex remains a disappointingly mediocre experience—then this is because my parents or society at large, by their rules and limitations, have crippled me and are unwilling to concede me that minimum of freedom needed for my self-actualization. This, of course, is Rousseau revisited: *Que la nature a fait l'homme heureux et bon, mais que la société le déprave et le rend misérable.* Robert Ardrey, in pointing to this opening sentence of "Emile," believes that it launched what he so aptly calls the Age of Alibi: nature made me happy and good, and if I am otherwise, it is society's fault. The Age of Alibi, he writes in "The Social Contract,"

presenting greater sympathy for the violator than the violated, has with elegance prepared us for maximum damage as we face a future of maximum civil disorder. A philosophy which for decades has induced us to believe that human fault must rest always on somebody else's shoulders; that responsibility for behavior damaging to society must invariably be attributed to society itself; that human beings are born not only perfectible but identical, so that any unpleasant divergences must be the product of unpleasant environments . . . such a philosophy has prepared in all splendour the righteous self-justifications of violent minorities, and has likewise prepared with delicate hands the guilts and the bewilderments of the violated.

Alfred Adler already was quite aware of this projective mechanism, e.g. when defining his concept of an individual's life plan. "The life plan of the neurotic demands categorically that if he fails, it should be through someone else's fault and that he should be freed from personal responsibility." And concerning paranoia, Adler wrote: "The activity [of the paranoiac] is usually of a very belligerent kind. The patient blames others for the lack of success in his exaggerated plans, and his active striving for complete superiority results in an attitude of hostility towards others. . . . His hallucinations . . . arise always when the patient wants something unconditionally, yet at the same time wants to be considered free from responsibility."

Since in spite, or perhaps just because, of their utopian nature, the proposed solutions are astonishingly pedestrian and inadequate—in Ardrey's words, the cliches of a century, all tried and found wanting—the belief in their uniqueness and pristine originality can only be maintained by a studious disregard for the evidence of the past. A deliberate disdain not only for the lessons of history, but for the whole idea that history has anything to offer, thus becomes yet another essential ingredient of the utopia syndrome. This not only prevents embarrassing comparisons between one's behavior and, say, the terror tactics of Nazi goon squads in the early Thirties, but has the additional advantage of enabling one to see one's own suffering and the sorry state of the world as a unique, unheard-of plight for which there are no valid comparisons. Those who ignore history, warned Santayana, are doomed to repeat it . . .

Common to all three aspects of the utopia syndrome is the basic fact that the premises on which the syndrome is based are considered to be more real than reality. What we mean by this is that the individual (or, for that matter, a group or a whole society), when trying to order his world in accordance with his premise and seeing his attempt fail, will typically not examine the premise for any absurd or unrealistic elements of its own, but will, as we have seen, blame outside factors (e. g., society) or his own ineptitude. The idea that the fault might lie with the premise is unbearable, for the premise is the truth, is reality. Thus, the Maoists argue, if after more than half a century the Soviet brand of Marxism has not managed to create the ideal, classless society, it is because the pure doctrine has fallen into impure hands, and not because there might be something inherently wrong with Marxism.

The main source of suffering in either form of the utopia syndrome is thus an age-old and universally known one: the painful discrepancy between what *is* and what, according to one's ideal, *should* be. In this sense there is nothing particularly new about this affliction; the teachings of Buddha state the predicament just as lucidly as existential writers from Kierkegaard and Dostoevsky to Camus. But there seems to have been only one earlier period in the history of mankind when the pathology of utopia reached comparable proportions. This was during the last decades of the first millennium A. D., when eloquent prophets of doom announced the imminent end of the world from plague and pestilence, and militant, secular religions rose against any manifestation of established order. Could it be that the approaching end of the second millennium afflicts us more deeply than we realize?

So much for the pathologies of the utopias. But what about their therapy? We must here distinguish between therapy in the narrower sense, that is, psychotherapy, and those measures which have wider social implications. As far as the former is concerned, the question arises if and to what extent psychotherapy is itself suffering from the affliction it is supposed to cure. With the possible exception of the writings of Alfred Adler, Harry Stack Sullivan and Karen Horney, most schools of psychotherapy (although not necessarily their individual adherents) have set themselves utopian goals, such as genital organization, individuation, self-actualization, and the like—to say nothing of the more modern and extreme "schools" mentioned in the introductory paragraph. With goals like these, psychotherapy becomes an open-ended process, perhaps humanistic, but more likely inhumane as far as the concrete suffering of patients goes. In view of the lofty magnitude of the endeavor, it would be unreasonable to expect concrete, rapid results and in a fascinating, almost Orwellian display of logical acrobatics, the concrete is thus labelled utopian and utopia defined as reality. As every high school student knows, the introduction of zero or infinity into an equation produces paradoxical results, and the human equation does not seem to be an exception to this mathematical rule. Make concrete change of a concrete problem dependent upon the reaching of a goal which is so distant as to border infinity, and the resulting situation becomes self-sealing, to borrow Leon Lipson's apt term. For instance, if an acute appendicitis is not cured by the power of the patient's prayer, this merely proves that his faith was not strong enough and his demise therefore vindicates rather than invalidates the teachings of Spiritual Healing. Open-ended, self-sealing systems win either way, and the bitter joke comes to mind about the patient who after years of treatment still wets his bed, "but it does not bother me any more."

Utopian attempts at solutions create situations in which it is often impossible to distinguish clearly between the "problem" and the "solution." As far as human problems go, two obvious facts should be (but are not always) borne in mind: a problem, in order to be solved, must first of all be a problem and, secondly, the solution has to be applied to *it* and not somewhere else. This enables one to separate problems from "problems." The unattainability of a utopia is such a pseudo-problem, but the suffering it entails is very real. If men define situations as real, they are real in their consequence, remarked W. I. Thomas. If, in a logical *salto mortale,* these consequences are seen as the causes of the problem, it then makes sense to attempt to solve them. If these attempts are unsuccessful (as they have to be), it then makes sense to try harder. "The possible we do right away, the impossible takes a little longer"—a cute aphorism, but a cruel trap for anyone who even half believes in it. The impossible, obviously, takes forever, but in the meantime, to quote Ardrey once more, "while we pursue the unattainable we make impossible the realizable." We smile at the joke about the drunk who is searching for his keys not where he really lost them, but under the street lamp, because that's where the light is best. It sounds funny, but only because here the fact is made explicit that a solution is attempted not only away from the problem (and is therefore doomed to fail), but also because the fruitless search could go on forever—in fact, the attempted solution *is* the problem. In real life situations this fact usually remains outside the awareness of all concerned; the cure is not simply worse than the disease, but rather *is* the disease.

To exemplify: Quite obviously few marriages live up to the ideals formulated in modern sex and marriage manuals. Whose problem is this? Those who accept these theses as to what a marital relationship should "really" be like, cannot escape the realization that they have a problem and are likely to start working towards its solution until divorce do them part. Their concrete problem, obviously, is not their marriage, but their attempts at finding the solution to a problem which in the first place is not a problem, and even if it were one, could not be solved on the level on which they attempt its solution. They are like a dreamer caught in a nightmare: no matter what he does *within* his dream, no matter how he runs, fights, screams, hides, it is to no avail and the dream can theoretically go on forever (as some psychotic nightmares evidently do). The solution lies in waking up, and waking up is no longer part of the dream, it is a different premise, a different level of problem-solving altogether.

From the foregoing one arrives at the perhaps shocking conclusion that the limits of a responsible and humane psychotherapy are much narrower than is generally thought. Lest therapy become its own pathology, it must limit itself to the relief of suffering; the quest for happiness cannot be its task. From aspirin we expect a lessening of our headache, but not also ingenious thoughts, and this, basically, is also true of therapy. When an eager pupil, in his frantic quest for satori, asked the Zen master what enlightenment was like, he answered: "Coming home and resting comfortably."

On the socio-economic and political levels, the situation does not appear to be essentially different, except that there the sobering conclusions to be drawn may appear, if anything, even more shocking and backward. A recent article in the *Neue Zürcher Zeitung* summarizes the international monetary situation in terms which sound surprisingly familiar: "We now recognize that for years we have been confusing causes and effects in monetary matters and have thus been engaged in purely symptomatic therapy. Without imposing a limitation on our futuristic expectations and their mythical implications, all attempts at fighting inflation are doomed to failure. It can even be said that modern expansionistic policies indirectly create the ills which they are supposed to combat."

Very similarly, in countries with very sophisticated and highly developed social welfare programs, like Sweden, Denmark, Britain, Austria, and others, the situation has reached a point where these programs are creating new needs and thereby defeating their own purposes. In the United States, the situation is not much different. In his Henry Margenau Lecture on what he so aptly calls "The Functions of Incompetence," Professor Lee Thayer recently pointed to the fact that between 1968 and 1970, that is, in just two years, social welfare expenditures increased about 34% from $11 billion to $14 billion. This not only proves the need for these welfare measures, but also something else: that thousands of specialized jobs are needed additionally for the implementation of these programs, "and that the continued growth of this part of our total economy will depend upon increasing—not decreasing—the incompetence of the citizenry in all of those dimensions for which there is a welfare program, or for which a program might be invented and funded."

But increased incompetence is not the only problem we are facing. As early as 1947, in his essay on Utopia and Violence, the philosopher Karl Popper warned that utopian schemes must perforce lead to new crises. It is unfortunately much easier, he points out, to propose ideal and abstract goals and to find enthusiastic followers, than to solve *concrete* problems. But, warns Popper, our fellow humans have a right to our help. No generation must be sacrificed on behalf of the happiness of future generations, an ideal happiness which can never be realized. The basic concern of rational public politics is human suffering, and happiness cannot be part of this concern. The attainment of happiness must be left to our private endeavors. And long before Popper, the poet Hölderlin remarked: "What has made the State into hell is that man wanted to make it his heaven."

*To end this chapter on a somewhat less somber note, there follows a paper written by the staff of the Brief Therapy project for a dual purpose: to summarize the approach developed at MRI, and to be itself an example of this approach. As in the course of time MRI's brief methods became known to larger numbers of colleagues, a good deal of the kind of professional resistance, mentioned on pages 266–273, was encountered. These reactions ranged from an ambiguous "That's interesting" to considerably less neutral terms like "That's just manipulation."*

*Since one of the best ways of dealing with resistance consists in preempting it by demanding it (a technique also referred to as symptom prescription), it was decided to write a tongue-in-cheek warning to colleagues who might be contemplating the use of brief methods.*

# ON UNBECOMING FAMILY THERAPISTS

R. Fisch, P. Watzlawick,
J. Weakland, and A. Bodin

In our day everything seems to be pregnant with its contrary.

—KARL MARX

Life is a game, of which rule number one is: this is no game; this is dead serious.

—ALAN WATTS

Like any other professional, the family therapist is threatened by professional deformations, none of which is as insidious as the gradual, almost

The authors are indebted to Milton H. Erickson, MD, whose creative work over 35 years has opened new pathways in humane manipulation.

Originally published in *The Book of Family Therapy,* edited by A. Ferber, M. Mendelsohn and A. Napier, New York, Science House, 1972. Reprinted with permission.

imperceptible straying from the established doctrine. Very little has as yet been said—let alone published—about these dangers, but we believe that the sounding of a note of warning can no longer be delayed. Our task will not be an easy one, for the phenomena which we have come to identify over the course of many years are subtle and do not readily meet the eye of the critical observer. They are of a multi-faceted nature and can perhaps best be referred to collectively as the Danger of Unbecoming Book Therapists (abbreviated DOUBT), wherein "book" refers to the right theory and technique of family therapy.

By and large, these dangers stem from two different sources, one of which is located in the therapist, the other in his patients. In the give-and-take of the therapy situation, these two influences are bound to be present simultaneously and to overlap, interpenetrate, and compound each other to the point of utter frustration. We present first these two classes of DOUBT phenomena, and then show some of the many ways in which their combination can corrupt the process and outcome of any treatment.


### The Therapist

Talking first about the *therapist* himself, we find that he is threatened by the ever-present danger of paying more than lip service to the idea that he is not treating individuals, but human relationships and systems formed of such relationships. While no reasonable objection can be raised against a colleague's defending family therapy against the orthodox schools of intrapsychic dynamics by the expedient of frequent references to interaction, systems behavior, and systems pathology, he should nevertheless realize that there is a limit to which he should push this philosophy in his practical work.

Family therapists are an unruly crowd; the quantum jump from their original training to family therapy has proved a heady wine for some of them, who in the seclusion of their private offices are experimenting with ideas of yet another jump, this time from the orthodoxy of family therapy to treatment methods which do not even yet have a name. Revolution as an aim in itself is an ever-present danger—witness the many East Europeans who first fought the Nazis, and then after their liberation fought the Communists. It seems to us that not all of our colleagues possess the moral fibre to resist the temptation of pushing the idea of interaction to extremes, such as taking it quite seriously. Then they are eventually beset by great doubt—or rather, great DOUBT. The main part of this chapter is, therefore, devoted to pointing out where these colleagues are losing contact with the established and accepted theory of family therapy, by what arguments they try to justify their deviations, and how these arguments can best be countered.

## The Patient

The danger which the *patients* unwittingly bring into the therapy game has been known for some seventy years. Regrettably, we all have become complacent about this danger during the last fifteen years or so. In fact, a recent survey conducted by the New Caledonian Institute of Experimental Psychopathology* shows that references in the literature to this phenomenon have dropped from 86.2% in 1917 to a mere 2.7% in 1968 ($x^2 = 17.351$, $p = > .000$)! We are here, of course, referring to the patient's persistent tendency to *escape into health,* a most exasperating problem, wrecking the successful course of many a well-planned therapy. Over the decades, this phenomenon has lost none of its importance, and it is in this connection that therapists in DOUBT are very likely to display one of their simplistic and yet so subtle sophisms: reduced to its simplest terms, these colleagues argue that if a therapist accepts the patient's complaint as a reason for *starting* therapy with him, he should by the same logic accept his statement of satisfactory improvement as a reason for *terminating* treatment. They further argue that there is no evidence in the literature of any crises arising in the lives of patients who stopped therapy simply because *they* felt better, no matter how their therapist felt. This second argument is especially specious, for one cannot demand the same rigorous evidence for a well-known fact of everyday experience as for a more unusual phenomenon. Indeed, the very absence of documented evidence for the danger of a patient's flight into health proves that this is something known to everybody in the field and hardly requires proof. It is almost as if somebody doubted the universally known fact that red-haired people have impulsive personalities, just because this fact has not yet been scientifically researched.

After these introductory remarks and warnings, we are now in a better position to appreciate the complications which arise as soon as the two propensities just described begin to compound each other. We shall next consider a number of particularly crucial issues, but do not claim our presentation to be exhaustive.

* Personal communication.

## Length of Treatment

An important issue is likely to arise early, usually in the first session—at least one family member will probably ask how long they will all have to come. We, of course, believe in the paramount importance of clear, unambiguous and straightforward communication. Yet, we doubt that you the therapist should come right out and tell them, "Anything from eighteen to thirty-six months." In all likelihood, some family members would create an unpleasant scene by gasping and asking rather pointedly, "Are you kidding?" There are better, less crude ways of firmly implanting in the minds of all concerned your own certainty that family therapy is a long-term, open-ended process of restructuring personalities and changing deep-rooted patterns of communication and of family homeostasis. It is usually best to deal with this question subtly. Announce in a matter-of-fact way, "I have Tuesday at three open now, so that will become our regular hour." One may then inquire about "parental models," the nature of their parents' marriage, how they were raised by their parents, etc. But perhaps the most effective way is to translate all marital or family complaints into forms of "communication difficulty." From long experience we can guarantee that with a minimum of effort you can thereby dispel any naïve notions of rapid change—so that even if rapid change were somehow to occur in the course of treatment, the family would themselves realize that they must be doing the right thing for the wrong reason, i.e., that they are merely escaping into health. By no means should the therapist encourage any discussion about concrete goals of treatment, since the family would then know when to stop treatment.

We do not exclude the possibility that circumstances beyond your control may at times force you to embark on a time-limited course of treatment. In these cases, emphasis on professional ethics will assist you to label your service as purely a stop-gap measure, something superficial and of temporary value only, and ease the family into long-term therapy as soon as circumstances will permit.

## Experimenter Bias and All That

The only reason for mentioning these well-known facts is that therapists in DOUBT are very likely to see the length of treatment as at least a partial function of the therapist's conviction that it has to be long. They quote the work of Robert Rosenthal (1966) who showed that the performance of laboratory rats (and of human beings in rat-like situations) depends on the bias (i.e., the basic assumptions and beliefs) of the experimenter. According to his regrettable conclusions, the actual outcome of the experimenter-subject interaction reflects much more the prejudices of the former than the pathology of the latter. Quite independently from Rosenthal, very similar conclusions have recently been reached by Spiegel (1969).

But this is not all. Certain colleagues of ours are quietly voicing their belief that all theories of psychotherapy have limitations which are logically inherent in *their own* nature (i.e., the premises of the theory). These colleagues insinuate such limitations are typically attributed to *human* nature. One of their examples is that in terms of the postulates of psychoanalytic theory, symptom removal without insight must perforce lead to symptom substitution and exacerbation of the patient's condition—not because this is necessarily inherent in the mental makeup of human beings, but simply because the premises of the theory permit no other conclusion. For example, they cite the work of Spiegel (1967), who has claimed to have successfully removed such symptoms without symptom substitution. (No lack of data to the contrary needs to stop *us* from predicting that untoward effects will show up sooner or later, even if it takes decades.)

Therapists in DOUBT are particularly prone to make such mistakes in their thinking, and this should be a matter for grave concern. We might overlook their tendencies to erroneous methods of practice (nobody is perfect), but they do not even *think* right; that is serious. The simplicity of their views (which will unfold itself in all its complexity in the following pages) about reasonable goals of treatment, and their unwarranted optimism about the possibilities of change are likely to produce in their patients a typical Rosenthal effect and thus encourage the patients' unhealthy tendency to escape into health before their problems can be explored in depth. No time and space need be wasted to uncover the fallacy of these views. Any well-trained therapist can see it clearly. And most therapists, as well as their patients, have a fairly acceptable view about how deep-rooted the problems they are trying to change are. Yet, there are some who need help and guidance even in this area. A word about problems is therefore called for.

## Difficulties, Problems, and "Problems"

As already mentioned, a patient's wish for change is usually accepted as the reason for taking him into treatment. Beyond this point of agreement, however, we again run into controversy. Engaging in what is strongly suggestive of semantic hair-splitting, some of our colleagues insist on a clear distinction between "difficulties" and "problems." According to them, there are at least three ways in which this distinction can be lost sight of: 1. when the presence of an ordinary difficulty is defined as a problem; 2. when the absence of a difficulty is defined as a problem; and 3. when the presence of a difficulty is denied altogether. Since these views are major challenges to our traditional assumptions of pathology, we want to present the reasoning behind them as objectively as possible, so that the reader can judge for himself as to how absurd they are:

1. There are countless difficulties which are part and parcel of the everyday business of living, for which no known ideal or ultimate solutions exist, and which become "problems" primarily as a result of the belief that there *should* be an ideal, ultimate solution for them. For instance, some therapists in DOUBT claim the problem is not that there *is* a generation gap (apparently there has been one for the past five thousand years), but that an increasing number of people have convinced themselves that it should be closed. Similarly, they believe that there is probably no other single book which has caused more havoc to marriages than van de Velde's classic *Ideal Marriage,* compared to which all *real* marriages are miserable failures.

2. According to these colleagues, an essentially similar situation arises when the *absence* of a problem comes to be considered a problem. Compared to 1., this is the opposite side of life's normal mixture of effort and enjoyment, pleasure and pain, in which someone so firmly holds the view that "life is real, life is earnest," that any occurrence of ease, spontaneity, and pleasure is perceived as signifying the existence of something wrong. The woman who upholds motherhood as a glorious sacrifice, the compulsive husband who lives only for work, are likely to define carefree behavior in others as "irresponsible," and therefore a "problem." In such cases, "no sweat" becomes something to sweat about even more.

3. Finally, they say that "problems" can arise out of the *denial* of *undeniable difficulties.* While alternative 1. acknowledges the existence of a difficulty, but insists that there must be a perfect solution, here we are faced with a basic contention: there is no difficulty and anybody who sees one must be bad or mad. This allegedly is done by people who refuse to see the complexity of our own highly complex and inter-dependent modern world and define this blindness as a "real," "genuine," and "honest" attitude toward life—thereby labeling those who struggle with these difficulties as uptight hypocrites or exploiters.

The specific ways in which therapists in DOUBT imagine these very ordinary and common views to lead to particular acute or even chronic "problems" will be described a little later, in connection with the goals of their treatment.

A moment's consideration will show where this kind of thinking would take us. First of all, what is the patient to think of a therapist who refuses to see a problem as a problem and calls it a difficulty for which no known solutions exist? He will either be encouraged to escape into health or else is likely to start looking for another therapist. Nothing needs to be said about alternative 2.—we are all only too familiar with the effects of such insidious re-definitions of established moral values. Only as far as alternative 3. goes, it does not have much of a chance to cause harm in an era in which encounter groups, politicians, and the military breed such a profusion of two-dimensional thinkers (or, as the French have come to call them since May and June of 1968, *terribles simplificateurs*).

## What? Instead of Why?

It is not difficult to see that this approach to problems is anti-historic and simply overlooks the paramount importance of causation. Here again we run into a subtle sophism: these colleagues do not question the fact that any behavior in the present is shaped and determined by experiences in the past. But they flatly deny that for the purposes of *therapy* there is essential value in discovering the relation between causative events in the past (pathogenesis) and the present condition (pathology), let alone in the need for the patient himself to grasp this connection, that is, to attain insight. They are even likely to disbelieve that any elucidation of the past has ever made the slightest difference to a patient's present condition. They are sarcastic about what they call the self-sealing argument that the absence of improvement in the present "proves" that the past has not yet been sufficiently explored and understood. To use their own reasoning: they are interested in the ways people are behaving in the here and now, instead of *why* people behave the way they behave. Basing their work, as they do, to an excessive degree on systems theory, they claim to have found clinical confirmation of von Bertalanffy's concept (1962) of equifinality, purporting that a system's behavior can be quite independent of its initial conditions and determined only by its present parameters. For them the current state of a system is its own best explanation, and they thus show a shocking disregard for insight as the *conditio sine qua non* of therapeutic change. One of their favorite comparisons is that of a man who, not knowing the game of chess, travels to a country whose language he does not understand and comes upon two people engaged in an obviously symbolic activity—they are moving figures on a board. Although he cannot ask them for the rules and the purpose of the game, a sufficiently long period of watching their behavior will enable him to deduce the lawfulness underlying their interaction. This, they stress, he manages to do without any knowledge of the past or of the inner states of the players, or of the "meaning" of their game. Of course, if he wanted, he could have fantasies about that meaning, but they would have the same significance for his understanding of this two-person system as astrology has for astronomy.

Having thus cavalierly dispensed with insight as the precondition for change, the question arises: how do therapists in DOUBT try to bring about change? The answer, blunt, simple and shocking, is: by something they call direct intervention, but we must plainly label "downright manipulation."

## To Thine Own Self Be True

It is generally accepted that a therapist's attitude must be one of complete honesty, that he should always say what he believes (and even believe what he says), that his communications should be open, clear, straightforward, and guileless, and that he should share his own feelings, problems, and anxieties with his patients. This is particularly true of family therapists, and it is refreshing to notice the growing trend toward using the sessions for an exploration of their *own* hang-ups, and of experimenting with additional techniques of honesty and spontaneity, such as nude sessions (barring, of course, any expression of sexuality). The effect on their patients must be immeasurable.

In stark contrast to all that, certain colleagues of ours seem almost proud to play chameleons; they employ something akin to judo techniques, using the nature and direction of a human system's pathology to bring about its own downfall. Thus, instead of disarming their patients with the counterthrust of their sincerity, they are likely to yield and in yielding, to manipulate. Like their hypothetical chess observer, they study the rules of a human system's game, asking themselves: *"What* are these people doing to each other?"* not *"Why* are they doing it?," and then do not shy away from even the most questionable direct interventions into the system's behavior. These colleagues are thus not true to their own selves, although it cannot perhaps be denied that in an odd way they are true to the *patients'* selves—very much like a good hypnotist who utilizes whatever the subject himself brings into the session by way of expectations, superstitions, fears, and resistances, rather than monotonously applying the one method which is most congenial to *himself*.

There exists, indeed, a large bag of tricks from which manipulative therapists can draw. They can meet the need of patients who believe in the magical by offering a magical rationale for improvement; they can oblige those who come into therapy in order to defeat the expert, by insisting that real improvement is impossible; they may heap responsibility on the incarnate caretaker until he demands to be taken care of himself for a change; they provide subtle challenge to those who challenge openly; they outdo the confirmed pessimist by sadly commenting on the unrealistic optimism of his views; and to the woman endangered by her own long-standing game of suicidal threats against her family, they may even offer helpful suggestions for a pretty funeral. It must be noted that despite their apparent "flexibility," in all these manipulations, in their frequent use of multiple therapists and assignments of so-called "homework" to patients, these therapists in DOUBT keep harping on a theme of influencing behavior by employing *paradox,* instead of being rigidly honest and straightforward whatever the costs. Nowhere does this slippery attitude become more manifest than in their outlook on the goals of therapy.

### Goals

While different schools of therapy set themselves different goals, a few common traits can be discerned. Most of us would agree that the outcome of treatment should be in the direction of what has variously been termed genital organization, individuation, heightened sensitivity, self-actualization, improved communication, or merely a positive attitude toward life. In this area we need not fear disagreement from our patients, even though in their lay language they may use more primitive terms. Thus, when asked what they expect from therapy, they may explain that they do not get enough out of life, that they would like to be happier, or especially that in their family they do not communicate. Although expressed in an unsophisticated way, these definitions are useful: they are broad enough to be all-inclusive, they permit an open-ended course of treatment and therefore leave room for spontaneous change, and they take into account the complexity of human beings, with their reasons behind reasons behind reasons. Are we not all familiar with the patient who only wants to stop biting his nails, but is unwilling to consider his deep-seated oral aggressive impulses? Or the parents who complain about the misbehavior of a child, but are blind to the subtle breakdowns of their communication and have difficulty learning how to communicate clearly and openly about all subjects, including their own sexual fantasies? *We* are familiar with all this—but not those in DOUBT.

They contend that when therapists regard problems as complex, firmly entrenched, reflecting limited patient or family resources, and requiring extensive or intensive change, treatment is likely to be complex, profound, severely restricted by limited patient resources, long in duration, and uncertain in outcome. Using the Rosenthal effect positively, they contend that change can be effected most easily and rapidly if the goal of treatment is reasonably small and refers to a clearly stated and well delimited area of a human system's behavior. They have to admit that this approach seems insensitive to the big, deep, and basic problems which some patients want to talk about, but which are so broad and vague that they perpetuate themselves by this very fact. Indeed, so our colleagues speculate, more often than not a patient's problem lies in the fact that he *says* he has a problem.

The setting of reasonable, reachable goals—stated as concretely and specifically as possible—thus becomes one of their most important steps, to be taken at the very beginning of treatment. Our colleagues claim that in this task many of Alfred Adler's postulates about life styles and goals (Adler, 1928, 1956) are of immediate relevance to their approach. They also believe they have shown that these goals can be reached in ten sessions or less with a wide variety of patients, and that once a patient has experienced a small change in the seemingly monolithic structure of his "real" problem, this experience of change then generates further, self-induced changes in other areas of his life.

Obviously, very little needs to be said to counter these assumptions and claims. As pointed out in earlier sections, they are anti-historic and anti-causal, but now we see that they also disregard a patient's manifestations of his intrapsychic and unconscious dynamics, as well as the deepest levels of family pathology.

Having disregarded these cornerstones of psychotherapeutic theory, our colleagues feel free to view even the longstanding nature of symptoms, not as chronicity in the usual sense of a basic structural defect in an individual or a family, but as the result of poor handling of everyday difficulties. Again, we shall let their simplistic views speak for themselves:

"Everyday difficulties" are considered those arising most commonly during the normal transitional stages in the careers of individuals and families, when shifts in family functioning and redefinitions of relationships become necessary. These transitions occur most often at certain specific points in time, e.g., from courtship to marriage, from the partial commitment to marriage to a fuller commitment at the arrival of the first child, from autonomy over the children to the surrender of part of that autonomy on the child's entrance into school, and even more so as the child becomes involved with peers in the adolescent period, from a child-oriented marital relationship back to a two-party system when the children leave home, from the work-scheduled marital arrangement itself to retirement or to widowhood and its single life (or from marriage to divorce), etc. At any one of these junctures a mishandling of the necessary adjustments is possible, and likely to perpetuate and exacerbate itself.

### The Game Without End

They argue that the way people perpetuate their problems by trying to resolve them in inappropriate, if time-honored, ways is the most important single vicious cycle that they have been able to observe in their work. This pattern can perhaps best be described as the presence of positive instead of negative feed-back loops. For instance, the typical rebellious teenager, when faced with parental discipline, will increase his rebelliousness, which in turn is likely to increase repressive action by his parents, which in turn makes the teenager more rebellious, etc. A similar pattern is often at work between a depressed patient and his family—the more they try to cheer him and make him see the positive sides of life, the more the patient is likely to get depressed. In all of these cases the action which is meant to *alleviate* the behavior of the other party in actual fact *aggravates* it, but this fact usually remains outside the awareness of everybody involved, and thus the "remedies" they apply are likely to be worse than the "disease." They behave very much like two sailors hanging out from either side of a sailboat in order to keep it from heeling over. The more one sailor leans overboard, the more the other will be forced to lean out himself, while the boat actually would be quite steady if it were not for their acrobatic efforts at "steadying it."

In this anti-historic, anti-causal view, then, problems are seen as always existing in the here and now, to have their own lawfulness and to perpetuate themselves by their own momentum, so to speak. Poor handling of any everyday problem will tend to lead to more of the same, and this process will inexorably place ever-narrowing constraints on, and produce increasing blindness for, the alternative solutions which are potentially available at all times. People in such a situation are caught in a Game Without End (Watzlawick, 1967), a system governed by increasingly rigid rules but without rules for the change of its rules. Indeed, the inability of human systems to generate from within themselves these meta-rules is, for our colleagues at least, the only useful criterion of pathology. This brings us back to the kind of therapy they practice and advocate.

## Therapeutic Interventions

If pressed for an answer as to how they expect to bring about change, having discarded most principles of psychotherapy and, in particular, of family therapy, therapists in DOUBT are likely to claim that a Game Without End can be broken up only by the introduction of new rules into the system. They are, therefore, particularly interested in studying how systems occasionally reorganize themselves as the result of an almost fortuitous outside event. For example:

On her first day of nursery school attendance a girl of four threw such a tantrum as her mother was preparing to leave that the mother was forced to stay with her for the whole school session. The same happened on the next and all following days, and the situation turned into a severe strain on the mother's (and the teacher's) emotions and time. After about two months and before the school psychologist had a chance to take care of the case, the mother was one morning prevented from taking the child to school. The father drove her over, left her, and went on to work. The girl cried a little, but quickly calmed down and never made a scene again, although the mother resumed taking her to school the following morning. Of course, it could be argued that this was not a case of "real" pathology, but be this as it may, there can be little doubt that the case would have taken a very different course had it been given the label of "school phobia" and treated routinely, exploring the symbiotic relation between mother and child, the marital problem of the parents, and the family's modes of communication, etc.—perhaps even a chance to discover "minimal brain dysfunction" was missed.

Another example of a spontaneous remission that our colleagues claim proves their assumption that a system is its own best explanation and that change can occur quite independently from the historic evolution and the deeper meaning of a symptom is the following:

An unmarried, middle-aged man, suffering from an agoraphobia, had reached the point where his anxiety-free territory had become so small that even the most routine aspects of his daily life could no longer be carried out. He eventually decided to commit suicide by driving to a mountain top, about fifty miles from his home, convinced that after a drive of just a few blocks a heart attack would put him out of his misery. To his amazement and utter elation, he not only arrived safely at his destination, but for the first time in many years found himself completely free from anxiety and has remained so for the last five years.

What our colleagues regard as most noteworthy about this example is the strong paradoxical element of this spontaneous remission which reminds one of the Zen tenet according to which enlightenment comes only after the seeker has given up any hope of reaching it.

At this point, we hope the reader will be sufficiently warned as to the nature and insidiousness of DOUBT. The contagion of DOUBTers can best be controlled by early recognition and prevention of its spread. Toward that end, we will now describe in more concrete detail the handling of two cases by therapists woefully infected with DOUBT. Read, and let the reader beware! The grim and appalling evidence speaks for itself:

The mother of a fifteen-year-old boy called to seek help. She mentioned on the phone that the boy was overly defiant and hostile to her, but even more so to her husband and, in general, difficult to control, not helping with chores around the house, etc. She implied that her husband's passivity and obtuseness contributed greatly to the alienation between him and the boy. Despite the fact that the therapist could easily recognize the situation as basically a marital one, he naïvely asked the mother to come in alone! In the initial session she described the problem with the son in greater detail, but included a great deal of not very veiled dissatisfaction with the husband: his lack of leadership in the home, his limited efforts at increasing the family income, and his aloofness toward her. She could sympathize with the boy for his anger and alienation, yet she herself was frustrated by the boy in her attempts to gain his cooperation at home. Book therapists will immediately recognize that the marital conflict was most important; that obviously the son was playing out the mother's hostility toward her husband and that the husband's passivity with the child served as a retaliation against his wife. The husband should have been called in and this central pathology explored. But what did our "DOUBTer" do? He gave priority to the mother's frustration with the *son*. To test out her readiness to deal more harshly with the son, he told her a joke—that "mental illness is inherited; you can get it from your children." She laughed quite openly at this and began to reveal punitive fantasies she had toward the son. She explained that she had felt quite angry, but had dealt with him too leniently for fear of alienating him and thereby losing *all* parental control.

What follows is hard to believe. The therapist suggested that she depart from honest, straightforward, direct discipline and use subterfuge, double-dealing, and sabotage! Specifically, she was instructed to complain to her son about her husband (in the second session the husband, in the wife's presence, was instructed to criticize any advice or recommendation that the mother made to the son). She was also asked not to cajole or threaten her son; all wishes for correct behavior were to be made as quiet, simple requests, with the reminder that, "I can't make you do that, but I wish it." If the son did not comply, the mother was then to use unobtrusive sabotage—to put lots of salt in his chocolate pudding, or sand in his bed, or "misplace" a treasured possession of his, etc. If any complaint were raised by the son, she was instructed to play dumb and helpless and apologize profusely for her "absent-mindedness."

In the second session, the one also attended by the husband, he was filled in as to the wife's instructions and he was asked to help her by devising other means of sabotage since his experience as a boy and man could add useful hints to the mother's implementation of this program. In front of the husband she was re-instructed to make the relationship between son and father quite difficult by complaining about her husband, and the husband was told that this was necessary since any ultimate improvement of the father-son relationship could be meaningful only if it were not made easy, especially not by the mother, and that her attempts to keep father and son apart would actually constitute a help in the long run.

We think the reader can see enough of the duplicity, insensitivity, and gimmick employed in this case. It is inconsequential that the son became more tractable at home, that the husband became more openly assertive with his wife, and that she was making efforts to supplement the family income through part-time work. *Results* are not the most important thing, and should always be treated as secondary to understanding, deeper experiences, heightened sensitivity, and awareness.

Now, should the reader have assumed that such DOUBTing is limited to marital and child behavior problems, consider the following case:

A woman in her fifties came in for help because her twenty-five-year-old chronic schizophrenic son seemed on the verge of another psychotic break. Since the age of fifteen, when he had been diagnosed as schizophrenic, he had spent the majority of his time in mental hospitals and had been in almost continuous treatment with a succession of psychotherapists. The son was asked to come in with her on the second visit, and he displayed the mannerisms and speech characteristics of schizophrenia. The therapist was naïve and callous enough to tell him to stop talking "crazy" if he wanted to be understood—and the unfortunate patient complied. He then described some power struggles he got into with his parents, especially his mother. These struggles usually centered on how much money he was to receive and when. Essentially he felt that he was entitled to more allowance and on a much more definite basis. The mother felt that his questionable mental state made it unfeasible to just hand over money

322    THE INTERACTIONAL VIEW

which he might squander, and she felt it more appropriate to dole out money on a week-by-week basis, never indicating in advance how much it might be. It appeared to the therapist that her major criterion for doling out money was the son's psychotic behavior, but her reluctance to come across inclined the son to utilize even more psychotic behavior. The therapist then instructed the son to *deliberately* utilize his psychotic behavior, explaining that since the son felt helpless to contend with his parents' intransigent refusals to comply with his monetary wishes, he had every right to defend himself by threatening to cause an even greater expenditure on their part by his having to go to a mental hospital again. The therapist suggested that this threat could best be conveyed by turning on the psychotic behavior. He made a few comments on what this behavior should look and sound like, comments which were mostly along the lines of what the patient was doing anyway.

This kind of case and its handling is most disturbing: there was no regard for the sensitivity of the schizophrenic son, no attempt made to translate the richness of his metaphoric speech, no exploration of the mother's dependency-overprotectiveness. There was little attempt to get the father in (one telephone call had been placed to him and he refused to come in to see yet another of the son's many therapists, saying that he had "had it"). No explorations were made into any of the many, many possible areas of the family dynamics. These were all ignored by the DOUBT therapist, who proceeded to make only the most crass and superficial interventions. Again, the fact that the mother no longer felt intimidated by the son's psychotic behavior, that she decided to avoid the constant struggle over money and simply arrange that a larger amount be paid on a definite basis, or the fact that the son saved this money until he purchased a car, which in turn gave him greater independence from the mother who had acted as his constant chauffeur—none of this is significant in the face of the therapist's depriving the family of the rich and rewarding experience of exploring, investigating, discussing, and understanding the depths of their family dynamics and its probable rottenness, which should, of course, have received the highest priority, regardless of the time and anguish that this would have entailed.

### Final Warnings

Whenever the reader who wishes to remain a book therapist is approached by a therapist who talks about specific goals of therapy, of strategies and tactics of therapy, of frank manipulation, of shortening therapy time, of dealing with family problems by seeing only one member of the family, and who concerns himself with concrete results, that reader should be most on guard. He is very probably dealing with a DOUBT therapist. Yet some of them can be quite convincing, influential, and even worse. Some therapists in DOUBT get so carried away with their fantasies that they begin to view problems of behavior in the wider social world—in schools, business organizations, social agencies, even politics and government—in a similar simplistic fashion. One shudders to think where *this* might lead. It is therefore especially important to scotch this trend before its infection spreads. To this end, we offer a few helpful methods for discrediting and dismissing the DOUBTers' arguments and statements, to save oneself and the public from total contamination:

1. Remind yourself and him that what he is saying is not really new or different—that it is something rather traditional, only phrased in new words. Cite supporting and authoritative references.

2. Tell him that you have already tried what he has been talking about and that while it was of mild interest, it was not really effective and you discarded it long ago.

3. Tell him that while what he says is intriguing, it really requires a charismatic (or some other deviant, perhaps psychopathic) character to do it effectively, or to *want* to do it at all, and that this obviously excludes you since you are normal.

4. After he has gotten through fully explaining the rationale for his innovations, insist that he is leaving out the one fundamental basis for his assumption and imply that if he were to state it, it would simply be a book assumption already in use.

5. As a last resort, nod approvingly throughout his explanation and finish it by ignoring the chronic cases and saying quite cheerfully that indeed you have long been convinced of the important place that "crisis intervention" plays in the armamentarium of treatment as a stop-gap until real therapy can tackle the basic, underlying problems.

Good luck!

## REFERENCES

ADLER, A. (1928), *Über den nervösen Charakter,* 4th ed. Munich: Bergmann.
——— (1956), *The Individual Psychology of Alfred Adler.* New York: Basic Books.
ROSENTHAL, R. (1966), *Experimenter Effects in Behavioral Research.* New York: Appleton-Century-Crofts.

SPIEGEL, H. (1967), Is symptom removal dangerous? *Amer. J. Psychiat.*, 123: 1279–1283.

—————— (1969), The "ripple effect" following adjunct hypnosis in analytical psychotherapy. *Amer. J. of Psychiat.*, 126:91–96.

VON BERTALANFFY, L. (1962), General systems theory: a critical review. *General Systems Yearbook*, 7:1–20.

WATZLAWICK, P., BEAVIN, J., and JACKSON, D. (1967), *Pragmatics of Human Communication*. New York: Norton.

# CHAPTER 6

# Family Medicine

*It is a well-known fact that part of the price mankind has to pay for the vertiginous advances of modern medicine is the increasing disintegration of medical knowledge into separate areas of sophisticated specialization. The consequences of this development are numerous, but none of them is probably more noticeable to the patient himself than a sense of alienation between him and the physician. During the last decade, this loss of the human element in medicine—as it is sometimes referred to—has become a matter of increased concern and attention. The old ideal of the family physician who lacked the sophistication and the technology of modern medicine, but in his simple ways "somehow" seemed to make up for it, is still very vivid in the minds of many, but apart from mere nostalgic remembrances there is solid evidence to be found both in our highly technical western world as well as in other cultures\*, showing that the interpersonal element in medicine is of crucial importance.*

*In several of the contributions to this chapter mention is made of the work of Robert Kellner†, the author of a study of elegant simplicity, showing that physical illness in families tends to occur in clusters even where such a simple explanation as mutual contagion can be ruled out. Kellner's work, while not being the only forerunner of what may be called the modern family perspective in general medicine, is a classic that highlights the renewed appreciation of the role of the family physician—a trend that has already led to the establishment of departments of family medicine in various medical schools in this country.*

*In a sense it is ironic that this trend originated, largely in isolation, at a time when family psychotherapy, with its insights into the dynamics*

---

\* Cf., for instance, the detailed study carried out by Bell in Africa and Asia before becoming MRI's director in 1968. (John E. Bell, *The Family in the Hospital: Lessons from Developing Countries.* Washington, D.C., U.S. Government Printing Office, 1970.)

† Robert Kellner, *Family Ill Health—An Investigation in General Practice.* New York, Thomas & Sons, 1963.

*and the pathologies of human systems, had already become an established form of psychiatric treatment. The comprehensive medical approach to family illness, the application of family psychotherapy principles to general medicine, has been a slow development. A pioneering paper by Don D. Jackson has lost none of its freshness and importance, although it was written ten years ago:*

# FAMILY PRACTICE: A COMPREHENSIVE
# MEDICAL APPROACH

*Don D. Jackson*

Despite medical schools newly opened, medical schools in the stage of building, and medical schools planned for the future, it appears, according to the Assistant Secretary of Health, Education and Welfare, Dr. Phillip R. Lee, that there will not be a relative increase in the number of doctors per capita in the United States, at least for the next ten years.

Although there is considerable interest in streamlining the practice of medicine to allow the doctor the major portion of his time for clinical work, and although the aerospace industry has many sophisticated ideas and techniques to offer, especially in the area of information-gathering and retrieval, the prospect of important technological changes is not rosy. This is for the simple reason that as our methods of speeding the availability of information increases, so does the amount of information available to physicians. This is not only obvious in the numbers of medical journals, or in figures that indicate a 300 per cent increase in words written about medicine in the past ten years, but in the very fact that more and more gadgets and testing devices are being invented which require great skill and, of course, time on the part of the physicians to utilize. Thus, it seems unlikely that the physician in the foreseeable future will have the luxury of "treating the whole patient," with the concomitant implication that he will have the time, energy, and interest to listen to patients' sexual and psychological problems as well as to the rales in his chest.

This investigation was supported by Public Health Service grants No. MH 12171 and No. MH 10001 from the National Institute of Mental Health, and by a grant from the Wheeler Foundation.

Originally published in *Comprehensive Psychiatry* 7:338–344 (1966). Reprinted by permission.

One possible bit of silver in the otherwise greying medical cloud is that the general practitioner will be more and more freed from the specially technical aspects of medicine by an increase in the number of specialists, and that the logistical problems which now require in some areas that he do major surgery, obstetrical complications, and other technical and time-consuming aspects of medicine may be relieved by new developments, such as proposed medical centers and the use of helicopters and other devices which will speed the flow of very sick patients to areas where they may be treated by specialists.

This may mean that the general practitioner can get back to one of his most important functions, if not *the* most important—namely, his position as the physician to the family.

It has been my experience, garnered through visiting several large medical centers and modern medical clinics, that medical charts of the members of a family are kept individually and are recorded in the history room only under an alphabetical system as are all other individuals, related or not, with the same last name. Even if the members in a family should all have the same internist, he may be too busy to recall that the outbreak of certain disorders in the family was suspiciously time-linked, and his records will not have been written in such a way as to let him see at a glance what the medical history of the family is and has been.

We know from the work of Haggerty in Buffalo (and others) that streptococcal infections have been shown to be more prevalent in certain families on a basis that can only be reasonably accounted for by the stressful nature of the family's situation. We know from the work of an English general practitioner, Robert Kellner,[1] that outbreaks of certain disorders in families are noticeably quite common if one keeps yearly cards that reflect the clinical visits of all family members so that they may be viewed at a glance. Kellner's simple, clear system should be read by every general physician.

The nature of family interaction has been studied largely in the past ten years in the United States, and although the surface has only been scratched, it is already clear that family members tend to be involved with each other in quite intensive ways and that situations which markedly affect one member of the family, either physically or emotionally, or both, are apt to have reverberations for other family members.

The idea of comprehensive family medical care involves a point of view that the physician will not have learned in medical school. The traditional unit for medical treatment is one patient and one physician. It is difficult for the physician, without having had it especially called to his attention, to think in terms of a family unit in relation to medical disorders.

The following example is an idea of what kind of a change in viewpoint is involved. I will remember how much I enjoyed Hermann Wouk's novel, *The Caine Mutiny,* when it was first published a few years after World War II. Later, I saw the play, *The Caine Mutiny Court Martial,* with a fine Broadway cast; and then a few years later, I saw Humphrey Bogart as Captain Queeg in the movie version of *The Caine Mutiny.*

Recently, I saw the movie on TV and enjoyed it again almost as much as on first viewing, yet it seemed in significant ways a different movie from my recollection. The causative factor was a change of viewpoint *in me* and not any lack of fidelity on the part of the television presentation. Originally, I had seen a movie with the main action revolving around Queeg's mental illness and the inevitable, yet disastrous action that Steve, his executive officer, had to take. One of the scenes that stood out most in memory was the courtroom action when Queeg, needled by the clever defense attorney, spilled his paranoid suspicions like vomitus upon the courtroom floor; and defense and prosecution alike became nauseated, and looked away as if the revolting mess might disappear. Although Queeg's breakdown momentarily appears to be a blow for the forces of good, it works out to be a kind of Mexican standoff where neither Captain Queeg nor his executive officer is vindicated. Initially, I found this a disappointing outcome, but I think I had not done sufficient justice to Mr. Wouk's brilliance.

In seeing the movie recently on television, the emphasis that took place in my mind was entirely different. What I found myself noticing was the nature of the interaction between Queeg and his officers. For example, he berates a sailor for improper uniform just after having given the order to execute hard right rudder. The helmsman, aware that they will come about full tilt and cut their own tow lines, protests once and is told by Queeg to "shut up." He and his buddy at the wheel exchange significant looks, say nothing further, and, of course, the inevitable happens. Not that Queeg is any rose, mind you. He contributes to all aspects of the increasingly difficult situation by evasion, obfuscation, and distortion, but his officers let him flounder.

It is obvious that a warship, especially one not part of a pack or flotilla, is a movable island where the natives are frequently presented with the problem of either hanging together or hanging separately. In this regard, the officers of the USS Caine are notable failures. When Captain Queeg calls a meeting of his officers following a second unfortunate experience, he attempts to explain that he meant well but may have done the wrong thing. He asks any of the officers who feel this to be true to speak up. No one raises his voice, and the next incident—a particularly mean bit of picayune discipline by Queeg—follows thereafter. The more that Queeg is rejected in his attempts to "reach" his officers, the firmer the wall of resistance and the more Queeg becomes absurdly punitive and thus increases the distance between himself and his men. Meanwhile, behind his back, his officers gossip and complain and feed the paranoid fires.

When one shifts from Queeg, as an individual, to viewing the movie as an *interaction* or examines what exists between a group of men with a common purpose and place (like a family), the view is very different. This is the way a physician should regard patients coming from the same family. There are no good guys or bad guys or long-suffering wives and bastardly husbands. There are patterns of interaction which have to be so conceptualized that it isn't possible to say the husband withdraws because his wife nags, *nor* the reverse.

In changing to a family point of view, one might look at something like coronary attacks. Studies in recent years, especially by Friedman and his associates at Mt. Zion Hospital, have indicated that regardless of other factors, such as blood pressure, cholesterol levels, smoking, etc., the individual's personality appears to be paramount in determining his chances in having a coronary occlusion, and especially a fatal one in his mid-years. Friedman has separated patients into two groups, group "A" and group "B." The former are hard-driving, ambition-ridden, executive types who often are assertive, aggressive, and accomplish a good deal. By contrast, the "B" group are more easy-going, even though they may be in a position of considerable importance, because they tend to delegate authority.

In looking at it from a family interactional standpoint, it might be hypothesized (and our limited clinical experience tends to verify this) that an individual of Friedman's "A" type requires reinforcement for his behavior patterns and that such reinforcement usually comes from his family and his immediate surroundings. Thus, at the plant the type "B" people may be using the type "A's" as someone to whom they can delegate authority and know it will be carried out. At home, the coronary-prone individual may be considered by family members as the main "mover" or "power" in the family whether it relates to finances, disciplinary action, social activities, or whatever. Family responsibilities, decisions, and so on, are often passed on to this individual who considers it his duty to accept the responsibility. Other family members may be thus driving the coronary patient to his doom (completely unwittingly), because they either will not or cannot take over themselves, and also because they simply don't recognize the family pattern. They assume (and the physician may also) that "A" is simply a driver and that's the way it has to be.

As an illustration, I was recently talking to a mother and father who had brought their son in because he was having school difficulties. The parents initially had declared that they had no problems at all, but when the marriage was examined, they began to see that there was considerable covert dissatisfaction between them. When we turned to the question of the father's work (he was a quite successful executive), he told me he was annoyed that particular evening because he thought he had botched a job that he had been supervising over the past several days. I asked his wife what she thought of this and she said it was very unlikely, that he was such a capable worker she doubted if he could possibly make any mistakes in his work. Her husband smiled, looked slightly pleased, and did not remark about his wife's statement. When I called his attention to it, he still seemed puzzled, and I told him that anyone who thought I was perfect made me nervous. I asked him if he had ever considered what an enormous responsibility it was to have his wife think that he could make no mistakes in his job, and how possible did that make it for him to go home and feel openly depressed, concerned, or whatever? This struck him as a novel idea, and within a few minutes he was corroborating my observation by recounting instances of this kind of interaction as far back as their courtship. Naturally, the wife felt I was picking on her until it became clear that she often felt useless and "stupid" because she had so little decision-making power.

It would be foolish for the family physician to simply tell a type "A" coronary risk to slow down. Such advice is worse than useless because the physician feels he has discharged his duty, but it has doubtless gone through the patient's ears without scratching his brain. If it has registered, even slightly, it will soon be forgotten once type "A" gets back in his usual milieu with the significant others in his family and they put him in charge again.

### Some Theoretical and Practical Considerations

The busy family physician will want to know of what use it is to him to become "family oriented." This is a pertinent question because he is being asked to change his usual point of view and if, for example, he is an internist, it may mean getting information from the pediatrician in order to keep some kind of family records. There are two considerations that are of importance. One is the theoretical point of view or the research data that may be collected from having more information, even of an actuarial type, about families and illnesses; and the other is the practical considerations that may emerge from the physicians being family oriented.

We have recently completed at the Mental Research Institute a pilot study of a group of families, each of whom have a child with ulcerative colitis. These families seem to have an overall restrictiveness in their interactional patterns with consequent restrictedness on the part of the family, and the individual members could be called "restricted" individuals. That is, the families seem to engage in limited behaviors between family members and were restricted socially as far as utilizing the contingency possibilities that the culture made available. There was also overt evidence of restrictiveness in that one member would monitor the behavior of another and limit the other's behavior to a very narrow range. If an individual in the family engaged in outside activities other than those prescribed by law and custom (such as school or church), the family might take it as evidence that there was an avoidance of other family members and this behavior would be stopped. In fact, it might be stopped before it started by the fact that the family would kill an idea proposed by a member which would involve him outside of the family. The families seemed to have a rule against changing rules, and hence virtually any new contingency possibility was treated in much the same way. There was thus an inability to handle novel situations or to enjoy novel and/or creative acts together. When presented with stimulus material, to which a large variety of possible responses could occur, the restricted family would usually settle the matter quickly and unimaginatively, or they would allow one member (often the father) to settle the matter quickly by edict. These families were quite different from a large group of "ordinary" families we have been studying at the Mental Research Institute since March of 1959. In these families, there is involvement in a wide range of activities, even if it is at a cost to other family members. Hence, if father and son go duck hunting and leave the women at home, the women will not like it but they will not deprive the men of this opportunity and will assume that they will be rewarded in time, or that they will engage in some special activity of their own. In ordinary families there appeared to be much larger exchanges of spontaneous behavior, such as laughter, critical comments, sarcasm, irony, etc., occurring in a nonregularized way.

In looking at the data from our other family studies and from the literature, it would appear that the concept of a restricted family may be useful in more than just the ulcerative colitis group. For example, it is possible to postulate that there should be six types of illness—medical care patterns—that would be revealed by having data about the entire family.

(1) Family members have *frequent illnesses but rarely consult physicians.* They are so restricted socially that they do not enter into the "social act" of calling a physician but treat illness as a family affair, and being ill may have more than a "physical illness" meaning within the family group. For example, illness may help restrict other family members because of the sick one's need for them and frequent illnesses will help the family stay restricted. (2) There would be families who have *rare illnesses but frequent medical consultation,* and these would correspond to a restricted family who follow a pattern of hypochondria, displaying a high degree of interest in medical matters, in the use of remedies which are nonspecific, and who would tend to use the subject of illness as a frequent topic for family interaction. Their social restriction would be aided by fear of illness, whether actual phobias, worries, or concerns such as not going skiing because one might break a leg.

The other four types of families do not suffer from a distortion of the ratio between frequency of illness and medical consultation but suffer instead from the restrictions imposed by illness pattern itself. For example, (3) the family has *frequent illnesses and frequent medical consultations* but without exhibiting restrictiveness, and the illnesses are usually genetic, constitutional, or occupational. Such families are logically restricted by their ill health, but because of genetics, ignorance, socioeconomic reasons, etc., they cannot do anything to change the illness pattern. (4) *Frequent illnesses plus frequent consultation without chronic organic illness:* Families with a predominance of so-called psychosomatic disorders where there is a high degree of correlation between the course of the illness and interfamily contingencies. Here the physician would expect outbreaks of family illnesses during times of stress. He would be guided in diagnosis and treatment by past experience with their pattern. (5) A family may have *rare illnesses and rare medical consultation* yet not appear restricted since there was neither excessive delay nor urgency in the seeking of medical care. The change of roles within the family in order to cope with illness are easily managed and accepted by the patient without resentment. This, obviously, would be the ideal family for the physician to have in his care and one where he would take seriously any complaints, since his past experience of knowing the family did not tend to use illness as a major means of communication would tell him "this illness is probably organic." (6) The family might have *rare illnesses and rare consultations* but the family would be a severely restricted one, and although the illness was not used within the family as tools for communication, the heavily overstructured pattern of interaction within the family would become terribly chaotic when a serious illness struck one member, and the physician would be presented with "over-reaction." Here he would recognize the urgency of the situation and the need for taking strong measures to quickly bring matters under control and to heal the sick one as soon as possible and reassure the other members, within reason.

It is possible that some such classification (although this is obviously a crude one) and its use in developing a typology of families would provide as much information for the physician as we now have from noting merely genetic tendencies in a family.

Even without the results of this sort of research yet available to us, there are practical considerations which will be of benefit to the busy physician in his becoming family oriented. For example, if he unfailingly notes the reactions of other family members to an illness in one of their lot, he has not only done possible homework for a future date, but this information may have considerable impact on the method of treatment utilized—for example, hospitalization versus home care, or local hospitalization versus distant hospitalization even though more adequate facilities are available further away. The decision as to whether to allow one family member to take charge of the medications of another can be of considerable importance. Let me give you a few examples that have come my way:

1. A man was elected to a high public office and shortly thereafter his wife had a malady that was difficult to diagnose. Her physician as well as her acquaintances considered this a tragedy occurring at an otherwise happy moment. If the physician had seen the couple at any time together, he would have recognized that she was extremely bitter about his "outside" activities, and it was several months before a diagnosis was made. She was feeding herself small amounts of arsenic.

2. A couple had an only "delicate" son who finally was hospitalized for a schizophrenic episode. With drugs and psychotherapy he made a considerable improvement, but his mother became severely alcoholic and the father committed the son to a state hospital. The mother had a physician, the father had another, and the son's psychiatrist was in contact with neither. Only after the son had been hospitalized for a long time was there a confrontation made: that is, that his being in the hospital was not because of his "mental illness" but because of the family's convenience. The son has remained in the hospital.

3. A middle-aged man was addicted to a synthetic narcotic which had been given to him originally by his internist for severe gastrointestinal symptoms. He was in many ways a difficult patient and his wife spent

long hours nursing him. When his internist was able to almost force him to cut down on medication, a discrepancy appeared in that the amount of medication ordered continued to be high. It then was revealed that the wife had been taking the narcotic along with several other medications and was more severely addicted than the husband. She had been overlooked as a possible patient for nearly a year.

I am sure that all physicians can recount similar experiences. Just as he would not treat a typhoid patient without inquiring as to the source of the water he drank, a family-oriented physician will not think of illness in one member of the family as a single instance, but will pool it with his knowledge of the family as a whole.

## REFERENCE

1. KELLNER, R.: Family Ill Health—An Investigation in General Practice. New York, Thomas and Sons, 1963.

*The pilot study of families with a child suffering from ulcerative colitis, mentioned on page 331 of the preceding paper, is described in detail in the following contribution to this chapter. It is probably the first study of ulcerative colitis within the framework of family interaction. As is known, this condition can take a very severe, even lethal, course, but its etiology is unknown. It is, therefore, not possible to determine from the data obtained from these families alone whether or not the illness was the cause or the result of the specific interaction observed in these families or—as we might expect in a cybernetically oriented, circular view of causation—an interdependent mixture of both. The obvious next step in this research, namely the comparison of ulcerative colitis families with other families in which a child was chronically suffering from an illness of clearly non-emotional etiology (i.e., cystic fibrosis), could not be completed because of Dr. Jackson's death.*

*In spite of these limitations, of which the authors of this study are fully aware, it was possible to identify certain patterns of restrictiveness which may very well be typical for the so-called ulcerative colitis families, and are therefore of interest to family researchers and therapists alike.*

# FAMILY RESEARCH ON THE PROBLEM
# OF ULCERATIVE COLITIS

*Don D. Jackson, M.D., and Irvin Yalom, M.D.*

Chronic ulcerative colitis is an enigma today, despite many years of study and voluminous publications by persons of diverse interests and backgrounds. As Lepore stated in 1965: ". . . its etiology remains unknown and its treatment unscientific."[1] Since Murray's paper in 1930,[2] which noted the connection between emotional factors and both mucus colitis and ulcerative colitis, there have been many inquiries into the psychological functioning of ulcerative colitis patients. In general, there has been agreement that ulcerative colitis patients usually suffer from serious psychological illness. Descriptions of personality organization in such patients, based on psychological testing or therapy observations, include the whole panoply of our nosological types. Frequently mentioned characteristics are: obsessive-compulsive character traits, narcissism, a marked pseudo-mature veneer covering a deeper petulant infantilism, rigidity, and guarded affectivity, underlying depressive trends, and psychosexual immaturity. Patients often exercise marked denial and have difficulty in effectively expressing aggression. The psychological aspects of the precipitating stress have been studied by several investigators with some consensus about the psychological vulnerability of the ulcerative colitis patient to separation, or the threat of separation, from a significant other.

Developmental studies and speculations have, in the main, been limited to descriptions of the pathological relationship in the ulcerative colitis patient and his mother. There has been little mention of other members of the family and to our knowledge, and according to Finch,[3] there have been no descriptions of conjoint family interaction in ulcerative colitis. Such data, of course, has not been easy to obtain. Students of psychosomatic illness have become increasingly dissatisfied with attempts to reconstruct the family atmosphere from histories obtained from patients. Wenar,[4] among others, has demonstrated the unreliability of histories received from mothers about such important events in the life of their off-

Originally published in *Archives of General Psychiatry* 15:410–18 (1966). Copyright 1966 by American Medical Association. Reprinted by permission.

This study was supported in part by National Institute of Mental Health grants No. MH-08720 and No. MH-11362-01, the Louis and Maud Hill Family Foundation, and the Wheeler Foundation.

spring as hospitalization and major illness; consequently, the recall of any effectively tinged material is suspect. This difficulty is at least partially overcome in the utilization of the conjoint family interview, which does not depend on retrospective history-taking. In the conjoint family interview, current interaction of the family is observed both by the interviewer and by observers behind a one-way glass screen, and audio and visual material is available for lengthy study following the interview. There are, of course, drawbacks to this technique. The family's behavior is observed in an unusual and artificial situation, and cannot definitely be considered typical of their everyday life. It is conceivable, for example, that parents in this study might be burdened with guilt over their child's ulcerative colitis, and might withhold "incriminating evidence" from the interviewer. The recent work of Rosenthal[5] has demonstrated, in striking fashion, the influence of the interviewer, and although this has not been shown to occur in family interviews, we assume such bias to be present. We consequently present our observations on ulcerative colitis families as tentative, incomplete, and lacking in scientific rigor. However, other investigators may profit from a chance to agree or disagree with our findings, and their interest may lead to further studies.

In the past decade, information derived from the study of families through the device of conjoint family therapy[6] has provided considerable information about the characteristics of certain types of families, especially those containing a schizophrenic or delinquent member. The interactional profile of abnormal families has been shown to vary when measured by a variety of methodological tools. It is not unrealistic to suppose that a typology of families might eventually be derived. The purpose of the present study was to explore whether or not psychosomatic families have a characteristic interactional profile. For this reason a severe psychosomatic disorder, namely ulcerative colitis, was chosen. Although it is unlikely, in our opinion, that ulcerative colitis is the specific etiological result of certain family interactional patterns, this does remain a possibility. It seems more likely that it is a disorder produced under stress where certain genetic factors already exist. It is also important not to overlook the possibility that a chronically ill child is the source of the stress, rather than one of its products. For this reason we are currently undertaking a larger study in which families with a child with ulcerative colitis will be compared with families in which a child has a chronic illness not related to psychological factors.

Our sample of eight families is small, but they displayed a strikingly high degree of similarity in certain interactional patterns and the data seemed worth reporting. The families attended 4 to 20 conjoint 90-minute sessions which were labeled as investigatory interviews. The interviews were tape-recorded and generally witnessed by observers. The identified patients were all children (six boys and two girls), ranging in age from 7 to 17 years. In all cases the original parents were living with their bio-logical children; the families were white and middle class; and they were not in the midst of current financial or other crises that would tend to obscure the effect of the chronically ill child upon them.

## The Iron Family

As a typical family in our group, the "Iron" family serves as an intro-duction to the characteristics we encountered.

The first thing one notices about all five members of the Iron family is their extreme quietness; one observer characterized them as the "most deadly quiet" family he had ever seen. All the interviews were char-acterized by embarrassment, soft voices, silence. The circumstances of their life are also quiet. The father, in his 60's, works for Civil Service, where his wife is also employed. He denies ever having had any specific ambitions except to work on a farm, which he did for several years. Shortly after his marriage, however, he took a job in a hardware store, and stayed there for 20 years before changing to his present job. The family now lives on a farm outside of the small town where both the parents grew up. They seldom go out, except to visit relatives. They do not travel. The eldest daughter, Anita, 21, remarked that she had to "push them out the door" on their anniversary. The parents explain that they used to go out but stopped when the mother started working—although this was ten years ago. They add that rather than spend $20 on a restaurant dinner they prefer to spend the money on their children. They are a very child-oriented family.

Besides Anita, there are two children: Susan, 17 (the identified patient), and Ken, 15. They confirm their parents' claim of family closeness, and indeed the family seems to "stick together." On several occasions in the family interviews, it appeared that this effort extended to the attempt to suppress any evidence of dissension within the family. They seemed afraid to express themselves, and any personal expression that occurred was quickly covered up by another family member's action. The eldest daughter mentioned that she had raised sheep when she was a teen-ager and added that although her father approved of this, her mother had been against it. There was a sudden tension in the room. Anita then said that this was the only time her parents had ever disagreed, and the topic was changed.

There were other instances of this apparent concealment. In one of the interviews it was learned that there had been some kind of "unpleasant episode" the previous Saturday morning. With persistent inquiry the therapist was able to find out that Ken—who was always polite, laconic, and virtually expressionless—had expected to be picked up by two other boys in his class at 7 AM and had arisen early and waited for them. At 10 AM he was still waiting and the father then suggested that he telephone the home of one of the boys and find out what had happened to him. Upon doing so, he learned that he had been "stood up." In the presence of the therapist, the father complimented his son on his not being upset by the incident, or at least not being "really" upset. When the therapist suggested to the boy that he had waited three hours before telephoning because he perhaps did not want to find out that he had been stood up and chose to hope that maybe at any moment the other boys might arrive, the boy showed some feeling, appearing to be at the point of tears. The father was mildly annoyed with the therapist and felt there was "no use making a big deal out of it." The family rallied, changed the topic, and the door was closed on this episode.

On another occasion it was revealed that there had been some dissension in the family over what televsion show to watch in the evening. Although it was apparent that this was a current issue, the mother said that it had only happened when the children were very young. The father, disqualifying the issue further, suggested that it was not much of a problem since the television was supposed to be turned off at 7 PM each night. It was never clear what rules, if any, were enforced.

The family was equally reticent about their physical disorders. At first they denied that these existed; later it was learned that aside from Susan's ulcerative colitis, there had been gastrointestinal trouble for the mother and father. The mother complained of some bowel trouble ("trouble down there," as she called it) which she said was very similar to Susan's problem. The father has had three severe ulcer attacks, the most recent one requiring hospitalization and blood transfusions.

The hesitation in the family became—as might be expected—a major subject of the interview sessions. Each time we mentioned their reluctance to answer they suggested that they simply could think of nothing to say. Finally, we advanced the question of whether they had really had nothing to say or whether they felt they were not permitted to say things within the family. At this, Anita blurted out a memory: she was younger, she would want to talk, and would come into the room, but everyone would tell her to be quiet because they were watching television. The mother and father quickly denied that this had happened; a few minutes later the girl herself denied she had ever mentioned such a thing.

### Observational Data from the Families

The style of behavior we discovered in the Iron family was characteristic of the other families as well. To describe it, we came to use two essential terms: "restricted family" and "restrictiveness." By a "restricted family" we mean a family whose members have a marked inability to engage in, or even to recognize, contingency possibilities, ie, opportunities for kinds of behavior outside the pattern of their immediate lives. White, middle-class individuals normally have all kinds of opportunities to engage in a wide variety of activities, endeavors, and styles of living. If there are no obvious physical or cultural reasons for the individual's not making use of a considerable number of these contingency possibilities, it would then appear that he has learned some prohibition against doing so. This seemed to be true in the restricted families we studied, and the learning process itself proved to be at least partially observable in the interview sessions. The ulcerative colitis families in our study seemed to back each other up in their acceptance of limited behavior, and to discourage such behavior as humor, novelty, creative response, etc. For this process we used the term "restrictiveness."

Our overall assessment of what was demonstrated by the conjoint family interviews follows.

1. Restricted families have observable rules and transactions that confine the members to few and limited interactions within the family group. There are rules as to who can say what to whom, with negative sanctions used against the individual who says more than he "should." Family members seem to hold each other in check by placating, nullifying, and subduing each other. Voice tone is often quiet and expressionless. Arguments and emotional comments, anger, and affective responses, are in most instances avoided. There appears to be a conscious awareness of pain, disharmony, and unhappiness in the family and yet an agreement that this will not be mentioned in front of other family members. Usually it was possible to obtain some statement of the unhappiness in the family by interviewing individual family members alone. In a few cases, after a number of interviews, some mention of family problems occurred but this situation was the exception rather than the rule. Furthermore, there is a lack of tender, affectionate interaction between the parents.

Families With Ulcerative Colitis

| | | FAMILY RULES | | | |
|---|---|---|---|---|---|
| Family | Response to "How Did You Meet" | Restrictiveness (Activities, Range of Behavior, Etc.) | Scapegoating of Parent | Parental Roles | Marital Relationship |
| 1 | Fate. Met in bowling alley. | Mo restricts because of phobias. Neatness and dietary demands. | Mother | Fa described as a "softie." Mother does the disciplining. | Mo bored by Fa's account of war exploits. Unfriendly to his fine description of his first impression of her. Parents rarely spend time together except for occasional bridge games. |
| 2 | Mothers forced meeting. | Parents never go out together. Maintain status quo of discord at all cost. | Father | Fa not in charge. Gains ascendency in family through violent outbursts of impotent rage. Parents act together only against IP. | Fa beats Mo. Says Mo has never shown him affection. Mo says she is unable to. Many attempts at separation; never final. Times parents spend alone together end in some kind of explosiveness. No one in family talks about caring for anyone. |
| 3 | Fate. Met through job. No positive reaction to each other. | Parents do not leave IP for vacations. Have gone out six times in two years in spite of opportunities for free | Father | Mo immersed in mothering role. Fa feels helpless, ignored and indecisive. Goes into ineffectual rages. | No feelings expressed by either partner. Fa complains Mo does not care about him. Mo says he is impossible to |

340

| | | | | | |
|---|---|---|---|---|---|
| | church. Were "only two single people there." | everyone else's feelings. Parents out together only twice in 5 years despite urging to the contrary by children. Only concerns are: first, safety; next achievement. | | | in parenting. Fa ostensibly protects Mo. |
| 5 | Fate. Met through the Grange. Lived in same town. | Feelings not discussed or expressed. Parents rarely go out together. | Conspiracy of silence. | Much time spent with family. | Fa is self-effacing. |
| 6 | Fate. Mo entertained servicemen & met Fa while he was in the Air Corps. | Parents never go out together. Never hire baby-sitters. | Mother | Fa sees Mo as inconsistent with the children. Fa retreats & fails to back her up. | No expression of positive feelings. Mo complains of Fa's undemonstrativeness. Fa very withdrawn. |
| 7 | Fate. Met because of war. | Mother is only one to express overt anger. Extreme restrictiveness of feelings otherwise. IP fearful of going places. | Conspiracy of silence. | Fa somewhat childlike, disorganized, unrealistic. IP often assumes adult role. | No expression of positive feelings. Fa immersed in work, spends little time in home. Previous separation. |
| 8 | Fate. Same town & school. Families knew each other. | Parents go out together once a month. Everyone nice to everyone else. Very guarded family. | Conspiracy of silence. | Fa self-deprecatory. | No overt feelings of any kind expressed, but Mo subtly undermines Fa. |

*Families With Ulcerative Colitis* (continued)

| HEALTH (MENTAL AND PHYSICAL) | | EXTRAFAMILIAL RELATIONSHIPS | | |
|---|---|---|---|---|
| Health of Parents | Health of Siblings | Father's Job Picture | Peer Relationships | Grandparents |
| Mo was hospitalized for Gyn disorder, which is discussed openly and at length. Mo is phobic. Had "nervous breakdown" when IP was 2½ yr old. Also had bowel trouble. Fa preoccupied with own physical injuries. | Sister has fainting spells, is sullen & withdrawn during sessions. | Passive. Ineffectual at work & at sessions. Lack of affect. Admits reluctantly that his problems have to do with lack of drive & ambition. | IP had few peer relationships when young. | No known difficulties. |
| Mo has had double hernia, D&C, deviated nasal septum, hysterectomy, thyroid difficulty. Mo had "nervous breakdown" prior to marriage to Fa, after losing boyfriend. | All siblings are emotionally disturbed. | Sees himself as a failure. | IP has few peer relationships. Fa has few. | Mo's father was a philanderer.<br><br>Fa's parents separated when he was 7 yr old; he felt fatherless. |
| Fa in good physical health. Mo has gastric ulcer & also many phobias. | Sibling age 4 yr. | No ambition toward job advancement in spite of financial worries. | Mo has few peer relationships. Asks Fa's permission to go to luncheon. | Mo's father rarely home when she was small, due to job. Fa's father died when Fa 2 yr old. Had weak stepfather. |

| | | underachieving. | peer relationships. | psychiatric hospital. |
|---|---|---|---|---|
| ...gical procedures. Somewhat phobic and emotionally unstable. | ...has trichotillomania & hysterical deafness. The other is depressed. | | | Fa's parents killed in auto accident with Fa driving. |
| Mo had acne & mucous colitis. Fa has recurrent bleeding peptic ulcer. | One sibling withdrawn, depressed, has acne. 21-year-old sister has acne, does not date, is attached to sheep. | Extremely low job satisfaction. Tends to overlook anything unpleasant. | Parents have no peer relationships. | Mo's father paralyzed. |
| Mo hospitalized 11 times in 17 years for "back trouble." Complains about pain but does nothing about it. Mo has tics & is extremely phobic. | Siblings tense. IP is calmest. One sibling has tics & temper tantrums. | Unhappy & frustrated at work. Uninvolved & noncommunicative. | Parents & IP have no close friends. | Mo's father became ill before IP was born, was ill for 12 yr until death. Fa's father was depressed, alcoholic, committed suicide. |
| Mo often depressed. Fa is unrealistic, disorganized, somewhat paranoid. | Insufficient information. | Spends long hours at work, but little job satisfaction. Many business failures. | IP has no friends. Blames this on his ulcerative colitis. | Mo's mother paralyzed with multiple sclerosis. Fa's parents separated; saw own father rarely. His mother was extremely religious. Unstable life. |
| Mo had Gyn surgery; also history of depression & "sleeping sickness" from mumps, back trouble. | Insufficient information. | Many business changes & failures. | Parents have few friends. | Fa's parents were divorced when Fa was 15 yr old. Fa's father was alcoholic. |

*Families With Ulcerative Colitis* (continued)

| | | IDENTIFIED PATIENT (IP) | | |
| Family | Sex and Age of Onset of Ulcerative Colitis | Onset of Ulcerative Colitis in Relation to Family Events | Mother-Identified Patient Relationship | Father-Identified Patient Relationship |
| --- | --- | --- | --- | --- |
| 1 | Male, age of onset of ulcerative colitis unknown. | 1 to 2 months following Mo's brief hospitalization for Gyn disorder. | Very close, dependent relationships. IP can talk with mother. | No closeness, though IP expects father to discipline him. |
| 2 | Male, 12 yr | Parental separation preceded onset of abdominal pains. Colitis followed Mo's hospitalization for hysterectomy. Flare-ups related to arguments between parents. | Coalition between IP and mother. | Intense, complex feelings between IP and father. Fa jealous of Mo's relationship to IP. |
| 3 | Male, 6 yr | Related to time of marital difficulties between parents when Fa was fire captain. | Mo focuses on IP to the exclusion of Fa and sibling. Passes phobias on to IP. | Fa has no investment in IP's health because of Fa's jealousy of him. |
| 4 | Male, 12 yr | Colitis associated in time with birth of the youngest sibling & with Fa's molestation of a schoolgirl. Later aggravated by Mo's gallbladder surgery. | "ESP" type of communication. | No communication. Fa knew IP was sick only because of weight loss. IP cannot talk with father. |

| | | | |
|---|---|---|---|
| 5 | Female, 16 yr | Colitis associated with gradual break-up with boyfriend. | Strong identification of Mo with IP. | Fa favors IP though at times may scapegoat her. |
| 6 | Male, 10 yr | Mo's father died one month prior to onset. Mo was very upset. | IP tuned in on Mo's back pain; sounds like her. Mo talks for IP, "reads children's minds." | No communication. |
| 7 | Male, 10 yr | Colitis began after Fa deserted family. | Unclear. | Peer-type relationship. |
| 8 | Female, 15 yr | Associated with financial difficulties and moves in family. Coincided with some difficulties with school. | IP assumes material role, while Mo becomes inactive. | Unclear. |

We also noted that within the family system an individual often behaves in such a way that he invites sanctions from others and responds to feedback from them as if it were a command. Thus someone may act reluctant to depart and his spouse may say, "Don't go." The reluctant spouse may then reply, "O.K., if that's the way you want it." An individual may utilize restricting techniques or behaviors on other family members and in the process also restrict himself. This is usually done in one of two ways: (A). His relationship to the one that he is restricting in turn restricts himself: For example, the husband of a phobic wife is restricted in turn by her anxieties and fears and yet he continues to reinforce her phobias by failing to provide her with exposure to novel contingencies. (B). The individual may influence others to join him in a restricted shared pattern, as is obvious in the case of a paranoid two-against-the-world union.

Restrictions on family interaction appear to lead to restrictions on behavior in the world at large. There seems to be a curtailment of geographical movements by these families, and a lack of participation in new contingency possibilities outside the family system.* It was difficult to imagine what they had done in pretelevision days. The parents remain aloof from the social community, they have few or no peer relationships, and are engaged for the most part in work or child-oriented activities. Most of the families have rarely, if ever, used baby-sitters. Many of the families seem to have little or no social life except for their relatives or in-laws. While this may have been a cultural phenomenon that was the result of a biased sample, it appeared through discussions held with the family members, that the extended family was used not only for solidarity purposes, but in some cases, because the parents in families suffering from ulcerative colitis were afraid *not* to visit their relatives. One exception to this "extended family ties" situation was more apparent than real. The parents had left the East and fled to California to get away from their mutual families,

---

* A supplementary concept to the idea of "restrictiveness" is "recursive arborization." The word "recursive" refers to the fact that the same basic set of rules are the building blocks for the rules generated in any situation, and "arborization" refers to the fact that there is a branching out of these sets of rules to meet new situations even though the same basic set of rules are simply recurring over and over again. Under the process of recursive arborization, novel situations will have to be treated similarly in order for the same basic rules to apply for all situations. One way to do this is for an individual to ignore new contingency possibilities or distort them so that the percepts will fit the sample rule in which system he operates. The term "recursive arborization" (borrowed in part from computer language) is discussed in another paper: "Schizophrenia: The Nosological Nexus", reprinted on pp. 193–207 of this volume.

but they were still preoccupied with their relatives, quarrelled over them with each other, and accused their parents of forcing them together in an unsatisfactory marriage.

The whole family seemed to behave as if reducing varieties of behavior would reduce the possibility of one's behavior being taken as a relationship message by another family member. Thus, if an individual engages in out-side activities, in addition to those prescribed by law or custom (for example, school and church) such behavior could be taken as an avoidance of the family or of some particular member within the family or of being interested in some other family more than in one's own. A corollary of this is that the family that restricts behavior in order to avoid negative relationship messages must also teach its members not to notice this restriction or it would lead to mutual blame, rebellion, etc. Evidence for this finding occurs in the fact that although none of the parents in these ulcerative colitis families used baby-sitters as often as twice a year, and some had not been out together in many years of marriage, they chose to think that this was typical for others in their socio-economic group. The parents wittingly or unwittingly supported the fiction of a close, loving family.

Another form of restrictiveness was an excessive concern with medical matters and physical health. In some of the families, there was not only the apparent overconcern with health conditions, but the mothers had had multiple surgical procedures and frequent hospitalizations. In addition, the mothers were frequently phobic, and their hypochondriasis and phobias caused further social and geographical restrictiveness.

In none of the families did the father feel satisfied with his job, nor was there evidence of any ambition. Thus, there were no work-oriented social activities to speak of and no chance for the family to extend its knowledge of new situations through the father's job contacts or through job travel. It seemed to us to be an unusual finding that in all eight cases the father's lack of ambition and low self-esteem were obvious, as was his resignation to the task of merely being a breadwinner. The father's low titer of self-esteem was a clearly visible part of the family tradition. Although the family rules permitted no one else to comment on this, most of the fathers openly discussed their dissatisfaction and resignation. For example, Mr. H commented that he wanted his daughters to get a good education in order to get "a better husband than their mother did." Mr. A and Mr. C held themselves up as bad examples for their sons. (See the Table for details of fathers' work history.)

2. Communication in these families was exceedingly indirect and seemed, on occasions, to be deliberately so. Thus, data would be given in a rather loose, tentative fashion so that it could easily be altered if an-

other family member complained or questioned it or disagreed. Mr. D, for example, commented that when he returned from another state he got a job and the family moved into their present neighborhood. Later on in the same interview, the mother commented on the same material but stated that it took him a considerable period of time to find a job. When Mrs. D was describing her "sleeping sickness" she said it took her several months to get over it. In the same interview, when her husband described her "illness," he commented that it took her "years" to get over it and there appeared to be some implication that she was still "nervous." The investigators were never quite sure what the illness was. One of the inviolable family rules was that there were to be no relationship comments made overtly and the children in these families were instructed in the rule both implicitly and explicitly. Thus, when Mrs. D stated that she had been "jumpy" as a result of the "sleeping sickness" and the identified patient remarked that his mother was still jumpy, the father immediately denied this. Then the identified patient said that all he meant was that if you said something to Mother when she was not expecting you to, she had a startle reaction. Father responded, stating that he (the patient) also had a startle reaction, so did he and so did everyone. The Iron family, as has been seen, repeatedly disqualified data to the point of denial. In C family, the father expressed some emotion by weeping when talking about his younger sister. Characteristically, he would not pursue the topic and it was never learned what was behind the tears. Mr. O explained that he cannot get involved or excited about family matters because he had been through so much in World War II and had seen things that were really emotional and everything subsequently paled in comparison.

3. The observers were impressed with the amount of apparent mental pathology in the siblings. It was not uncommon for the parents to comment that they would be surprised if nerves had anything to do with ulcerative colitis because the identified patient was frequently the least nervous and most stable of the children. Outwardly, this appeared to be true. In the O Family, the sibling, an older sister, had had several syncopal episodes, severe menstrual disorders, and was surly and withdrawn. In the Iron family, all the siblings had very severe acne, the younger brother appeared markedly depressed, the oldest girl, 21, had no heterosexual experimentation. She felt inferior to her boyfriend, and unable to talk to him, so to remedy this she took the inappropriate step of enrolling in a night course in basic English. The two siblings in the H family were severely disturbed, one, age 15, continually pulled out her hair and ate it, the other, age 18, was very depressed, dependent, and had had no dating experience. Both the male siblings in the R family appeared socially retarded, neither having any peer relations. One, age 16, had multiple tics

and many phobias, refusing, for example, to drive or date. All of the C children appeared to be quite disturbed, had many rebellious episodes with various authorities, had run away from home, and one of them appeared to the observers to be actively psychotic during at least one of the family sessions.

4. The communication of restrictiveness from generation to generation is apparent in all of these families. The parents do not push the children out of the family circle and although they may comment on the child's lack of socialization, little or nothing is done about it. In most cases, the fact that a child has ulcerative colitis appears to be an excuse for the restricted family, but the accuracy of this observation will need to be verified by studying other families with chronically ill children. It appears that in subtle ways, the parents deliver a message to the child that branching out and leaving home is fraught with danger. Mrs. C, although she seemed unhappy in the fact that her 6-year-old boy was not riding his bicycle or leaving the house, repeatedly warned him not to walk with his hands in his pockets because he would have no way to protect himself when he fell. The H family actively restricted their daughter's dating, commenting on the frequency with which people get robbed, raped, or knifed. The O family were cautioned by Mother on the danger of germs and the family nourished the myth that "Mother would crack up at the slightest injury to any of us." It was also stated on another occasion, "She wants us in a straightjacket so we won't get hurt." The parents set an example for the children, as has been seen, by being severely restricted themselves in their social activities. In some cases this was unbelievably rationalized. The C family went out occasionally but said that they were afraid that the children might burn the house down and so were reluctant to go out very often. The A family, who had not been out together in years, attributed this to the husband's long working hours, and said they did not take trips as a family because "it was too much of a chore to be constantly preoccupied with looking for rest room signs." Mrs. O asked for help from Mr. O in taking over the socialization of the little boy, but forbade them to go hunting or fishing (Mr. O's sports) because she did not like the idea of "animals getting gored."

It appeared also that restrictiveness was enforced through physical posture; almost invariably members of both observations held themselves in rigid, wooden attitudes.

5. In nearly every family the father of one, or more frequently of both spouses, had died when the child was young, or was an alcoholic or deserter, or had committed suicide (Table). As in the previous items, this could be a simple chance finding, but it also could be a source of the family's restrictive behavior. One wife remarked that she did not say as

much to her husband as she would like to because his father had committed suicide and she was afraid she might push him in that direction. The lack of a model of a father provided difficulty for these parents in relating to their own children.

### Summary and Conclusions

From a study of eight families in which the identified patient had ulcerative colitis, from observation of several other such families, and from discussions with family therapists, who had treated such families, we were struck by the similarity of behavior among these families when interacting in conjoint family therapy. All the families appeared to be severely socially restricted and actively restricted each other in the range of permissible behavior. Data collected on individual family members as to their "outside the family" behavior corroborated the impression that they existed in a narrow band of social participation when compared to the group of "ordinary" families under study at the Mental Research Institute. The limitation in the range of interaction, the careful dealing with each other, the handling of a variety of situations in a similar fashion, suggest at one and the same time a feeling of despair and yet a feeling of family sameness that almost seemed like solidarity. Wynne's term "pseudomutuality" best describes the apparently false solidarity of these families.

Our sample was a white, middle-class one and we have no data to control for the effect of a chronically ill child on family interaction. It is obvious that the study needs to be broadened, both in the size and range of the sample, and a control instituted for the effect of a chronic illness by utilizing disorders that have no known emotional etiology, such as cystic fibrosis and muscular dystrophy. We would like to check on the social habits of the ulcerative colitis families by comparing them on a variety of measurements with a normal sample, as well as the above-mentioned chronically ill child sample.

Three terms: "restrictiveness," "restricted family," and "recursive arborization" are introduced as possible conceptual aids in the study of family interactional patterns.

### REFERENCES

1. LEPORE, M. J.: The Importance of Emotional Disturbances in Chronic Ulcerative Colitis, *JAMA* 191:819 (March 8) 1965.
2. MURRAY, C. D.: Psychogenic Factors in the Etiology of Ulcerative Colitis and Bloody Diarrhea, *Amer J Med Sci* 180:239 (Aug) 1930.

3. FINCH, S. M.: Personal communication to the authors, 1965.
4. WENAR, C.: The Reliability of Developmental Histories, *Psychosom Med* 25:505–509 (Nov–Dec) 1963.
5. ROSENTHAL, R.: Three Experiments in Experimental Bias, *Psychol Rep* 12:491–511, 1963.
6. JACKSON, D. D.: "Family Homeostasis and Family Therapy," in Masserman, J. (ed.): *Science and Psychoanalysis,* New York: Grune & Stratton, Inc., 1959, vol IV.

*The next paper, by Norma Davies and Elaine Hansen, reports on a highly successful program in which family interaction and brief therapy principles are applied to a problem area that has so far received very little attention from the family perspective: what happens to patients with a physical disability upon discharge from the hospital and return to their families. Traditionally, and at best, these families may get rather brief and didactic instructions on how they should deal with their handicapped relative. The result is that they are often left to their own devices and to what they, sincerely but quite mistakenly, may consider to be the best procedure. If we add to this their possible misconceptions about the nature and the seriousness of their relative's disability, it is not too difficult to see that here, as with many other human difficulties, the attempted solution may be a large part of the problem and seriously complicate a disability or greatly prolong a convalescence. The implictions of this pilot project for family medicine are obvious.*

# FAMILY FOCUS: A TRANSITIONAL COTTAGE

# IN AN ACUTE-CARE HOSPITAL

*Norma H. Davies, Ph.D., Elaine Hansen, R.P.T.*

The idea for the "Family Focus" program came into existence in 1971. The impetus for this new program was the view that patient care often excluded a factor of major importance—the patient's family. The guiding

The Family Focus project was designed by Katherine F. Shepard, Division of Physical Therapy, Stanford University School of Medicine, and John E. Bell, of the Stanford University Department of Psychiatry and formerly Director of the Mental Research Institute. The project is sponsored by the Division of Physical Therapy (Helen Blood, Director) and is a service of premise for Family Focus is the belief that prior to discharge the patient, especially the patient needing post-hospital care, is usually best served by treating and training both him and his family in an environment that closely approximates the home setting.

During its first years of operation the format for the program has been as follows: Stanford Hospital patients who are receiving physical therapy and who are willing to participate are referred by the attending physician. For the last three days of hospitalization the patient is transferred to a specially constructed "cottage" located on Stanford Hospital grounds where he resides with his family and/or whoever will be of assistance upon his return home. The cottage is a prefabricated modular house that has been divided into a family living area and a staff office. The family area has a kitchen, family room, living room, bedroom, and bathroom—all comfortably furnished with second-hand donations. A few special adaptations have been made. These include a ramp to the front entrance, a widened bathroom door and several bathroom grab bars.

The adjacent staff office is equipped with one-way mirrors and an audio system to the family area so that the treating therapist and family can be observed at prearranged times with family consent. The psychologist, physical therapy student, and other staff can observe these sessions without actually participating in the activities.

Family members are encouraged to function as if they were in their own home. They purchase food to prepare their own favorite meals, rise and sleep at their convenience, invite guests or family for social and business affairs, and utilize an outdoor area for walks or "fresh air." In our experience, families quickly adapt to the setting and view themselves as proprietors and hospital or Family Focus staff as guests. In support of this relationship, all staff members visiting the patient make prior appointments and present themselves by knocking at the family's front door. If the family desires to talk to a staff member before a scheduled appointment, they can do so by phone.

This transitional setting stands in sharp contrast to the traditional direct patient discharge from hospital to home. Ordinarily, the family members may be invited for a last-minute hour or half-hour of quick instruction on special care for the patient: his medication and dietary needs, special equipment needs, exercise instruction, and any other special disability

the Stanford University Hospital. It is supported by DHEW Grant No. 5 D12 AH 00097. In addition to the two clinical physical therapy instructors, physical therapy interns assist as part of their graduate training. Originally published in *Family Process* 13:481–8 (1974). Reprinted by permission.

training. The shortcomings of this traditional "watch me" approach are evident when observing the families struggle through the first day at Family Focus. The absence of any family involvement in the hospital exacerbates these problems.

The goal of Family Focus transitional living is to prevent, or shorten, difficult post-hospital adjustment periods that a patient and family usually face alone at home. When they first arrive at Family Focus, family members generally exhibit considerable anxiety about how they will manage, but there is comfort in the knowledge that hospital personnel are available twenty-four hours daily and Family Focus staff are prepared to teach them the technical skills they require. This is a time to define and hopefully resolve problem areas (medical, physical, emotional) in order to assist the patient and family to function optimally. To accomplish this goal, the needs of all relevant parties must be considered. Suggestions are offered based on these needs and in keeping with the previous life style of the family.

In the process of treatment and training, the physical therapist discusses goals and expectations and identifies present or potential interpersonal problems. In this context of defined tasks for patient and family training, the physical therapist is the most appropriate staff member to deal with behavioral problems. When difficulties arise or are anticipated, the family advisor, a psychologist, consults with the physical therapist and occasionally with the family.

In the early stages of the program, the psychologist always entered the family scene to deal with behavioral problems. The liabilities of this direct intervention within this three-day residence period became clear in short order. Although rapport, trust, and openness might exist between physical therapist and family, the psychologist was a stranger. It seemed more realistic to have the physical therapist observe trouble spots as they arose naturally and easier for patients and family members to talk about problems as they related to the tasks they performed. As a result, the psychologist now functions as consultant to the physical therapist and the physical therapy interns.

A systematic follow-up evaluation is under way to compare the outcomes for families who have had pre-discharge intervention through Family Focus with families who have not, but results will not be available for some time to come. A detailed case presentation is offered to illustrate the ways in which an in-hospital family transition period may facilitate readjustment of patients and families to home. In addition, two brief cases are reported in order to indicate the variety of patients served and common difficulties encountered by them.

## Case I

The B.'s, a middle-class Philippine couple, had lived in the United States for six years when Mrs. B., age 26, gave birth to their first child. The delivery and the baby were normal. Several hours later, however, Mrs. B. had a subarachnoid hemorrhage that left her with a right hemiplegia and severe expressive aphasia.

During the course of her month in the hospital, she learned to walk and to care for herself independently despite remaining weakness and sensory deficits. She continued to have difficulty writing, performing simple calculations, and occasionally remembering appropriate words. Her greatest problem, however, centered around her relationship to her newborn child. Shortly after the delivery, her mother, Mrs. S., arrived from the Philippines and cared for the infant daughter at the B.'s home. Although Mrs. S. brought her granddaughter to the hospital daily, Mrs. B. played little part in her care. In her hospital bed she sometimes held the child and gave her a bottle at feeding time, but on only one brief occasion was she left alone with her. Mr. B. visited after work and then took his mother-in-law and daughter home.

"I don't feel like her mother," Mrs. B. said despondently. To be a mother, Mrs. B. believed that she should be able to do everything for her daughter. Her sense of detachment began with her inability to recall the delivery and was accentuated by her lack of experience in caring for and comforting her child. The fear of being an inadequate mother was coupled with her more general concerns about whether she would ever be normal again: able to drive a car, to climb steps in their newly purchased home, to prepare a meal, and eventually to return to work. In capsule, her anxieties centered around her competence as an independent person and her role as a mother.

Mrs. B.'s expressed apprehensions and the hospital staff's concerns about potential problems of role-definition for the B.'s and Mrs. S. were the bases for referral to Family Focus.

The B.'s, the baby, and Mrs. S. lived in the Family Focus cottage for the last three days of Mrs. B.'s hospitalization. Mr. B. was employed during the day and returned each evening. The B. family slept in the bedroom, while Mrs. S. used a convertible sofa in the family room.

From the first moment Mrs. B. was eager to experiment with all the activities she had been unable to perform on the hospital ward; caring for her daughter, cooking, keeping house. In the course of accomplishing a task that required organized planning, she viewed herself as extremely slow and forgetful. She was afraid to use pins to diaper her baby or to prepare food on a hot stove, believing that her sharp-dull and hot-cold sensations were impaired. Each minor stumbling block simply reinforced her notion that she would be inadequate to the demands of the situation and those she was making upon herself.

During the early part of her residence, steps were taken by the Family Focus physical therapists to clarify and delineate her weaknesses. As it turned out, she could feel a pin prick and a hot stove but could not identify the position of her arm unless she observed it. Isolating and learning to cope with this specific problem relieved some of the vague, ill-defined apprehension she was experiencing. In other instances it was difficult to determine whether problems encountered were the result of stroke-related disabilities or confusion normally faced by a new mother unaccustomed to caring for an infant and a household. In her case this confusion was accentuated by the prolonged hospitalization. While the staff were careful to be realistic in their appraisal of Mrs. B.'s special difficulties and accepting of her fears, they attempted to refocus her self-concept from "disabled patient" to "new mother adjusting to a novel and complex role."

If Mrs. B. were to become "mother," it was necessary that Mrs. S., who until this time was in complete charge of the infant's care, accept a different role. Mrs. S.'s importance as helper was reinforced throughout this period so as to strengthen and reward this view of herself and to prevent her from maintaining the role of baby's primary caretaker. At one point Mrs. S. suggested that another relative from the Philippines replace her when she departed. Mrs. B. asserted that she would hire someone for the job. This idea was encouraged, since establishing Mrs. B. as independent mother and household manager had been a major goal and it was deemed a simpler task to dismiss a paid employee than to dislodge a relative.

By the second day Mrs. B.'s attempts to experiment with every conceivable household and child-care responsibility had taken its toll. She looked exhausted, her frustration becoming increasingly apparent. She spoke again of her feelings of inadequacy as a mother and was generally depressed and tearful. She was overwhelmed by her high expectations of functioning immediately as expert mother and housewife. Among other things, we were concerned that her mother might be interfering with child care when no observers were present. It was suggested that if Mrs. S. were extremely busy with household duties she would be too tired to care for the baby. This idea that Mrs. B. had the power to control her environment and the relationships within it was reinforced throughout the physical therapy sessions. On this particular occasion she calmed down and expressed gratitude for having the opportunity to discuss her discouragements and anxieties. Her new outlook was reflected in her conclusion, "This is the way I am, so I'll have to figure things out." Now she was eager to begin learning the program of rehabilitation activities that she would continue to follow at home.

By the third day, Mrs. B. reported that the previous night had gone exceedingly well. Mrs. B. had responded to her infant's cry in contrast to the night before when her husband had tended to the baby's needs because his wife was too exhausted. Her optimism was still guarded, but her tone and appearance were brighter and more hopeful. During the evening of her departure she expressed some apprehension about adjusting to her own home, but she was eager and ready to leave when her husband arrived from work.

At this juncture Mrs. B.'s attending physician arrived for a final hospital visit. He first spoke to the Family Focus therapist in the adjoining office. He mentioned his discomfort of the previous evening when he had appeared in formal write laboratory coat to find a warm, comfortable, home atmosphere. Now he was attired in street clothes and during the family visit answered questions while sitting comfortably and smoking his pipe.

### Follow-up

On the physical therapist's first follow-up visit two weeks later, Mrs. B. answered the door holding her daughter comfortably in her arms. The observed interaction between Mrs. B. and her mother gave the impression that Mrs. B. was in complete control, although she might occasionally request assistance. As far as her progress was concerned, she was physically stronger but still dissatisfied with her slowness and disorganization. Although acknowledging her improvements, Mrs. B. wanted more immediate results.

The second home visit, approximately five weeks later, took place at the B.'s new home. Mrs. B. was doing all the housework, cooking, and child care. Her mother had been ill for two weeks. This circumstance coupled with continued physical improvement prompted the final steps towards complete independence.

### Case II

The F.'s arrived at Family Focus in a state of high anxiety and turmoil. In Mr. F.'s eyes, his nervous wife seemed incapable of learning to properly assist him in the exercises necessary for a good recovery after hip surgery.

The result was a constant harangue about his suffering and her incompetence. Guided by an observation of their traditional pattern of interacting, the psychologist suggested to the physical therapist a simple shift in focus. The physical therapist lifted the responsibility from the wife and placed it with Mr. F. As a result, he was taught the exercise program and informed that its correctness was dependent on the clarity of his instructions to guide Mrs. F. In this manner the problem was dramatically resolved.

## Case III

Mr. and Mrs. D. were an elderly couple in their 70's. Mr. D. had been hospitalized following his second stroke. Although physically well, Mrs. D. had a faulty memory. They were particularly distraught because failure to prove their ability to live independently would lead to nursing home residence—an isolated and often dreary existence. Mrs. D. expressed her fear and anxiety when she questioned, "How am I going to handle all of this at home? It is all so new to me." As is often the case, the patient agreed to Family Focus because of the needs of his spouse rather than his own expressed needs.

In this case, Mr. D.'s medications were the prime concern. He was no longer able to administer them to himself as he had done in the past. Mrs. D. became easily confused about the proper dosages and time schedule. Many methods were attempted during their three-day Family Focus stay. The solution proved to be a combined effort with a neighbor calling to signal medication times, Mr. D. overseeing the proper mixture of his numerous medications, and Mrs. D. actually grinding the appropriate pills. Thus their problem did not prove insurmountable, and both were able to return home.

## Conclusion

The Family Focus philosophy enlarges the scope of hospital services in two important ways. First, family members, as well as patients, are recognized as affected by the patient's disability. Their lives, too, may require considerable readjustment. The manner in which they cope is not unrelated to the patient's ability to accept, or overcome, his disability. Second, difficulties do not terminate with hospital discharge. Rather they often escalate when the family must assume functions previously performed by hospital personnel. We believe that hospital care should look beyond the discharge date and prepare the patient and family with the skills and support necessary for optimum out-of-hospital living. Although designed and implemented primarily by physical therapists, this mode of intervention may serve as a model for other allied health professionals in both medical and psychological hospital settings.

*Another area of family interaction in which helplessness and problem-engendering wrong solutions are particularly frequent are the difficulties inherent in old age. Here, too, traditional attempts have focused predominantly on the aging individual and his idiosyncrasies or partial disabilities rather than on an examination as to how these influence, and are in turn influenced by, the behavior of the entire human system of which he is a part.*

*In 1973, MRI obtained a grant to undertake a combined service and research project, directed specifically at assisting families with geriatric patients. It is called the Family Interaction Center and the following paper by Elaine Sorensen, the project director, describes its rationale and functioning.*

# FAMILY INTERACTION WITH THE ELDERLY

## Elaine M. Sorensen

There is an abundance of statistics to verify what most of us have observed in our own families—population profiles are changing significantly. From the turn of the century until 1930 the number of persons over 65 years of age doubled. The number doubled again between 1930 and 1950, and today (1973) some 20 million people, or one in ten Americans, are over 65 (1). It is further projected that the population over 65 will have increased to 23 million in 1980, 28 million in 1990 and may reach 48 million by 2030 (2).

While the population over 65 years of age is growing very fast, the group over 75 is growing even faster. By 1990 the 65 to 74 age group will be 7-½ times as large as in 1900; however, the group over 75 will be 11-½ times as large (3). Because of the decline in the female mortality rate, by 1990 there also will be 170 aged women for every 100 aged men (2).

Original contribution.

## Theoretical Foundations

As people live longer and die more slowly, new social roles emerge for the elderly and necessary shifts in inter-personal and family relationships occur.

Several theories have been proposed to explain this adjustment in life style. Activity theory would describe the highly satisfied older person as the one who is active physically, socially and mentally, and has frequent association with family and society as a whole (4). Since according to this orientation the activity norms for old age are the same as those for middle age, this theory postulates that if older people are to relinquish some formerly useful roles, they must be given new useful roles to take their place (5).

Continuity theory maintains that in the process of becoming an adult, the individual develops habits, commitments, preferences and a host of other dispositions that become a part of his personality. The person's life-long experience thus creates in him certain predispositions that he will maintain if at all possible. Therefore, Continuity Theory does not assume that lost roles need to be replaced (5).

According to Disengagement Theory there is a "thinning out of the number of members in the social structure surrounding the individual, a diminishing of interactions with these members, and a restructuring of the goals of the system" (6). This is probably the most controversial theory in social gerontology. Among other things it has been criticized for the assumption that disengagement is both natural and good (5). However, according to Cumming, the notion of disengagement was postulated from the findings of a study of a special population and never included, or intended, any moral or value judgments.

Since the family is the universal primary social system, family theory occupies a special position in any consideration of social theory. Every human group has devised traditional prescriptions and proscriptions to make sure that the family fulfills its biological and enculturating tasks (7).

In recent years the emphasis on the nuclear family concept has been modified to include a focus on the extended family or kin network concept and its functions of mutual aid and services (8). Speck and Attneave (9) include in their network not only the nuclear family and kin, but also friends, neighbors and numerous "significant others." They postulate that such a network "has within it the resources to develop creative solutions to the human predicaments of its members." The feasibility and effectiveness of these kin networks is due to the existence of modern communication and transportation systems as well as to increased leisure time, all of which facilitate interactions of individuals.

### The Family Interaction Center

The Family Interaction Center (FIC) of MRI is a service and training project designed to meet the special needs of families with older members, who together are seeking information or help in order to deal more effectively with the stresses of their daily lives. The program arose in response to the unmet needs of senior citizens as defined by professionals, citizens and agencies.

In order to maximize successful aging and extend the period of independent living (both physically and psychologically), the FIC program is designed to assist older persons and their families (nuclear and/or extended) in solving a broad range of problems common in today's culture. Above all the staff seeks to bridge barriers which may have isolated family members from each other, thereby re-establishing communication and support systems within the family.

It is around this basic concept that a staff of ten professionals has been recruited and trained by the Family Interaction Center. They represent the areas of psychiatry, nursing, psychology, anthropology and theology, and utilize the team approach in problem-solving. The continuing emphasis is on the strengths of clients with an orientation toward learning and growth at any age.

We still do not fully understand why some people are devastated by old age and others seem to adjust, even thrive (5). In general, it appears that persons who retain the youthful, vigorous, problem-solving view of life tend to make a better adjustment to old age (7). However, in solving problems, older individuals may be at a disadvantage if many items of information must be dealt with simultaneously. Some have trouble defining goals, remembering information or separating relevant material from irrelevant (5). Other, younger members of the family who find the presenting situation frustrating or stressful may experience similar difficulties. However, as an individual finds someone listening and accepting him, he becomes more confident of himself—as he becomes more confident he also becomes more accepting of others, and circumstances are thereby created where change and growth can occur (7).

Problem-solving counseling utilizes an individual and/or team outside of the family system to facilitate communication and subsequent decision-making within the family group. The general goals of counseling are 1) to define the presenting situation, 2) to explore possible alternatives/solutions, 3) to select and implement the desired solution, 4) to accept the things about the situation that cannot be changed. The team approach allows not only for the matching of client and counselor but also for the utilization of co-counseling and "guest counseling" when indicated to facilitate this process.

Discussion groups with specially trained leaders offer similar opportunities for growth. Multi-generation groups also help to dispel the myths the young have about older people and vice versa (10). Kastenbaum (11) suggests that the layman and the professional alike avoid intimate contact with the aged because they cue off death-related anxieties that people prefer not to confront. Kastenbaum and Aisenberg (12) also raise the question, "In a society that does not encourage grief work does bereavement overload explain much of the behavior of the elderly that is labeled 'bad aging?'" Death is also the unspoken variable in many geronotological studies and discussions. However, death is a crucial component in the life-death continuum. It has been postulated (13) that only after older generations have come to terms with death can younger generations come to terms with life.

## Summary

Because of this orientation, the primary goal of the FIC program is to enable the older person and other significant family members to operate as a functional problem-solving system by:

1. Enhancing families' sense of efficacy and ability to obtain and use resources germinal to productive problem-solving.

2. Increasing opportunities for choice and self-direction of older family members.

3. Promoting self-respect and mutual regard among members of family, kin/social networks.

4. Acquainting more individuals with the stimulation and satisfaction possible in association with creative programs serving individuals 55 or over.

5. Enhancing the skills of individuals providing services to older people.

6. Promoting community-service continuity.

7. Developing or assisting in developing services to fill unmet needs as defined by existing programs and agencies.

8. Providing training opportunities for professionals working in agencies which deal with families and other social systems having members affected by the aging process.

9. Contributing to knowledge expansion and model program development.

## REFERENCES

1. ANDERSON, NANCY N. Services to older persons. *Evaluation 1,* 1973, 4–6.
2. RILEY, MATILDA W. and FONER, ANNE & ASSOCIATES. *Aging and Society. Volume One: An Inventory of Research Findings.* New York: Connecticut Printers, Inc., 1968.
3. BROTMAN, HERMAN. Who are the aged: A demographic view. *Occasional Papers in Gerontology, Vol. 1.* Ann Arbor: University of Michigan-Wayne State University Press, November, 1968.
4. HAVIGHURST, R. J., NEUGARTEN, BERNICE, and TOBIN, S. Disengagement and patterns of aging. In Neugarten, Bernice (Ed.). *Middle Age and Aging.* Chicago: University of Chicago Press, 1968.
5. ATCHLEY, ROBERT C. *The Social Forces in Later Life: An Introduction to Social Gerontology.* Belmont, Ca.: Wadsworth Publishing Co., 1972.
6. CUMMING, ELAINE and HENRY, W. E. *Growing Old: The Process of Disengagement.* New York: Basic Books, 1961.
7. FREEDMAN, A. M., KAPLAN, H. and SADOCK, B. J. *Modern Synopsis of Comprehensive Textbook of Psychiatry.* Baltimore: Williams and Wilkins, 1972.
8. SUSSMAN, MARVIN and BURCHINAL, LEE. Kin family network: Unheralded structure in current conceptualizations of family functioning. In Neugarten, Bernice (Ed.). *Middle Age and Aging, A Reader in Social Psychology.* Chicago: University of Chicago Press, 1968.
9. SPECK, ROSS and ATTNEAVE, CAROLYN. *Family Networks.* New York: Pantheon Books, 1973.
10. WHITE HOUSE CONFERENCE ON AGING, U.S. Government Printing Office, Washington, D.C., 1971.
    Report of the Special Concerns Section on:
       a) Planning
       b) Retirement Roles and Activities
       c) Roles for Old and Young
       d) The Aging and Aged Blacks
       e) The Asian American Elderly
       f) The Elderly Indian
       g) The Spanish Speaking Elderly
       h) Training
11. KASTENBAUM, R. Epilogue: Loving, dying and other gerontologic addenda. In Eisdorfer, C. and Lawton, M. P. (Eds.). *The Psychology of Adult Development and Aging.* Washington, D.C.: American Psychological Association, Inc., 1973.
12. KASTENBAUM, R. and AISENBERG, R. *The Psychology of Death.* New York: Springer Publishing Co., 1972.
13. KUBLER-ROSS, ELIZABETH. *On Death and Dying.* New York: MacMillan Co., 1969.

*In his article on family practice (page 329), Don D. Jackson mentions some hypotheses on the interaction in families of heart attack patients. He frequently expressed the opinion that the notorious inability or unwillingness of these patients to cut down on their high-risk behavior (smoking, overeating, drinking, lack of physical exercise, etc.) did not exist in a vacuum, but—especially in view of its very possible lethal consequences— was bound to influence their family interaction and be influenced by it. A study of these families would, therefore, not only have great theoretical interest, but eminently practical medical importance as well.*

*In 1974 Fred Hoebel undertook a pilot study along these lines and made it into the subject of his Ph.D. thesis. What follows here is a brief description of his work and its implications. As the reader will appreciate, they are indeed far-reaching. Hoebel's work shows not only that Jackson's clinical assumptions were correct, but that significant and perhaps even life-saving changes can be brought about in the families of heart attack patients through simple, brief interventions. But it also shows the converse, namely that quite frequently the efforts by the patient's spouse, well-intentioned and reasonable as they may appear, actually feed into the vicious cycle of the difficult heart patients' high-risk behavior.*

# CORONARY ARTERY DISEASE
# AND FAMILY INTERACTION:
# A STUDY OF RISK FACTOR MODIFICATION

*Fred C. Hoebel*

## Introduction

Numerous coronary related "risk factors" over which the individual can exercise control, such as dieting, smoking, exercising, and the competitive time-harried "Type A" behavior described by Friedman and Rosenman (1,2) are believed to be implicated in coronary artery disease (CAD). While the degree of importance attributable to each, and the relationship of these various factors to one another and to CAD remains speculative,

Original contribution.

it is generally agreed that once CAD has been diagnosed, the patient must modify his life style—i.e., his high risk behaviors—if he is to prevent a worsening of his heart condition. Nonetheless, a significant number of heart patients—including those with a history of the most severe symptoms—fail to make such changes in spite of the obvious serious personal consequences involved. How to deal effectively with such difficult to manage heart patients is a serious problem confronting physicians—and more recently behavioral scientists.

Common to all past reported efforts to deal with this problem has been the assumption that the problem of heart disease lies within the heart patient, with the primary focus being on the dynamics of the patient's personality structure and this structure's relationship to the patterns of bodily dysfunction being observed. There has been little more than a tentative recognition of the possibility of approaching CAD—or for that matter, other disease entities conventionally seen as "organic" in nature—from a family or social interaction perspective, in spite of the obvious impact which the family has on the individual throughout his lifetime. In the exploratory work reported below, a fundamental shift in focus from the individual heart patient as the unit of study and treatment to the interaction *between* the heart patient and his wife was examined.

The study was based on the guiding assumption that difficult-to-manage heart patients—i.e., those who failed to modify their at-risk behavior patterns following a life threatening cardiac event—and their families, in their attempts to deal with the threat of heart disease, would interact with one another in a manner which would maintain the patients' high risk behavior pattern.* Conversely, "non-difficult" patients—i.e., those who had modified their at-risk behaviors—and their wives would interact with one another in a manner appropriate to a modification of the patients' coronary-prone behavior. It was hypothesized that the wife's attempts to modify her husband's high risk behaviors following a cardiac event was a key factor contributing to the maintenance of such behaviors, and that if her behavior could be appropriately altered, a modification of the heart patient's behavior would follow suit.

---

* In therapeutic work involving a wide range of human problems seen by the Brief Therapy Center, it has been observed that quite often the attempted solutions employed by the "identified patient" and/or others in his social system act to maintain or exacerbate the original difficulty. In effect, the attempted solution becomes the problem. Further elaboration of this theoretical position can be found in Watzlawick, P. et al, pp. 31–39 (7).

## Method

The heart patients included in the project were obtained from physicians in the Palo Alto area. They were asked to refer families in which they had found the heart patient to be among their *most difficult*-to-manage patients due to his lack of cooperation with the prescribed medical regime, lack of satisfactory progress in changing his physical conditions, and/or repeated complaints, concerns, etc. from the patient's spouse as to the nature of the patient's high risk behavior in the home. Other than these somewhat general guidelines, the criteria for evaluating a patient as "difficult" was left up to the discretion of the referring physician. This approach was followed in order to better meet the physician's clinical needs, but also to gain further insight into the types of patients and problems which the physicians found to be difficult to deal with, as well as an impression of how they chose to deal with such patients.

To be eligible for the project, heart patients also had to meet the following criteria: (a) the patient had to have been clinically diagnosed as having CAD; (b) the patient had to have been explicitly warned by the referring physician to modify his high risk behaviors; (c) the patient had to be living with his spouse; and (d) the patient's most recent hospital discharge for matters related to CAD must have occurred at least one month previous to the time of the family's first contact with the project. This time period was imposed to allow for "re-normalization" of the family's interactive pattern.

Once the name of a family was obtained, the patient's spouse (in all cases, the wife) was contacted and informed of the nature of our service —i.e., that we could provide brief (five hour maximum) counseling designed to help her to modify her husband's coronary-prone behavior, and that contract with her husband would be minimal, if at all.

The clinical process followed with each wife can be conceived of in three main phases: During the first phase the *specific* (behavioral) nature of the heart patient's high risk behaviors *of concern to his wife,* and how she was attempting to modify or deal with these was established. In addition, each wife was asked to indicate a *minimal behavioral* change which, if it were to occur, would indicate that a significant first step had been taken in dealing with her husband's behavior. Contact with the heart patients (husbands) also occurred at this point in our work, if this was agreeable to both husband and wife and would not interfere with realizing the goals of treatment. Such contact was used for information-gathering purposes—e.g., to verify the wives' reports.

During the second phase, the focus was on modifying the problem-solving behaviors being used by the wives to deal with their husbands' high risk behaviors. The rationale for this treatment approach was based on the aforementioned assumption, that even the most well-intended problem-solving efforts often maintain or even exacerbate human problems. Thus, if such efforts were to stop or to be modified in a prescribed manner, a change in the high risk behaviors might also be expected to follow suit.

The final evaluation phase of the project occurred approximately one month after the last treatment contact and involved a telephone contact with both wives and referring physicians. The wives were asked to report on two main areas: (a) had they carried out the suggested changes in their own problem-solving behaviors, and if so, (b) had their husbands' high risk behaviors changed for the better, remained the same, or worsened? The referring physicians were asked to participate in evaluating behavioral changes in their patients. At the time of the referral, each physician had been asked to identify those behaviors of most concern to him and show what a minimal but significant change in the patient's behavior might look like. At the time of the one month follow-up, he too was asked if the patient had demonstrated any change in his high risk behavior(s) to the better, the worse, or not at all.

To date nine difficult-to-manage heart patients and their wives have participated in the project. In Table A below, the diagnoses and high risk behaviors reported for each patient at the time of referral to the project are summarized.

Before turning to a discussion of the results of our work with these nine families, I have included the following case summary in order to more specifically illustrate the clinical rationale and procedures employed in the project.

## CASE SUMMARY: HEART FAMILY 4

I. *Family Members:* Mr. A was 41 years old and his wife 39 years old. Both had attended two years of college and had no religious preference. He had been retired from a public service job following his by-pass surgery and had remained unemployed to date. Mrs. A had recently held a part-time clerical position, but was currently unemployed. The specific family income was not mentioned but was primarily dependent on disability pay. They had two teen-age children living at home.

II. *Medical Information*
A. Mr. A:
    1. CAD History: He underwent coronary artery by-pass surgery in early 1973.

**Table A.**—*Patient Diagnoses and High Risk Behaviors at the Time of Referral*

| Families | D$_x$ | Cig. Smoking | Blood Fats | High Bld. Pressure | Lack of Exercise | Obesity | Type A Behavior | Others |
|---|---|---|---|---|---|---|---|---|
| 1 | MI | X | X | X | | | X | |
| 2 | MI | X | X | | X | X | X | Excessive Drinking |
| 3 | MI | | | | X | X | X | Excessive Drinking |
| 4 | S | | X | | X | X | | Depression |
| 5 | MI | X | X | | X | X | X | |
| 6 | SA | | X | | X | X | X | |
| 7 | SA | | X | | | X | | |
| 8 | MI | | X | | X | | X | |
| 9 | MI | | | | | X | X | |

"Type A Behavior" refers here to overwork, tension and/or habitual explosive anger; "MI" to Myocardinal Infarction; "S" to By-pass surgery; and "SA" to severe angina.

2. Current CAD Symptoms: Anginal pain; arrhythmias; dizziness; fatigue; and shortness of breath.
3. Current Risk Factor Status: Mr. A did not smoke, and his cholesterol was being controlled with medications and diet. He was overweight by approximately 20–25 pounds, and was not exercising.
4. Other Health Problems: Mrs. A reported that her husband had arthritis, depression subsequent to his heart surgery, and a tendency to be hypochondriacal.
B. Mrs. A: She reported that she and the children had no significant health problems.

III. *Referral Information*
A. Referral Source: A community based cardiac rehabilitation program.
B. Referral Process: Mrs. A had stated concern with regard to her husband's behavior. The family's name was subsequently forwarded to the Family Heart Project and Mrs. A was contacted.

C. Family Understanding of the Referral: Mrs. A wanted help in coping and adjusting to her husband's illness and guidance in helping her husband to adjust "mentally" to his heart problem. Mr. A was unwilling to cooperate, but was aware and agreeable to our meeting with his wife.
D. Referral Problems: Mr. A was 25 pounds overweight. Weight was listed as the main problem by the physician. In addition, Mr. A was not exercising, was adjusting his own medications, and was "chronically depressed" since his heart surgery.

IV. *Wife's Presenting Complaint*
A. Heart-Related Problems: Mrs. A listed her husband's depression as the problem of most concern to her—e.g., "Since his surgery, he has just been sitting, waiting to die." She also listed his weight and lack of exercise as problems, but saw these related to the depression.
B. Other Problems: Mrs. A felt "anxious" and "panicky," especially with regard to being able to do the "right thing" if confronted with a cardiac emergency.

V. *Attempted Solutions and the System's Feedback Loop*
A. Wife's Behavior and Rationale: Mrs. A described herself as "optimistic" and with a tendency to encourage and point out the positive side of things to her husband in response to his "pessimism and depression." Her behavioral repertoire was based on the assumption that, if someone is down, it is best to cheer them up.
B. Husband's Behavior and Rationale: Mr. A was not interviewed, but judging from Mrs. A's description, he tended to vacillate between verbal optimism —i.e., "I should exercise, diet, etc.,"—and verbal despair—e.g., "What's the use. I am going to die anyway." He took no *action* with respect to dieting, exercising, or other activities.
C. Significant Others: The Cardiac Rehabilitation staff was operating in the same basic way and on the same assumptions as Mrs. A. Mr. A's heart surgeon, on the other hand, was "pessimistic" and "stern" with him—e.g., "Continue as you are and you are going to shorten your life even more."
D. System's Feedback Loop: The more depressed Mr. A became, the more Mrs. A and the rehabilitation program's staff would try to cheer him up and encourage him. Likewise, signs of optimism from Mr. A were met with increased encouragement from his wife. Mr. A made no positive change in his high risk behaviors in response to either of these general problem solving behaviors, but instead either stayed the same or became more depressed. In general, the more things failed, the harder they tried. The surgeon, on the other hand, with his "pessimism," was able to get Mr. A to lose weight and exercise for approximately six months, at which time their contacts became less frequent.

VI. *Goals*
A. Wife's Goals:
   1. She felt that "improving his attitude" was the most important goal.

For Mr. A to go back to work or school and/or find a hobby would, she believed, be an indication of this attitudinal change.

2. For Mr. A to lose weight or at least to take action in this area, as opposed to continued talk about his need to diet.

3. For Mr. A to exercise—e.g., to return to the cardiac exercise program.

B. Therapist's Goals: These were the same as Mrs. A's, with the main focus being on the first.

VII. *Treatment Strategy:* To get Mrs. A to stop optimistically encouraging her husband to exercise, lose weight, find interest, etc., and, rather, to become pessimistic with regard to his chances for improvement and/or compliance with his medical regime, and in general to make things harder for him.

VIII. *Major Interventions and Behavioral Reactions*

A. Session 1: Mrs. A's anxiety was most apparent in this session. In the case of a cardiac emergency, she wanted to act appropriately. She was afraid that she might overreact—e.g., to take her husband to the hospital unnecessarily. She felt sure that her husband would be critical if she "goofed." She was asked to recall for us the birth of her first child and how her husband behaved at that time. She appeared more relaxed as she recalled her husband's anxiety and overreaction to her labor pains.

B. Session 2: Mrs. A was ending her employment and looking forward "to really getting *our* (her and her husband's) diet and exercising started. With me home, I know he will be happier and he has been excited about beginning the diet." This well-meaning, but problem-maintaining, behavior was countered by the therapist with: "You've been the bread-winner now for two years. Your husband has become accustomed to keeping the house. Adjusting to your new roles is bound to take time. Therefore, we suggest that we take only one step at a time. We would recommend that you place a moratorium on changing or beginning anything new this week and instead simply enjoy being together and adjusting to your new life. Take a vacation, sleep late and eat well! If Mr. A asks about the diet or exercise, explain this to him and add that 'Next week is soon enough to begin.'" Mrs. A agreed that this made sense.

C. Session 3: Mrs. A took the suggested "vacation" and reported that Mr. A went along with it, albeit reluctantly—i.e., he repeatedly stated his interest in losing weight and exercising. In keeping with her basic position, she was eager to oblige her husband's wishes in the upcoming week. She was encouraged not to do this and appeared to understand that, to do so, would once again result in his "backing off" and becoming more depressed. We suggested—this time explicitly—that she "drag her heels" with regard to dieting, etc. and, in addition, to agree with any pessimistic statements that he might make. She agreed to carry out these suggestions.

D. Session 4: Mrs. A had carried out the assignment well. Mr. A continued to ask about the diet and exercising, but took no action himself. Mrs. A continued to have difficulty believing that no action on her part was powerful action in and of itself. She was reinforced to continue "dragging her heels" and to add pessimism of her own—e.g., "We both know that your intentions are good, but let's face facts; we both know you won't really be able to stick to a diet or exercise program. Therefore, why try?"

E. Session 5 (3 weeks later): Mrs. A had again carried out the assignment relatively well. She reported that Mr. A had begun dieting on his own and she believed that he had lost weight judging from his appearance. Her good work was reinforced and she was warned to expect normal set-backs.

IX. *Follow-up Results*
A. Wife's Report:
  1. It was ascertained that Mrs. A had continued to behave in the suggested matter vis-a-vis her husband.
  2. "When you first came to the Family Heart Project, you were concerned about your husband's attitude. Is that the same, better or worse?"
  "Better. He's taking an interest in things again." She cited as an example of this improvement the fact that he had gone on a week-long fishing trip without her. Previously, he had remained at home or went out only with her.
  3. "You were also concerned about his weight. Has his weight gone down, stayed the same or increased?"
  "Gone down. He has been dieting on his own for a month, though I'm not sure how much he's lost. He looks better."
  4. "You were also concerned about his lack of exercise. Is this the same, better or worse?"
  "Better. He now is working in the garden and riding his bicycle."
  5. "Have any new problems arisen in the family since our last contact?"
  "No. He's complaining more about being bored and wanting to get out, but I know this is what we want. Anyway, I haven't bailed him out."
  6. "Have any old problems not worked on directly cleared up since our last contact?"
  "No."
  7. "Have you sought any additional help in dealing with your husband's behavior."
  "No."
B. Referring Physician's Report: There had been no further contact with the family since the referral was made. (3)

## Results and Discussion

The results of the study supported the hypothesis that the wife's attempts to modify her husband's high risk behavior play a role in maintaining these behaviors, and that effecting a change in her problem-solving behavior will lead to a modification in the family system and, thus, in her husband's behavior. In seven of the "difficult" cases (Families 1, 2, 3, 4,

5, 6, and 7 as listed in Tables A and B), suggested changes in the wives' behaviors occurred and were accompanied by subsequent desirable changes in their husbands' coronary prone behaviors. In the remaining two "difficult" cases (Families 8 and 9 in Tables A and B), changes in the wives' behaviors were not effected and, as expected, no change occurred in the husbands' behaviors. In Table B below, both the status of the wives' problem-solving behaviors and the high risk behaviors of their husbands one month after treatment are summarized.

The extent of the changes which occurred in the husband's high risk behaviors were limited—i.e., in each case, only partial changes were re-

**Table B.**—*Status of Wives' and Heart Patients' Behaviors at the Time of the Follow-Up*

STATUS OF THE HEART PATIENTS' HIGH RISK BEHAVIORS

| Family | Status Wives' Behaviors | Cig. Smoking | Blood Fats | High Bld. Pressure | Lack of Exercise | Obesity | Type A Behavior | Others |
|---|---|---|---|---|---|---|---|---|
| 1 | PC | S | UK | UK | | | B | |
| 2 | PC | S | UK | | S | S | B | B |
| 3 | C | | | | B | W (+5 lb) | B | B |
| 4 | C | | UK | | B | B | | B |
| 5 | PC | B | UK | | S | S | B | |
| 6 | PC | | UK | | S | B (−6 lb) | S | |
| 7 | C | | UK | | | B (−9 lb) | | |
| 8 | NC | S | | | S | | S | |
| 9 | NC | | | | | S | S | |

The abbreviations used above refer to: Desirable Change (C); Partial Change (PC); No Change (NC); Unknown (UK); Better or Improvement (B); Same (S); Worse (W).

ported within one or two such behaviors, among the usual three or four requiring modification. The implications of these changes are nonetheless considered significant for the following reasons: They occurred as a consequence of very limited treatment exposure, without the cooperation or the presence of the heart patients in treatment, and in families which had previously experienced little or no success in modifying these behaviors. Furthermore, in each of these cases, the desirable change(s) which occurred, did so in the high risk behavior described by the wife as of *most concern* to her and within the suggested context that such change, if it were to occur, would represent only a "significant first step" in the elimination of the problem—*not* an end product. To the extent that this suggested definition of change was accepted, modifications in the husband's behavior—albeit minor—could be taken by the wife as an indication that her problem-solving behaviors were meeting with success—thus, setting the stage for the continued use of her new behavior and a beneficial shift in the family system.

The degree of significance which can be attributed to these findings must also be weighted against such factors as limited sample size and the brief amount of time allowed between the end of treatment and the follow-up evaluation. They are, nonetheless, sufficiently substantial to suggest that continued research of the post-cardiac adjustment of heart families from an interactional perspective could prove useful.

### Conclusions

Due to the predominantly individual focus and implied linear cause-effect model subscribed to in most cardiac prevention and rehabilitation programs, attempts to modify high risk behaviors have consistently proven unsatisfactory when the heart patient was unwilling to cooperate—for whatever reason—with treatment. The social interaction model used in this study, with its focus on problem-maintaining behaviors and feedback loops, proved to be a useful conceptual tool for dealing with this specific clinical difficulty. Most significant in this regard was the finding that the clinician need not be bound to the direct treatment of the individual patient for modification of high risk behaviors to occur: One-to-one treatment of the patient's wife, in which prescribed changes in her behavior vis-a-vis her husband were initiated, was sufficient for bringing about a change in the heart patient's behavior. The therapist, in dealing with such cases, has the option, therefore, to work with the family members most likely to be accessible to change—thus, improving the chances for an efficient and successful outcome to treatment.

The findings of the present study suggest other clinical advantages to be gained by the application of the interactional perspective to the problem of risk factor modification in difficult patients as well: 1) Because this therapeutic approach does not focus on the modification of specific high risk behaviors per se, but rather on those family behaviors which are believed to be maintaining the high risk behavior, the elimination of these behaviors can lead to modification in more than one high risk behavior. This is particularly advantageous in working with heart patients who are at-risk in a number of areas, and not likely to tolerate multiple therapies. 2) Modification of such behaviors can also occur rapidly, especially, but not exclusively, in those cases in which the wife is motivated to change her husband's behavior. 3) With the focus on how the behaviors in a particular family act to maintain the "problem behavior," the therapist is in a better position to establish ongoing, implicit social reinforcement of the desirable behaviors—i.e., a negative feedback loop between husband and wife. It is the belief of this author that this crucial factor is often lacking in therapy which, while successful in changing behavior in the controlled milieu of the therapist's office, fails to sustain such change when the patient is returned to an unchanged family system.

The role of social interaction and its potential for structuring and maintaining high risk behaviors need not be confined to the family system, as was the case in this study, but might extend to other social systems as well. The doctor-patient relationship would appear to be especially important in this regard, due to the significance which is attributed to it by both patient and doctor alike when a life-threatening disease such as CAD has been diagnosed. Especially in those cases in which the patient has proved difficult to manage and in which the medical personnel charged with the patient's care have become concerned and/or attempted numerous unsuccessful approaches in dealing with him, an evaluation of the interaction between doctor and patient would appear to be in order. Well-meaning, but nevertheless, problem-maintaining behaviors on the part of the physicians were observed although not systematically investigated in the course of conducting the study.

It is likely, too, that the effects of social interaction on CAD are not confined to the post-cardiac phase of the illness, or to those behaviors which lie under the direct voluntary control of the patient—i.e., high risk behaviors—as was the case in this study. The bulk of CAD research has focused on factors which are believed to stress the cardiovascular system, thus predisposing the individual to the development of CAD. It is not inconceivable, however, to imagine social interactional patterns operating in such a manner. Friedman and Rosenman, for example, hypothesize that "Type A Behavior Pattern" produces such a stress on the individual, but such behavior might well be found to represent a "Type A" *interaction*—as opposed to an inherent personality characteristic. The "double-bind" interactional pattern (8) and other, as yet, unidentified no-win interactional situations also likely influence bodily functioning and could be found to correlate with the development of CAD.

## REFERENCES

1. FRIEDMAN, M. and ROSENMAN, R. H. Overt behavior patterns in coronary heart disease. *Journal of American Medical Association,* 1960, 173, 1320–1325.
2. FRIEDMAN, M. and ROSENMAN, R. H. *Type A Behavior and Your Heart.* New York: Alfred A. Knopf, 1974.
3. HOEBEL, F. C. *Coronary Artery Disease and Family Interaction: A Study of Risk Factor Modification.* A doctoral dissertation submitted to the California School of Professional Psychology, San Francisco, July 1975.
4. HONEYMAN, M. S., EISENBERG, H., GLUECK, B. C., RAPPAPORT, H. and REZNIKOFF, M. Psychological impact of heart disease in the family of the patient. *Psychosomatic Medicine,* 1968, 9, 34–37.
5. MCALISTER, A., FARQUHAR, J., THORESEN, C. and MACCOBY, N. Behavioral science applied to cardiovascular health: A survey of progress in the modification of risk-taking habits in adult populations. Unpublished manuscript.
6. MEISSNER, W. W. Family dynamics and psychosomatic processes. *Family Process,* 1966, 5, 142–161.
7. WATZLAWICK, P., WEAKLAND, J. H. and FISCH, R. *Change: Principles of Problem Formation and Problem Resolution.* New York: W. W. Norton, 1974.
8. WEAKLAND, J. H. The double-bind theory by self-reflexive hindsight. Reprinted on pp. 241–248 of this volume.

*The preceding papers may give the impression that since the publication of Jackson's article on family practice a good deal of work on the impact of somatic illness on family interaction has been performed at MRI and, by implication, elsewhere. However, as the reader undoubtedly knows, the idea that family therapy is not merely a treatment for psychi-*

*atric disorders, but holds great promise for practically all the other fields of medicine, has remained largely just that—an idea. Even the papers included in this chapter deal with first steps only, with pilot studies and with tentative formulations. The study of the somatic aspects of family pathology are truly a neglected edge, and this is precisely the title of the concluding paper of this chapter.*

*It was written by John H. Weakland for presentation at the Nathan W. Ackerman Memorial Conference in Cumaná (Venezuela) in February 1974, and it lays some foundations for a family-oriented conception of physical illness.*

# "FAMILY SOMATICS"—A NEGLECTED EDGE

## John H. Weakland

If I appear to sound a negative note in my title with "A Neglected Edge," it is because I take our conference theme, "The Growing Edge," seriously. The positive aim of growth can at times be served by negative— or at least critical—means. To cite an example especially relevant here, constructive criticism of individual treatment was a significant factor in Nate Ackerman's laying of foundations for family therapy. So I will make some critical comments in this paper about what we are not doing in one particular area, with the positive aim of stimulating useful thought and action.

Our field of interest, as stated on our journal's masthead, is "family study, research and treatment." There are ample grounds in our work, I believe, for an even wider definition: that we are concerned with applying an interactional systems viewpoint, focused mainly but not exclusively on family systems, to the study and better handling of human problems. Either statement, however, leaves undefined exactly what sort of problems are to be examined and treated. This seems all to the good, especially since ours is still a new field. It avoids premature closure, and the accompanying danger of possibly excluding potentially relevant problem areas from our purview—at least by formal definition.

Nevertheless, such exclusion could still take place, in practice and in effect, simply by concentration of our interest and effort on certain areas and neglecting other possibilities. This paper will suggest that this has indeed been the case concerning the potential relevance of family interaction for illness generally—that is, including even clearly organic pathology—and will suggest possible steps toward rectifying this apparent neglect. This area of inquiry I have termed "family somatics," by an obvious analogy to "psychosomatics."

## Background

I am, of course, not maintaining that there is *no* current interest in disease from a family interaction viewpoint. Neglect, and even exclusion, are relative terms; in this instance, relative in two respects. First, disease appears to be receiving less attention from workers in the family field than it did formerly, although meanwhile our field has grown considerably. Second, this approach to problems of disease appears to receive scant attention overall, in comparison to the time, money, and effort expended on genetic, physiological and biochemical research.

When family interaction studies and family therapy were just getting started—only fifteen to twenty years ago—all of our work involved moving, somewhat tentatively, into new territory. Even if the problems involved were old; perhaps *especially* when they were old and therefore "known"—applying a new viewpoint made it a new ball game, and a dubious one to many observers holding established views. Nate Ackerman's interest in the family originally appeared, in the New York analytic context, a wild idea. The case was similar for the early work on schizophrenia and the family, which constituted a point of entry into wider family concerns for many—including Wynne, Bowen, and Lidz, as well as my Palo Alto colleagues and myself. When this work began, schizophrenia certainly was not generally seen, either by laymen or professionals, as a problem of interaction, especially current interaction. Rather, it was viewed by some in a very "mentalistic" way, and by more (at least among professionals) in a physiological framework, though with varying emphases on genetics, neurology, and biochemistry. This latter kind of opinion, indeed, is still very strong. Nevertheless, such uphill work based on the family interaction viewpoint produced significant and lasting contributions to the understanding and treatment of schizophrenia—that is, in an area where this viewpoint had widely been considered to be irrelevant to the nature of the disease.

Interest then developed at MRI (which I use for exemplification because of familiarity) in looking at some other more or less clearly "physical" problems—from asthma and ulcerative colitis at the more evidently psychosomatic end of the scale to coronary disease at the other. But although some suggestive ideas and observations developed, none of this work ever was pursued beyond a stage of preliminary inquiry—in part because of the untimely death of Don Jackson, in part because of changes in research funding, and in part because greater involvement in treatment as such.

If a broader view is taken, the situation appears much the same. The content of *Family Process* probably offers the best single indicator of work in our field. The first five volumes included just two articles clearly concerned with the family and physical illness. Bursten's (1) article on "Family Dynamics, the Sick Role, and Medical Hospitalization," though interesting, is largely limited to an interest in family exacerbation or emphasis of existing disease. Meissner's (9) article on "Family Dynamics and Psychosomatic Processes" is an important survey of psychosomatic ideas about a wide range of diseases—including duodenal ulcer, ulcerative colitis, hypertension, hyperthyroidism, arthritis, tonsillitis, tuberculosis, diabetes, cancer and leukemia—together with pertinent suggestions about the advantages of a family rather than individual viewpoint in considering the "psychological" factors in disease: "The awareness has grown in recent years that human disease, in addition to a pathology, also has an ecology. The understanding of disease, then, must comprehend the pertinent aspects of that ecology if it is to be at all meaningful. The patient's emotional involvement in the family system constitutes a major aspect of that ecology which we can no longer afford to ignore." (9, p. 157). Yet this paper was only a beginning, as Meissner himself recognized—"a tentative formulation which might serve as a heuristic basis for further much needed study". And it has not been followed up as he hoped. In the next five volumes of *Family Process,* there is no article directly concerned with this area. At most, Spark and Brody's (12) "The Aged Are Family Members" has some implicit relevance for the problem of senility. If anything, in view of the growth of publication in the journal, this evidence suggests a decline in interest in problems of physical illness. But relevant articles are so scarce at best that it is probably most accurate to conclude that this adventurous and promising, though difficult, line of work never really got off the ground.

This examination, however, has not considered the established field of psychosomatic medicine sufficiently. Perhaps relevant work has been done, but published only in its journals? This, however, also does not seem to be the case. A brief survey of *Psychosomatic Medicine* and *Psychosomatics* is enough to see how completely they are still concerned with an individualistic, or at most a mother-child orientation, to psychological factors in disease. And this point is documented extensively, though unintentionally, by Grolnick's (5) recent *Family Process* article, "A Family Perspective of Psychosomatic Factors in Illness; A Review of the Literature". Grolnick obviously searched diligently for examples of "Family Perspective", as his 129 references attest. Yet again, many of his references are concerned with essentially psychological or hypochondriacal problems, and many deal with only individuals or dyads; very few are really concerned with the relationship of interaction patterns and physical illness.

In sum, since the early days referred to above, the family interaction viewpoint has become more widespread, and family therapy in particular has become much more established, accepted and widely practiced; variations in therapeutic approach and technique also continue to develop. But it does not seem that there has been a parallel growth in the range or variety of problems that the interactional viewpoint is applied to practically, or even theoretically. Rather, treatment and even thinking and observation, are largely concentrated on problems which—at least to those associated with the field—now appear as plainly and manifestly emotional or behavioral in nature; that is, on the traditional, though now relabelled, area of "psychopathology." Nor, meanwhile, has our basic interactional viewpoint appeared to spread and influence those more immediately concerned with "psychological" factors in illness to any significant degree.

Obviously, I am here proposing that efforts might be made to alter this situation—that family therapists and researchers might themselves devote more attention to problems of physical illness, and that we might also promote wider understanding and utilization of our interactional viewpoint among those already concerned with illness—certainly those involved in psychosomatic medicine, and perhaps in medicine more generally. On the other hand, promoting such change would not be an easy task, and since so little work along these lines has actually been done, proposals for such action and change cannot be supported by much direct evidence of relevance and utility. As with all original research, if we had the sort of information hoped for, the work would not be needed; it is rather a question of proceeding on the basis of reasonable expectations.

In the circumstances, therefore, I will attempt to support my proposals by presenting: 1) A discussion of the rationale for work on illness and interaction—the general grounds for believing this approach relevant; 2) Suggestions of how such work might at least be begun; and 3) Some consideration of the probable consequences—both difficulties and benefits —of such work.

## Rationale

The fundamental basis for investigating interaction and illness actually is obvious. There exists the same general situation that historically has been the basis for important research in many other areas: We know just enough to recognize that there is much we don't know that might be significant. Most simply, there is some evidence that interaction can and does influence bodily functioning. Therefore, it *may* be significant for some or even all those sorts of functioning or dysfunctioning—this distinction being one of semantics and point of view—that we term illness. Yet it is equally plain that we know little, generally or specifically, about either the extent of this potential significance or its limits. A clue concerning major problems is at hand, but—some possible reasons will be mentioned later—we have not got on with the inquiry needed to determine whether this clue is of great, or only minor, significance for those problems.

It is not necessary here to set forth the existing evidence for the influencing of bodily function by social interaction in any detail. All that is required as a reasonable basis for inquiry—especially in the circumstances of general neglect of this area of possible relationships—is an indication that such influence is possible rather than impossible. And, in fact, evidence for the influencing of bodily function by interaction abounds. One could even fairly say that this is a matter of everyday common knowledge, among both laymen and medical men. Only it is conceived and phrased differently. Thus it is a matter of everyday experience that emotions often affect such bodily functions as blood circulation and hormonal secretion obviously and markedly. Such effects have also been studied scientifically at least since the days of Cannon (2), and continuing reports of such work appear in the psychosomatic journals currently. Considerable changes in bodily function also can be rather readily produced in hypnosis. The question of more lasting and profound bodily changes, such as are involved in disease, is a more difficult one, but again both lay and professional observers—from Dunbar (4) to Selye (11)—have been seriously concerned with the significance of experience for the gravest diseases. Perhaps the worldwide folk belief connecting disease and evil personal influence should be considered more seriously. At least, Cannon (3) believed death by witchcraft to be a real and scientifically explainable possibility. All in all, it seems that Herman's (7) statement is quite a moderate and reasonable one: "That emotional phenomena accompany or lead to physical phenomena is undisputed. It is also well known that factors in the psychological pattern or events in the life of the patient have great influence on the progress or amelioration of the disease state."

Most of the above points simultaneously to the significance of this area and—but only implicitly—to the fundamental problem involved. That is, these views of bodily influence and changes largely focus on the individual, in relation to "emotions," on the hypnotic "state," or general "stress"; they fail to note that emotions, hypnosis (6), and stress all depend greatly on communicative interaction, which can be observed and studied. This, as mentioned, may be only a difference of conception and phrasing—but our own work with families is based on just such a difference, and has shown how important this can be for theory, research, and practice.

Thus there is, usually under other names, considerable and varied evidence that bodily function can be and is influenced by communicative interaction. At the same time, much is unknown about what patterns may be significant for long-term or continuing effects on such functioning, let alone the matter of possible structural changes, and probably still less for particular diseases. Again, this means only that a field of great possible importance is lying open and fallow. Perhaps such relationships do not exist, or cannot be discerned with our present scientific resources. But perhaps they can, and we only know by trying, by checking it out. At this point, there may not be a total absence of such inquiry, but certainly such inquiry is minimal in comparison to individual-centered psychosomatic studies, let alone the enormous expenditures of time and money routinely poured into biochemical and physiological studies of disease.

We may also consider several different ways in which interaction might be relevant to illness somewhat more specifically.

If, proceeding chronologically or developmentally, we begin with the onset or etiology of illness, there are at least three general ways in which interactional situations or patterns might be significant. First, a certain sort of interaction, presumably continuing over some length of time, might itself constitute the sufficient conditions for the beginning of a certain disease. "Itself" in this instance would not mean in isolation, but in connection with otherwise healthy persons and generally obtaining environmental circumstances. Probably, if any such instance exists, the sort of interaction involved would have to be very special, though this is not equivalent to obvious or blatant. It is not easy even to imagine a possible example, but this logical possibility should not be ignored. Second, a certain sort of interaction might constitute a necessary but not sufficient condition for the onset of a certain disease. That is, while the development of a disease might definitely require the presence of some virus or other noxious agent, it could concurrently require some particular sort of interactive situation for the agent to be effective. Therefore, attention should be paid to both aspects; even if an agent is essential, it should not be seen as *the* cause of its associated disease. In this connection, one might think of those many diseases whose active agents are ubiquitous or at least occur widely, but which only certain individuals actually develop. Such selectivity at present often does not seem well accounted for by strictly medical factors such as general health; interaction might be significant for susceptibility. It is even conceivable, and worth considering, that even if these is little or no correlation between specific interaction patterns and specific diseases, there may be some broader correlation—that is, that some form or forms of interaction may increase susceptibility to illness generally, with the particular disease contracted being dependent on other factors. Finally, there might be diseases for which certain sorts of interaction, while not necessary, would contribute as sensitizing or predisposing influences.

Once an illness exists, interaction may be relevant to its course and outcome, for better or worse. Such an influence might be direct—that is, one form of interaction might interfere with the body's functions of resistance and healing, while another might facilitate these, as hypnotic suggestion appears to do in certain cases. Less directly, yet perhaps equally significantly, interactive factors might function to help or hamper the useful application of medical treatment for a given problem. To take a relatively simple example, the success of current therapies for cancer depends greatly on whether the disease is recognized and treated early or not. As Shands (10) and others have noted, failure of recognition in many cases appears to involve active avoidance or denial, not just the overlooking of minor signs; certainly interaction might be important in this.

In another respect, however, the interactional viewpoint might lead towards some useful questioning of this usual distinction between etiology and course of disease, with the related major emphasis on etiology that is especially common in research and public health work. Our own work in family research and therapy—again the early work on schizophrenia is a clear example, followed by many others—has largely involved such a shift of viewpoint and emphasis concerning behavioral problems. From seeking for some original etiology and linear causation of problems, we have moved toward much greater concern with circular causality involving feedback loops, and the corresponding importance of reinforcements that keep a problem going, or worsening. Evidence collected from this perspective suggests that how a problem got started—which may involve rather ordinary or minor matters—is often less important than what causes the problem to persist and develop. It is quite possible that such an orientation might also be very relevant for a new look at physical illness; again, we simply cannot tell *a priori*.

## Approaching Such Research

While it is not possible to lay out a specific research program in advance because so little is yet known about this area, this level of ignorance itself suggests certain broad guidelines for productive study. That is, such study should initially be correspondingly exploratory and flexible, guided by general principles rather than rigid prescriptions. Since what is specifically significant about interaction in relation to illness is not known, but the very subject of inquiry, any attempt to predetermine just what must be viewed and the means of viewing is apt to be not only useless but self-defeating. In such an enterprise, fixed targets and instruments can only focus attention on things that are prominent, or that one assumes *must* be important—but it is more likely that if these matters were significant, important discoveries would have been made from them already. Meanwhile, wide-ranging but careful scanning of the terrain is obstructed.

This, again, is the sort of approach taken in our early studies of schizophrenics and their families. It led to discerning the double-bind interaction pattern which, though actually fairly simple and plain, previously went undetected amid many inquiries seeking factors dramatic or drastic enough to account for such a dread illness, and much psychological testing bound up by categories precise but not pertinent. What people know must be important is not always what really matters.

In the present case, a similar approach might mean beginning with some form of natural history study, utilizing direct observation of interaction related to illness, rather than collection of masses of discrete data by questionnaires, for instance. This might be begun by interviewing and observing at length a small sample of families with a member having a particular sort of illness, and simply looking for any discernable patterns of interaction they have in common—as a first step.

A few tentative suggestions may be offered on the general orientation of such family interviews, although too much specificity still appears a greater danger than looseness. Beyond the ordinary gathering of family demographic data, interviews might initially be focused on three matters. First, the family's conception of the disease, its nature and its history—which might include inquiry about any similar previous disease in the same or preceding generations. Second, in what concrete ways the disease is presently a problem, for the patient and for other family members, in daily life. Third, how are the patient and other family members attempting to handle these problems? Where feasible, this might include investigation of their responses to any suggestions that could be made as to possibly more useful ways of dealing with the disease, since reactions to potential change are often especially illuminating about family behavior. Hopefully, examination of the data gathered in this way might lead to the perception of regularities in how particular diseases are conceptualized— their perceived nature, causes, who or what is to blame—and handling— by avoidance, frantic activity, reassurance or whatever, which might provide leads for further inquiry.

It is plain that the simple approach suggested above starts from existing identified cases of illness. Therefore, it may not relate most directly to the question of interactional causes of the illness, and it also involves the perennial worry that observed interaction may be mainly a result of the illness. Two factors seem to outweigh these potential difficulties, however. First, as suggested earlier, our professional experience, together with the whole theory of cybernetics and systems of interaction, increasingly suggests that the old distinction, cause vs. course of problems, may not be so valid or significant as formerly believed; it may even be a misleading focus for thought and observation. Second, this appears to be the only feasible way to arrange *direct* study of interaction related to illness at the start, and this is the most likely source of fresh observations and ideas. Later, perhaps, leads gained in this way might be used to search for cases of potential illness to be followed over time.

Obviously, this is only one possible line of exploration among various others, and only a first step along that line. Another possible way of beginning inquiries is to follow Freud's suggestion for help in understanding human situations: "Go to the poets". That is, the study of literary accounts of illness in a family context might offer leads and insights, much as such an approach has been useful at times in both psychiatric and anthropological studies of problematic behavior. But the particular method is not the main point; what matters is to take seriously the possible significance of interaction for illness, and to initiate exploratory inquiry based firmly on this *viewpoint*.

## Potential Benefits—And Some Caveats

Most of the direct potential benefits of the sort of work proposed here are rather obvious, or plainly implied in the earlier discussion of its rationale. Such work might lead to significant alterations and advances in our understanding of particular diseases that are important because of their spread or severity. In turn, better understanding could lead to improvements in prevention and treatment, individually and more widely. It is worth noting, however, that the relationship between greater understanding and practical importance is apt to be complex and unpredictable For instance, the discovery of some interaction pattern that merely predisposes persons to a certain disease could be more readily applicable, and therefore practically important, than some more sweeping finding. The whole question of the economics of illness and its control, in the broadest sense, is involved here in much the same way as in public health generally. If various factors are seen to be involved in the onset and course of any disease, the problems of its costs and its control might correspondingly be attacked in various ways, focusing on one another, or several of the factors. There is no intrinsically best way; the approach of choice will depend on the existing knowledge, evaluations of the importance of the problem, and the given social context, which includes both available material resources and, not least, preferred modes of thinking and action about disease generally.

Such prospects are large, but also uncertain. It is certain that such inquiries and their application would require much difficult work. This would be difficult enough intrinsically, given its complexities and exploratory nature. It would be more difficult because it would be an attempt, both conceptually and practically, to make headway against the mainstream of current medicine—at the same time that some medical cooperation would be needed to carry it out.

If any such work were done, however, it would also contribute toward developing and promoting a broader and potentially more useful general conception of illness—essentially a behavioral or even ecological view of disease. In much the same way that we now increasingly see "mental illness" not as separate disorder but as ordered through unfortunate behavior, explainable in terms of interaction, we might contribute toward a view of disease that would diminish the separation of "pathology" from "health". Rather, both might be seen, and seen better, as sorts of functioning to be understood in terms of interaction—of the human organism with other humans, as well as with other sorts of organisms and with the inorganic environment.

To mention this possibility might appear to be suggesting a simple but grandiose inversion of the old imposition of the medical model on "mental illness", about which we have justifiably complained, but this is not the case. For one thing, the interactional viewpoint, based on cybernetics and systems theory, is inherently more general and comprehensive than the traditional medical model of illness and treatment. For another, I am not suggesting a takeover but an expansion or supplementing of medical views—and in a general direction some medical thinking is already struggling toward.

Still, such a broad interactional conception of illness would hardly be immediately and widely welcomed by the medical world. Yet it might gradually find some welcome and use. For one example, psychosomatic medicine already involves a related framework, but one that to a considerable extent is implicit, narrow, and piecemeal. A broader and more explicit interactional viewpoint could be useful there. For another, there is the newly-christened field of family medicine. Kellner (8) and other perceptive physicians have in recent years observed and reported clusters and associations of illnesses occurring in families, and students are increasingly being trained in family medicine as a specialty. Yet so far, there appears to be no general framework in use to help these physicians go beyond simple noting of temporal association and sequence in interrelating such illnesses, or to help the students view in a unitary way the families whose members they are to treat. Our viewpoint might be useful here also, where a related need is unusually manifest.

Finally, we may conclude by considering the pursuit of the interactional viewpoint, beyond those areas where it is already established, in the widest perspective. That is, keeping in mind that throughout this paper we are not concerned with abstract truth, but with the utility of viewpoints—ways of observing and conceiving our experiential world, and their consequences—one may examine the prospects, positive and negative, that are inherent in the nature of the interactional viewpoint, as compared to other viewpoints.

Throughout history, both laymen and a variety of professionals have been concerned with examining and explaining human events, especially any kinds of events seen as difficult or problematic. Until recently, most such explanation has followed one of two general lines of thought. Human events and problems have often been seen as the outcome or consequence of powerful impersonal forces, external to the human realm. Such forces may be physical, social in a broad sense, or supernatural—such as climate or geography, economics or class structure, fate or God's will. To this list, in a modern and scientific age, one may add small yet powerful microbes and viruses. Or, human events and behavior have been explained as a consequence of intrinsic human factors—physical, mental or moral attributes seen as characteristic of individual persons or groups and determining their behavior. These two broad viewpoints appear to be very different, even polar. Yet like many polar opposites they have much in common at a more general level. Both lead toward considering the nature of any given situation or problem as evident, usually achieved either by the sharp division of problems into separate and discrete kinds, or lumping them into a global category, and focusing inquiry rather on their "why" or "who." Both lead toward an orientation to ultimates—primal causes or final solutions, or both. Both tend to place the locus of responsibility for problems and their handling beyond one's own human sphere, whether by attribution to nonhuman forces, or by labelling some other party as inherently bad or mad, and as causing the problem. Both easily lead either to resigned acceptance, or a call for the power of some higher authority, whether this be God, a leader, or science, to resolve matters.

The interactional viewpoint appears as rather new, as yet rather limited, and as very different from all this. It looks at human events and problems —concretely various yet generally similar—primarily in terms of behavior occurring between persons in some system of social relationships. It assumes that the nature of difficulties often is *not* self-evident, and focuses inquiry on the "what" and "how" of the situation in question. Such inquiry is less concerned with ultimate origins or ends than with the present situation, how this is being maintained and how it might be altered for the better, though no solution will ever be final or perfect. Viewing of problems in relation to interaction also puts them on a human scale, and in terms of *joint* responsibility: "All in it together" rather than an "all or none" or "either you or me" responsibility of specific parties. This implies further that better problem handling is a joint enterprise, and potentially mutually beneficial, not mainly a matter of winners or losers.

It seems plain that it is this general interactional viewpoint that provides the main common bond among us, beyond our specific differences of idea and practice, and that has led us to a more human, behavioral, and useful understanding of "mental illness". This viewpoint, however, is general; it is not inherently restricted to mental or emotional problems. It might quite similarly, and perhaps as usefully, be applied to other problems, and specifically to illness. Yet, even if inquiry based on a similar viewpoint began to discern significant relationships between interaction and illness—in fact, perhaps especially then—a serious difficulty probably would arise. "We're all in it together" is a more humane and generally more useful view of problems than "We're right and he's wrong." Yet this is not the usual view, blame is more popular than sharing of responsibility, and as we know, people are seldom eager for change in their basic views.

This difficulty, of course, is not unfamiliar. We face it constantly in promoting the interactional viewpoint in our own work with families. But there we have some experience and methods of dealing with it; for physical illness, the situation would be new, and quite possibly more severe. Any positive findings about interaction and disease might well, at least initially, be seen more as accusations that people are making their loved ones sick

than as a realistic and helpful recognition of how, without benefit of ceremony even, we are in life together, for better or worse, in sickness and
in health, until death do us part—and sometimes even beyond.

In the wider application of our interactional viewpoint, then, there is a
prospect of progress, but no certainty except of hard work and conflict.
Perhaps, after all, we should just mind our own business and not get involved?

## REFERENCES

1. BURSTEN, B. "Family Dynamics, The Sick Role, and Medical Hospital
   Admissions," *Family Process 4,* 206–216 (1965).
2. CANNON, W. B. *Bodily Changes in Pain, Hunger, Fear and Rage.* 2nd
   edition, New York, Appleton, 1920.
3. CANNON, W. B. "Voodoo Death," *American Anthropologist 44:*169–81,
   1942.
4. DUNBAR, FLANDERS. *Emotions and Bodily Changes.* New York, Colum-
   bia University Press, 1954.
5. GROLNICK, L. "A Family Perspective of Psychosomatic Factors in Illness:
   A Review of the Literature," *Family Process 11,* 457–486 (1972).
6. HALEY, J. "An Interactional Explanation of Hypnosis," *American Journal
   of Clinical Hypnosis 1,* No. 2, 41–57 (1958).
7. HERMAN, M. "A Critique of Psychosomatics." Read at the Fifth Annual
   Institute in Psychiatry and Neurology, Veterans Administration Hospital, Lyons, New Jersey, April 13, 1955.
8. KELLNER, R. *Family Ill Health—An Investigation in General Practice.*
   New York, Thomas, 1963.
9. MEISSNER, W. W. "Family Dynamics and Psychosomatic Processes," *Family Process 5,* 142–161 (1966).
10. SHANDS, H. C. *Semiotic Approaches to Psychiatry.* The Hague, Mouton,
    1970.
11. SELYE, H. *The Stress of Life.* New York, McGraw-Hill, 1956.
12. SPARK, G. M. and BRODY, E. M. "The Aged are Family Members," *Fam-
    ily Process 9,* 195–210 (1970).

# Epilogue

*It seems appropriate to end this volume, as a report on work still in progress, with an article that, while based on a now familiar interactional viewpoint, illustrates its utilization in a quite new and different area of study.*

*This brief piece by John Weakland is one product of a long-term research on the content of modern Chinese films. Like other reports in this book, it is concerned with interaction and behavior, family systems, and the interrelation of permanence and change. But it also indicates how the interactional viewpoint can be applied to fictional images of families as well as to actual observation of families, and to the relationship between family systems and their environing sociocultural systems.*

*The scope and power of an interactional view of behavior, we may conclude, are still just beginning to be explored and applied.*

## CONFLICTS BETWEEN LOVE AND FAMILY

## RELATIONSHIPS IN CHINESE FILMS

### John H. Weakland

The People's Republic of China's admission to the U.N. and President Nixon's visit to China have created a sudden interest in this country for

Though this paper is based on research on Chinese mass communications supported by a contract between the Group Psychology Branch of the U.S. Office of Naval Research and the Mental Research Institute, Palo Alto, California, the views expressed are solely those of the author.

Originally published in the *Journal of Popular Film* 1:290–8 (1972). Reprinted with permission.

the heretofore little known popular culture of the Chinese people. Chinese ping-pong players have been written up in the sports pages of most of our newspapers and a popular Chinese revolutionary ballet has been presented on nationwide American television. So far, however, little serious attention has been given to one of China's most popular entertainment forms, the movies.

This paper examines a group of popular Chinese films from the People's Republic of China, from Taiwan, and from Hong Kong, in which the film content is observed and considered as reflecting and projecting significant socio-cultural patterns. That is, these films manifestly give depictions of Chinese social behavior and interaction. Of course, film depictions are not "real" everyday behavior, but only constructed images. Yet, these images are easy to examine compared to real behavior in large societies, and they have their own value toward recognizing and understanding real patterns of thought and action. Mao Tse-Tung at least thinks so: "The creative forms of art and literature supersede nature in that they are more systematic, more concise, more typical, and therefore more universal" (from *Problems of Art and Literature*).

Any film, closely observed, is an almost inexhaustible mine of images of behavior, and relationships among them. Drastic selective attention is therefore necessary, and this account accordingly discusses only its films' depiction of the nature, source and resolution of conflicts between love and family relationships. This single chosen theme, however, appears to be a fundamental one. It is very prominent in these films, as it has also been in Chinese literature traditionally, and it is closely related to many other facets of Chinese social life.

The sample of films examined is also restricted, but these films appear fairly representative of their source and period generally. Regardless of differences in detailed content or style among individual films, the films from each particular source essentially present a reiterated picture of the basic theme with only minor variations. The films are, therefore, discussed here essentially as three groups, except that the Chinese Communist films are subdivided into those depicting "Old China" before the Communist revolution, and "New China" thereafter. A major comparison is made between the Chinese Communist films and those from Taiwan, as presenting two contrasting official or semi-official images of social relationships. The Hong Kong films, made commercially with a minimum of political influence, offer some useful contrast to both other groups.

Considering the extent of the socio-political differences among them, it is striking how much the films from each of these three sources focus on conflicts between parents and children in the traditional Chinese family system, and how similarly their nature is depicted (Table I). Of the 21 Chinese Communist films studied (dating from 1949 to 1962), 16 were concerned at least partly with "Old China" and only 5 entirely with "New China." Among these 16, 8 put major emphasis on conflict between parents and children, and one on similar conflict between a young widow and her mother-in-law. Three of the 5 Taiwan films (all from the 1960's) emphasized conflict between parents and children, and of the 12 non-Communist Hong Kong films studied, 7 emphasized this theme.

In all three groups of films, with the exception of a single Hong Kong film, these conflicts consistently centered around parental opposition to the romantic sexual attachments of young people in their late teens or early twenties or, from a different viewpoint, personal love versus socially arranged marriages or betrothals. In some instances other bases of conflict such as money, education, career or political views were shown, but only in a secondary way. It is in their images of the genesis of these conflicts, and of their resolution, that the basic differences among the three groups of films are evident.

Among the Chinese Communist films, the "Old China" films present the Communist picture of the nature of the conflicts in an evil society, while the "New China" ones depict their solution of these conflicts in the ideal new society. In the "Old China" films, there is an intensity about the nature of the recurrent conflict between youthful romance and parentally arranged matches which often leads to suicide attempts or flight from home. The young lovers are sympathetically portrayed as right and good, while the "feudalistic" parents are wrong and bad. They cause the conflicts by insisting on arranged matches, often over their children's protests, in order to increase family wealth, position and power.

In these "Old China" films, the young heroes or heroines may struggle hard, but they are always defeated, except in a few cases of obvious fantasy solutions, such as the reunion of the lovers after death as a pair of butterflies in the film *Liang Shan-po and Chu Ying-tai*. The clear implication is that there is no resolution possible within the old system; within it the parents will not change and the children cannot.

The resolution envisioned outside that system is depicted in the "New China" films. In these films we do indeed see young people get together and marry those whom they wish to, but only under certain significant conditions. First, the love involvements never appear intense to begin with—the great romances of the old days are absent. Second, although this aspect is so de-emphasized that it is easy to overlook, the marriages in large part are still arranged. Only the arranging, which is depicted largely as a matter of facilitating the young people's getting together, is now done by government officials or Party leaders. They take over much of the former parental role, but are shown as helping set up only good and desirable unions. Third, even after marriage, the couple is linked by a common and parallel involvement in socially productive work, rather than by personal love, and indeed they may appear to have minimal contact with each other. This is exemplified especially clearly in the film *Singing Above the Reservoir,* in which Party leaders arrange for a village girl to join her fiance at the Ming Tombs Reservoir construction site, since she will gain valuable knowledge there. Later, arrangements are made for them to be married in the construction headquarters. Immediately after the ceremony, he and she go out to work separately on the night shift in the men's and women's construction teams.

Within the limits of the small sample in this study, the Taiwan films put no less emphasis on the difficulties within the family over arranged marriages, in spite of Chinese cultural myths of family harmony. They too vividly show much suffering and frustration among the young. But they also show frustration among their elders, and the depiction of causes of the conflicts is quite different than in the Communist films. The causes also are less easy to describe clearly. Largely, things just seem to happen that way. This in itself is probably significant; taken together with certain more specific indications, it suggests that basically these problems are ascribed to fate—that's just the way life is. (In one film, however, the Communists get a large share of the blame, being shown as ordering a Communist girl to seduce the married son in the family; this leads to many of the subsequent family difficulties.) One major difference is clear, although it must be stated negatively. The parents are not overtly blamed, even though from an outsider's view of their behavior they might well be judged as at least partly responsible for the conflicts. This exculpation of the parents is quite consistent with the Taiwan films' prescription for resolution of these conflicts. Again, this appears more variable in detail than the simple line of the Communist films, but highly consistent in basic elements. The three Taiwan films all propose that the young should *adapt* to the status quo, by various combinations of: 1) Fortitude and endurance, oriented toward accepting continuing performance of one's given social role despite its difficulties. In the Communist films, fortitude and endurance are also valued highly for youth, but are to be used in a struggle *against* one's given role—in the old system only; but not in the "New China," where there again is struggle to fulfill one's social role, though its definition now is different. 2) Avoiding disruption of family ties, or their reestablishment if disrupted; thus these films uphold the myth of family harmony. 3) Service to a social group beyond oneself, which may involve the family, wider social organizations, or especially the country.

Two examples will illustrate how these elements appear in different combinations. In *Four Loves*, a family of the 1920's is disrupted when all its three sons fall in love with a beautiful orphan girl who was raised in the household and betrothed to the eldest son by the parents. This parental order is resisted, yet the young people cannot resolve the problem even among themselves—the sons all try to defer to each other, and the girl cannot make any decision among them. Finally, one by one, they leave, but eventually send word home of their involvement in the Nationalist Revolution; they devote themselves to country instead of love. In *Days of Cheer and Sorrow*, a complex plot involves love relationships between two children of a man's original family and two of a second family he established after becoming temporarily involved with the Communists, leaving home, and losing track of the original family. When the man finally finds his first wife again—the second is now dead—the young people are shocked to find that they are related to each other. They then discover they are really not related, biologically; the second two children were adopted. Yet the final outcome is not resumption of their love relationships, but the joining of all together as brothers and sisters in one big family under an old grandfather.

The theme of conflict between parents and children occurs in the commercial films from Hong Kong with about the same frequency as in the ones from Taiwan and Communist China, but their handling of this theme takes a middle ground in several respects.

Three of the Hong Kong films having this theme are versions of old stories, of which the Communists have also made films. The two versions of *Dream of the Red Chamber, Liang Shan-po and Chu Ying-tai,* and *Yang Nai-wu and Hsiao Pai-tsai* differ little with respect to this theme. The conflict in these three Hong Kong films is also depicted as stemming from the authoritarian nature of the old, traditional family and its concern to arrange marriages that are desirable in terms of family wealth and power. While the Hong Kong films are sympathetic to the young lovers, as are the Communist films, they are probably a little easier on the older generation. They incline toward an attitude of "that's just the way it was" more than blaming them, yet without defending the parents as the Taiwan films did. These three films parallel the Communist versions in their depicted resolution of the conflicts. They also show that true love loses out to the family system except in *Liang Shan-po and Chu Ying-tai* with its fantasy reunion of lovers as butterflies.

*The Female Prince*, which is another story set in ancient times, is very similar to the three preceeding cases. The conflict arises when a step-mother of the heroine insists on breaking a prior engagement to a youth the girl loves, since his family has lost its high political position. The girl is betrothed to the son of the new prime minister, who is also related to the stepmother. In this case, the power of the Emperor is invoked to support the cause of the lovers, who are finally united. This too seems largely a fantasy resolution, as is also the case for the films *Temple of the Red Lotus* and its sequel, *The Twin Swords.*

It thus appears, in summary, that both Communist and Nationalist Chinese films strongly emphasize the existence of conflicts between parents and children over love and marriage in the traditional family system. However, their ascriptions of cause and prescriptions for resolution of these conflicts differ markedly, and in ways which are quite consistent with the radical and conservative political stances of the societies—that is, the Communists advocate change in the traditional family system (although their view of the ideal working of these changes itself probably is largely a fantasy solution), while the Nationalists advocate its maintenance and adaptation to it. The less official Hong Kong films have similarities to both groups of more official films from Taiwan and Communist China. Half of the Hong Kong films stressed the fantasy resolution which also appeared in a few of the "Old China" Communist films. Half reflected the Taiwan solution of acceptance of fate.

Although the Communist-Nationalist differences are so marked at the level of relatively specific images of social organization and personal goals that are promoted, there remain major similarities at a more basic and general level. Neither Communist nor Nationalist films suggest that love should conquer all, as American films might. Instead both, in the different forms described, ultimately advocate traditional Chinese values such as acceptance of authority, even in matters of marriage, faithful performance of one's given social role, and subordination of personal love to wider social ends seen as more important and desirable.

Thus even this limited study suggests the potential value of film analysis for the thorny general problem of exploring and understanding not only social patterns but social change. Statements about social change usually tend to be either oversimplified yes-or-no characterizations or detailed accounts that provide no basis for discriminating specific or superficial and basic or general changes. There has been little serious thought about the fundamental nature of change in complex yet unitary social *systems,* and direct empirical observation of large scale societies is beset with problems. For revolutionary situations, the problem of studying social change is further compounded in difficulty at the same time that it is increased in urgency. The speed and extent of overt change involved, its practical political significance, and the heavy investment of various parties in rapidly and firmly affixing their own labels and definitions on the revolutionary developments all tend to restrict and obscure any systematic and objective viewing of such change.

The most general significance of this brief study therefore lies in its indication, by analysis of a limited but significant body of concrete data, that the essential problem must be viewed not as one of change *or* continuity, but as one of change *and* continuity, and the ways in which these are interrelated. The continuities with traditional Chinese culture observable in Communist films, such as the covert continuation of marriage arrangement by authority figures, the general similarities of attitudes and values despite new specific content or contexts, demonstrate and clarify how particular changes not only co-exist with continuities at other levels or in other areas, but are dependent on them.

**Table I.**—*Chinese Films and Family Conflicts*

| TITLE | PARENT-CHILD CONFLICT | |
| --- | --- | --- |
| | Occurrence | Arranged matches focus |
| 1. Chinese Communist Films—21 | | |
|   a. "Old China" (at least in part)—16 | | |
|     Daughters of China | – | – |
|     The White-Haired Girl | – | – |
|     The Scholar and the Fairy Carp | x | x |
|     The Letter with Feathers | – | – |
|     Liang Shan-po and Chu Ying-tai | x | x |
|     The Family | x | x |
|     New Year Sacrifice | x (Mother-in-law) | x |
|     Hua Mu Lan | – | – |
|     Woman Basketball Player No. 5 | x | x |
|     Lin Tse-hsu | – | – |
|     Song of Youth | x | x |
|     Cool Mountain's Bright Pearl | – | – |
|     Women Generals of the Yang Family | – | – |
|     Dream of the Red Chamber | x | x |
|     The Jade Hairpin | x | x |
|     Yang Nai-wu and Hsiao Pai-tsai | x | x |
| | 9 | 9 |

b. "New China"—5

| | | |
|---|---|---|
| Young Footballers | – | – |
| Flames on the Border | – | – |
| Singing Above the Reservoir | – | – |
| Blossoms in the Sun | – | – |
| New Story of an Old Soldier | – | – |
| | 0 | 0 |

2. Taiwan Films—5

| | | |
|---|---|---|
| No Greater Love | – | – |
| Lady General Red Jade (Joint Taiwan-HK) | – | – |
| Four Loves | x | x |
| The Silent Wife | x | x |
| Days of Cheer and Sorrow | x | x |
| | 3 | 3 |

3. Hong Kong (non-Communist)—12

| | | |
|---|---|---|
| Liang Shan-po and Chu Ying-tai* | x | x |
| Hua Mu Lan* | – | – |
| Dream of the Red Chamber* | x | x |
| Yang Nai-wu and Hsiao Pai-tsai* | x | x |
| Empress Wu | x | – (Power |
| Rear Entrance | – | – Struggle) |
| The Female Prince | x | x |
| Stranger than Fiction | – | – |
| The Golden Buddha | – | – |
| Come Drink with Me | – | – |
| Temple of the Red Lotus | x | x |
| The Twin Swords | x | x |
| | 7 | 6 |

* Films of certain stories have been made both by Communists and Hong Kong producers.

# Name Index

*(Asterisks refer to footnotes)*

# Subject Index

Please remember that this is a library book,
and that it belongs only temporarily to each
person who uses it. Be considerate. Do
not write in this, or any, library book.

WITHDRAWN